Religious Reading and Everyday Lives in Devotional Hinduism

AMERICAN ACADEMY OF RELIGION

RELIGION IN TRANSLATION

SERIES EDITOR
John Nemec, University of Virginia
A Publication Series of
The American Academy of Religion
and
Oxford University Press

THE HISTORY OF THE BUDDHA'S RELIC SHRINE
A Translation of the Sinhala Thūpavamsa
Stephen C. Berkwitz

DAMASCIUS' *PROBLEMS & SOLUTIONS CONCERNING FIRST PRINCIPLES*
Translated with Introduction and Notes by Sara Ahbel-Rappe

THE SECRET GARLAND
Āṇṭāḷ's Tiruppāvai *and* Nācciyār *Tirumoḻi*
Translated with Introduction and Commentary by Archana Venkatesan

PRELUDE TO THE MODERNIST CRISIS
The "Firmin" Articles of Alfred Loisy
Edited, with an Introduction by C. J. T. Talar
Translated by Christine Thirlway

DEBATING THE DASAM GRANTH
Robin Rinehart

THE FADING LIGHT OF ADVAITA ĀCĀRYA
Three Hagiographies
Rebecca J. Manring

THE UBIQUITOUS ŚIVA
Somānanda's Śivadṛṣṭi and His Tantric Interlocutors
John Nemec

PLACE AND DIALECTIC
Two Essays by Nishida Kitarō
Translated by John W.M. Krummel and Shigenori Nagatomo

THE PRISON NARRATIVES OF JEANNE GUYON
Ronney Mourad and Dianne Guenin-Lelle

DISORIENTING DHARMA
Ethics and the Aesthetics of Suffering in the Mahābhārata
Emily T. Hudson

THE TRANSMISSION OF SIN
Augustine and the Pre-Augustinian Sources
Pier Franco Beatrice
Translated by Adam Kamesar

FROM MOTHER TO SON
The Selected letter of Marie de l'Incarnation to Claude Martin
Translated and with Introduction and Notes by Mary Dunn

DRINKING FROM LOVE'S CUP
Surrender and Sacrifice in the Vārs *of Bhai Gurdas*
Selections and Translations with Introduction and Commentary by Rahuldeep Singh Gill

THE AMERICA'S FIRST THEOLOGIES
Early Sources of Post-Contact Indigenous Religion
Edited and translated by Garry Sparks, with Sergio Romero and Frauke Sachse

GODS, HEROES, AND ANCESTORS
An Interreligious Encounter in Eighteenth-Century Veitnam
Anh Q. Tran

POETRY AS PRAYER IN THE SANSKRIT HYMNS OF KASHMIR
Hamsa Stainton

THE UBIQUITOUS ŚIVA VOLUME II
Somānanda's Śivadṛṣṭi and His Tantric Interlocutors
John Nemec

FIRST WORDS, LAST WORDS
New Theories for Reading Old Texts in Sixteenth-Century India
Yigal Bronner and Lawrence McCrea

THE LUMINOUS WAY TO THE EAST
Texts and History of the First Encounter of Christianity with China
Matteo Nicolini-Zani

RELIGIOUS READING AND EVERYDAY LIVES IN DEVOTIONAL HINDUISM
Emilia Bachrach

JEWISH PIETY IN ISLAMIC JERUSALEM
The Lamentations Commentary of Salmon ben Yerūḥīm
Jessica Andruss

AMERICAN ACADEMY OF RELIGION

Religious Reading and Everyday Lives in Devotional Hinduism

EMILIA BACHRACH

OXFORD
UNIVERSITY PRESS

OXFORD
UNIVERSITY PRESS

Oxford University Press is a department of the University of Oxford. It furthers the University's objective of excellence in research, scholarship, and education by publishing worldwide. Oxford is a registered trade mark of Oxford University Press in the UK and certain other countries.

Published in the United States of America by Oxford University Press
198 Madison Avenue, New York, NY 10016, United States of America.

Library of Congress Control Number: 2022936389
ISBN 978-0-19-764859-9

DOI: 10.1093/oso/9780197648599.001.0001

1 3 5 7 9 8 6 4 2

Printed by Integrated Books International, United States of America

Contents

List of Figures vii
Acknowledgments ix
Note on Transliteration and Translation xiii

Introduction: An Ethnography of Reading 1

1. Dialogical Reading: The Pushtimarg's Performative Canon 30
2. Commentarial Reading: Historicizing Hagiography and Making Modern Readers 67
3. Public Reading: Debating Text, Temple, and Religious Authority 99
4. Community Reading: Learning Affective Piety 128
5. Women's Reading: Navigating Family, Gender, and Devotion 157

Conclusion: Religious Reading and Everyday Lives 187

Appendix: Select Translations of Key Texts 195
Glossary 205
Bibliography 211
Index 227

List of Figures

I.1. Home shrine with Krishna icon (Thakurji) and milk pudding offering. 2

I.2. 19th-century painting of Thakurji asking the widowed disciple for food "like a small child" from an illustrated manuscript. 22

I.3. 19th-century depiction of Pushtimargi hereditary leaders bathing Krishna in his form as Shrinathji. 26

I.4. (Left) Devotees making flower garlands for a Krishna *svarūp* in an Ahmedabad temple. (Right) Women gathered to read in a devotee's living room. 28

Acknowledgments

This book has had a long gestation period and has developed with the incredible patience, enthusiasm, support, and generosity of many people and institutions. In many ways, the research I present here would not have been possible without the mentorship I received in the study of South Asian religions from Andy Rotman while an undergraduate at Smith College. Likewise, my work as a scholar, and therefore this book, would not be possible without the immeasurable support I have found from the friends and mentors—namely, Kathryn Hardy, Arti Gujrati, and Ramachandra Pandit—with whom I spent so much time during my very first visit to India in 2000 with the University of Wisconsin Madison's "College Year in India Program."

Research that appears in this book was supported by a Junior Fellowship from the American Institute for Indian Studies (AIIS) and through research funding from Oberlin College. Intensive language learning in Hindi and Gujarati with AIIS, in Jaipur and in Ahmedabad, respectively, and at the University of Texas at Austin has also been essential to my ability to carry out the research for this book (funding for this language study was supported by AIIS, Critical Language fellowships, and Foreign Language and Area Studies fellowships). Many thanks to the administrative staff and teachers at all of these institutions and programs. Between 2011 and 2017 I conducted research in several libraries and archives in India and the United States, including the University of Texas at Austin Libraries; the Vidya Vibhag Library in Kankroli, Rajasthan; the Pratham Peeth Archives in Kota, Rajasthan; the Gujarat Vidyapith Library in Ahmedabad, Gujarat; the Gujarat University Library in Ahmedabad; the Vallabh Sadan Library in Ahmedabad; the B.J. Institute of Higher Learning and Research in Ahmedabad; the L.D. Institute of Indology in Ahmedabad; and the Oriental Institute of Baroda in Baroda, Gujarat. I owe thanks to the staff at all of these institutions, but particularly to Dr. Ramji Savaliya at the B.J. Institute of Higher Learning and to Adhikari Ashok Paliwal at the Vallabh Sadan. I am also grateful to scholar and artist Amit Ambalal, who granted me access to his personal library and image collection. Thanks are also due for Amit's permission to include images from his private collection in this monograph. Thanks also to Murtaza Gandhi, who patiently and enthusiastically helped me to transcribe and decipher several recorded Gujarati materials I worked with during 2012.

As this book grows out of a doctoral dissertation that I completed at the University of Texas at Austin, I owe many thanks to my dissertation co-supervisors, Rupert Snell and Kathryn Hansen, both of whom have remained ever supportive mentors, colleagues, and friends as I have revised this work from dissertation to book. Likewise, I owe thanks to the rest of my dissertation committee, Cynthia Talbot, Martha Selby, and Kathleen Stewart, whose support and feedback on my work at various stages has been invaluable. This is a book about practices of reading, and as mentors, each of these individuals has taught me to read lovingly, critically, enthusiastically, inquisitively, carefully, and patiently in different and treasured ways.

Though I have written various parts of this book at many institutions—the University of Texas at Austin, Millsaps College, Elon University, and High Point University—the bulk of the writing and revision for this book took place between 2017 and 2021 while teaching at Oberlin College. Many Oberlin students—too many to mention here—have inspired me to rethink aspects of my research in the classroom, and many colleagues whom I have had the honor to work alongside have offered their support in a variety of ways as I have completed this project. Special thanks to: Joyce Babyak, Corey Barnes, KJ Cerankowski, Cynthia Chapman, Rishad Choudhury, Cheryl Cottine, James Dobbins, Brenda Hall, Margaret Kamitsuka, Andrew Macomber, Amir Mahallati, Greggor Mattson, Kathryn Metz, Patrick O'Connor, Swapna Pathak, Shari Rabin, Paula Richman, Daniel Schultz, and Ellen Wurtzel.

For incisive feedback on my research for this book in the context of colloquia and conference and seminar presentations, I offer thanks to Dean Accardi, Neelima Shukla Bhatt, John Cort, Oliver Freiberger, Jack Hawley, Nell Hawley, Syed Akbar Hyder, Anne Monius, Patrick Olivelle, Heidi Pauwels, Karen Pechilis, Andy Rotman, Samira Sheikh, Caley Smith, Frederick Smith, Hamsa Stainton, and Steven Vose. I am likewise grateful to everyone who participated in an AIIS Dissertation to Book Workshop in 2016, but especially to Joyce Flueckiger, Brian Hatcher, Jennifer Ortegren, Claire Robinson, and Tulsi Srinivas for their feedback. For their guidance, intellectual companionship, and support at various stages of book writing and revision, I am grateful to the following individuals: Asiya Alam, Isabel Huacuja Alonso, Amy L. Allocco, Arun Brahmbhatt, Ishan Chakrabarti,

Richard Delacy, Joyce Flueckiger, Kathryn Hardy, Margaret Kamitsuka, Constance Kassor, Hanna Kim, Priya Kothari, Deonnie Moodie, Priya Nelson, Nikola Rajić, Jennifer Ortegren, Dinyar Patel, Shruti Patel, Shital Sharma, Rupert Snell, Hamsa Stainton, and Vallabhdas. Several of these people—Isabel, Arun, Constance, Joyce, Kathryn, Margaret, Shruti, and Rupert—have read parts of this manuscript and have offered invaluable comments that have improved my written work. Others—Amy and Jenn—have read nearly every word of this monograph many times over, becoming book doulas, without whom the final manuscript would never have been born. Many thanks are also due to the two anonymous reviewers of this manuscript for Oxford University Press, to OUP's religion editors Cynthia Read and Theo Calderara, to my Title Manager Brent Matheny, and to John Nemec—the outstanding *Religion in Translation* series editor, and most patient correspondent.

This book is dedicated to all members of the Pushtimargi community who have, over the past several decades, welcomed me into their homes and places of worship, sharing with me the intimate details of their devotional lives and reading practices. There are too many people to mention here by name, but named thanks must be given to Jitubhai and Surekhaben Shah and to Paulomi Shah for their gracious hospitality and friendship: thank you for always providing me with safe and comfortable homes during my research trips to Ahmedabad. I thank also Ashok, Ranjan, Avdesh, and Siddharth Paliwal for their generosity, care, and good humor. Endless gratitude to Yoginiben, Maheshvariben, Kailashben, and Krutikaben for their friendship and willingness to teach me about all things Pushtimargi. Many Pushtimargi hereditary leaders have offered their support and wisdom during my research for this book. Special thanks go to Madhusudhanlalji Goswami and his family, including Rajabetiji, in Ahmedabad and to the late Goswami Indirabetiji of Baroda. Finally, I offer deep gratitude to Shyam Manoharji Goswami of Mumbai, who has been especially patient and generous with his scholarship, time, and boundless knowledge.

Finally, infinite thanks to my immediate family: my two young children Max and Sebastian, for knowing me only as mother and not as scholar, and my spouse Zoran, for knowing and supporting me as co-parent, scholar, partner, and so much more. Special thanks to my mother, Judi, for reading parts of this manuscript and offering her always insightful readerly impressions, but also for being a model writer, reader, and author and most graceful human being. My sister Marion, too, is a writer-author and bookworm par excellence, and to her I owe thanks for her tacit support of my work on this book. And finally, I owe oceans of gratitude to my late father Richard (1950–2018), who, along with my mother, supported my academic—and all life—pursuits with unconditional love.

Note on Transliteration and Translation

All translations from Hindi and Gujarati to English are my own unless otherwise noted. All translations from Sanskrit are attributed accordingly. Indic words in transliteration will, for the most part, appear italicized and with diacritical marks. Indic words that do not appear italicized with diacritical marks include proper names and terms widely used in English. These words will be rendered as they are most commonly transcribed (e.g., *guru* = guru, Vallabhācārya = Vallabhacharya, Vaiṣṇava = Vaishnava, Kṛṣṇa = Krishna, Braj Bhāṣā = Braj Bhasha, etc.). The exception to this rule is that in my citations and bibliography I use conventional diacritical marks for the names of authors whose works were composed in Indian languages (the same goes for names of publishers, but not of place names). The first letter of all words (except for post-positions) are capitalized in the titles of Indian language texts, such as *Caurāsī Vaiṣṇavan kī Vārtā*. When discussing Sanskrit sources and terms therein, I have followed common conventions of contemporary Sanskritists. For example, भागवतपुराण = *Bhāgavatapurāṇa* and जीव = *jīva*. In the context of discussing Hindi and Gujarati literature and terms therein, however, I omit the inherent *a* vowel, so जीव = *jīv*—except in the case of certain conjunct letters that are commonly pronounced with the vowel (e.g., द्रव्य = *dravya*, but सिद्धांत = *siddhānt*). The first time an italicized Indic word or text title appears I will provide an English gloss or title translation. Thereafter, these words and titles will not be glossed or translated unless discussed in a specialized context. Repeatedly used Indic words, text titles, and proper names, with or without diacritical marks, will appear in this book's Glossary. Words that appear with diacritical marks will correspond to the following chart:

अ *a*	आ *ā*	इ *i*	ई *ī*	उ *u*	ऊ ū[1]
ऋ *ṛ*	ए *e*	ऐ *ai*	ओ *o*	औ *au*	
क *ka*	ख *kha*	ग *ga*	घ *gha*	ङ *ṅa*	

[1] This table is adapted from R.S. McGregor, *The Oxford Hindi-English Dictionary* (Oxford: Oxford University Press, 1993), xvii.

च *ca*	छ *cha*	ज/ज़ *ja/za*	झ *jha*	ञ *ña*
ट *ṭa*	ठ *ṭha*	ड/ड़ *ḍa/ṛa*	ढ/ढ़ *ḍha/ṛha*	ण *ṇa*
त *ta*	थ *tha*	द *da*	ध *dha*	न *na*
प *pa*	फ/फ़ *pha/fa*	ब *ba*	भ *bha*	म *ma*
य *ya*	र *ra*	ल *la*	व *va*	
श *śa*	ष *ṣa*	स *sa*	ह *ha*	

Words transliterated from Gujarati follow this Hindi syllabary chart except in the case of *ḷa*, which is specific to the Gujarati syllabary. Vowel nasality is shown with *ṃ* (e.g., नहीं = *nahīṃ* etc.). The nasal consonant ङ will be transliterated as *ṅa* (hence *satsaṅg*), and ञ as *ña* (hence *jñān*).

Introduction: An Ethnography of Reading

The Theology of Pizza

At a small neighborhood temple in Ahmedabad, Gujarat, ten women have gathered to read and discuss devotional literature specific to their Hindu tradition, the Pushtimarg, or the "Path of Nourishment."[1] The literature in question is a collection of 17th-century hagiographies, which are key to the Pushtimarg's scriptural canon and provide life stories of the community's first charismatic leader, Vallabhacharya (1479–1531), and his beloved disciples. The women, who come together each Thursday afternoon, begin their weekly gathering with a collective prayer, recited in Sanskrit, and end with *kīrtan* (devotional songs) sung in a form of Old Hindi. In between prayer and songs, the women take turns reading aloud in Modern Gujarati from their own copies of the hagiographies. Although each gathering is organized around a predetermined selection of narratives, the readings are also informal and can be paused at any time for questions or comments by the designated reader or by her fellow devotees. On this day, a woman named Leena has just read aloud from one hagiography that tells the story of a widowed disciple of Vallabhacharya and her relationship with Thakurji, a form of the deity Krishna who is worshiped as a fully animate being in temples and in devotees' homes (see Figure I.1).[2] As the hagiography recounts, the widow decides to prepare ritual food offerings for Thakurji in bulk so that the supply might last a full ten days. This way, the widow reasons to herself, she will be

[1] Although many scholars translate Pushtimarg (Puṣṭimārg) as Path of Grace, in my experience "nourishment" is a more accurate translation of *puṣṭi* than is "grace." For example, when asked to describe (in Hindi or Gujarati) what *puṣṭi* means, many community members will use the word *poṣaṇ*, which is regularly translated as "nourishment" or "fostering," rather than terms regularly translated as "grace," such as *kṛpā*.

[2] Members of the Pushtimarg commonly refer to Krishna as Thakurji (*ṭhākur* meaning lord; chief; master. *Jī* is an honorific suffix). According to Institutional Review Board agreements with the University of Texas at Austin and Oberlin College, individuals who are *not* public figures are given pseudonyms to protect their identities. In some cases, I have also changed other particulars about these individuals (e.g., where they live, social position or relationships, temple affiliation, etc.) to further protect their anonymity.

Religious Reading and Everyday Lives in Devotional Hinduism. Emilia Bachrach, Oxford University Press. © Oxford University Press 2022. DOI: 10.1093/oso/9780197648599.003.0001

Figure I.1. Home shrine with Krishna icon (Thakurji) and milk pudding offering (© ELAKSHI CREATIVE BUSINESS/Shutterstock).

able to attend to her spinning work, from which she earns a living. Thakurji, however, who loves only freshly cooked items, gobbles down the entire food supply in one sitting and then speaks directly to his devotee, chastising her for being lazy.

In response to hearing this episode read aloud, another woman, named Megha, shares an anecdote about how she and her sister-in-law were recently debating which kind of milk pudding to prepare for their family's household deity. According to Megha, she herself had suggested that they prepare a somewhat complicated and time-consuming dish, while her sister-in-law was insistent that they prepare a more simplified version of the pudding. "Well," says Megha, wrapping up her story, "I told her, fine then! If we don't have time to cook something special, we might as well just order Him a pizza!" Some women fall into fits of laughter over the anecdote, while others quiet the group so that they can respond to Megha's comment. "But why *not* pizza?," one woman, Kumud, asks sincerely. "Isn't He supposed to eat what we eat? Isn't He a part of our family?" "But He'll burn His mouth," Megha exclaims. "Imagine all the cheese from the hot pizza getting stuck on His lips! Like that widow from the hagiography learned, we should never be so lazy as to disregard His comfort." The debate over which food items to offer Thakurji continues for well over an hour, weaving in and out of references to devotional literature and to the women's own experiences as ritual practitioners. In doing so, the women ask each other, and the hagiographies, many questions: Do the norms for feeding Thakurji shift when one is traveling by airplane or visiting family in an American suburb without a grocery store that carries familiar ingredients? What if feeding Thakurji milk pudding is "traditional" according to seasonal customs, but where one is living—say, in Sydney, Australia—the seasons are different than in northwest India? If one is stuck late at work and cannot cook something fresh for Thakurji, does one ask a family member or friend to help out? Questions about caring for Thakurji, inspired by the women's reading, are therefore directly linked to daily concerns about personal and familial diets, schedules, and human relationships. Before returning home, where many of these women will prepare meals for Thakurji and for themselves and their families, it is decided that pizza could potentially be on the menu, but only if it is made by hand in the devotee's home, and only if it is fed with loving care to Thakurji so that he does not burn his mouth.

In India's western state of Gujarat, which is currently home to a majority of Pushtimargi Hindus, exchanges such as the one just recounted are a regular feature of weekly gatherings in which these hagiographies are read and discussed.[3] As illustrated in the debate over whether or not Krishna should be served pizza, many contemporary readers engage with the narratives in ways that help them to navigate their own roles as devotional caretakers of Krishna in the context of their everyday lives and in light of shifting social

[3] Pushtimargi (Puṣṭimārgī; Puṣṭimārgīy) is adjectival, meaning "belonging" or "pertaining" to the Pushtimarg.

realities and religious ideals. Though particularly significant for understanding changing dynamics in Pushtimargi Hinduism, studying the ways in which devotees read and interpret these hagiographies also offers important insight into how religious reading functions more broadly: as a distinct set of practices that enable devotees—as individuals and in community—to make centuries of tradition mesh with, and transform, their contemporary worlds. For the purposes of this study, "reading" points to far more than consuming written words on a page. Rather, reading includes various analytic and affective modes of individual quiet and collective "out loud" engagement with religious texts, primarily as they appear as printed books, but also various forms of oral and written discourse. Through these practices, devotees put their personal lifeworlds into dynamic conversation with the landscapes of their beloved texts. In the iterative process, both readers and texts are transformed.

Hagiographies of the Pushtimarg's early followers are enshrined in several distinct collections of 17th-century Braj Bhasha (a form of Old Hindi) prose texts referred to as *Vārtā Sāhitya*, or Chronicle Literature.[4] Within the broad category of "hagiography," or narratives of "saintly" lives, *Vārtā Sāhitya* is somewhat distinct: like the story of Vallabhacharya's widowed disciple read aloud by the women in the Ahmedabad temple, the most popular Pushtimargi *vārtā*s (chronicles; hagiographies) consist of devotional stories about the lives of those who *followed* the Pushtimarg's primary "saint," rather than stories focused on Vallabhacharya as a "saint" himself. While steeped in the social world of early modern North India, these stories of Vallabhacharya's followers (in Braj Bhasha and in Gujarati translation) have continued to be immensely popular among generations of devotees whose various techniques of reading and exegesis have allowed them to maintain the written *vārtā*s as primary guides for devotional living in modern western India and beyond. Accordingly, *Vārtā Sāhitya* is integral to how Pushtimargi readers cultivate their own devotional experiences and relationships—a common and significant function of many narratives categorized as hagiography.[5]

[4] Braj Bhasha refers to a regional form of Hindi often associated with medieval and early modern literary traditions (devotional and courtly) of northern India.

[5] For an annotated bibliography of scholarship on hagiography in Hindu traditions, and other South Asian religious traditions more broadly, see Emilia Bachrach, "Saints and Hagiography in Hinduism," in *Oxford Bibliographies in Hinduism*, ed. Tracy Coleman (New York: Oxford University Press, 2019).

My initial interest in the devotional literature of Pushtimargi Hinduism emerged in 2008, while studying Modern Hindi in the Rajasthani city of Jaipur. In preparation for my upcoming graduate studies, I had also started to learn older forms of Hindi with the aid of Rupert Snell's *The Hindi Classical Tradition: A Braj Bhāṣa Reader*, which fortuitously included brief selections of *Vārtā Sāhitya*.[6] The hagiographies, I quickly realized, had a dialogical quality that seemed to beg for reading partners: many *vārtā*s are built around what amounts to transcribed conversations (such as those between Thakurji and his widowed devotee) that include questions for the reader, which then prompt further dialogue and interpretation (e.g., "what can we say the inner meaning of this *vārtā* might be?"). While Rupert Snell himself would soon become a mentor and fellow reader of the *vārtā*s at the University of Texas at Austin, where I completed my doctoral work, my first reading partners of this literature were several women who gathered daily for collective worship at a temple in Jaipur's old city. When I first met these women, to whom I was introduced by one of my Hindi language teachers, I still knew very little about the Pushtimarg, also known as the Vallabha Sampraday (the *sampradāy*, or following of Vallabhacharya), and clearly bored them with seemingly irrelevant technical questions about terminology that I could not find in my Hindi dictionaries or glossaries. "It doesn't seem like you understand *anything*," I remember one of the women, Manju, saying as I scribbled in my notebook something about the surprising spelling of a Persian loan word. Though initially I may have missed the point of what it meant to read *Vārtā Sāhitya* as devotional literature—as literature that demands savoring, questioning, and engaged dialogue—I was immediately excited to have learned that the texts are still widely read today. As the women at the Jaipur temple proclaimed,

> These texts are read by everyone. Even if people don't read daily in this way, they will know these stories. They are primary for followers of the Pushtimarg and they put us in a devotional mood each time [we read/hear them]. They are an ocean for us.

The word *sāgar* (ocean) is often used by Hindi speakers to refer to things that are enduring, "deep" in significance, and dynamic. This assertion about the

[6] Rupert Snell, *The Hindi Classical Tradition: A Braj Bhāṣā Reader* (London: School of Oriental and African Studies, 1991).

sāgar-like quality of the hagiographies has remained key to how I approach the Pushtimargi *vārtā*s in relationship to those who read them.[7]

For devotees, such as the women in the Ahmedabad and Jaipur temples, *vārtā* texts are not stable and prescriptive so much as they are invitations to discussion, dialogue, and performance. Devotees use the texts to argue among themselves, to nurture relationships with each other and with Krishna, to define their own best practices, and to work through modern problems—and they do this through various modes of reading. I therefore approach *Vārtā Sāhitya* as a performative canon: a repertoire of written texts *and* the different modes through which people engage with these texts. While the core body of texts that comprise *Vārtā Sāhitya* has stayed relatively static since the 19th century (that is, it is a "closed" canon in the sense that new *vārtā*s are not, to my knowledge, composed), the collection's performative qualities distinguish it from others. As Elaine Fisher writes,

> The term "canon" is commonly used in the field of religious studies to refer to the codification of a sacred text, thereafter held as authoritative in either knowledge or practice by a particular community. A canon comes to be viewed, often, as inevitable, eternal, or beyond human control or contestation.[8]

While authoritative, the *vārtā*s as part of a performative canon are not viewed as fully beyond human control, and their various modes of reception,

[7] While no other published works attend to Pushtimargi reading practices or the living tradition of *Vārtā Sāhitya*, the Pushtimarg has received attention in academic (namely, English-language) scholarship. Research on the tradition's visual culture and temple arts has been especially popular and includes Peter Bennett's *The Path of Grace: Social Organisation and Temple Worship in a Vaishnava Sect* (Delhi: Hindustan Publishing Corporation, 1993); Amit Ambalal's *Krishna as Shrinathji: Rajasthani Paintings from Nathdvara* (Ahmedabad, India: Mapin Publishing, 1987); Anne-Marie Gaston, *Krishna's Musicians: Musicians and Music Making in the Temples of Nathdvara, Rajasthan* (New Delhi: Manohar, 1997); and Tryna Lyons' *The Artists of Nathadwara: The Practice of Painting in Rajasthan* (Bloomington: Indiana University Press, 2004).Vasudha Dalmia, Shital Sharma, and Shandip Saha are among a handful of scholars to have published on the Pushtimarg's social history. See, for example, essays in Dalmia's *Hindu Pasts: Women, Religion, History* (Albany: State University of New York Press, 2017); Sharma's "Middle-class Modernities and the Reproduction of Sectarian Identity Among Puṣṭimārg Vaiṣṇavas in the Bombay Presidency," *The Journal of Hindu Studies* 10, no. 1 (2017): 86–111; and Saha's "The Darbār, the British, and the Runaway *Mahārāja*: The Transformation of the Nathdvara-Mewar Relationship," *South Asia Research* 27, no. 3 (2007): 271–291. Frederick M. Smith, among others, has written on Vallabhacharya's philosophical legacy as recorded in Sanskrit literature (e.g., "The Hierarchy of Philosophical Systems According to Vallabhācārya," *Journal of Indian Philosophy* 33, no. 4 [2005]: 421–453). Among Richard Barz's publications on Pushtimargi literature, *The Bhakti Sect of Vallabhācārya* (New Delhi: Munshiram Manoharlal, 1992) has been a favorite introductory text on the tradition that also introduces *Vārtā Sāhitya*.

[8] Elaine Fisher, "Public Space, Public Canon: Situating Religion at the Dawn of Modernity in South India," *Modern Asian Studies* 42, no. 5 (2018): 1498.

physical forms, and readerly interpretations change according to social and historical contexts. Though the *vārtās* may be distinct in how they invite performance and dialogue, all written texts live in and do things in the world—they are themselves "performative"—and, as such, exist on a "continuum" with the performances of humans (authors and readers of texts) in their everyday lives.[9]

Approaching *Vārtā Sāhitya* as a performative canon is not inevitable. This methodology requires a commitment to studying readers and texts as *relationally* performative. Simply put, to study a canon of religious literature as "performative" is to study the lives of texts alongside the lives and religious practices of the people who author and read them. The women devotees whose readings of *Vārtā Sāhitya* I observed over my two-month stay in Jaipur did not leave a written record of their engagement with the hagiographies. To study religious texts without also studying the contexts in which said texts are read, then, is not only to miss the richness of emergent and affective relationships *between* texts and readers, but also to miss the *plurality* of reading practices and readerly interpretations—including women's interpretations, which are often absent from the written record. Moreover, the failure to take seriously the living, embodied performances and interpretations of religious texts can produce impoverished conclusions about the liturgical, didactic, ethical, political, and devotional functions of such texts, past and present.[10] At the same time, however, an ethnographic study of how religious texts are read should also attend to the form and content of written texts themselves. Just as devotees' life experiences and shifting community contexts influence their reading practices and interpretations of devotional literature, *Vārtā Sāhitya*, like any type of literature, has a distinct "ecology" or "literary grammar," which also informs how devotees read.[11]

[9] Richard Schechner, *Performance Studies: An Introduction* (New York: Routledge, 2013), 170.

[10] Linda Hess also makes this claim in *Bodies of Song: Kabir Oral Traditions and Performative Worlds in North India* (Oxford University Press, 2015), as does William A. Graham in *Beyond the Written Word: Oral Aspects of Scripture in the History of Religion* (New York: Cambridge University Press, 1993).

[11] For a discussion of literary "ecology," see A.K. Ramanujan's "On Translating a Tamil Poem," in *The Collected Essays of A.K. Ramanujan*, ed. Vinay Dharwadker (Oxford: Oxford University Press, 1999), 198. For a discussion of "literary grammar," specifically in oral poetry, see John M. Foley's *How to Read an Oral Poem* (Urbana: University of Illinois Press, 2002), 86. Susannah Laramee Kidd's dissertation, "Genres of Reading/Genres of Agency: An Ethnography of Protestant Women's Reading Groups" (Emory University, 2013), makes this case as well. As Laramee Kidd's work shows, specific genres of religious texts provoke specific genres of reading, while different reading practices in turn influence how people experience texts.

This book therefore begins by exploring the unique literary grammar of the written hagiographies (Chapter 1) and then moves on to show how specific written *vārtā* texts and contexts stimulate certain modes of reading (Chapters 2–5). Many of these modes share similarities with genres of reading engendered by texts from various other religious traditions. For instance, many kinds of religious texts, including those in the performative canon I discuss here, provoke what I call "commentarial reading" (see Chapter 2). Commentarial reading refers to different types of reading practices that aim to record a commentary (often in writing) that may have "systematic, theoretical, or practical interests of its own" and is therefore intended to guide *other* readers in their engagement with a particular written text.[12] Other modes of reading that this book attends to include those that transpire during *pravacan*s, a type of public, performative oral "religious lecture" that requires a live or virtual audience. As discussed in Chapter 3, *pravacan*s (and other related modes of reading) make space for Pushtimargi leaders and devotees to read aloud from and orally analyze carefully chosen selections from written texts with the aim of advancing their own strongly held positions on community-wide debates, such as how to care for Krishna *svarūp*s (icons of the living deity) in temple spaces. *Satsaṅg*s, or "gatherings of the faithful," where devotees (sometimes in the company of religious leaders, as discussed in Chapters 4 and 5) sing devotional songs and collectively read and discuss literature in pairs or larger groups, are common to various South Asian religious traditions. However, as stimulated by those who take turns reading aloud directly from the written hagiographies in a storytelling mode (that is, with some embellishments and with gusto, but not theatrically per se), Pushtimargi *satsaṅg*s also function as spaces in which readers may openly discuss how to best interpret written texts in relationship to their own experiences as Krishna's caretakers. Central to caring for Krishna are the rituals of *sevā* (loving service), which include feeding and dressing Krishna *svarūp*s that many devotees keep in their private homes. In this way, then, rituals of *sevā*—which are integral to the written *vārtā* narratives and to how people discuss the significance of these narratives—also become part of the performative canon. These various modes of engaging with written texts therefore tell us a great deal about how practices of reading contribute to people's well-being and devotional and social relationships, and about how contemporary readers make sense of ideals inherited from the past in terms of daily life in the present.

[12] Paul J. Griffiths' *Religious Reading: The Place of Reading in the Practice of Religion* (New York: Oxford University Press, 1999), 84.

Although there are certain discrepancies in how different members of the community live (e.g., between hereditary religious leaders descending from Vallabhacharya and devotees without inherited authority), for many contemporary Pushtimargis, "daily life" is grounded in relatively affluent urban lifestyles as well as caste privilege. Male hereditary leaders and their families are Brahmins, as are a considerable number of devotees. The majority of devotees, however, hail from *baniyā*, traditionally "merchant caste," groups based in western India. Pushtimargis' caste privilege is distinct from, but also connected to, class privilege, as well as the privilege of being part of a Hindu group that has generally been favored by local and national political leadership since the mid-20th century.[13] While I rarely hear class or caste privilege discussed explicitly, such privileges are certainly implicit in how Pushtimargis bring their personal experiences into conversation with devotional literature (e.g., as they are reflected in discussions about everyday habits of eating, traveling, managing one's household, etc.).

My questions about how Pushtimargis navigate their everyday experiences and well-being through practices of religious reading have taken me to multiple places in North and northwest India over the past fifteen years, though my research has primarily been based in the pilgrimage town of Nathdwara, Rajasthan, and in the western Indian cities of Ahmedabad, Gujarat, and Mumbai, Maharashtra. In each of these places, I have conducted archival research based on reading written texts as well as ethnographic fieldwork. My ethnographic research has relied heavily on participant observation during *pravacan*s and *satsaṅg*s, where Pushtimargis—hereditary leaders and devotees, both men and women—read and discuss devotional literature, often in temples or in their private homes, but also on a variety of virtual platforms. Years of continuously attending these events and gatherings has resulted in long-term professional connections and friendships with Pushtimargi devotees and hereditary leaders, many of whom I have formally interviewed for this book. I have spent countless hours with many others speaking informally and "hanging out"[14] over tea, en route to vegetable markets, during pilgrimage processions, while waiting for children to be dismissed from school, in

[13] Shital Sharma has attended to matters of class vis-à-vis Pushtimargi ritual here: "Consuming Krishna: Women, Class, and Ritual Economies in Pushtimarg Vaishnavism," in *Ritual Innovation: Strategic Interventions in South Asian Religion*, ed. Amy L. Allocco and Brian Pennington (Albany: State University of New York Press, 2018), 149–167.

[14] See Clifford Geertz's widely read article, "Deep Hanging Out," *The New York Review of Books* 45, no. 16 (1998): 69–72.

the wings of peoples' professional workspaces, and via Skype, Zoom, and WhatsApp when I am back in the United States.

My "outsider" status as a white American scholar who has not been initiated into the Pushtimarg is an ongoing topic of conversation, and my interlocutors have interpreted my positionality in various ways. Since the 1960s there has been a small, but growing, number of Europeans and Americans—who are not of South Asian descent—who have been initiated. Some of my conversation partners urge me to seek formal Pushtimargi initiation, which, they argue, would earn me greater access to the tradition's devotional literature as well as greater acceptance in the community as a researcher. Others—particularly hereditary leaders—do not seem concerned with my non-Pushtimargi status and instead seem to valorize my efforts to learn about devotional literature from a community that is not "my own." Regardless of the nuances of how I am perceived by different interlocutors, I rarely feel unwelcome in Pushtimargi spaces. On the contrary, most everyone I meet seems exceedingly hospitable and eager to speak with me.[15]

In order to study how different members of the Pushtimargi community have read and reworked *Vārtā Sāhitya*, I have, in addition to ethnographic research, pursued the literature's recorded reception history (namely, from the 19th century onward) by turning to written commentaries on and translations of the *vārtā*s, which I have found in manuscripts (mostly housed in private temples or personal archives), print publications, and on the Internet. While all of my interlocutors are literate—often across several languages including Gujarati, various forms of Hindi, and English—"reading" in this book, as I have already emphasized, includes more than consuming the written word.[16] Just as I count individual quiet reading and collective "out loud" reading of this literature as performative acts, I also count practices of commentarial writing and oral exegesis (including informal discussion)

[15] My "access" to Pushtimargi spaces in part hinges on how I have been perceived by certain religious leaders and devotees as a non-threatening religious "other"—namely, as Jewish. For further information on my positionality as a researcher, see my article, "The Uncertain Self in Ethnographic Research and Writing," *Fieldwork in Religion* 15, no.1–2 (2020): 113–125.

[16] Charles Briggs' meditation on literacy is useful to consider here. Briggs suggests that literacy is not "simply the ability to read, though it is partly that. It is a complex cultural phenomenon with powerful ideological implications, which vary depending on the time, place and milieu one is looking at" ("Literacy, Reading, and Writing in the Medieval West," *Journal of Medieval History* 26, no. 4 [2000]: 397–420, 398). Further, Briggs writes, "any discussion of literacy must take into account the oral mode of communication which it complemented, substituted for, and often competed with" (ibid). This corresponds to my approach to reading as a dynamic, performative set of practices that moves beyond literate engagement with written texts.

on the texts to be integral to what reading is and does for Pushtimargis. In this way, my approach to "reading" moves beyond the perhaps predictable elements of literate engagement with written texts to consider how readers' varied oral and written discourse in relationship to texts functions vis-à-vis the social environments in which reading itself occurs, but also the contexts in which readers' lives unfold more broadly.

The discussions and commentaries that arise from reading these hagiographies vary widely to include public, community-wide debates about sectarian history, doctrine, leadership, and temple rituals, as well as more intimate and often gendered negotiations of family relationships and domestic worship (as we saw in the opening conversation about Thakurji and milk pudding). In considering the diversity of conversations that arise from reading devotional texts, I also highlight how devotees' commentaries on matters often dismissed as trivial (e.g., ritual food preparations) in academic studies of scriptural exegesis in fact exist alongside, and not in subordination to, discussions about doctrine and religious history. Concern for domestic ritual practices is *primary*, just as the vernacular hagiographies are themselves *primary* religious texts. This is an important distinction to make in terms of etic as well as emic perspectives on the primacy of vernacular Indian texts, particularly in relationship to their Sanskrit-language counterparts. In focusing more heavily on Sanskrit language texts than on their vernacular counterparts, much of the extant academic scholarship on the Pushtimarg, in English and other Indian languages, falsely suggests that *Vārtā Sāhitya* is secondary in terms of its reception by devotees and in terms of its literary value. Though contemporary devotees themselves almost universally acknowledge *Vārtā Sāhitya* as "sacred" literature and read and engage with these and other vernacular texts on a more regular and sustained basis than they do with Pushtimargi Sanskrit literature (e.g., philosophical treatises attributed to the Pushtimarg's first teacher Vallabhacharya), Sanskrit texts are generally acknowledged as distinctly authoritative, though not always "primary" in a practical sense. As I address in this book's first chapter, the *vārtās*' authors themselves acknowledge these differences in textual authority, linking the primacy of the hagiographies not only to the wider canon of written Pushtimargi literature, which includes many Sanskrit texts, but also to the record of both Vallabhacharya's and Krishna's own speech acts as recorded in the written *vārtās*.

Though men and women alike discuss *Vārtā Sāhitya* in relationship to a broad spectrum of ritual and social issues, women, who are among today's most avid devotee-readers, are especially focused on reading devotional literature in ways that help them to mediate their social and devotional commitments. As I discuss in detail in Chapter 5, this is in part because women, even those who have demanding familial and professional commitments, are often the primary caretakers of Krishna in Pushtimargi households.[17] My attention to women readers highlights not only the gendered ways in which Pushtimargis read, but also that by paying attention to readers in the first place—rather than to the texts alone—we turn what is often a "linear" model of reading on its head. Scholar Elizabeth Long, whose ethnographic work considers women's book clubs in the United States, suggests that a reader-centered model "focuses our attention on reading as one kind of cultural practice, a form of behavior that performs complex personal and social functions for those who engage with it."[18] When Pushtimargis convene to read and discuss devotional literature, they are not merely sharing religious knowledge and cultivating devotion. They are also making and remaking themselves as individuals and as a wider community. As Long puts it, reading enables people "not merely to reflect on identities they already have, but also to bring new aspects of subjectivity into being."[19] Further, reading provides fodder for discussions during which "tradition" is, in a certain sense, reauthorized, but also remade. For instance, the conclusion that women at the Ahmedabad temple came to about feeding Thakurji handmade pizza at home—with the caveat that extra care should be taken so that the deity does not burn his lips—attends to conventional Pushtimargi

[17] Anthropologist Anishka Gheewala-Lohiya's forthcoming dissertation, "Everyday Play in Mothering Krishna; Rethinking Devotional *Seva* (Service) and Prayer in the Pushtimarg" (London School of Economics), will attend in detail to women's practices of *sevā* in contemporary Pushtimargi communities.

[18] Elizabeth Long, *Book Clubs: Women and the Uses of Reading in Everyday Life* (Chicago: University of Chicago Press, 2003), 22. Other books that consider reading ethnographically include Jonathan Boyarin's edited volume, *The Ethnography of Reading* (Berkeley: University of California Press, 1993), and Tamara Bhalla's *Reading Together, Reading Apart: Identity, Belonging, and South Asian American Community* (Champaign: University of Illinois Press, 2016). Janice A. Radway has authored two books that consider reading practices ethnographically: *Reading the Romance: Women, Patriarchy, and Popular Literature* (Chapel Hill: University of North Carolina Press, 1984) and *A Feeling for Books: The Book-of-the-Month Club, Literary Taste, and Middle-class Desire* (Chapel Hill: University of North Carolina Press, 1997). Similarly, Tanya Erzen's book, *Fanpire: The Twilight Saga and the Women Who Love It* (Boston: Beacon Press, 2012), offers some ethnographic reflection on different modes of reading. Few published books consider *religious* reading ethnographically. Two exceptions are Anna Gade's *Perfection Makes Practice: Learning, Emotion, and the Recited Qur'ān in Indonesia* (Honolulu: University of Hawaii Press, 2004) and Pieternella van Doorn-Harder's *Women Shaping Islam: Reading the Qur'an in Indonesia* (Bloomington: University of Indiana Press, 2006). As with Laramee Kidd's dissertation, "Genres of Reading/Genres of Agency," Mugdha Yeolekar's dissertation, "Gurucaritra Pārāyaṇ: Social Praxis of Religious Reading" (PhD diss., Arizona State University, 2014), also uses ethnographic methods to consider how religious readers engage with their scriptures to make sense of concerns in the present.

[19] Long, *Book Clubs*, 22.

concerns as outlined in written *vārtā* narratives, but also to distinctly contemporary circumstances. The norms of feeding Thakurji have shifted, while the "essential" point of loving care through feeding itself has remained largely consistent. In this way, by studying the hagiographies themselves as well as the social contexts of their reading, this book provides a distinct example of how changing religious, regional, class, gender, and other social identities continue to shape debates over premodern religious texts, and how in turn these debates influence ongoing projects of self- and community fashioning.

"Reading" as a lens through which to situate my study of Pushtimargi Hinduism is distinct: religious studies scholarship that focuses explicitly on reading practices remains somewhat limited,[20] particularly in the field of Hindu studies.[21] Though religion scholar Vincent L. Wimbush and others (particularly scholars of biblical studies)[22] have argued that the "point of departure for and even the crux of" biblical studies interpretation should not be texts alone, but rather "worlds, viz. society and culture and the complex textu(r)alizations of society and culture,"[23] there continues to be a commitment

[20] In addition to Gade's *Perfection Makes Practice* and van Doorn-Harder's *Women Shaping Islam*, Graham's *Beyond the Written Word* and Griffiths' *Religious Reading* examine religious reading explicitly. Graham and Griffiths both consider oral and aural experiences of religious texts, looking comparatively across geographical regions and religious traditions. While Graham's major theoretical contribution is a re-examination of "scripture" as a social and historical category, Griffiths argues that religious reading brings readers closer to their scriptures and that practices of religious reading are informed by "authoritative tradition" and are always distinct from so-called secular ways of reading. This latter issue is also taken up in Alan Jacobs' *A Theology of Reading: The Hermeneutics of Love* (New York: Routledge, 2001) and *Discovering the Riches of the Word: Religious Reading in Late Medieval and Early Modern Europe*, ed. Sabrina Corbellini et al. (Leiden: Brill, 2015). Finally, Velma E. Love's *Divining the Self: A Study in Yoruba Myth and Human Consciousness* (University Park: Pennsylvania State University Press, 2012) attends to the embodied and performative nature of "scripture and scripturalizing practices," and Femke Molekamp's *Women and the Bible in Early Modern England: Religious Reading and Writing* (New York: Oxford University Press, 2013) considers the centrality of the Bible in women's interpretative and literary agency in early modern England.

[21] In addition to many publications that attend to adjacent issues, Bhakti Mamtora's ongoing research is an important exception. See, for example, Mamtora's "Smartphone Applications and Religious Reading Among Swaminarayan Hindus," *Postscripts* 12, no. 1 (2021): 21–44.

[22] Lynn S. Neal's *Romancing God: Evangelical Women and Inspirational Fiction* (Chapel Hill: University of North Carolina Press, 2006) discusses reading in the context of Protestant women's reading groups in the United States. Relatedly, Wesley A. Kort describes a shift in how non-biblical texts have been received as scripture in *"Take, Read": Scripture, Textuality, and Cultural Practice* (University Park: Pennsylvania State University Press, 1996). Mary Kelley's "'A More Glorious Revolution': Women's Antebellum Reading Circles and the Pursuit of Public Influence" (*The New England Quarterly* 76, no. 2 [2003]: 163–196) also addresses Protestant reading practices historically. Vincent Wimbush's edited volume, *Theorizing Scriptures: New Critical Orientations to a Cultural Phenomenon* (New Brunswick, NJ: Rutgers University Press, 2008), contains essays that address scripture in relationship to interpretation across various cultural contexts—a topic taken up more explicitly in James Bielo's edited volume, *The Social Life of Scriptures: Cross-cultural Perspectives on Biblicism* (New Brunswick, NJ: Rutgers University Press, 2009).

[23] Vincent L. Wimbush, ed., *African Americans and the Bible: Sacred Texts and Social Textures* (Eugene, OR: Wipf and Stock Publishers, 2021), 19.

across subfields of religious studies to written texts themselves as necessary, and often exclusive, points of departure. While I have taken Wimbush's invitation to study "sacred texts" alongside their "social textures," my research also builds on significant work by South Asia studies scholars who have attended to adjacent issues, such as storytelling,[24] theatrical-musical performances of text traditions,[25] and text reception (past and present) more broadly.[26] These studies provide important perspectives on some of the ways that South Asian religious communities engage with texts, oral and written. For instance, Paula Richman's career-long attention to the *Rāmāyaṇa* ("The Adventures of Rama") narrative—in text, theatrical performance, and the visual arts—has been instrumental in highlighting the myriad ways in which the widely loved narrative of Rama and Sita continues to spark conversation and debate among a range of readers, listeners, and performers in India and beyond.[27] Likewise, Philip Lutgendorf's scholarship continues to provide a wonderful template for how to study the *Rāmāyaṇa* as a living text tradition. Lutgendorf's book, *The Life of a Text: Performing the Rāmcaritmānas of Tulsidas*, considers both the contexts of theatrical and musical performance that surround Tulsidas' 16th-century Hindi epic telling of Rama's story, and how such performances continue to instigate controversy and debate over the social and religious teachings of the *Rāmcaritmānas*.[28] More recently, Syed Akbar Hyder's *Reliving*

[24] See Kirin Narayan's *Storytelling, Saints, and Scoundrels: Folk Narrative in Hindu Religious Teaching* (Philadelphia: University of Pennsylvania Press, 1989) and Joyce B. Flueckiger's *Gender and Genre in the Folklore of Middle India* (Ithaca, NY: Cornell University Press, 1996).

[25] See Hess, *Bodies of Song*.

[26] For example, Deven Patel's *Text to Tradition: The Naiṣadhīyacarita and Literary Community in South Asia* (New York: Columbia University Press, 2014) offers a reception history of a Sanskrit *mahākāvya* (great poem). Other monographs in this vein that have informed my approach to Pushtimargi literary culture include Anne Monius' *Imagining a Place for Buddhism: Literary Culture and Religious Community in Tamil-Speaking South India* (New York: Oxford University Press, 2001); Tony K. Stewart's *The Final Word: The Caitanya Caritāmṛta and the Grammar of Religious Tradition* (New York: Oxford University Press, 2010); Robin Rinehart's *Debating the Dasam Granth* (New York: Oxford University Press, 2011); and Vasudha Narayanan's *The Vernacular Veda: Revelation, Recitation, and Ritual* (Columbia: University of South Carolina Press, 1994).

[27] Richman's articles on the *Rāmāyaṇa* are numerous, as are her contributions to edited collections, including the forthcoming *Performing the Ramayana Tradition: Enactments, Interpretations, and Arguments*, co-edited with Rustom Bharucha (New York: Oxford University Press, 2021)). Richman also edited *Ramayana Stories in Modern South India: An Anthology* (Bloomington: Indiana University Press, 2008)), *Questioning Ramayanas: A South Asian Tradition* (Berkeley: University of California Press, 2001)), and *Many Ramayanas: The Diversity of a Narrative Tradition in South Asia* (Berkeley: University of California Press, 1991). Richman's forthcoming monograph, *A Narrative and a Region: Rama and Sita in Tamil Country and Beyond* (New Delhi: Permanent Black, forthcoming), focuses on the *Rāmāyaṇa*'s reception in southern India.

[28] Philip Lutgendorf, *The Life of a Text: Performing the Rāmcaritmānas of Tulsidas* (Berkeley: University of California Press, 1992). More recently, one chapter of Jennifer Saunders' *Imagining Religious Communities: Transnational Hindus and Their Narrative Performances* (New York: Oxford University Press, 2019) discusses how selections of Tulsidas' *Rāmcaritmānas* are

Karbala: Martyrdom in South Asian Memory (2006), shows how readers/listeners and writers/performers "relive" the narrative of Karbala in radically different places, from Houston to Hyderabad. Hyder's book also challenges the notion that religious narratives only elicit performances and interpretations that stay within the realm of theology (or even religious history).[29] Interpretations of the Karbala narrative, Hyder writes, are dependent on the "readers/listeners' (interpretive community's) situational hermeneutics."[30] And these interpretive communities include those engaged in the politics of nation-building as well as those focused on deeply personal devotional practices (two aims that are not mutually exclusive).[31] In this way, Hyder's material highlights how people's engagements with religious texts go far beyond the normative, often exclusive, ways that those deemed "authoritative" interpret scripture. As Tamara Bhalla writes with respect to South Asian Americans' book clubs in the United States, reading (here, novels) should not be considered "as an anointed, elite tradition but as a living and breathing cultural practice."[32] Of course, some religious texts are used in ritually specific and "elite" ways intended to be separate from the "mundane," but this is rarely the *only* way that they are used. As the opening conversation about feeding Krishna pizza shows, that which is "sacred" for Pushtimargi devotees is not entirely separate from ordinary aspects of daily life. On the contrary: forming a relationship with Krishna through rituals of *sevā*, and the reading practices that support this formation, are also part of people's everyday decisions about what and how to eat, which clothes to wear, when to depart for one's office job or travel for pleasure, and how to engage in the social world more broadly.[33] While for many Pushtimargis these decisions are anchored in class and caste

read and recited by a diaspora Hindu community in the United States to cultivate both social and religious community and to gain merit.

[29] This challenges Griffiths' theoretical framework in *Religious Reading*, which ultimately perpetuates a binary between "sacred" and "mundane" (or, as he writes, "consumerist") modes of religious reading—a binary that also emerges from the essays in Boyarin's *An Ethnography of Reading*. Matthew Rosen addresses this binary in an article on "footpath libraries" in Pune, India. As Rosen notes, Boyarin's study attends primarily to the reading of literary and or sacred texts, separating "important" reading from reading that is "routine" ("Ethnographies of Reading: Beyond Literacy and Books," *Anthropological Quarterly* 88, no. 4 [2016]: 1060).

[30] Syed Akbar Hyder, *Reliving Karbala: Martyrdom in South Asian Memory* (New York: Oxford University Press, 2006), 74.

[31] Hyder draws on the term and concept popularized by reader response critic Stanley Fish.

[32] Bhalla, *Reading Together, Reading Apart*, 130.

[33] Joyce B. Flueckiger argues for the "everyday" to be included in what is counted, by scholars, as "religious." As Flueckiger writes, "Given the centrality of everyday practices in Hindu traditions, over both time and space—including the foods one cooks at particular ritual occasions—I would prefer to expand the boundaries of what counts as 'religion' to include 'ways of life' rather than to exclude

privileges specific to urban life in western India, the observation that daily-life concerns influence people's negotiations of text-based precept and practice is not unique to this community: that which is "prescribed" and "practiced" vis-à-vis religious texts is, as Leela Prasad has shown, dynamic and elastic even in relationship to elite Sanskrit treatises like the *Dharmaśāstras* ("Dharma Manuals"), which are often considered to be rigid, "authenticated," as they are, "by the [male Brahmin] monastic authority."[34] This book expands on this body of South Asia studies and religious studies scholarship by emphasizing religious reading in order to re-center text and reader as inherently interdependent in performative practice.

While I study Pushtimargi texts in relationship to actual readers, past and present, most scholarship has taken a disembodied approach to the subject by diligently avoiding real readers in theorizing about reading. Since we cannot get inside a person's head to watch "live" how they receive and analyze a text, as many literary theorists have asserted, we must consider reading through theoretical or "ideal" readers.[35] This, of course, reifies not only the reader, but also the text: if both exist only as ideal types, then it is easy to avoid the diverse and sometimes unpredictable relationships that real readers have with written texts. The scholarly impulse to sidestep the dynamic relationships that people have with religious texts is also connected to the notion that if we are speaking of "reading"—rather than, say, distinct genres of oral recitation or singing of a text—then we are only speaking of something silent, private, and personal. However, as anyone who has spent significant time in and around religious communities in South Asia knows, even quiet reading to/for oneself often happens among others, whether in one's home, on the train, or at a temple or shrine. Reading, in other words, is a social practice: Pushtimargis read written texts both "silently" and "out loud" among and with other people

Hinduism. This inclusion may cause us to see practices in other religious traditions, such as cooking, in a new light—as *religious* practices" (*Everyday Hinduism* [West Sussex: Wiley-Blackwell, 2015], 4).

34 Leela Prasad, *Poetics of Conduct: Oral Narrative and Moral Being in a South Indian Town* (New York: Columbia University Press, 2006), 12. The term *dharma* has varied connotations in different contexts but broadly refers to socio-religious norms and may be translated as "duty" or "righteousness." Beyond the study of modern South Asia, Corbellini et al. have likewise discussed religious reading as an "intensive, physical and emotional" practice that accompanied readers in all aspects of their public and private lives (*Discovering the Riches of the Word*, 3).

35 There are many overlapping scholarly lineages that have theorized about the "ideal" or "implied" reader. For instance, 20th-century "reader response" theorist Wolfgang Iser, drawing on German phenomenological philosophy, proposed that the act of reading be considered via the construction of an "implied reader," who is not a "real" reader (*The Act of Reading: A Theory of Aesthetic Response* [Baltimore: Johns Hopkins University Press, 1978], 36).

and in order—among many reasons—to strengthen their relationships with other people, and with Krishna.[36] It is my assertion that regardless of how important the inner aesthetics of reading may be, and regardless of the desire to theorize some ideal type, religious reading is embedded in the messy realities of real people's lives and in the ways in which they make and remake their moral, social, and devotional worlds.[37]

If reading is social, then so, too, are texts, and not merely because they are read. As Edward W. Said has suggested, a reader "may often be, but is not merely, the alchemical translator of texts into circumstantial reality or worldliness." Texts on their own,

> have ways of existing, both theoretical and practical, that even in their most rarefied form are always enmeshed in circumstance, time, place, and society—in short, they are in the world, and hence are worldly. The same is doubtless true of the critic, as reader and writer.[38]

While texts are not "just like" living human interlocutors, they are, of course, written by humans and inevitably communicate with their readers: the text is inescapably a communicative act across time and space. In this process of communication, *both* readers and texts change. *Both* text and reader are "ordered in accord with codes of perception" that neither text nor reader solely controls.[39] In *The Practice of Everyday Life*, Michel de Certeau offers a wonderfully vivid analogy, comparing the reader to a renter making habitable an apartment (the text): "renters make comparable changes in an apartment they furnish with

[36] My thinking about this has been influenced by the work of historian of religions Robert Orsi, who writes that religion "exists not as a medium of making meanings" but, rather, as a "network of relationships between heaven and earth involving humans of all ages and the many different sacred figures together" (*Between Heaven and Earth: The Religious Worlds People Make and the Scholars Who Study Them* [Princeton, NJ: Princeton University Press, 2005], 2).

[37] In the article, "'More than 'Alone with the Bible': Reconceptualizing Religious Reading," Emily K. Ronald emphasizes the need to dissociate religious reading with the solitary reader, namely, in the context of Protestant and Catholic American communities (*Sociology of Religion*, 73, no. 3 [2012]: 323–344).

[38] Edward W. Said, "The Text, the World, the Critic," *The Bulletin of the Midwest Modern Language Association* 8, no. 2, 1975: 5. See also, Edward W. Said, *The World, the Text, and the Critic* (Cambridge, MA: Harvard University Press, 1983).

[39] Michel de Certeau, *The Practice of Everyday Life*, trans. Steven Rendall (Berkeley: University of California Press, 1984), 171. I am both drawing from and also pushing back against de Certeau here. The sentence from which I have pulled this quote is speaking of the ways in which texts, not readers, change. I am asserting that texts change *with* readers, and readers *with* texts. Writing about digital Bible reading, Tim Hutchings has noted something similar: "texts and their readers shape each other" ("Design and the Digital Bible: Persuasive Technology and Religious Reading," *Journal of Contemporary Religion*, 32, no. 2 [2017]: 205–219, 216).

their acts and memories; as do speakers, in the language into which they insert both messages of native tongue, through their accent, through their own 'turns of phrase,' etc., their own history [. . .]."[40] While de Certeau's project is more generally concerned with how people navigate and make their own the "everyday" in relationship to popular culture, daily rituals, language, and laws, this assertion about readers as "renters" provides a useful way to think about how texts and readers cohabitate. When discussing *religious* reading, however, we must modify de Certeau's analogy.[41] Religious readers, or perhaps any reader who is in a close and sustained relationship with a particular text tradition, cannot be thought of in terms of mere renters in an apartment. Rather, religious readers tend to take up permanent residence in the habitats built (at least in part) by their beloved texts. For Pushtimargi devotees, practices of reading also quite literally occupy their own physical dwellings, as does Krishna, who often resides as a *svarūp* at the center of devotees' homes.

By exploring how Pushtimargi devotees have engaged with their devotional literature as readers in a variety of social and historical contexts, this book's five chapters showcase these vibrant relationships between texts and readers and exhibit how reading functions as a primary vehicle for individuals and communities to navigate their "habitats"—their everyday spaces of living—as well as to navigate broader social and religious change. In so doing, I invite my own readers to consider how a text's medium is essential to its communication with readers, but also how people's readings of texts emerge out of specific contexts, such as personal and social-historical circumstances.

Navigating This Book and the Devotional-Social Worlds of Pushtimargi Hinduism

This book is organized both thematically and chronologically: the first two chapters consider the distinct textual ecology of *Vārtā Sāhitya* and the modern history (starting in the late 19th century) of Pushtimargi literature and reading practices, while the following three chapters are anchored in the ethnographic present as I explore the various sites and manners in which

[40] de Certeau, *The Practice of Everyday Life*, xxi.

[41] In asserting that scripture, too, can be worldly, Said writes about interpretations of the Qur'an, suggesting that in some schools of exegetical practice, the text—an "event"—can be viewed as "absolutely circumstantial and worldly, without at the same time making that worldliness *dominate* the actual sense of the text" ("The Text, the World, the Critic," 7). In other words, by claiming that texts are worldly Said is not negating scripture's devotional and more-than-human qualities.

contemporary Pushtimargis read and analyze devotional texts. Familiarity with the form, content, and social history of this devotional literature is essential, I maintain, for understanding how Pushtimargis read today. All five chapters, however, blend literary and ethnographic analysis, as I aim to show how readers' personal relationships with *vārtā* texts are connected to the literature's form and history.

Chapter 1, "Dialogical Reading: The Pushtimarg's Performative Canon," begins by describing a key textual episode from *Vārtā Sāhitya* as it is read aloud by Goswami Shalini Bahuji, a hereditary leader's wife, to a group of newly initiated Pushtimargi devotees in 2017. The episode in question comes from one of today's most widely read and discussed *vārtā* texts, the *Caurāsī Vaiṣṇavan kī Vārtā* ("Chronicles of Eighty-Four Vaishnavas").[42] As shown in my translation here, the episode is intended to justify the text's own authority in relationship to the *Subodhinī* ("That Which Is Greatly Enlightening")—one of the most prominent Sanskrit theological treatises attributed to the Pushtimarg's first teacher Vallabhacharya. A small portion of this episode may be translated as follows:

> One day, Shri Gokulnathji was discussing the eighty-four Vaishnavas with Kalyan Bhatt and some other devotees . . . [43] By midnight he still hadn't begun his daily recitation of the *Subodhinījī*. Then, a devotee said to Shri Gokulnathji: "My Lord, when will you begin the recitation? It is already midnight!" Then, from his lotus-like-mouth Shri Gokulnathji said: "Today the fruits of my recitation will be known through a discussion of the eighty-four Vaishnavas. There is no principle superior to the Vaishnavas and it is by means of the Vaishnavas that our path will come to fruition.[44]

I discuss how Shalini Goswami, after reading this episode aloud in Braj Bhasha, explains to those gathered that her own reading from the *Caurāsī Vaiṣṇavan kī Vārtā* in the 21st century is "proof" that reading devotional literature will continue to "nurture the Pushtimarg into the future." The chapter

42 Though the word *vārtā* in this title (*Caurāsī Vaiṣṇavan kī Vārtā*) might be translated as "chronicle," I have rendered it "chronicles" to indicate that the text in fact contains multiple *vārtās*. The term "Vaishnava" can refer broadly to devotees of the Hindu deity Vishnu and to his various *avatars* (manifestations), including Krishna. However, its use in this text's title is specific to followers of the Pushtimarg. In contemporary Gujarat, too, people often use the designation to refer specifically to *Pushtimargi* Vaishnavas.

43 Shri (*śrī*) is an honorific prefix.

44 Dvārkādās Puruṣottamdās Parīkh, ed., *Caurāsī Vaiṣṇavan kī Vārtā* (*Tīn Janma kī Līlā Bhāvnā Vālī*) (Indore, India: Vaiṣṇav Mitra Maṇḍal, 2011), 1–2.

then further elaborates on how Shalini Goswami's reading and exegesis point to the modes through which Pushtimargi literature and textual interpretation have traditionally been authorized. In so doing, I also introduce the tradition's broader textual landscape, arguing that the intertextual content and aesthetics of *Vārtā Sāhitya* are essential to how these particular written narratives continue to be read in contemporary contexts.

Perhaps the most widely read Pushtimargi texts in their own right, the *vārtās* are also inextricably linked to other vernacular literature and also to works produced in Sanskrit, particularly those attributed to Vallabhacharya, such as the *Subodhinī*.[45] The *Subodhinī* itself is a commentary on the *Bhāgavatapurāṇa* ("The Legend of God"), a Sanskrit poetic work redacted in southern India during the 10th century CE. As with myriad Krishna-devoted theologians before and after him, Vallabhacharya's commentary is especially focused on the *Bhāgavatapurāṇa*'s tenth canto, which famously describes the *līlā* (divine pastimes) of Krishna as a playful child and amorous youth in the idyllic and eternal land of Braj.[46] One of the *Subodhinī*'s primary concerns is to apply Vallabhacharya's *śhuddhādvaita* (pure non-dual) theology, as well as concepts borrowed from Indian theorists' writing on the aesthetics of theater, to explain how Krishna's Braj *līlās* become a model for the proper cultivation of the devotee's love for the divine.[47] As indicated in the *vārtā* episode previously cited, one of *Vārtā Sāhitya*'s stated aims is to use stories about the Pushtimarg's early disciples as a preferred way to relate Vallabhacharya's teachings to the reader/listener. And indeed, for a majority of modern devotees, the most accessible—but also the most beloved and widely read—texts of the tradition are not those attributed to Vallabhacharya himself but, rather, those by and about his early disciples.[48]

[45] For further information on this text, see James D. Redington's *Śrīsubodhinī: Vallabhācārya on the Love Games of Kṛṣṇa* (Delhi: Motilal Banarsidass, 1983).

[46] Braj is conceived of as both an otherworldly place and also a physical, geographical location. While the Pushtimarg has been present in urban western India since the mid-17th century, its roots are in the rural North Indian region of Braj (Vallabhacharya's own family hailed from the Telugu-speaking region of India). The physical Braj is not recognized administratively. Rather, it has largely been defined by popular Krishna devotion. Much of the region as people experience it today (e.g., via pilgrimage routes) falls within the contemporary state of Uttar Pradesh's Mathura District. For a comprehensive study of the region, see Alan W. Entwistle's *Braj: Centre of Krishna Pilgrimage* (Groningen, the Netherlands: Egbert Forsten, 1987) and David Haberman's *Journey Through the Twelve Forests: An Encounter with Krishna* (New York: Oxford University Press, 1994).

[47] *Vārtā Sāhitya* describes Vallabhacharya's passion for the *Bhāgavatapurāṇa* as central to his writings, proselytizing pilgrimages, and to his modes of religious instruction.

[48] Chapter 1 further discusses authorship of *vārtā* texts, but, in short, these texts are attributed to Vallabhacharya's descendants and their followers living between the 17th and 19th centuries. Scholar Priya Kothari's forthcoming doctoral dissertation, "Preaching and Public Memory: Storytellers of

In addition to considering how the *vārtā*s fit into the Pushtimarg's broader textual landscape, Chapter 1 also examines the literature's form as distinctly conversational. Texts like the *Caurāsī Vaiṣṇavan kī Vārtā* are constructed around records of direct speech known as *vacanāmṛt* (nectarous speech) in the form of dialogue between Krishna, Vallabhacharya and his descendants, and their disciples. The following episode from the *vārtā* about a widowed woman and her Thakurji (her Krishna *svarūp*), the same figure discussed in this Introduction's opening vignette, is one of many examples of how *vacanāmṛt* appears in the *vārtā*s:

> After completing *sevā* for her Krishna *svarūp*, the widow would spin cotton and sell it to support herself. Whenever a vegetable seller would come by the house of the widow, Shri Thakurji would call out, "O' Ma! The vegetable lady has come, go get me something!" Then the widow would go and buy a small amount of everything. [. . .] One day, when a vegetable seller was passing by the widow's home, Shri Thakurji ran to the door and called out, "Come quick! My mother is coming to fetch something!" The vegetable seller heard Shri Thakurji's beautiful voice and came running, but Shri Thakurji quickly went back inside the house and was never seen by the vendor. "My darling! You mustn't run out like that, you may be given the evil eye," the widow scolded Shri Thakurji. [. . .] Then, just like a worldly child, Shri Thakurji began to argue with the elderly woman saying, "Now that vegetable woman has left! How will I eat? How will you feed me my meal?" The woman assured Shri Thakurji, telling Him that she would get vegetables from another vendor or from the bazaar. "Don't argue with me—just be content!" Then, like a small child, Shri Thakurji climbed up on the widow's shoulders and whined, "but when will you bring me food?" In this way, Shri Thakurji bestowed much grace on the woman.

This episode, depicted in Figure I.2, is poignant for readers because of its refrain about how Krishna behaves "like a small child," showing his familial relationship with the widow as he *speaks directly* to her, telling her what he

Krishna in the Vallabha Tradition of Western India" (University of California, Berkeley), will consider the growing popularity of the *Bhāgavatapurāṇa* for modern Pushtimargis, focusing especially on how the text is performatively read to an audience in a genre called *kathā* (the recitation and exegesis of a text, often religious in nature).

Figure I.2. 19th-century painting of Thakurji asking the widowed disciple for food "like a small child" from an illustrated manuscript (Source: the Amit Ambalal Collection).

desires.[49] I show how these records of *vacanāmṛt*, as *Vārtā Sāhitya*'s primary dialogical feature, are essential to the way modern readers like Shalini Goswami engage with the narratives intertextually and dialogically, giving rise to distinct types of public readings, sermons, and both oral and written commentaries. In this way, when received by readers, *vārtā* narratives as written texts become part of a performative canon, re-establishing social and devotional networks each time they are read.

While the quote from the *Caurāsī Vaiṣṇavan kī Vārtā* about "discussing" the lives of Vallabhacharya's disciples shows how the *vārtā*s emerged from an oral storytelling tradition, since the end of the 19th century Pushtimargis

[49] Figure I.2 also appears and is discussed here: Emilia Bachrach, *In the Service of Krishna: Illustrating the Lives of Eighty-Four Vaishnavas from a 1702 Manuscript in the Amit Ambalal Collection* (Ahmedabad, India: Mapin, 2019), 31.

have primarily engaged with these texts as printed and published books. The movement from manuscript culture to book culture, and from oral storytelling culture to book-reading culture, along with broader social changes of the period, inspired Pushtimargi readers to engage with their devotional literature in new ways. One significant change was the proliferation of written commentaries on the hagiographies, many of which emphasized the "correct" manner in which to read and interpret the texts in terms of contemporary circumstances. Chapter 2, "Commentarial Reading: Historicizing Hagiography and Making Modern Readers," discusses these contemporary circumstances by introducing a series of pivotal moments in the modern formation of the Pushtimarg, all of which hinged on shifting perceptions of the tradition's devotional literature. I first look at the social climate that led to the well-known Maharaja Libel Supreme Court Case of 1862, during which the scriptural authority of *Vārtā Sāhitya* and the texts' representation of the Pushtimarg as an "authentically Hindu sect" were called into question in the national spotlight. While 19th-century disputes over Pushtimargi identity have been well documented, little attention has been paid to how the community itself responded to the libel case and its aftermath.[50] I demonstrate how Pushtimargis restored a sense of community not through a rejection of but, rather, through a deliberate cultural reauthorization of their vernacular literature. This reauthorization was achieved in part by translating *Vārtā Sāhitya* into modern Gujarati and embedding within the hagiographies new styles of written commentary aimed at making the texts palatable to modern readers—both Pushtimargis as well as those beyond the fold. The rise of late 19th-century print capitalism, which initiated the circulation of the *vārtā*s as published and increasingly affordable books, was an important factor in facilitating this cultural reauthorization. Examples of the late 19th- and 20th-century written commentaries that I discuss in Chapter 2 reveal a distinct concern for how Pushtimargis might continue to find devotional inspiration from their premodern literary tradition.

Chapter 3, "Public Reading: Debating Text, Temple, and Religious Authority," further examines how Pushtimargis have approached

[50] For example, see Amrita Shodhan, "Legal Representations of Khojas and Pushtimārga Vaishnava Polities as Communities: The Aga Khan Case and the Maharaj Libel Case in Mid-Nineteenth Century Bombay" (PhD diss., University of Chicago, 1995); David L. Haberman, "On Trial: The Love of Sixteen Thousand Gopees," *History of Religions* 33, no. 1 (1993): 44–70; J. Barton Scott, "How to Defame a God: Public Selfhood in the Maharaj Libel Case," *The Journal of South Asian Studies* 38, no. 3 (2015): 387–402; and Makrand J. Mehta, "Maharaj Libel Case: A Study in Social Change in Western India in the 19th Century," *Indo-Asian Culture* 19, no. 1 (1970): 26–39.

17th-century hagiographies as models for contemporary devotional living by considering how public readings of *vārtā* literature have been used by a diverse set of 21st-century interlocutors (e.g., a contentious hereditary leader, temple trustees, and a female devotee-blogger) to negotiate changing physical and social-institutional structures. The chapter's primary example is an ongoing community debate over temple (re)construction and corresponding changes in the ritual worship of Krishna in temple spaces. Practically speaking, temple (re)construction projects include such measures as building new "hygienic" kitchens in older temples and increasing the size of spaces in which devotees can gather for *darśan* (auspicious sight) of Krishna deities. Those who oppose (re)construction argue that such projects are not only antithetical to the teachings embedded in Pushtimargi literature but also strip the tradition of its distinct identity by rendering the community's temples, known as *havelī*s (palatial homes), ordinary *mandir*s (*mandir* being the most common, trans-sectarian term in Hindi and Gujarati for "temple"). *Havelī*s, some argue, were traditionally intended to function as private homes for Krishna deities and their immediate caretakers, not as public centers of collective worship. The chapter analyzes the nuances of these debates, including how interlocutors with various commitments defend their positions via specific styles of public reading and textual exegesis (e.g., during *pravacan*s, *carcā sabhā*s, or "debate colloquiums," and on social media platforms). The debates analyzed in this chapter reveal the diverse ways in which individuals rely on practices of publicly reading and interpreting *Vārtā Sāhitya* to articulate a vision of the Pushtimarg's future as an increasingly affluent and transnational Hindu community.

Shifting from public debates to more private ones, Chapters 4 and 5 take a closer look at the contexts of community reading, or *satsaṅg* (gathering of the faithful) among contemporary readers in Ahmedabad city (the primary site for my ethnographic research). Chapter 4, "Community Reading: Learning Affective Piety," considers how devotees use the context of *satsaṅg* to cultivate Pushtimarg-specific, though highly personalized, modes of affective piety. Devotees also use *satsaṅg* as a site for learning: about Pushtimargi doctrine and about how better to navigate between being Krishna's caretakers and fulfilling various social and familial expectations. Drawing on participant observation from several *satsaṅg*s in Ahmedabad, I analyze the features of these ritualized gatherings, which are grounded in reading aloud from the prose hagiographies in a "storytelling" mode as well as active dialogue that includes affirmations and challenges to sectarian authority and long-standing theological, ritual, and social ideals. Readers' personal circumstances come to the fore as they make sense of the 17th-century hagiographies in terms of their own 21st-century lives. Ultimately, I argue, community readings provide a forum in which *laukik* (worldly) and *alaukik* (otherworldly) narratives can be allowed to coexist for contemporary devotees whose practices of reading in turn sustain *Vārtā Sāhitya* as canonical.

As illustrated by the examples of *satsaṅg* gatherings in Ahmedabad, readers' personal circumstances, including life stage and gender, can significantly influence how they use religious reading as not only an exegetical, but also an affective and embodied, practice. This book's final chapter, "Women's Reading: Navigating Family, Gender, and Devotion," picks up on this theme by following the lives and reading practices of several women, namely, the Pushtimargi hereditary leader Goswami Indirabetiji (d. 2016) and three devotees. Goswami Indirabetiji, the first and only female hereditary leader to initiate her own followers into the Pushtimarg, used her role as a public reader-exegete to gain authority in a male-dominated tradition where, historically, authority has been inherited through male primogeniture, descending from Vallabhacharya. This public leader's mode of textual interpretation and her emphasis on the centrality of reading are also connected to how ardent female devotees describe their own practices of reading. For many women, reading is essential to how they maintain their and their families' well-being and also to how they balance Krishna's ritual care and social obligations (e.g., marriage, child care, and professional life).

Key to ritual worship in the Pushtimarg is the loving service of Krishna *svarūp*s, who are cared for in temples and devotees' homes (Figure I.3 depicts temple *sevā*). While *Vārtā Sāhitya* depicts men and women alike as Krishna's caretakers, contemporary domestic *sevā*, which typically involves the daily feeding, bathing, and dressing of Krishna *svarūp*s, is frequently performed by women. As Chapter 5 delineates in greater detail, women's primacy as *both* ritual practitioners *and* religious readers is often explained to me (by men and women) in terms of women's "inherent qualities" of devotional nurturing and, as one female interlocutor put it, the ability to "balance multiple commitments at once." The gendered nature of Pushtimargi *sevā* and the way that devotees describe women's practices as dominant are also more broadly connected to pan–South Asian *bhakti* (devotional) theologies that mark female figures as models for forming relationships with the divine. In the context of Krishna *bhakti*, such role

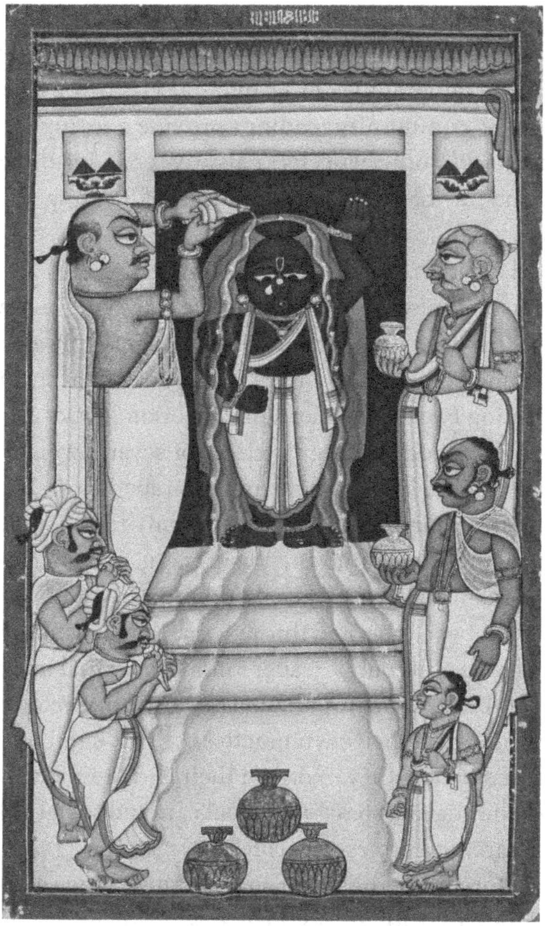

Figure I.3. 19th-century depiction of Pushtimargi hereditary leaders bathing Krishna in his form as Shrinathji (Source: the Amit Ambalal Collection).

models famously include the *gopīs*, the otherworldly cow-herding women of Krishna's celestial and earthly home in the region of Braj, as well as Krishna's adoptive mother Yashoda.[51]

As *Vārtā Sāhitya* itself details, devotees should become so attuned to Krishna's daily needs and desires that they ought to know if the deity is feeling

[51] Karen Pechilis discusses the gendering of *bhakti* more broadly in *Interpreting Devotion: The Poetry and Legacy of a Female Bhakti Saint of India* (New York: Routledge, 2016). With respect to my use of the term *bhakti* (which I translate as "devotion" and "devotional" throughout this book), I follow the lead of Jain studies scholar John Cort, who argues that "*bhakti*" is many things: "Bhakti is

hot and needs a drink of water, or cold and could use an extra pair of wool socks or a shawl. While each devotee's *sevā* practices are unique, lunisolar calendars managed by the Pushtimarg's hereditary leaders in Nathdwara, Rajasthan (a sort of headquarters for the community), are published annually to suggest a particular sequence of worship throughout the year. Such calendars, however, do not consider the regular dilemmas of professional work outside the home, international travel, and any other number of daily matters, including gender-specific concerns (e.g., such as those related to menstruation), that Pushtimargis face. Juggling the assumed norms of a demanding ritual calendar—and the directly articulated demands of Krishna himself!—is therefore key to women's ongoing dialogue about navigating precept and practice in their daily lives. *Vārtā* narratives, much like the one about the widowed devotee with which this Introduction opened, model ways in which one might juggle the roles of Krishna's caretaker and, for instance, busy parent for whom pizza is a convenient weeknight food item. As Goswami Indirabetiji told a room full of devotees—most of them women—during a seven-day *pravacan* on *Vārtā Sāhitya*: the *vārtā*s are unique in that they provide both *siddhānt* (doctrine) as well as *dṛṣṭānt* (an "illustration" of said doctrine in practice).[52]

Today many Pushtimargi women in western India are professionally employed outside their homes and express anxiety about fulfilling social, familial, and professional expectations while also cultivating a relationship with Krishna through rituals of *sevā* (such as making flower garlands, as shown in Figure I.4). Chapter 5 argues that both female devotees and their hereditary leader counterparts have strategically innovated traditional techniques of reading and exegesis to renegotiate not only the structure of their personal social-devotional relationships as women, but also the very structure of community leadership and the public identity of the Pushtimarg. In so doing, women's practices of readings—which are as affectively significant as they are analytically meaningful—contribute directly to the way that women cultivate their own personal well-being, as well as the well-being of their household *svarūp*s, families, and broader community.

not restricted to what scholars say it is; rather, it is primarily what bhaktas have said it is . . . " ("Bhakti in the Early Jain Tradition: Understanding Devotional Religion in South Asia," *History of Religions* 42, no. 1 [2002]: 59–86, 62).

[52] "Indira betiji pravachan 84 vaisnav varta- 1 of 71," https://www.youtube.com/watch?v=okx9DILLBgI, accessed January 10, 2018.

Figure I.4. (Left) Devotees making flower garlands for a Krishna *svarūp* in an Ahmedabad temple; (right) women gathered to read in a devotee's living room. (Photos by author.)

When I returned to the United States after a research trip to India for this book project in 2017, I spoke with Mona Desai, a long-time conversation partner, on the phone about my journey home. "Did you get any research done on the plane?" Mona asked me. "Well, not so much, I was really tired and feeling sad about not being able to see you and others for a long time," I replied. "Just read the *vārtās*," Mona instructed me in a comforting voice. "Can't you find anyone to read with?" While there are study guides available today for reading the *vārtā*s solo (see more on this in Chapters 2 and 5), the possibility of reading alone continues to be difficult to imagine for many Pushtimargis. Some younger devotees manage separation from their home communities by reading and discussing literature virtually, but for Mona, now in her seventies, it is not ideal to replace in-person gatherings with technologically mediated ones.[53] "Emilia!" Mona said, excitedly. "You can just ring me up on the phone on Thursdays and you can join us that way. I'll put the phone in the center of [our *satsaṅg*], and that way you can hear us all. I did that once when I was traveling in Canada. It made my heart happy even though I felt great *viraha* (pangs of separation, specifically from one's object/s of devotion)!" My conclusion to this book, "Religious Reading and Everyday Lives," returns to the question of how studying Pushtimargi readers like Mona points more broadly

[53] During the COVID-19 pandemic beginning in 2019, devotees have shared with me their anxiety around reading in isolation and being separated from other community members. Even older devotees like Mona, however, have been innovative about virtual gatherings and solo reading.

to how religious reading functions as a dynamic set of practices that influence and are influenced by devotees' personal circumstances and unique relationships to their beloved texts. For my interlocutors, reading takes place in multiple contexts, including ritualized meetings and public debates during which *Vārtā Sāhitya* may be read aloud, quoted, casually referred to, formally commented on, actively questioned, and interpreted in ways that validate and challenge long-standing exegetical paradigms and values. Practices of reading and interpretations of texts are as emergent as people's real-life situations, but they are also dependent on the form and content of texts themselves. The form of written *vārtā* texts as vernacular prose hagiographies is uniquely inviting for devotees to contemplate their own modes of devotional living in dialogue with others. As Tony K. Stewart has written with respect to the 16th-century hagiographies of a Hindu tradition similar to the Pushtimarg, "Each generation [of devotees] was charged with the responsibility of revalorizing its tradition without destroying it, to make it relevant to a contemporary world without having to diverge from the general consensus of its broad normative ideals, to make its history relevant [. . .]."[54] This happened, Stewart suggests, through writing hagiography, which might be thought of in terms of a process of "fixing a 'grammar' of Vaiṣṇava ritual and theology," which eventually works in "structuring individual and group experience, structuring community, structuring the tradition's own history."[55] As this book shows, it is not only acts of writing, but also acts of reading hagiography, that contribute to the ongoing process of celebrating and (re)articulating individual and community identity and devotional practice. In modern contexts this process is ongoing. Devotees do not read to merely perpetuate didactic accounts of sectarian orthodoxy. Rather, devotees approach *Vārtā Sāhitya* as part of a performative canon that animates an *ever-expanding* grammar of tradition in ways that speak directly to readers in the here and now.

[54] Stewart, *The Final Word*, 9.
[55] Ibid.

1

Dialogical Reading

The Pushtimarg's Performative Canon

Megha Choksi is hosting a formal gathering for newly initiated Pushtimargi devotees in the backyard of her Ahmedabad home. Shalini Goswami Bahuji, the wife of Megha's guru, is presiding over the event and is seated on a platform beneath a white tent that has been erected adjacent to Megha's well-tended rose garden. Megha and several other women are seated on either side of Shalini Goswami, while the rest of those gathered—about forty men and women, mostly adults and a few teenagers—sit on mats on the ground in front of the platform. Like Shalini Goswami herself, Megha and the other women seated on the platform are all seasoned Pushtimargis who have been bestowed with two sets of initiatory mantras meant to cleanse devotees so they are fit to pursue a relationship with Krishna. The first mantra, *Shri Krishna śaranaṃ mama*, translates to "Shri Krishna is my refuge," and the second, the *brahmasambandha* (the "binding with Brahman"), is meant to bind devotees to Brahman, the Supreme Being, who is one and the same as Krishna.[1] It is only after receiving this second mantra, along with explicit *ājñā* (permission) and guidance from the initiating guru, that devotees may begin Krishna's loving service, or *sevā*, through the domestic ritual care of the deity in his embodied form as a *svarūp*.[2]

Many of these newly initiated Pushtimargis received their initiation mantras and performed the associated rituals on the same day as one

[1] The first mantra is also called the *nām nivedan* (dedication to the name) or *aṣṭākṣara* (eight syllables) mantra. Some devotees receive the first mantra as children, while others receive it as adults, often just before their *brahmasambandha* mantra (also known as the *ātmanivedan*—"the soul's supplication"). For more on the *aṣṭākṣara mantra*, see Priya Kothari, "The Aṣṭākṣara Mantra: Spiritual Growth from 'Śrī' to 'Ma' in Puṣṭimārga," *Journal of Vaishnava Studies* 24, no. 2 (2016): 197–212. For further information on the relevance of mantra in the Pushtimarg, see Shital Sharma and Emilia Bachrach, "Beyond Initiation: The Social Lives of Mantra in the Puṣṭimārg," *Journal of Vaishnava Studies* 24, no. 2 (2016): 177–196. The *brahmasambandha* mantra asks initiates to dedicate their body, senses, life breaths, inner faculties, and possessions to Krishna. An English translation of the mantra can be found in James D. Redington's *The Grace of Lord Krishna: The Sixteen Verse-treatises (Ṣoḍaśagranthāḥ) of Vallabhacharya* (Delhi: Shri Satguru Publications, 2000), 67.

[2] *Svarūps* are often crafted of metal or stone and are just a few inches in height.

Religious Reading and Everyday Lives in Devotional Hinduism. Emilia Bachrach, Oxford University Press. DOI: 10.1093/oso/9780197648599.003.0002

another: in their respective homes they had fasted, bathed, and donned new clothing. Once in the ritually pure state known as *aparas* (> Skt. *asparśa*, "untouched"), they had traveled from their homes to the temple run by their to-be guru, Shalini Goswami's husband, with a monetary donation for the Krishna *svarūp* housed there. Now, just a few weeks later, this group of newly initiated devotees is gathered in Megha's backyard as "Vaishnavas ready to begin a journey together." This journey, as Shalini Goswami announces in her welcoming address, will help them to increase their "knowledge and devotion" and learn what it means to "be a Pushtimargi Vaishnava." In the subsequent ninety minutes, those gathered will hear Shalini Goswami discuss the responsibility they assume when beginning Krishna's *sevā* and how the *sevak* (loving servant) can live faithfully in the "modern world." She will also read aloud from several Pushtimargi texts, but primarily from the hagiographies of the Pushtimarg's first followers as they are enshrined in the *Caurāsī Vaiṣṇavan kī Vārtā*—a text at the heart of the tradition's literary canon and the foremost text within the genre of *Vārtā Sāhitya*.

In conversations with Shalini Goswami prior to the backyard event for new devotees, she shared with me her own memory of initiation upon marriage. She had not been raised Pushtimargi and had to quickly learn the norms of public wifehood in her husband's Vallabha Kul (Vallabha Dynasty) family.[3] Her husband, who is directly descended from the community's first teacher Vallabhacharya, has inherited the authority to initiate new devotees into the fold and to be the custodian of a prestigious Krishna *svarūp* who has resided in his family's *havelī* for generations. Upon joining this Vallabha Kul family, Shalini Goswami also had to learn Gujarati (her first language is Hindi), and—most importantly, she said—the numerous rituals associated with temple and domestic *sevā*. What was most interesting during our conversation, however, and what likewise came to the fore during the event Shalini Goswami presided over in Megha's backyard, was how deeply intertwined the rituals of initiation and subsequent *sevā* practices are with people's readings of Pushtimargi literature. "I read a lot," Shalini Goswami told me, as she described her own experience of becoming Pushtimargi. "Shri Mahaprabhuji (one of several titles for Vallabhacharya) also received the *brahmasambandha* mantra directly from Shrinathji (a localized form

[3] For many Pushtimargis, particularly for members of the Vallabha Kul, caste, not affiliation with the Pushtimarg, governs marriage practices. The name "Shalini Goswami," as with the names of other interlocutors in this chapter, is a pseudonym, and I have therefore left the name and other identity markers for her husband and their family intentionally vague.

of Krishna and chief Pushtimargi *svarūp*). This is all told in *vārtājī* [*Vārtā Sāhitya*] and in Shri Mahaprabhuji's *granths* (texts)," she explained, "and these texts continue to guide Vaishnavas today." As Shalini Goswami told those gathered in Megha's backyard, their initiation in the 21st century was "proof" that reading the *Caurāsī Vaiṣṇavan kī Vārtā* will continue to "nurture the Pushtimarg into the future."

This chapter attends to the centrality of reading in the process by which people become Pushtimargi and argues that the *Caurāsī Vaiṣṇavan kī Vārtā* (hereafter *84VV*) and related texts contribute to a shared grammar of devotional experience and praxis that animates devotees' everyday lives. Throughout this book I show how Pushtimargis engage with devotional literature in ways that are unique to their own social positions and historical circumstances, but this chapter emphasizes that Pushtimargis also participate in an ever-emergent but shared "grammar of tradition" as readers.[4] This grammar emerges from the distinct style and content of the written hagiographies themselves and is formed and reformed each time devotees gather together to read, analyze, and discuss the narratives in community settings. In this way, practices of reading and textual exegesis become primary modes through which devotees—as individuals and in community—continuously make their traditions relevant to the contemporary world.

In what follows, I analyze this shared grammar of tradition vis-à-vis two texts: the *84VV*, which provides hagiographies of Vallabhacharya's disciples, and its sister text, the *Do So Bāvan Vaiṣṇavan kī Vārtā* ("Chronicles of Two Hundred and Fifty-Two Vaishnavas"; hereafter *252VV*), which provides hagiographies of devotees initiated by Vallabhacharya's son and successor Vitthalnath (1515–1585). Likely composed during the 17th century, these collections of hagiographies tell intensely sweet, and sometimes funny and polemical, stories about Vallabhacharya and Vitthalnath's followers and the growth of the Pushtimarg during the early modern period.[5] After introducing the *84VV* and *252VV*, I consider how the hagiographies are characterized by their use of direct speech in the form of dialogue between the narratives' human protagonists and Krishna himself. This *vacanāmṛt*—particularly when uttered by Krishna and Vallabhacharya—is central to the

[4] Tony K. Stewart suggests that any attempt to understand hagiographies must bear in mind the "theological assertions, the rhetorical strategies, and the traditional narrative conventions of the genre [. . .]" (*The Final Word*, 13).

[5] I discuss the texts' provenance further later in this chapter.

authority of the *vārtās* and has directly contributed to the *vārtās*' canonical status within the broader collection of Pushtimargi Sanskrit and Hindi literature. Even contemporary translators and commentators suggest as much, often including lists of "nectarous speech" as appendices in printed editions of the *vārtās*.[6] As we will see in this chapter and throughout this book, these records of speech also model the ways in which today's devotees may wish to cultivate relationships with their Krishna *svarūps*, one another, and their gurus.

Records of conversations in the *vārtās* enter into yet another layer of dialogicality[7] as the *84VV*'s and *252VV*'s authors emphasize the hagiographies' relationships to other Pushtimargi texts, specifically those attributed to Vallabhacharya. Significantly, these intertextual elements of the *vārtās* also include records of performative reading and storytelling themselves: Vallabhacharya and Vitthalnath, for instance, are often depicted as attracting new devotees through their public recitations of, and commentaries on, the *Bhāgavatapurāṇa*. After unpacking these and other intertextual and conversational features of the hagiographies, I consider a final way in which the *vārtās* exhibit dialogicality through a late 17th-century commentary called the *Bhāvprakāś* (the "Illumination of [the text's] Inner Meaning"), which circulates with most versions of the *84VV* and *252VV* as they are

[6] A salient example is hereditary leader Shyam Manohar Goswami's *Vārtānkī Saiddhāntik Saṅgati* ("The Chronicles Harmonized with Key Principles"), a transcribed *pravacan* on *vārtās* from the *84VV*, which includes as an appendix each instance of Vallabhacharya's *vacanāmṛt* that appears in the hagiographies under consideration (the appendix is titled *amṛtvacanāvalī*, or "a list of nectarous speech"). As an excerpt from one of Shyam Manohar Goswami's transcribed lectures tells us, "Just as speech and meaning are bound together, in the same way are scriptures and Shri Krishna bound through the lotus-like-mouth of Mahaprabhuji. I humbly bow to his speech and its meaning wherever I find or use it" (Śyām Manohar Gosvāmī, *Vārtānkī Saiddhāntik Saṅgati* [Mumbai: Ramā Arts, 2011], 1). Collected utterances of Vallabhacharya's ancestors are also recorded as nectarous speech. See, for example, Vāgīśkumārjī Mahodayśrī, ed., *Śrī Girdharlālјī Mahārājśrī nā 120 Vacanāmṛt* (Vadodara, India: Vākpati Foundation, 2012).

[7] My use of this term is distinct, though not entirely disconnected from its use by 20th-century Russian philosopher Mikhail Bakhtin. Bakhtin's use of the term is wedded to an argument about the difference between literary monologism and dialogism. Privileging polyvocal modes of literary discourse, Bakhtin argues that monologism narrows the possibility for plural interpretations: "in the unity of a monologically perceived and understood world [. . .] there is no presumption of a plurality of equally-valid consciousnesses, each with its own world" (Mikhail Bakhtin, *Problems of Dostoevsky's Poetics* (1929), ed. and trans. Caryl Emerson [Minneapolis: University of Minnesota Press, 1984], 7). While the *84VV* and *252VV* are built around records of dialogue *between* the narratives' protagonists, *between* various layers of the narratives themselves, *between* the *vārtās* and other texts, and *between* text and reader, a Bakhtinian reading of Pushtimargi literature is complicated. The *vārtās* exhibit dialogue, polyvocality, and even the type of humor that Bakhtin looked for in instances of dialogism. At the same time, however, the hagiographies promote a single "truth" insofar as they promote unquestionable devotion to Krishna and guru. In this way, it is difficult to mark the *vārtās* as dialogical in a Bakhtinian sense.

received by modern devotees (from the late 19th century onward).[8] While the commentary functions in various ways, one of its most interesting features is hypophora: the commentary speaks directly to the reader by posing and then answering its own questions. These distinct features of the hagiographies are essential to the *84VV*'s and *252VV*'s positioning at the heart of *Vārtā Sāhitya*'s performative canon and therefore to the ways in which readers continue to actively engage with these written texts—carrying the Pushtimarg "into the future," to use Shalini Goswami's words.

Introducing the *84VV* and *252VV*

Aside from the *84VV* and *252VV*, most modern Pushtimargis accept the following hagiographic texts as inherent to *Vārtā Sāhitya*: the *Bhāvsindhu* ("The Ocean of Devotion"), which offers extended accounts of certain characters from the *84VV* and *252VV*; the *Gharu Vārtā* and the *Nij Vārtā* ("The Domestic Chronicle" and "The Intimate Chronicle"), which focus on Vallabhacharya and his immediate family; the *Caurāsī Baiṭhak Caritra*, which narrates Vallabhacharya's proselytizing pilgrimages to eighty-four locations; the *Śrī Ācāryajī* (or *Mahāprabhujī*) *kī Prākaṭya Vārtā* ("The Emergence Chronicle of Acharyaji"), which provides accounts of Vallabhacharya's life drawn from earlier *vārtā*s and reiterates them in one narrative; and the *Śrīnāthjī* (or *Śrī Govardhannāthjī*) *kī Prākaṭya Vārtā* ("The Emergence Chronicle of Shrinathji"), which traces the 15th-century emergence of Shrinathji in Braj and the deity's subsequent movement to Rajasthan during the 17th century (I specifically discuss this text further in Chapters 2 and 3).[9] Other distinct

[8] The most widely disseminated editions of the *84VV* and *252VV* are based on that of devotee and commentator Dwarkadas Parikh, who first published his redaction of the texts in 1948. Parikh's version of the *84VV* is based on the earliest extant manuscript of the *84VV* with the *Bhāvprakāś*, which contains a colophon bearing the date of Vikram Samvat 1752 (1695 CE). In his edition of the *252VV*, Parikh refers to a manuscript with Hariray's *Bhāvprakāś* from 1730 CE. The Vikram Samvat calendar is generally fifty-seven years ahead of the Gregorian calendar, though in Gujarat, due to calendrical distinctions, it is frequently just fifty-six years ahead. For further information on this, see Helen M. Johnson, "Conversion of Vikrama Saṃvat Dates," *Journal of the American Oriental Society*, 58, no. 4 (1938): 668–669.

[9] Besides the *Prākaṭya Vārtā*, these other texts are often read as a single collection. See, for example, Dvārkādās Puruṣottamdās Parīkh, ed. *Mahāprabhujī kī Nijvārtā, Gharuvārtā, Baiṭhak Caritra ityādī* (Indore, India: Vaiṣṇav Mitra Maṇḍal, 2010). Though not hagiographic per se, Pushtimargis often refer to the *Baḍe Śikṣāpatra* ("The Great Teaching Letters")—along with Vallabhacharya's treatises, which I discuss in this chapter—in the context of *Vārtā Sāhitya*. The *Śikṣāpatra* is composite and dialogical, written partly in Braj Bhasha and partly in Sanskrit, and takes the form of letters sent from *vārtā* commentator Hariray to his brother Gopeshvar on the event of the death of Gopeshvar's wife. In addition to Hariray's letters, Gopeshvar's commentary on the letters is also included. The

"emergence" *vārtās* likewise chronicle the stories of different prestigious Krishna *svarūps* of the *sampradāy* but are not widely read or circulated beyond the specific temple communities where the *svarūps* in question reside. Although there are examples of Pusthimargi texts written in the *vārtā* genre well into the 19th century, the written canon of *Vārtā Sāhitya* as it is received by most devotees today refers explicitly to the aforementioned texts, which focus on Vallabhacharya and Vitthalnath and their devotees as well as the primary *svarūps*, such as Shrinathji, that were directly in their care.[10]

Due in large part to their emphasis on Vallabhacharya and Vitthalnath as founding figures of the tradition, the *84VV* and *252VV* are today by far the most beloved and widely read collections of hagiographies in the corpus of Pushtimargi *Vārtā Sāhitya.* Both the *84VV* and *252VV* consist of a series of prose narratives written in what is meant to represent the everyday spoken language of the North Indian region of Braj from the 15th through 17th centuries.[11] The hagiographies that appear in the *84VV* and *252VV* vary in length, averaging at about fifteen-hundred words per *vārtā*, each of which is arranged in several episodes known as *prasaṅgs*. Taken as a whole, these *vārtās* offer a coherent account of how the charismatic first theologians of the Pushtimarg attracted a diverse following of Krishna devotees across the subcontinent. Though it is not always entirely clear that the ordering of the hagiographies in the *84VV* and *252VV* is significant, the opening account in all versions of the *84VV* that I have encountered is fittingly Vallabhacharya's first disciple, Damodardas Harsani. Harsani's hagiography, which I heard Shalini Goswami read out loud from during the 2017 gathering for new devotees in

forty-one letters focus on devotional living and emotional well-being. Versions of this text that my conversation partners read include Hariräy and Gopeśvar, *Śrī Hariräy kṛt Baḍe Śikṣāpatra: Śrī Gopeśvar kṛt Vrajbhāṣāṭikāsahit*, ed. Śrī Subodhinī Sabha (Lucknow, India: Janakprasād Agravāl, 1972), and Dvārkādās Puruṣottamdās Parīkh, ed., *Śrī Harirāyjī Mahāprabhupraṇīt 41 Baḍe Śikṣāpatra* (Ahmedabad, India: Pūjā Prakāśan, 2011).

[10] For an example of a 19th-century *vārtā*, see Vasudha Dalmia's chapter, "The Sixth *Gaddi* of the Vallabha *Sampraday*: Narrative Structure and Authority in a *Varta* of the Nineteenth Century," in *Hindu Pasts* (pp. 189–209).

[11] Though not all translations of the hagiographies strive to retain the everyday speech that characterize the Braj Bhasha originals (see Chapter 2 for one example of this), the most widely read versions of the texts today stay close to the original language. It is worth noting that more than eighty-four and two hundred and fifty-two hagiographies appear in the *84VV* and *252VV*, respectively: accounts of multiple devotees may be included under the title of one figure (e.g., the parent of an entire family of devotees). The significance of the numbers eighty-four and two hundred fifty-two (84 x 3) is tied to the belief that there are eighty-four *lakh* (eight million four hundred thousand) categories of beings in the universe, or similarly that the average soul passes through this number of births as plants and animals before being born in human form. It is for this reason that the texts' authors kept the official number of narratives to eighty-four and two hundred fifty-two.

Megha's backyard, narrates how this lauded first follower of the Pushtimarg received initiation from Vallabhacharya just after the theologian himself had received the *brahmasambandha* mantra directly from Shrinathji. As the opening *vārtā* in the *84VV*, Harsani's hagiography also establishes what is one of the text's most fundamental teachings and formulas: initiation through Vallabhacharya (and his descendants) is essential to cultivating a devotional relationship with Krishna. Each of the hagiographies that follow in the *84VV* and *252VV* tell stories of men and women—some seemingly extraordinary and some exceedingly ordinary—whose lives are transformed through the Pushtimarg's cleansing initiation mantras, the charismatic guru's teachings, and, ultimately, intimacy with Krishna.

While authorship and provenance of the *84VV* and *252VV* remain matters of scholarly debate,[12] both texts are understood by devotees to have been composed by two of Vallabhacharya's illustrious descendants: Vallabhacharya's grandson Gokulnath (1551–1640) is said to have authored and arranged the hagiographies, while Vallabhacharya's great-grandson Hariray (1590–?) is attributed with the texts' final *praṇīt* (editing and compilation).[13] Hariray is also said to have authored the *Bhāvprakāś* commentaries, which are attached to one recension of the *84VV* and one recension of the *252VV* in their manuscript forms, and which is considered inherent to both texts by most Pushtimargi readers with whom I am in conversation today.[14] As the following chapters of this book show, the ways in which Pushtimargis over the

[12] The *84VV* is the earliest *vārtā* text, predating the *252VV*, which has a less clear history than its earlier counterpart. The earliest *84VV* manuscript without the *Bhāvprakāś* is dated at Vikram Samvat 1697 (1640 CE). Hereditary leader Vrajeshkumar Maharaj graciously permitted me to view this manuscript during a visit to Kankroli, Rajasthan, in March 2012. More on the manuscript history of both texts can be found here: R.S. McGregor, *Hindi Literature from Its beginnings to the Nineteenth Century* (Wiesbaden: Otto Harrassowitz, 1984), 209; Hariharnāth Ṭaṇḍan, *Vārtā Sāhitya: Ek Vṛhat Adhyayan* (Aligarh, India: Bharat Prakāśan Mandir, 1960), 125–130; Galina Rousseva-Sokolova, "Sainthood Revisited: Two Printed Versions of the Lives of the Eighty-Four Vaishnavas by Gokulnāth," in *Bhakti Beyond the Forest: Current Research of Early Modern Literatures in North India, 2003–2009*, ed. Imre Bangha (New Delhi: Manohar, 2012), 91–104; Shandip Saha, "A Community of Grace: The Social and Theological World of the Puṣṭi Mārga Vārtā Literature," *Bulletin of SOAS* 69, no. 2 (2006): 225–242 (see especially fn. 22); Premnārāyaṇ Ṭaṇḍan, *Sūrdās kī Vārtā* (Lucknow, India: Nandan Prakāśan, 1968); and Richard Barz, "The *Caurāsī Vaiṣṇavan kī Vārtā* and the Hagiography of the Puṣṭimārg," in *According to Tradition: Hagiographical Writing in India*, ed. Winand M. Callewaert and Rupert Snell (Wiesbaden: Harrassowitz, 1994), 44–64.

[13] Traditional sources list Hariray's death year as 1717, suggesting that he had a more-than-human life span. Vallabhacharya's son Vitthalnath had six sons; Gokulnath was his fourth. Hariray's father was Kalyanray, who was the eldest son of Govindray, Vitthalnath's second son. Some contemporary Pushtimargis suggest that Gokulnath only arranged the *vārtās* in oral form, while others claim that he left written stories that Hariray compiled and edited.

[14] Multiple Pushtimargi texts are attributed to Hariray. For further information, see Viṣṇu Caturdevī, *Gosvāmī Harirāy aur unkā Braj Bhāṣā Sāhitya* (Mathura, India: Javāhar Pustakālya, 1976).

centuries have authorized the *vārtās* as canonical texts include questioning and contesting the narratives in various ways. The hagiographies, however, are ultimately recognized by Pushtimargi readers to be embodiments of Krishna himself. In this way, "textual autonomy,"[15] so to speak, is an illusion for the Pushtimargi reader, as is the belief that the author (and reader) exists as separate from Krishna as the Supreme Being.[16]

This understanding of the *vārtās* as inherently authoritative and imbued with divinity is written into the texts themselves and appears in the opening narrative of Hariray's *Bhāvprakāś* as a framing for the hagiographies that follow in the *84VV*:

> One day, Shri Gokulnathji was discussing the eighty-four Vaishnavas with Kalyan Bhatt and some other devotees. . . .[17] By midnight he still hadn't begun his daily recitation of the *Subodhinījī*. Then, a devotee said to Shri Gokulnathji: "My Lord, when will you begin the recitation? It is already midnight!" Then, from his lotus-like-mouth Shri Gokulnathji said: "Today the fruits of my recitation will be known through a discussion of the eighty-four Vaishnavas. There is no principle superior to the Vaishnavas and it is by means of the Vaishnavas that our path will come to fruition."[18]

In this oft-cited textual episode, which I also heard Shalini Goswami read out loud to those gathered in Megha's backyard in Ahmedabad in 2017, Gokulnath recounts the life stories of Vallabhacharya's beloved disciples (the very same life stories that appear in the body of the *84VV*). Gokulnath asserts that his own recitation of the *Subodhinī*—Vallabhacharya's commentary on the *Bhāgavatapurāṇa*—will be "known through a discussion of the eighty-four Vaishnavas." Vallabhacharya's commentary, as we will soon consider, is

[15] Paul Griffiths uses this term "textual autonomy" in *Religious Reading*. As Griffiths writes, "I prefer the word 'work,' or 'literary work' [from the word 'text'], though, to emphasize the importance of human agency and human labor, and to de-emphasize the idea of textual autonomy, which is a fundamentally irreligious idea" (Griffiths, *Religious Reading*, 22).

[16] In light of this, we might say that the Pushtimargi literary canon as a sectarian canon with a clear "religious account" could be an example of Bakhtinian monologism, while performative aspects of the texts that comprise said canon (the rhetorical strategies used by the texts themselves and by their readers) present us with multiple instances of dialogism.

[17] The Braj Bhasha here reads, "*Caurāsī vaiṣṇavan kī vārtā karat*." *Vārtā karat* is used as a verb "to discuss." The word *vārtā* is cognate with the Modern Standard Hindi word *bāt* (speech, though the word has various meanings depending on context). For a brief study of how the *vārtās* as conversational chronicles relate to other similar types of regional literature, see Norman P. Ziegler, "The Seventeenth Century Chronicles of Mārvāṛa: A Study in the Evolution and Use of Oral Traditions in Western India," *History in Africa* 3 (1976): 127–153.

[18] D. Parīkh, ed., *Caurāsī Vaiṣṇavan kī Vārtā*, 1–2.

described both in the hagiographies and also in contemporary discourse as one of Vallabhacharya's most defining works. In this way, Gokulnath employs a familiar rhetorical flourish by claiming that the *84VV* offers its listeners/readers the essence of the *Subodhinī*, a commentarial text meant to describe the essence of the *Bhāgavatapurāṇa*, which itself is understood to describe the essence of Krishna as Supreme Being! That is, Gokulnath is claiming that the hagiographies, too, reveal Krishna's essential nature. South Asia studies scholar Vasudha Dalmia makes a parallel observation about the relationship between the *vārtā*s and the *Bhāgavatapurāṇa*, writing,

> Thus it is that while tales of community-formation shape the *vartas*, the compendium in its turn acquires the function of further forming and perpetuating the community. This makes for the canonic status of the *vartas*, raising them to a level above that of the *Bhagavatapurana* and even of the *Subodhini*, Acharyaji's own commentary on the *purana*. The *Bhagavatapurana* remains central, but it is superseded, at least in their own representation, by the *vartas*, which had clearly originated as oral texts composed in everyday speech.[19]

Gokulnath's claim also implies that the *84VV* functions as a "practical canon." According to Buddhist studies scholar Anne Blackburn, a "practical canon" consists of the texts that are employed by religious readers in the regular practices of reading, commenting on, listening to, and "preaching sermons," which may be distinct from texts in a "formal canon."[20] This self-referential assertion of functional authority is true in terms of contemporary Pushtimargi practice: while modern hereditary leaders and devotees alike continue to read the *Bhāgavatapurāṇa* and Sanskrit commentaries and treatises attributed to Vallabhacharya and Vitthalnath (and their descendants), the majority of today's Pushtimargis know these texts through *Vārtā Sāhitya*'s vernacular synthesis. Yet *vārtā* texts are not *mere* syntheses of their Sanskrit counterparts. While their intertextuality is meant to offer readers an accessible way to engage with various layers of Pushtimargi history and theology, they are also, in their own right, primary and beloved texts with a distinct and complex literary aesthetic of their own, to which we now turn.

[19] Dalmia, *Hindu Pasts*, 166–167.

[20] Anne Blackburn, "Looking for the Vinaya: Monastic Discipline in the Practical Canons of the Theravada," *Journal of the International Association of Buddhist Studies* 22, no. 2 (1999): 284.

"Krishna Speaks to Me Directly": Nectarous Speech in the *84VV* and *252VV*

"After doing *sevā* for some time the Vaishnava will come to know what Shri Thakurji needs, what He desires," Megha Choksi explained to me as we sat in her kitchen drinking tea one morning in the winter of 2015. Her initial remarks came in reply to my somewhat straightforward question about when she had started to perform Krishna's *sevā* in her home. "How exactly does one come to know what Thakurji needs?" I had asked her. "It's just as Shri Harirayji describes it: *Shri Thakurji sānubhāvatā janānā*," Megha said, using the Braj Bhasha phrase that appears throughout the *84VV* and *252VV* to explain how Vallabhacharya's and Vitthalnath's disciples come to experience Krishna. This phrase—which not only appears frequently in the *vārtā*s but is also repeated by hereditary leaders and devotees in their conversations about the texts—can be translated literally as "causing the intimate experience of Thakurji." The implication of the phrase is that if the devotee intimately experiences Krishna, she will naturally know what the deity needs. Contemporary devotees like Megha strive for such intimate knowing of Krishna through practices of *sevā* (clothing, bathing, and singing to the deity), even though they maintain that experiencing Krishna is not contingent on performing any specific rituals—it is entirely up to Krishna as to how he will reveal himself to his caretakers. All ways of knowing Krishna, devotees frequently tell me, depend on the deity's own *icchā* (desire) and *kṛpā* (grace). As ethnographers of religion know well, asking a person directly to describe their "experience" of the divine does not generally yield straightforward or satisfying answers. To ask someone directly about such experiences could also appear insensitive, as it invites a person to uncover sentiments that may be deeply private and intimate, or perhaps ineffable. However, when I am with Pushtimargis I regularly hear solicited and unsolicited accounts of what happens when one encounters Krishna. For many *sevā* practitioners like Megha, such encounters are as profound as they are commonplace: "When Shri Thakurji begins to reveal Himself—slowly, slowly—the Vaishnava can hear Him say whatever it is that He wants. I'm hungry! It's cold in here!" Megha explained, changing her voice to imitate the voice that a sweet, but impatient child might use to request something from a doting parent. "Does Thakurji speak to you?" I asked her. "Of course, yes! He is always telling me things—in my sleep, while I'm dreaming, and during the day when I'm awake, too."[21] Megha's comments about Krishna's modes of communicating with her clearly echo how *vārtā* texts themselves describe their protagonists' epiphanies. In this way, the grammar of devotional experience and praxis that animates Pushtimargis' daily lives today is grounded in their tradition's devotional literature and reaffirmed—though also expanded on and changed—each time devotees read and discuss texts like the *84VV* and *252VV*.

Although protagonists of the *84VV* and *252VV* are shown to experience divinity in various ways, records of Krishna speaking directly to his human interlocutors is one of several types of encounters that stand out as thematic in the *vārtās*. Some hagiographies even feature Krishna explaining the significance of his own utterances by suggesting that only the initiated devotee, blessed with the grace of Vallabhacharya or Vitthalnath through initiation, can fully experience the deity's nectarous speech. Take, for example, what Krishna tells Vitthalnath (known as Gusainji in the *vārtās*)[22] in the hagiography of a poet named Raskhan: "It's my vow to only speak to, accept food-offerings from, and touch those you have first initiated. Without your *sambandha* (lit. "connection," with reference to initiation) these three things will be granted to no one."[23] While occasionally formulaic, one of the most distinctive features of Krishna's utterances in the *vārtās* is that they reflect—in the speech itself—specific protagonists' characteristics and circumstances. I should reiterate that all dialogue in the *vārtās*, whether from the mouth of Krishna or not, is generally depicted as *real-life* speech acts: it is rarely meant to be poetic. This makes hearing and reading the *vārtās* feel very much like reading/hearing a transcribed set of orally recounted stories and conversations from the early modern period![24] As we will see, Raskhan's *vārtā* lucidly demonstrates these features of dialogue in the hagiographies.

21 Devotees' communication with Krishna is akin to how religion scholar Tanya M. Luhrmann describes evangelical Christians' communicative relationship to Jesus. See *When God Talks Back: Understanding the American Evangelical Relationship with God* (New York: Vintage, 2012).

22 Gusain (*gusāīṁ* or *gosāīṁ* in Braj Bhasha; *gosvāmī* in Sanskrit and modern Indian languages) literally means "lord of the cows" but is generally an honorary title affixed to religious leaders' names in the Pushtimarg and in other Hindu communities.

23 Raskhan's *vārtā* is normally featured as the forty-fifth *vārtā* in the *252VV*.

24 This sets the *vārtās* apart in terms of their literary texture from other hagiographies of the early modern period. For instance, the *Caitanyacaritāmṛta*—a hagiography of theologian Chaitanya, which is attributed to Krishnadas Kaviraj in c. 1557—is a poetic text, written in Bengali with a number of Sanskrit verses. While direct speech does appear in the text, it is not intended to appear as if it were a real-life speech act. John S. Hawley offers a comparison of the Pushtimargi hagiographies and those in the traditions that developed around Chaitanya as a charismatic figure. See John S. Hawley, *A Storm of Songs: India and the Idea of the Bhakti Movement* (Cambridge, MA: Harvard University Press, 2015), 139–189.

Raskhan is one of a handful of Muslim-born protagonists who, according to *Vārtā Sāhitya*, received initiation into the Pushtimarg. Raskhan's status as Muslim is articulated (and mocked) in part through the way the character speaks, and in turn through how Krishna speaks to Raskhan. To show this, I offer here a translation of the second of two episodes in Raskhan's *vārtā*, marking all dialogue, including "thinking out loud" speech (which *vārtā* characters are shown to do quite often), in bold. The interested reader can find a translation of Raskhan's complete *vārtā* in this book's Appendix. Leading up to the following episode we learn that Raskhan is ethnically "Pathan," lives in Delhi, and has what his family feels to be an unhealthy infatuation with the son of a Hindu merchant.[25] This reference to his homoerotic desires aligns with early modern (and enduring) stereotypes about certain groups of South Asian Muslims, but as we will see, this trope is also used as a way to explain Raskhan's eventual attachment to Krishna.

> One day, while visiting Delhi, two Vaishnavas observed Raskhan's behavior toward the merchant's son. One Vaishnava said to the other, "**Look, brother. This Raskhan models attachment. He follows that Hindu boy everywhere. He cannot live without the boy and is totally unashamed of what people say about him with respect to caste or the rest. Is this not the type of attachment one should have for the Lord?**" Meanwhile, the lovestruck Raskhan was standing nearby and saw how one of the Vaishnavas clapped his hand to his forehead and stuck his nose up into the air. "**Was it about me that you just did that? Tell me or I'll knock you out cold!**" Raskhan drew his sword and the Vaishnava cautiously explained, "**If you loved the Lord as you do that boy, you'd find fulfillment.**" Raskhan asked, "**Whom do you call "Lord"? I don't know anything about this.**" The Vaishnavas responded: "**The Lord is the one from whom the world's magnificence emerges.**" Raskhan asked, "**How do I come to recognize the Lord?**" One of the Vaishnavas took out of his turban a painting of Krishna in the form of Shrinathji. Immediately upon viewing the painting, Raskhan's eyes welled with tears and his mind spun. His love for the boy then came to an end.
>
> ***Bhāvprakāś***: Here it is shown that attachment, even if worldly, is divine and therefore, if sincere, can be transformed, taking a being towards God.

[25] Pathan here refers to people with ancestors in today's Afghanistan (Pathan = Pashtun, someone who speaks Pashto).

Raskhan's attachment to that boy was sincere and real, and so he was therefore able to take that affection and become attached to Shrinathji.

Raskhan then inquired, **"Where does this *mahbūb* (beloved one) stay?"** One of the Vaishnavas replied, **"The Beloved lives in Braj."** Raskhan demanded, **"Give me that painting."** The Vaishnava, recognizing Raskhan to be a *daivī jīv* (godly being), gave the painting to him, and Raskhan departed for Braj. He went to many temples on his way, but nowhere did he find a deity with Shrinathji's form. At last his travels took him to Mount Govardhan, but when he tried to go into the temple there, the temple guard threw him out rudely.[26] Raskhan went to Govind Pond nearby, thinking to himself, **"I have never been thrown from a Hindu temple. This place, with such strict measures of security, must therefore be where my Beloved resides."** So Raskhan sat there staring at Shrinathji's temple, saying again and again, **"My Beloved resides in that temple,"** and swearing to not leave without having *darśan* there. Three days passed and Shrinathji thought to Himself, **"Raskhan will soon die from hunger."** Feeling compassion, Shrinathji appeared, along with His retinue of cows and cowherds, playing His flute at the top of Mount Govardhan. He looked exactly as He did in the painting, and so Raskhan recognized Shrinathji as his Beloved and ran to grab Him. But Shrinathji disappeared and went to the town of Shri Gokul where He awakened the sleeping Gusainji by gently stroking the hair on his head. **"Praise the one who removes his devotees' suffering,"**[27] Gusainji said. Shrinathji then said, **"There is this *daivī jīv* who has been born into the *baṛī jātī*** [lit. **"senior community"; Muslim community**]**. I gave him *darśan* but then he ran to grab me. You initiate him, and then I shall give him refuge."** Gusainji asked, **"Why have You come in such a rush?"** Shrinathji replied, saying, **"Because he tried to touch me and it's my vow to only speak to, accept food-offerings from, and touch those you have first initiated. Without your initiation these three things will be granted to no one."** Pleased, Gusainji got up, went to the banks of the Yamuna and

[26] Mount Govardhan is a sanctified landmark specific to Krishna devotion in the region of Braj. According to classical texts (e.g., the *Bhāgavatapurāṇa*) and other devotional narratives, Krishna lifted Govardhan to protect his cowherd counterparts in a battle with the Vedic deity Indra. Krishna also revealed himself as manifest in the stones of Govardhan. Today Govardhan is a popular pilgrimage destination. For a comprehensive study of Govardhan's significance, see David L. Haberman, *Loving Stones: Making the Impossible Possible in the Worship of Mount Govardhan* (New York: Oxford University Press, 2020).

[27] The Braj Bhasha here reads, "*bhaktāpanivārakāya namaḥ*."

> crossed the river in a boat. Reaching the other side, he mounted a horse and went toward Mount Govardhan where he then proceeded directly to Govind Pond where Raskhan was seated. Upon seeing Gusainji, Raskhan thought, **"This man who just got down from his horse appears to be a close *mitra* (friend) of my Beloved who lives atop Mount Govardhan."** He approached Gusainji and said, **"My Beloved lives in that house on the hill. I am very attached to Him. I also know that you are His close associate. If you would let me meet Him, that would be truly wonderful."** Gusainji was pleased with Raskhan's words and asked him, **"How do you know that He's my friend?"** Raskhan replied, **"As you were approaching I saw that your gaze was fixed on His temple."** Gusainji replied, telling him, **"Now bathe in the Govind Pond's cleansing waters."** After returning from his bath, Gusainji initiated Raskhan through his grace. Gusainji then had a servant take Raskhan up to Mount Govardhan, and he himself climbed to the temple and sounded the conch to wake up Shrinathji. When the temple opened, Gusainji prepared some fruits for Shrinathji's early afternoon food offering. A bit later, Raskhan entered Shrinathji's temple and was thrilled again to have *darśan*. As Raskhan was departing from the temple, Shrinathji emerged from His shrine and grabbed hold of Raskhan's arm, saying, **"Hey you bastard,[28] where are you going?!"** And from this day on whenever Shrinathji left to graze the cattle He would take Raskhan along. The *līlā* that Raskhan saw there he would then illustrate through his verses. It was in this manner that he acquired the *bhāv* (devotional sentiments) of *gopī* (a female cowherd). Raskhan was Shri Gusainji's blessed follower; to what extent can his story be praised?

While Raskhan's *vārtā* provides us with a great deal to analyze, let us begin by considering the patterns of dialogue in the narrative. Even a quick glance at my English rendering shows how frequently *vārtā* characters speak directly to each other, and to themselves: nearly half of the words in my translation appear in the bold font I have used to indicate *vacanāmṛt*. This dialogical feature of the story, which is common throughout the *84VV* and *252VV*, can prove difficult to translate. When the *vārtā* is read aloud in its original Braj Bhasha or in Gujarati translation, however, the

[28] The Braj Bhasha term used here is *sāre*—a vocative of Modern Standard Hindi's *sālā* (wife's brother or brother-in-law), and a harsh, though sometimes playful, term of abuse (the implication being that the person hurling the insult is sleeping with the other person's sister).

repetitive dialogue lends itself to the type of performative styles of narration commonly employed by contemporary Pushtimargis who read aloud from the texts during community gatherings and public lectures. For instance, some contemporary readers will adopt distinct voices for different protagonists. One woman, Dipa, whom we will meet briefly in Chapter 4, is often chosen by her fellow devotees to read aloud during *satsaṅg* because she has the "best voices" and because she also has a very loud voice, which adds to the intended drama of her readings. In the aforementioned selection from Raskhan's *vārtā* there is only one instance of the *Bhāvprakāś*, in which Hariray briefly clarifies the matter of worldly and divine attachment. Hariray's commentarial voice, which normally appears at least several times in the course of any given hagiography, provides what I have observed to be a natural stopping point during readings for people to discuss the text with fellow devotee-readers, drawing connections between what the stories are perceived to teach and their own individual experiences. In doing so, the *Bhāvprakāś* implicitly provides a fertile juncture in peoples' readings at which to enter into "conversation," not only with Hariray's commentary, but also with other interlocutors within and beyond the text.

Chief among the experiences that devotees like Megha bring to discussions about the *84VV* and *252VV* are those specifically related to their own relationships with Krishna. While I have yet to hear Raskhan's *vārtā* read aloud and discussed among Pushtimargis, I asked several of my interlocutors about their interpretation of the story and its primary significance for modern devotees. Megha replied to my inquiry as follows:

> See, Shri Govardhannathji [another title for Krishna as Shrinathji] spoke directly to Raskhanji. He [Raskhan] was a *daivī jīv* but he was *kāco* (raw) and so Shri Govardhannathji spoke to him just the way that he would understand [i.e., crudely!]. Otherwise he wouldn't understand, if He [Krishna] spoke very sweetly.

I asked Megha if Krishna speaks to all devotees in ways that match their own *bolī* (dialect). "Yes, yes," Megha said emphatically. "Shri Thakurji will speak whatever *bhāṣā* (language) His devotees speak—Gujarati, Hindi, English, Chinese, whatever. This is all Shri Thakurji's *līlā*."

While the *vārtās*' markedly dialogical prose in Braj Bhasha is distinct among other early modern traditions of *bhakti* hagiography, the texts' emphasis on the spoken word is not unique within South Asian narrative traditions writ large.[29] Brian Black and Laurie Patton, editors of the volume *Dialogue in Early South Asian Religions: Hindu, Buddhist, and Jain Traditions* (2016), discuss some of the shared ways in which dialogue functions and is emphasized as primary across literature from the subcontinent.[30] Using as a template the *Kauṣītaki Upaniṣad*'s opening scene—a set of dialogues about "paths to the other world" between the youthful Shvetaketu, his father Uddalaka Aruni, and King Citra Gangayayani—Black and Patton explain how dialogue occurs both inside and beyond the text. "Within the text," they write, "this *upaniṣad* places its content within a dialogical context, presenting its teachings as emerging from a conversation."[31] Because the genre of *upaniṣad* is understood to be orally transmitted, it is clear that the dialogical narrative in the written text is a "self-conscious mirror of the text's own transmission."[32] The *vārtā*s function in precisely this way as well, showing within the narratives themselves the ideal way in which Pushtimargi teachings should be transmitted, namely, by way of dialogue between fellow devotees, between devotees and Krishna, and between gurus and their followers. I return to such instances of dialogue at various points throughout this book as I discuss the contexts of *pravacan*s and *satsaṅg*s during which hereditary leaders and devotees read and analyze devotional texts.

Black and Patton also consider how dialogue can provide a way for authors and readers to distinguish difference and negotiate relationships between and across religious traditions. In the material they consider, this means explicit conversation across Buddhist, Jain, and Hindu traditions through texts. Well-known examples of textual dialogue across religions are also found throughout the *Rāmāyaṇa* tradition. A.K. Ramanujan, for example, shows how different tellings of the Rama story reflect the distinct cultures, languages, politics, and religious traditions of the tellers themselves. For

[29] While there are examples of Braj Bhasha prose that likely predate the *84VV*, most of these examples are from commentarial texts, rather than from prose hagiographies or other types of prose literature. This has been noted as distinct by Hindi literary scholars. See, for example, R.S. McGregor, *A History of Indian Literature: Hindi Literature from Its Beginnings to the Nineteenth Century* (Wiesbaden: Harrassowitz, 1984), 210; and Barz, "The *Caurāsī Vaiṣṇavan kī Vārtā*," 44–64. For more on the development of Braj Bhasha, specifically as a classical, rather than a devotional, language, see Allison Busch, *Poetry of Kings: The Classical Hindi Literature of Mughal India* (New York: Oxford University Press, 2011).

[30] Brian Black and Laurie Patton, eds., *Dialogue in Early South Asian Religions: Hindu, Buddhist, and Jain Traditions* (New York, Routledge: 2016).

[31] Black and Patton, *Dialogue in Early South Asian Religions*, 1.

[32] Ibid. The term *upaniṣad* itself might be translated as "sitting down"—that is, sitting down beside a person giving some type of oral discourse. More broadly, *upaniṣads* are texts that represent theological, and often argumentative, portions of the *Vedas*.

instance, in tellings attributed to Jain authors—for whom the philosophy of nonviolence is paramount—Rama's killing of the antagonist Ravana is too problematic an act for the narrative's presumed hero. To remedy matters, some Jain authors make Rama's brother Lakshmana the villain's slayer, thereby promoting Jain values and maintaining Rama as a nonviolent protagonist.[33] While several narratives that appear in the *84VV* and *252VV* also appear "retold" in texts attributed to authors of distinct traditions, namely, other Vaishnava traditions that had competing philosophies and interests during the early modern period in the region of Braj (e.g., the traditions that formed around the 15th-century theologian Chaitanya), this feature of dialogue as distinguishing difference between traditions, or at least between community identities, also appears *within* particular *vārtā*s, as it does in the example of Raskhan's hagiography. As Rupert Snell writes in "Raskhan the Neophyte: Hindu Perspectives on a Muslim Vaishnava," "this hagiography provides an unusually graphic illustration of Hindu attitudes towards the Muslim community, whose leaders held temporal power throughout the heyday of North Indian Hindu *bhakti* from the early sixteenth century."[34] Thus, the dialogue between Krishna and Raskhan is significant not only because it shows the conversational nature of the *84VV*, but also because it shows, through the *bhakta*'s (devotee's) speech patterns, how the hagiographies' authors indicate "Otherness" and belonging in the Pushtimargi community.[35]

In one sense, all protagonists in the *84VV* and *252VV* are depicted as starting their worldly lives outside the Pushtimargi fold: each *vārtā* includes the protagonist's initiation as part of the narrative formula. This formula is emphasized by Hariray's commentary, which often frames each hagiography with an introduction that provides protagonists with divine counterparts within Krishna's *alaukik* (otherworldly) and eternal realm of Braj. Raskhan, therefore, like his fellow *bhakta*s, is considered a "godly being" who just

[33] A.K. Ramanujan, "Three Hundred *Rāmāyaṇas*: Five Examples and Three Thoughts on Translation," in *Many Ramayanas: The Diversity of a Narrative Tradition in South Asia*, ed. Paula Richman (Berkeley: University of California Press, 1991), 22–49.

[34] Rupert Snell, "Raskhan the Neophyte: Hindu Perspectives on a Muslim Vaishnava," in *Urdu and Muslim South Asia: Studies in Honour of Ralph Russell*, ed. Christopher Shackle (London: SOAS, 1989), 29.

[35] In addition to Snell's article, other considerations of how "Otherness" is portrayed in the hagiographies include Saha, "A Community of Grace," 225–242; Barz, *The Bhakti Sect of Vallabhacarya*; Frederick M. Smith, "Dark Matter in Vārtāland: On the Enterprise of History in Early Puṣṭimārga Discourse," *The Journal of Hindu Studies* 2, no. 1 (2009): 27–47; and Charlotte Vaudeville, *Myths, Saints and Legends in Medieval India* (Delhi: Oxford University Press, 1996).

happens to have been born into the "senior community," or *baṛī jātī* as it reads in the Braj Bhasha.[36] While Raskhan's *laukik* (worldly) name (Raskhān) could be interpreted in various ways, it is a name that readers of the past and present would likely recognize as Muslim, a "typical Pathan designation."[37] Raskhan's otherworldly name—the name of his form as a *gopī* in Krishna's eternal land of Braj—however, is rendered as Rasasiddha (Rasasiddhā), which can be translated as "he who is endowed with the sentiment of passion." Indeed, as clearly depicted in the portion of Raskhan's *vārtā* that I have translated, this protagonist is a caricature of passion.

Raskhan is at once violent and crude in his communication with others: he threatens to strike his interlocutors and to "grab" Krishna, and he speaks to both his human and divine counterparts in ways that are supposed to mark him as utterly clueless about the divine (and very sectarian) nature of Krishna, Vitthalnath, and the Pushtimarg. Examples of this are Raskhan's use of the words *mahbūb* (an Arabic-derived word meaning "beloved" or "sweetheart") and *mitra* (a Sanskrit-derived word for "friend") to refer to Krishna, and the title *sāhib* (sir) to address Vitthalnath.[38] Krishna in his various local forms, such as Shrinathji (also known as Govardhannathji or just Shriji) is known by several honorific titles in the *vārtās*, but never as *mahbūb* or *mitra*, which are intended to sound pedestrian. For Vitthalnath, as for Vallabhacharya, an even fewer number of strictly sectarian-specific honorifics are used throughout the hagiographies. Most prominently in the context of dialogue is the term "Maharaj" (*mahārāj*, lit. "great king," though "my Lord" is a more accurate translation into English. Maharaj is often used as a vocative—as in "O my Lord!"). In addition to his crude and out-of-place word choices, Raskhan is depicted as passionately attached to the son of a Hindu merchant. Both his "hot" temper and his romantic attraction to the Hindu boy are typical ways that early modern non-Muslim authors disparaged Muslim characters in their texts. Here, however, Raskhan's unchecked passion—a passion due, namely, to his worldly birth into the *baṛī jātī*—is used as a teaching device in the *vārtā* to show how passion and attachment are precisely the emotions that one *should* cultivate when forming a relationship with Krishna. Krishna appears ready to engage Raskhan as an unlikely, but

[36] Snell notes that this term is a "revealing indicator of a social as opposed to a spiritual hierarchy": the ruling elite of the early modern period were Muslim ("Raskhan the Neophyte," 31).

[37] Snell, "Raskhan the Neophyte," 30.

[38] For a discussion on the use of all three of these terms, and others, see Snell, "Raskhan the Neophyte," 34–45.

fully eligible, devotee after he receives initiation from Vitthalnath. Krishna's uncouth use of the term *sāre* (which I have translated as "bastard") to call out to Raskhan is meant to show the deity's deep affection for his Muslim *bhakta*, even while also being humorous and mocking as it imitates Raskhan's own rough and "foreign" word choices throughout the narrative. As Snell puts it, Krishna's use of the term *sāre*,

> . . . is an affectionate one, and in suggesting a close rapport between Krishna and Raskhān is of course a vindication of the Pathan's status as a devotee of the inner circle; but at the same time there is no escaping the disparaging tone of the language, and the Vaishnava author of the text is clearly enjoying the implied subjugation of this non-Hindu devotee while yet praising his innately spiritual character.[39]

Raskhan's *vārtā* provides a telling example of how the Pushtimargi hagiographies model devotional behavior (or offer "spiritual guidance," as Shalini Goswami often describes it to me in English) through dialogue between various interlocutors, human and divine. At the same time, the example of Raskhan highlights the way the *vārtā*s mark relationships between insiders and outsiders, the worldly from the otherworldly, and the inherently divine from the pedestrian.[40] While much is negotiable in people's interpretation of the *vārtā*s, these certain, though sometimes subtle, aspects of the texts' vocabularies continue to be used by today's readers. In other words, these terms and the related speech patterns of the hagiographies' protagonists are key to how the *vārtā*s continue to provide a grammar of tradition for contemporary devotees. Moreover, contemporary readers elevate these instances of dialogue, such as those considered in Raskhan's *vārtā*, as among the most "truthful" and "accurate" ways to access Pushtimargi teachings—particularly when the utterances in question are delivered directly from the "lotus-like" mouths of Vallabhacharya, Vitthalnath, or Krishna.[41]

39 Snell, "Raskhan the Neophyte," 35–36.

40 Another way that the *vārtā*s distinguish divine from pedestrian is through titles that are given to sacred places. Revered places are referred to respectfully with the honorific prefix *śrī* and an honorific suffix *jī*. For example, Shri Mathuraji, for Krishna's birthplace, but simply Agra for the once Mughal capital. So, too, can one find examples of marking particular actions and exchanges with ritually specific and formulaic language. For example, when *vārtā* protagonists are bestowed with *svarūp*s, the exchange is inevitably written in the Braj Bhasha as *Ṭhākurjī mathu padhrānā*—literally "to bestow" or "mount" Thakurji on the forehead (of the devotee).

41 For instance, during *Bhāgavata kathā*s or recitations and commentaries on the *Bhāgavatapurāṇa*, which are becoming increasingly popular in Pushtimargi communities, *kathākār*s (exegetes) may use *vacanāmṛt* found in the *vārtā*s to facilitate their analysis of the *purāṇa*. It is also significant to

Vārtā Sāhitya as Intertextual Hagiography

Yet another dialogical feature of the *Kauṣītaki Upaniṣad* that Black and Patton discuss is intertextuality. The *Kauṣītaki Upaniṣad* scene they examine also appears in two other *upaniṣads*, both of which offer some variation of the conversation between the three characters of Shvetaketu, his father Uddalaka Aruni, and King Citra Gangayayani, and therefore different expressions of the text's teaching. This points more broadly to how many South Asian textual traditions "explicitly refer to dialogues in other texts, invoking their authority, while also taking the formal features of the dialogue in new directions."[42] This assessment accurately describes both how the *84VV* and *252VV* refer to other texts *and* also to how today's readers speak and write about the *vārtās* in relationship to other texts. Just as contemporary readers emphasize *vacanāmṛt* in the *vārtās* to establish the hagiographies' authenticity, authors of the *84VV* and *252VV* (as well as contemporary readers) refer to works attributed to Vallabhacharya (and others) as a way to authenticate the texts and to bring them into conversation with the Pushtimarg's broader intertextual landscape.

One of the primary ways that the *84VV* and *252VV* refer to works attributed to Vallabhacharya is by providing a narrative context for these texts' composition. When the hagiographies are read aloud among devotees, such references therefore provide natural segues into conversations about how the *vārtās* provide "examples for Vallabhacharya's teachings," as female hereditary leader Goswami Indirabetiji told me. Likewise, when the primary topic of a *pravacan* is a text attributed to Vallabhacharya, rather than the *vārtās* per se, exegetes often use the hagiographies' framing of the treatise in question to help impart its teachings to their audience. This literary device of providing narrative contexts for works attributed to Vallabhacharya appears in the *vārtā* of Damodardas Harsani in the *84VV*. In Harsani's *vārtā* the reader vicariously witnesses Vallabhacharya's own initiation by Shrinathji, and then, in the same story, the initiation of Harsani as the Pushtimarg's first disciple by Vallabhacharya. This divine encounter, we learn in the *vārtā*, was also recorded by Vallabhacharya himself in his Sanskrit treatise called the

note here that one of Vallabhacharya's many titles is Mukhavatar, or the "manifestation of [Krishna's] mouth."

[42] Black and Patton, *Dialogue in Early South Asian Religions*, 1.

Siddhāntarahasya ("The Doctrine's Secret"). Vallabhacharya's treatise reports his meeting with Shrinathji as follows:

> *śrāvaṇasyāmale pakṣe ekādaśyām mahāniśi /*
> *sākṣādbhagavatā proktaim tadakṣaraśa ucyate //1//*
> At midnight on the eleventh day of *śravana*'s bright half,
> The Blessed Lord Himself appeared before my eyes.
> And what He proclaimed to me then I repeat here, word for word.[43]

The following verses of the treatise relay the "Doctrine's Secret"—that is, that according to Krishna himself, the devotee must remove physical and mental impurities through the *brahmasambandha* mantra.[44] The *Siddhāntarahasya* is one of sixteen short treatises compiled into what is known as the *Ṣoḍaśagrantha* ("Sixteen Treatises"), and it is inferred from Harsani's *vārtā* that Vallabhacharya composed this particular treatise for the benefit of his first disciple ("this path has been manifest for you," Vallabhacharya tells Harsani in the *84VV*).[45] As the first, and perhaps most lauded, of the devotees whose stories are recounted in the *84VV*, Harsani is seen as particularly worthy of receiving "The Doctrine's Secret."[46]

While Vallabhacharya's and Vitthalnath's disciples whose stories are told in the *84VV* and *252VV* are marked as *daivī jīvs*, we know from Raskhan's *vārtā* that not all of these figures are shown to be as "traditionally" good-natured or pious as Damodardas Harsani.[47] Each character has distinct qualities, and each narrative imparts different, though certainly related and sometimes formulaic, lessons to the reader. Collectively, the protagonists from the *84VV* and the *252VV* represent a diversity of socioeconomic,

[43] Redington, *The Grace of Lord Krishna*, 64. *Śrāvaṇa*, a month in the Hindu calendar, roughly correlates to July.

[44] By doing so, Vallabhacharya writes, "all become Brahman" and "just as all faulty things become [the River] Ganges (upon entering it), and just as it is relevant to discuss their virtues, defects and so forth before they enter the Ganges, but not after, the case is precisely the same here" (Redington, *The Grace of Lord Krishna*, 65).

[45] According to hereditary leader Shyam Manohar Goswami, the anthologizing of the "Sixteen Treatises" likely occurred over nearly a century as commentators redacted and interpreted the texts (personal communication, July 23, 2012).

[46] It is not clear that when Vallabhacharya refers to the *brahmasambandha* that he is referring to an initiation mantra (Hawley, *Storm of Songs*, 186–187).

[47] For further information on the concept of predestination of souls initiated into the Pushtimarg, see Frederick Smith, "*Nirodha* and the *Nirodhalakṣāṇa* of Vallabhācarya," *Journal of Indian Philosophy* 26, no. 6 (1998): 589–651 and "Predestination and Hierarchy: Vallabhācārya's Discourse on the Distinctions Between Blessed, Rule-Bound, Worldly, and Wayward Souls (the *Puṣṭipravāhamaryādābheda*)," *Journal of Indian Philosophy* 39 (2011): 173–227.

religious, and cultural backgrounds from a variety of geographical regions (from as far north as Kabul, as far south as Tamil Nadu, as far east as Bengal, and as far west as Gujarat). The reader encounters men, women, children, kings, queens, farmers, carpenters, thieves, jewelers, beggars, Brahmins, Shudras, merchants, Jains, yogis, Muslims, goddess worshipers, tribal people, prostitutes, orphans, child brides, and widows. In addition to presenting the (idealized) social diversity of the Pushtimarg's early followers, the texts also emphasize the diversity of human emotions and behaviors. Some characters—like Damodardas Harsani—exhibit conventional qualities of humility, patience, and unwavering faith in Krishna's divine grace and Vallabhacharya and Vitthalnath's authority as gurus. Others, however—like Raskhan—are irascible, vain, tactless, or even violently aggressive.[48] In the *84VV* and *252VV*, these rough-around-the-edges characters provide numerous teaching moments and inspire Vallabhacharya and Vitthalnath to author treatises to address their fumbling followers' confusions and questions.

For example, in what is traditionally the seventy-second hagiography in the *84VV*, Vallabhacharya's character is inspired to compose the *Saṃnyāsanirṇaya* ("A Judgement on Renunciation") for one of his disciples, Narhar Sannyasi. In the *vārtā*, the misguided disciple stubbornly tries to follow a path of renunciation by practicing extreme austerities (e.g., sitting out under the summer sun with fires built around him or sitting in a tub of ice water during the winter) until he realizes the essence of the Pushtimarg through Vallabhacharya's teachings and *renounces* his *renunciation*. In the *vārtā*, which contextualizes the teachings of the *Saṃnyāsanirṇaya* treatise, Vallabhacharya responds to his disciple's question, "Which is the better path, devotion or renunciation?," by explaining that while all mental and physical attributes should be fully dedicated to Krishna, one should not live removed from the social world. Why? Because, in the *kaliyug* (degenerate age), traditional forms of renunciation lead to pride and egotism rather than devotion. "What did you achieve by practicing so many austerities?" Vallabhacharya asks Narhar Sannyasi. The answer, of course, is nothing good at all (Narhar Sannyasi does, in fact, achieve some things, namely, shame

[48] For an article on an irascible devotee, see Richard Barz, "Kṛṣṇadās Adhikārī: An Irascible Devotee's Approach to the Divine," in *Bhakti Studies*, ed. Greg M. Bailey and Ian Kesarcadi-Watson (New Delhi: Sterling, 1992), 236–262. For a similar study, see Richard Barz, "Kumbhandas: The Devotee as Salt of the Earth," in *Krishna: A Sourcebook*, ed. Edwin F. Bryant (Oxford: Oxford University Press, 2007), 477–504.

and humiliation!).[49] This is one of many examples throughout the *84VV* and *252VV* that shows how significant texts attributed to Vallabhacharya and his descendants are introduced to readers through accounts of devotees stumbling ungracefully along the Path of Nourishment (the Pushtimarg).

These intertextual moments, such as the one described in Narhar Sannyasi's *vārtā*, also inspire today's readers to refer to the wider corpus of Pushtimargi literature and likewise to consider their own interpretations of particular teachings as they pertain to life in contemporary contexts. As we will see throughout this book, devotees frequently discuss the theme of negotiating between a householder lifestyle and performances of Krishna's *sevā*—a theme that is undoubtably central to the hagiographies themselves. While this theme manifests in various (and occasionally divergent) ways in the hagiographies and in real-life practice, the emphasis on maintaining a so-called householder lifestyle (that is, marrying, having children, and financially supporting one's family) is due in large part to how Pushtimargis from the 17th century onward have interpreted Vallabhacharya's writings to indicate that the theologian looked unfavorably on traditional practices of renunciation.[50] These views are connected both to the Pushtimarg's emphasis on caring for Krishna *svarūps* in domestic settings, and also to the perpetuation of the Vallabha Kul through male primogeniture.

Without straying too far from the theme of intertextuality, it is important to note here that Vallabhacharya's positions on caste and gender also permeate the *84VV* and *252VV*. Vallabhacharya's writings suggest that he promoted *varṇāśramadharma* (a Brahminical system by which people are ranked and expected to act in certain ways according to birth community, life stage, and gender), while at the same time implying that any person predestined to be

[49] Krishna is said to have commanded Vallabhacharya to marry and raise a family. It was only in his final days of life, according to the *vārtās*, that the theologian renounced the material world. For more on this, see James D. Redington, "The Last Days of Vallabhacarya," *Journal of Vaishnava Studies* 1, no. 4 (1983): 109–134. For more on Vallabhacharya and renunciation, see Frederick Smith, "The *Saṃnyāsanirṇayaḥ*: A Śuddhādvaita Text on Renunciation by Vallabhācārya," *Journal of Vaishnava Studies* 1, no. 4 (1993): 135–156. For further information on debates over renunciation in the medieval period, see Patrick Olivelle, *Renunciation in Hinduism: A Medieval Debate* (Vienna: Institut für Indologie der Universität Wien, 1986).

[50] John S. Hawley considers this perception of Vallabhacharya's views—that is, his negative views on the householder lifestyle—to be amplified by the tradition after the theologian's death. As Hawley writes, while discussing the *Siddhāntarahasya*, "In a similar vein we find Vallabha far more ambivalent about the value of householdership than would be suggested by the way in which the *sampradāy* named after him championed that form of life. In two of his pithy treatises, Vallabha does indeed struggle with the obstacles that a life of a renunciant wandering can pose to cultivating an awareness of Krishna's freely given grace (11.7, 14.2–6), but he is also attuned to the difficulties that a householder's life can throw in one's spiritual path (11.2–3, 11.8) and recommends a measure of travel on that account (11.8) (Hawley, *Storm of Songs*, 187)."

accepted by Krishna (that is, *daivī jīvs*) could join the fold. In the *vārtās*, we see protagonists who hail from many different social groups within and beyond the *varṇa* system. Though sectarian logic claims that Vallabhacharya travelled wherever *daivī jīvs* were in need of "uplifting," historians argue that Vallabhacharya and his ancestors went to places where economic and political unease produced willing converts to a new *sampradāy*, which, according to the *vārtās*, included the downtrodden and allowed for the maintenance of community-based interpretations of *varṇāśramadharma*.[51] This coupling of traditional *bhakti* tropes of accepting the downtrodden, which includes women, and also maintaining *varṇāśramadharma*, which generally is restrictive to women, makes the *vārtās*' positions on gender complicated.[52] Issues around purity and pollution—traditional issues in matters of *varṇāśramadharma*—are often attached to female characters, who appear less frequently than their male counterparts but do account for a significant number of the *84VV*'s and *252VV*'s lauded devotees.[53] These characters are shown to navigate in unique ways between gender-specific *dharma* prescriptions and their passionate devotion for Krishna and their gurus.[54] The bottom line across the hagiographies, however, is that caste and gender do not necessarily determine one's status in the community. It is unwavering devotion to Krishna *and* guru that is paramount. Take, for example, how Mirabai—the 16th-century poet-saint and Krishna devotee adored within communities across Rajasthan and Gujarat—is described in the *84VV*. In the hagiography of Krishnadas Adhikari, Krishnadas encounters Mirabai,

[51] For more on this, see Norbert Peabody, *Hindu Kingship and Polity in Precolonial India* (Cambridge: Cambridge University Press, 2003); and Shandip Saha's "The Movement of *Bhakti* Along a North-West Axis: Tracing the History of the Puṣṭimārg Between the Sixteenth and Nineteenth Centuries," *International Journal of Hindu Studies* 11, no. 3 (2008): 299–318.

[52] For more on such *bhakti* tropes, see Snell and Callwaert, eds., *According to Tradition*; and W.L. Smith, *Patterns in North Indian Hagiography* (Stockholm: Department of Indology, University of Stockholm, 2000).

[53] Galina Rousseva-Sokolova makes a similar comment about female protagonists in "Voices from the Past. Rearranging Values in Times of Crisis: The Example of North Indian Vaishnava Hagiographies," *Journal of Human Values* 26, no. 1 (2020): 64–74. For a general account of how female saints are treated in Indian hagiographies, see A.K. Ramanujan's "On Women Saints," in *The Collected Essays of A.K. Ramanujan*, ed. Vinay Dharwadker (Oxford: Oxford University Press, 1999), 270–278. Ramanujan also discusses female saintly voices, including their expression through male authors, in "Talking to God in the Mother Tongue," *Manushi* 50–52 (1989): 9–14.

[54] I am in agreement with Gil Ben-Herut, who writes, with reference to "Talking to God in the Mother Tongue," that Ramanujan's interpretation of "female voicing by male authors is illustrative of how female agency within the devotional discourse is rarely straightforward and comprehensive but rather involves multiple concentric circles of appropriation, caveats, and containment" (*Śiva's Saints: The Origins of Devotion in Kannada According to Harihara's Ragaḷegaḷu* [New Delhi: Oxford University Press, 2018], 111). Ben-Herut notes that "these sensibilities apply also in the case of the early Kannada saintly imaginaire" (*Śiva's Saints*, 111).

who attempts to give an offering to Krishnadas for Shrinathji. As Mirabai is *not* an initiated disciple of Vallabhacharya, Krishnadas refuses the offering. Contemporary devotees have various positions on the poet. As one woman named Saloni shared with me, "Some say that she was a great devotee, but she was crazed in her devotion, she was selfish and took her own life instead of doing Krishna's *sevā* . . . Krishna is part of our family." Saloni does not emphasize Mirabai's status as non Pushtimargi but, rather, her choice to end her life in the human world, which Saloni sees as an affront to Krishna devotion. Women like Saloni, who are among today's most avid Pushtimargi readers, are, as future chapters exhibit, particularly drawn to discussing matters of family, gender, and devotion to Krishna in relationship to what they perceive the *vārtās*' protagonists to model.

Although the *vārtās* are keen to emphasize their connection to Vallabhacharya's philosophies by providing narrative contexts for his treatises, the texts most frequently referred to throughout the *84VV* and *252VV* are not authored by Vallabhacharya and are in fact poetic in nature. These include multiple references to poems or bodies of poems, many of which are attributed to some of the hagiographies' most beloved protagonists. For instance, the final four hagiographies in both the *84VV* and *252VV* are dedicated to a group of eight particularly lauded Pushtimargi poets, known as the *aṣṭachāp* (eight seals). This group of eight poets wrote in Braj Bhasha, and anthologies of their poems are canonical in their own right.[55] Poems attributed to the *aṣṭachāp* are sung, rather than read, in a musical style known as *havelī saṅgīt* (temple music) that has come to characterize the worship of Krishna *svarūps* in Pushtimargi temples, but also increasingly in devotees' domestic practices.[56]

[55] *Chāp* refers to the "seal," or signature of a poet, which, appearing in a line of verse, confirms or alleges authorship by that named poet. John S. Hawley notes that the establishment of the *aṣṭachāps*' *vārtās* at the end of the *84VV* and *252VV* point to the efforts of the texts' authors to "give liturgical coherence to their fledgling *sampradāy*" (*Storm of Songs*, 182). It is notable that while these eight poets' connection to the Pushtimarg is not questioned by devotees, their identity as sectarian poets is a narrative written by hagiographers, rather than a historical fact (Hawley, *Storm of Songs*, 183).

[56] For further information on *havelī saṅgīt*, see Meilu Ho, "The Liturgical Music of the Puṣṭi Mārg of India: An Embryonic Form of the Classical Tradition" (PhD diss., University of California, Los Angeles, 2006); Guy L. Beck, "Vaishnava Music and the Braj Region of Northern India," *Journal of Vaishnava Studies* 4, no. 2 (1996): 115–148; Guy L. Beck, "Haveli Sangit: Music in the Vallabha Tradition," *Journal of Vaishnava Studies* 1, no. 4 (1993): 77–86. For further reading on changing *kīrtan* performances, see Shital Sharma, "A Prestigious Path to Grace: Class, Modernity, and Female Religiosity in Puṣṭimārg Vaisnavism" (PhD diss., McGill University, 2014), 33, 214–263. See also Anne-Marie Gaston, *Krishna's Musicians*; "Continuity of Tradition in the Music of Nathdvara: A Participant-Observer's View," in *The Idea of Rajasthan: Explorations in Regional Identity*, Vol. I, ed. Karine Schomer et al. (New Delhi: Manohar, 1994), 238–277. In addition to appearing embedded within the hagiographies, modern commentators often list the *84VV*'s and *252VV*'s references to

The other type of poetic work referred to, though not always cited from, throughout the *vārtā*s is neither vernacular nor distinctly Pushtimargi: it is the Sanskrit *Bhāgavatapurāṇa*, which is attributed to the more-than-human *ṛṣi* (seer)-poet Vyasa, also said to have authored the *Mahābhārata* ("The Great Narrative of the Bharatas' War") and to have "split" (*vyāsa*) the *Veda* ("Knowledge").[57] By all accounts, Vallabhacharya accepted that *Veda*, or *śruti* (that which is heard), was unquestionably a valid expression of Truth. However, Vallabhacharya (like other theologians of his time) also asserted that the era in which he lived was that of the disastrous *kaliyug*, an age in which humans could no longer comprehend the truth of the *Veda*. *Parabrāhmaṇa*, the Supreme Being, had fortunately revealed himself on earth as Lord Krishna in order to restore and protect righteousness during the degenerate age. For Vaishnava theologians of Vallabhacharya's time, and still for countless devotees across the Hindu spectrum, one of the most popular records of Krishna's manifestation on earth is told in the *Bhāgavatapurāṇa*.[58]

The *84VV* and other *vārtā* texts describe Vallabhacharya's passion for the *Bhāgavatapurāṇa* as central not only to his theological writings, but also to his proselytizing pilgrimages and modes of religious instruction. The Braj Bhasha *Caurāsī Baiṭhak Caritra*, for instance, describes eighty-four of the primary places where Vallabhacharya read and commented upon the *Bhāgavatapurāṇa*, transforming the lives of those who heard him.[59] In the *84VV* and *252VV* would-be-devotees often become attracted to the Pushtimarg because they catch a glimpse of or hear the charismatic teachers Vallabhacharya and Vitthalnath as they are on "tour" reading from and giving teachings on the Sanskrit text. It is therefore no surprise

poems in the introductory pages of printed versions of the texts. See, for example, a list of intertextual references including *kīrtan*, *kāvya* (poetry), *śloka* (Sanskrit verses), etc., here: Dvārkādās Puruṣottamdās Parīkh, ed., *Do Sau Bāvan Vaiṣṇavan kī Vārtā-Tīn Janma kī Līlā Bhāvnā Vālī: Pratham Khaṇḍ*, Vol. 1 (Indore, India: Vaiṣṇav Mitra Maṇḍal, 2009), 75.

[57] The *Veda* is a "collection of poems or hymns composed in archaic Sanskrit by Indo-European-speaking peoples who lived in northwest India during the 2nd millennium bce. No definite date can be ascribed to the composition of the Vedas, but the period of about 1500–1200 bce is acceptable to most scholars" (*Britannica Academic*, s.v. "Veda," accessed January 8, 2021, https://academic-eb-com.ezproxy.oberlin.edu/levels/collegiate/article/Veda/74939).

[58] Edwin F. Bryant, trans., *Krishna: The Beautiful Legend of God (Śrīmad Bhāgavata Purāṇa Book X)* (London: Penguin, 2003), xvi.

[59] For more on this text, see David L. Haberman, "A Theology of Place: Pilgrimage in the *Caurāsī Baiṭhak Caritra*," in *Studies in Early Modern Indo-Aryan Languages, Literature and Culture*, ed. Alan. W. Entwistle and Carol Solomon, with Heidi Pauwels and Michael C. Shapiro (New Delhi: Manohar, 1999), 155–166.

that one of Vallabhacharya's most widely known compositions is his *Subodhinī* commentary on the *Bhāgavatapurāṇa*. Recall that in the *84VV*'s opening *Bhāvprakāś* episode Gokulnath says that the *Subodhinī*'s essence is contained in the hagiographies of Vallabhacharya's disciples. The *Subodhinī* itself highlights the *Bhāgavatapurāṇa*'s tenth canto, which establishes Krishna as Supreme Being and describes the deity's *līlā*—including his *rāsa-līlā*, or dramatic enactment of "amorous divine play" with the *gopī*s in the eternal land of Braj.[60]

One of Vallabhacharya's primary concerns in the *Subodhinī* is to apply concepts borrowed from Sanskrit aesthetic theory, known as *rasa* theory, to explain how Krishna's *rāsa-līlā* as it is depicted in the *Bhāgavatapurāṇa* becomes a model for the proper cultivation of the devotee's love for the divine. *Rasa* (lit. "juice" or "essence") is generally understood as distilled aesthetic emotion that arises when everyday human feelings (such as love or anger) are depersonalized and transcend their social contexts.[61] Premodern theorists writing on *rasa* selected eight *sthāyībhāva*s (stable feelings) from the gamut of human emotions for the dramatic representation of life on stage or in literature.[62] Early *rasa* theorists described how through a "rigorously specified compositional process," these stable feelings could be "metamorphosed into corresponding dominant moods or emotions (*rasas*)."[63] Vallabhacharya's *Subodhinī* suggests that Krishna himself is the divine embodiment of *rasa*. In Vallabhacharya's view, as in Vaishnava accounts from other traditions, experiencing Krishna as the embodiment of *rasa* (namely *śṛṅgāra*, or the amorous *rasa*) becomes the primary goal of the *gopī* (the metaphoric human devotee). The *gopī*, like the *sahṛdaya* (cultivated viewer or reader of poetry or drama), reaches her goal when the *rāsa-līlā* is performed with all the

60 These *līlā* episodes are famously described in a five-part section of the *Bhāgavatapurāṇa*'s tenth canto known as the *Rāsapañcādhyāyī*.

61 *Rāsa* should be distinguished from *rasa*. The former can mean "a dance of cowherds" or "specif. the round-dance of Kṛṣṇa with the herd-girls of Braj"; "a Kṛṣṇa festival including enactment of the round-dance, celebrated in the month of Kārttik"; "a type of popular drama dealing with the exploits of Kṛṣṇa" (McGregor, *The Oxford Hindi-English Dictionary*, 863). *Rasa* can mean "juice, sap; liquid; liquor"; "flavor"; "pleasure; joy; elegance, charm, wit" (ibid., 855).

62 These emotions include love, joy, grief, fear, energy, disgust, humor, and wonder.

63 Leela Prasad, *Ethics in Everyday Hindu Life* (Ranikhet, India: Permanent Black, 2007), 174. These *rasas* include *śṛṅgāra* (erotic), *hāsya* (comic), *karuṇa* (tragic), *raudra* (furious), *bhayānaka* (fearsome), *vīra* (heroic), *bībhatsa* (disgusting), and *adbhuta* (wondrous) *rasas*. Some medieval philosophers, namely, Anandavardhana (c. 850) and Abhinavagupta (fl. c. 975–1025), would add a ninth *rasa*, *śanta* (serenity) to this list. One of the first texts to theorize *rasa* is the *Nāṭyaśāstra* ("A Treatise on Theater")—a Sanskrit treatise on drama likely composed between 200 BCE and 200 CE. For further information on this text, see Adya Rangacharya, ed. and trans., *The Nāṭyaśāstra: English Translation with Critical Notes* (New Delhi: Munshiram Manoharlal, 1996).

requisite devotional sentiments.[64] While Vallabhacharya's account of how to experience *rasa* as a devotee is not as clearly delineated as those of some of his near contemporaries (e.g., Rupa Gosvamin of the Chaitanya Sampraday), his writing lays the groundwork for Pushtimargi discourse on how the human devotee can, through the establishment of ritual techniques in *sevā*, imitate and thus actually come to inhabit the world of Krishna's *nitya* (eternal) *līlā* while still living in a human body in the mundane world.[65] Vallabhacharya himself did not, however, leave a detailed manual on the ritual techniques of *sevā*. Likewise, *sevā* in the *vārtā*s is not depicted as a strictly formulaic set of acts. It does, though, often include offering Krishna *bhog* (special food items), as well as *rāg* (lit. a "musical mode," but with reference to devotional singing) and *śṛṅgār* (dressing and adorning Krishna as a *svarūp*). As long as *sevā* is performed with loving devotion, the *vārtā*s suggest, it is not necessary to follow any one fixed system. In fact, those who become too attached to the rituals of *sevā*, as rituals themselves, are mocked in the *vārtā*s for losing their values specific to the Pushtimarg and for following the *maryādāmārg* (a path of rules and regulations, as opposed to the path of *puṣṭi*, or nourishment). Instead of following strict ritual guidelines, *vārtā* protagonists rely on fellow devotees, their guru, and Krishna himself to navigate their way as *sevā* practitioners. If a devotee makes a misstep, Krishna himself steps in to correct his *sevak* or calls upon Vallabhacharya, Vitthalnath, or a seasoned devotee to set matters straight (recall an example of this in Raskhan's *vārtā*). Even what would be seemingly basic prescriptions for Vaishnava ritual practice, such as refraining from *sevā* during times of physical "pollution" (e.g., during menstruation or after the death of a family member), are shown to be negotiable in the presence of sincere and fervent love for Krishna. We will return later to how Hariray's *Bhāvprakāś* deals with the presentation of such potentially questionable actions and in turn how devotees today navigate

[64] Devotional sentiments delineated in the *Bhāgavatapurāṇa* and adopted by later *bhakti* traditions include *dāsya* (the *bhāva* of servitude); *śānta* (the *bhāva* of serenity); *sakhya* (the *bhāva* of friendship); *mādhurya* (also known as *śṛṅgāra*, the *bhāva* of sweetness with reference to erotic intimacy); and *vātsalya* (the *bhāva* of parental affection).

[65] For a comprehensive description of *bhakti rasa*, see David L. Haberman, *Acting as a Way of Salvation: A Study of Rāgānugā Bhakti Sādhana* (Delhi: Motilal Banarsidass, 1998). While *bhakti* was considered an aesthetic category prior to the 16th century, it was during this period—during Vallabhacharya's lifetime—that Vaishnava (and Shaiva) theologians popularized the use of *rasa* theory to delineate the devotional sentiments of *bhakti*. For more on Pushtimargi ritual in relationship to other similar Vaishnava traditions, see Monika Horstmann and Anand Mishra's "Vaishnava Sampradāyas on the Importance of Ritual: A Comparison of the Two Contemporaneous Approaches by Viṭṭhalnātha and Jīva Gosvāmī," in *Bhakti Beyond the Forest: Current Research of Early Modern Literatures in North India, 2003–2009*, ed. Imre Bangha (New Delhi: Manohar, 2012), 155–176.

between what the hagiographies and Vallabhacharya's treatises are perceived to teach about ritual propriety and more contemporary perspectives on issues of "purity and pollution." Suffice it to say that the hagiographies build on Vallabhacharya's theological writings on Krishna-centered theology, especially as it is found in the *Bhāgavatapurāṇa*, to demonstrate how initiated devotees might cultivate passionate, other-worldly love for their personal *svarūps* while still living their daily lives in the mundane world.

As I have discussed here, the *vārtās*' authors use intertextual references, namely, references to treatises attributed to Vallabhacharya, both to *authorize* the hagiographies as primary religious texts and to build on and develop Vallabhacharya's theologies and doctrines through narrative descriptions of devotees' lives. We now turn to a final dialogical and intertextual layer of the *vārtās*, Hariray's *Bhāvprakāś*, which aims to align the *vārtās* with Vallabhacharya's teachings in still distinct ways.

Hariray's *Bhāvprakāś* Commentary

While not all devotees and hereditary leaders see eye to eye on the significance of Hariray's commentary, the *Bhāvprakāś* circulates with most contemporary versions of the *84VV* and *252VV* and is therefore considered inherent to the texts by a majority of readers today.[66] One explanation offered by a devotee named Manish about how the *Bhāvprakāś* functions is fairly representative of the ways in which today's readers understand the commentary:

> Without Shri Harirayji's *ṭīkā* (commentary), the *vārtās* will be very difficult to read. What he did was join together all the teachings of Shri Mahaprabhuji with all of the *vārtās* told by Shri Gokulnathji. He [Hariray] is our guiding light who knows our questions [about the texts] before even we ourselves know them.

Manish's observation about Hariray's commentary being a "guiding light" (as he says in English) points not only to the commentary's title as the *Bhāvprakāś*—the "Illumination of [the text's] Inner Meaning"—but also to

[66] As the following chapter explores, some modern editors and translators omit the *Bhāvprakāś* in their versions of the *84VV* or *252VV*, only to add new, contemporary commentaries, which mimic aspects of the *Bhāvprakāś*. However, in most contemporary versions of the texts, Hariray's commentary is left intact and new commentaries are included alongside it.

how Manish understands Hariray to be a guide for understanding the hagiographies in light of Vallabhacharya's teachings. Hariray's commentary does this in several ways: first, by fleshing out the biographical details of each protagonist and linking their *laukik* lives to their roles as favored devotees who also have a place in Krishna's *alaukik līlā*; and second, by anticipating and quelling readers' doubts about seemingly dubious actions of certain protagonists.

The *laukik* biographical details that Hariray adds to the hagiographies refer to such matters as caste or birthplace, while *alaukik* details refer to the protagonists' roles in Krishna's *nitya līlā*. The *laukik* and *alaukik* aspects of *vārtā* characters' lives are essential to the structure of Hariray's *Bhāvprakāś* and relate to another common title for the commentary: the *Tīn Janma kī Bhāvnā*, or the "Recollection of the Three Lives."[67] The three lives refer to the protagonists' *laukik* and *alaukik* lives as well as to a third life stage: the condition of each character after he or she has encountered either Vallabhacharya or Vitthalnath and has entered the Pushtimargi fold through the formulaic initiation mantras.[68] Though without the textual markers that tell the reader otherwise it is sometimes difficult to distinguish where the root text ends and Hariray's commentary begins, it is generally the case that the "first" and "third" portions of protagonists' lives are revealed in the *Bhāvprakāś*, which help to explain and expand upon the events that unfold in their "second lives" described in the root text.[69]

Hariray frames and introduces most of the hagiographies in the *84VV* and *252VV* by providing "extra" biographical details of protagonists' this-worldly *and* otherworldly lives. Therefore, when introducing the *laukik* name and birthplace of each protagonist, Hariray also assigns them *alaukik* roles as specific *sakhī*s (female friends; a term used interchangeably with *gopī*s in

[67] *Bhāvnā* can mean "perception, consciousness"; "feeling; mood spirit; moral"; "mental process; recollection; imagination; premonition"; "thought; meditation" (McGregor, *The Oxford Hindi-English Dictionary*, 766).

[68] In most cases, initiation as it is described in the *vārtās* consists of the following: *snān* (taking a ritual bath); receiving the initiatory *nām nivedan* and *brahmasambandha* mantras and a *tulsī mālā* (necklace made of Tulsi wood); and, finally, receiving either a Krishna *svarūp* or another physical object (e.g., a printed cloth with Vallabhacharya's footprints) for which *sevā* should be performed.

[69] In manuscripts of the *84VV* and *252VV*, scribes will indicate the beginning and end of commentarial sections by using red ink. In printed versions of the texts in which the *Bhāvprakāś* appears, the editor will normally indicate the commentarial sections by printing them in a font that is smaller than the root text. In some versions of the *84VV* and *252VV*, the root text and commentary are elided. See, for example, Shyamdas, trans., *Eighty-four Vaishnavas* (Baroda, India: Shri Vallabha Publications, 1985). For a brief study of the differences between the manuscript recensions of the *84VV* with and without the *Bhāvprakāś*, see Rousseva-Sokolova, "Sainthood Revisited," 91–104.

the *vārtās*) in Krishna's *līlā*. Vallabhacharya and Vitthalnath are also given roles in Krishna's eternal realm: Vallabhacharya is none other than Krishna's divine partner Svamini (Radha), while Vitthalnath's divine counterpart is Svamini's primary *sakhī* Chandravali. Hariray describes all other devotees as *sakhī*s of Svamini and Chandravali (recall Raskhan's divine role as a *gopī* by the name of Rasasiddha).[70] While the "three lives" narrative is a novel construction of the *Bhāvprakāś*, Hariray's discussion of protagonists' otherworldly characteristics represents one way in which he works to align the *vārtās* with Vallabhacharya's theological writings on the human aspiration to find union with Krishna.[71]

One example of how Hariray's *Bhāvprakāś* draws connections between the *laukik* and *alaukik* lives of the *vārtās*' protagonists can be found in the account of Vallabhacharya's disciple Parvati from the *84VV*. In Hariray's opening comments on the *vārtā* he writes that Parvati was a devotee who was *rājasī* (full of passion).[72] We learn that Parvati's divine counterpart is a *sakhī* named Sucharita, who "decorates her body a great deal, but from her pride in her beauty has fallen down from *līlā*."[73] When she falls from *līlā*, Parvati loses knowledge of her *alaukik* role. In the *laukik* world Parvati performs *sevā* lovingly. However, one day she develops leprosy and feels great disgust and humiliation. "Then she recalled her previous form as a *sakhī*," Hariray chimes in. In recognition of her *alaukik* form she sends a letter to Vitthalnath, who responds to the distressed devotee, telling her not to worry because Krishna will remove the illness. Indeed, after several months, Parvati's leprosy vanishes, and she learns to perform *sevā* lovingly and without pride.

While Hariray does not always draw such clear connections between the *laukik* fate or actions of protagonists and their *alaukik* positions, protagonists' divine roles in *līlā* are key to the theology of the *Bhāvprakāś* and

[70] The *aṣṭachāp* poets are assigned roles as *sakhī*s and as *sakhā*s in *līlā*. The implication is that these eight individuals had a special kind of spiritual insight, which, through devotional song, allowed them to access to Krishna's *līlā* as both female and male counterparts.

[71] It is not clear that Vallabhacharya and Vitthalnath had themselves established a clear map of connections they or their devotees had to divine figures in Krishna's *līlā*.

[72] In the opening pages of the *84VV* and *252VV*, Hariray asserts that the eighty-four followers of Vallabhacharya were *nirguṇ* (without qualities) and that Vitthalnath's two hundred and fifty-two devotees were *rājasī*, *tāmasī* (irascible), and *sāttvikī* (virtuous). These enumerations and the reference to the *guṇ*s (qualities) are familiar to many Hindu, Jain, and Buddhist traditions. As previously noted, eighty-four is considered to be an auspicious number, in part because there are understood to be eighty-four *lakh* categories of living beings, each of which is assigned a *guṇ*. The exemplary devotees of the tradition are representative of each of these categories. Even though Vallabhacharya's followers are said to have been *nirguṇ*, Hariray still assigns them *guṇ*s.

[73] D. Parīkh, ed., *Caurāsī Vaiṣṇavan kī Vārtā*, 53. The Braj Bhasha term used here is *girī*. *Sucarita* can mean "right conduct" or "good behavior."

to the *vārtā* stories themselves. As scholar Richard Barz notes in his writing on the hagiographies, "the bypassing of the ego to discover true identity as a transcendent woman, a *sakhī*, or as both a *sakhī* and a transcendent man, a *sakhā*, is the mystery that lies at the heart of the Pushtimarg as presented in the *CVV* (*Tīn Janma kī Līlā Bhāvnā Vālī*)."[74] Recognizing this "true identity," however, does not necessarily distance the *vārtās*' protagonists from their *laukik* circumstances. It is the relationship between the devotee and his or her Krishna *svarūp* that creates a bridge, so to speak, between the two worlds. It is only when intimacy is achieved between devotee and *svarūp* that the deity acts in the *laukik* world as a speaking, loving, playful, sweet, and mischievous counterpart, often as a sort of divine member of a devotee's family (see, for example, the *vārtā* of the Kshatriya woman, discussed in this book's Introduction, in which Krishna speaks to his caretaker "just like a small child").

The second way the *Bhāvprakāś* functions in the *84VV* and *252VV*, and its most significant function as a dialogical feature of the texts, is to anticipate and quell readers' doubts about seemingly dubious actions of certain protagonists and therefore to smooth over theological tensions in the narratives. In this way, we are able to witness how Hariray, himself a reader of the hagiographies, struggles to make sense of how Vallabhacharya's teachings align—or do not align—with the stories told in the *vārtās*. An example of this function of the *Bhāvprakāś* is found in an account from the *84VV*, when a devotee named Virbai is told by her Krishna *svarūp* to carry on with his *sevā* even though she is in a state of impurity due to childbirth. Hariray is quick to justify the character's behavior. Don't misunderstand, Hariray tells the reader, since Virbai was much loved by Thakurji and was given permission by the deity to carry on with *sevā*, her actions were neither wicked nor impure.[75] In Chapter 4 I analyze a discussion among contemporary devotees who have just heard this *vārtā* read aloud by their guru in *satsaṅg*. As we will see, Hariray's assessment of Virbai's behavior in the text prompts a lively debate about women's propriety during *sevā*—a matter about which devotees and certain hereditary leaders have differing opinions.

Another example of the *Bhāvprakāś*' justifying function is found in the *vārtā* of Krishnadas Adhikari, known to have been a "manager" of

[74] Barz, "The *Caurāsī Vaiṣṇavan kī Vārtā* and the Theology of the Puṣṭimārg," 60.

[75] Virbai's *vārtā* is normally the sixty-first account in the *84VV*. See D. Parīkh, *Caurāsī Vaiṣṇavan kī Vārtā*, 339–344.

Shrinathji's first temple at Mount Govardhan. In the *vārtā*'s fifth episode we learn that Krishnadas has gone to the imperial (Mughal) capital of Agra to collect provisions needed for Shrinathji's *sevā*. While in the bazaar, his attention is caught by the sight of a prostitute teaching her daughter to dance:

> The prostitute's daughter was a girl of around twelve who was extremely beautiful. Krishnadas was so impressed and charmed by that young prostitute's singing that he stopped his chariot right there, got down, and pushed his way through the crowd until he could gaze upon the beauty of the girl. He stood there for some time charmed by her song.

Here the *Bhāvprakāś* interrupts the root text's narrative with the following comment:

> This episode may cause doubt, for some will wonder how Krishnadas, who was a faithful servant of Shri Acharyaji, could be charmed by the song of a prostitute. Further doubts may arise when one recalls that even the charms and beauty of heavenly nymphs should not interest devotees like Krishnadas, who are completely drowned in their love for Shri Krishna. As Shri Acharyaji wrote in his *Jalabheda* ("Distinctions vis-à-vis Water") treatise on the topic of singers and prostitutes: "Singers who stay with prostitutes and other lowly people and become intoxicated and sing songs for their living are like dirty gutter water."[76]

The commentary continues to explain how Vallabhacharya's *Jalabheda* treatise (included in the *Ṣoḍaśagrantha*) describes the danger of taking the company of prostitutes and other "debased" individuals.[77] So why, Hariray continues, was Krishnadas, a person of great wisdom and a defender of "correct behavior," so charmed by the singing of a prostitute? How could Krishnadas, who had appeared in the *laukik* world to assist in the instruction and uplifting of all souls be charmed by a prostitute? All doubt, assures Hariray, will be dispelled by the following commentary, which explains—using a rhetorical flourish well-known to early modern *bhakti*

[76] D. Parīkh, *Caurāsī Vaiṣṇavan kī Vārtā*, 690–693. I have used Richard Barz's translation of the Sanskrit from the *Jalabheda* as quoted in the *vārtā* (Barz, *The Bhakti Sect of Vallabhacarya*, 229).

[77] The *Jalabheda* describes different categories of souls in terms of different kinds of water. For more on the *Jalabheda*, see Frederick Smith, "Vedic and Devotional Waters: The *Jalabheda* of Vallabhācārya," *International Journal of Hindu Studies* 10, no. 1 (2005): 107–136.

narratives—that the prostitute was herself a godly being who maintained a role as a *sakhī* in Krishna's *līlā*.

Hariray again refers to the prostitute's *alaukik* role when the *vārtā* tells us how the girl became so immersed in joy while singing for Shrinathji that she was released from her *laukik* body to live eternally with Krishna as her divine incarnation. Here, Hariray inserts yet another comment in order to rationalize the prostitute's liberation without ever having received "proper" Pushtimargi initiation. "The *brahmasambandha*," the commentary reminds us, "may only be given by a member of the Vallabha Kul." However, because Vallabhacharya was enshrined in the heart of Krishnadas, the prostitute actually *did* receive proper initiation when Krishnadas taught her a verse of his poem to sing before the deity. Hariray acknowledges that one might still have doubts about how any person could enter into *līlā* without the help of a guru. However, he reassures the reader, such doubts are dispelled by the fact that the girl was already a godly being before she received initiation and, in *līlā*, is a companion of Krishnadas' divine manifestation as Lalitaji, one of Svamini's foremost *sakhīs*.

The episode as it exists *without* the *Bhāvprakāś* suggests that Krishnadas was blessed by the grace of Krishna and was therefore able to facilitate the girl's liberation. Hariray, on the other hand, rewrites the narrative through his intervening comments and concludes the *vārtā* with a reminder about how to correctly receive Pushtimargi initiation. In this way, the commentary employs two distinct narrative strategies: first, it refers to Vallabhacharya's doctrines, and then it uses the *alaukik* life of the character to provide justification and causal explanation for a story that could potentially be read as transgressive. Both of these strategies are deployed through Hariray's use of hypophora, which in this case means he is "speaking" directly to readers, anticipating their confusions, but also suggesting which kinds of questions they *should* be asking of the hagiographies, and, of course, providing answers to said questions.[78]

While inherent to the hagiographies for many contemporary readers, Hariray's *Bhāvprakāś* is not the final word on the *vārtās*. Rather, as this chapter has shown, the commentary is one of several features of the *84VV* and *252VV* that provides a way for readers to enter into a conversational and even argumentative relationship with the texts. Contemporary commentators

[78] Hawley discusses this *vārtā* and Hariray's efforts to smooth over theological tensions in the hagiographies here: *Storm of Songs*, 180–182.

openly contest Hariray's interpretations as well as those of fellow devotees and hereditary leaders, often coming to disparate conclusions about which behaviors are worthy of emulation and in which circumstances, etc. As Shalini Goswami explained things to me, "Shri Harirayji's *Bhāvprakāś* does not always answer our questions about the eighty-four and two hundred and fifty-two Vaishnavas, but he [Hariray] does encourage us to ask how the *vārtās* tell us about Shri Vallabhacharya's teachings and the application of these teachings to our own lives."[79] This particular function of Hariray's commentary and of the hagiographies themselves also echoes what scholar Robin Rinehart has observed about hagiography. At its most essential level, Rinehart writes, hagiography is "the history of how the saint's followers have chosen to remember him or her," and therefore the job of hagiographers is to "serve as mediators, creating a bridge between the saint and his followers through their texts."[80] The *84VV* and *252VV* certainly function as meditating bridges, as does Hariray's commentary. But as my interlocutors' comments make clear, the *vārtās* also function as conversation partners and starters, inviting readers to engage in dialogue with each other, with the narratives, and directly with Krishna, as they make sense of ideals inherited from the past in terms of their present, everyday lives.

Final Thoughts on Dialogicality in Pushtimargi Texts

In this chapter I have shown that the form and content of the *84VV* and *252VV* as dialogical and intertextual hagiographies are integral to how devotees read and interpret these (and other) Pushtimargi texts. I have also suggested that the *84VV* and *252VV* aid devotees as they forge relationships with one another and with the divine. I want to conclude by clarifying how these arguments build on and challenge other scholarly frameworks for approaching texts and readers in order to pave the way for this book's subsequent chapters.

My approach to the *84VV* and *252VV* as dialogical texts that are part of a performative canon is inspired not only by the hagiographies themselves and by those who read them, but also by broader conversations in South Asian literary and intellectual history. Amidst a diverse record of theoretical writing

[79] Personal communication, August 25, 2010.

[80] Robin Rinehart, *One Lifetime, Many Lives: The Experience of Modern Hindu Hagiography* (Atlanta: Scholars Press, 1999), 11–12.

on matters of epistemology and reception indigenous to South Asia (e.g., theories of aesthetic response, which I have gestured to in my discussion of *rasa*), the *Kauṣītaki Upaniṣad*—on which Black and Patton draw in their edited volume—provides us with a theory for what merits our attention in understanding acts of reception. The following appears in the *upaniṣad*'s third chapter (3.6) and is situated within a broader teaching about how coming to know another person requires knowledge of their soul: ". . . speech is not what one should desire to understand. One should know the speaker. . . . Sound is not what one should desire to understand. One should know the hearer."[81] Though not referring specifically to relationships between texts and readers, the *upaniṣad* might well have extended its examples to suggest that one should not focus on knowing the text (not to mention the author) but, rather, the reader. While *Religious Reading and Everyday Lives* may seem to favor the reader over the text, my observations of how Pushtimargis read make it impossible to fully adopt the logic of the *Kauṣītaki Upaniṣad*'s position on reception, namely, that it is to the hearer/reader that we should turn, rather than to the speaker or text. Instead, I—as others before me—study readers and texts as interlocutors who influence each other, albeit in different, and certainly not always equal, ways.[82] Even in this chapter, in which I examined rhetorical strategies in the *vārtā*s as written texts, real readers have been with me every step of the way.

Emphasis on the reader, rather than the text and author, has been favored in many schools of modern literary criticism. For instance, reader response critic Stanley Fish's concept of "interpretive communities"—which suggests that a text's "meaning" is realized through acts of readerly interpretation, themselves grounded in specific cultural contexts—is helpful for thinking about the community-making power of texts for Pushtimargis past and present.[83] For Fish, the act of reading should be approached as an "event," which is primarily understood through making sense of a text's intended audience, or the "informed reader."[84] The *84VV* and *252VV* have clear target audiences,

[81] An echo of this formula is found in the *84VV* when Vitthalnath asks Damodardas Harsani, "which is greater, the gift or the giver?" Harsani replies that it is the giver, without whom the gift could not be received. The teaching here, as the text elaborates, is that Vallabhacharya as guru is supreme as the "giver" of Krishna to initiated devotees. This teaching, however, is specific to emphasizing initiation and guru, rather than suggesting a broader theory of reception.

[82] In this book's Introduction I referred to Edward W. Said's position on how texts and readers enter into conversations. See "The Text, the World, the Critic," 5. See also Lutgendorf, *The Life of a Text*.

[83] Stanley E. Fish, "Interpreting the *Variorum*," in *Reader-Response Criticism: From Formalism to Post-Structuralism*, ed. Jane P. Tompkins (Baltimore: Johns Hopkins University Press, 1980), 182.

[84] Stanley E. Fish, *Self-Consuming Artifacts: The Experience of Seventeenth-Century Literature* (Berkeley: University of California Press, 1972), 407.

namely, initiated devotees like those who gathered in Megha Choksi's backyard to listen to and learn from Shalini Goswami so that they could become "informed readers," in turn becoming Pushtimargi. However, what is missing from Fish's approach to reading, and from others similarly based on ideal or abstract readers, is the nuance that comes from including real *living* readers in one's analysis. Living people's reading practices and interpretations of texts are far less stable or predictable than their ideal reader counterparts, even though they share common devotional grammars with their beloved texts and with one another. Like scholar Linda Hess, whose monograph *Bodies of Song: Kabir Oral Traditions and Performative Worlds in North India* presents a model for merging textwork and fieldwork, my own research has led me to a methodology that approaches Pushtimargi narratives and rituals as both grounded in written texts and also enlivened by real, living readers. As Hess writes,

> Written texts have a quasi-sacred status in the humanities partly because they are convenient. Texts hold their shape. We can xerox them. Performances are dizzyingly varied, changing through different times and locations. We have to go out of our way to experience them. [. . .] I am trying to develop a method in which fieldwork and textwork inform and change each other. Perhaps we can imagine together a larger world of "text," where one mode of inquiry does not need to eclipse the other.[85]

It is in part due to my intentional merging of textwork and fieldwork that I use the term "performative canon": "canon" because I am analyzing a relatively fixed set of written texts that continue to be approached as canonical (though the texts' canonicity shifts in different historical contexts), but also "performative" because the modes of reading and exegesis that readers bring to these written texts are always grounded in places, bodies, and sociohistorical contexts, which are dynamic and fluid.

It should come as no surprise that Pushtimargi literature and those who read this literature resist being analyzed in terms of any one theoretical model. While the intertextual and dialogical features of the *vārtā*s make them ripe for comparison across literary and religious traditions, the Pushtimarg's performative canon has a logic of its own—one that has been questioned, loved, debated, and renegotiated by religious readers past and present.

[85] Hess, *Bodies of Song*, 4.

2

Commentarial Reading

Historicizing Hagiography and Making Modern Readers

Founded in 1858, the Naval Kishore Press of Lucknow was a prominent feature of what became a robust and dynamic culture of Indian print in the latter half of the 19th century. Even in its early days, a significant number of texts printed by Naval Kishore were Vaishnava in nature. By the 1880s, the press's collection of Vaishnava titles quickly expanded to include many of the key vernacular works associated with the Pushtimarg, including the *84VV*. Other burgeoning presses, including those based in rapidly growing centers of the Pushtimargi community—namely, Mumbai (then Bombay) and nearby Gujarati cities—also began to publish Pushtimargi titles in increasing volume. The demand for these titles clearly corresponded to the demand from readers: Pushtimargis wanted to read their vernacular texts, but specifically in the "quintessentially modern venue"[1] of the published book. The printing press and the production of Pushtimargi vernacular literature (such as *Vārtā Sāhitya*) as published books was also closely linked to broader "metadiscursive regime[s]" that organized "intellectual interventions in oral tradition" as a key element in the "symbolic construction of modernity."[2] Simply put, books became sites for Pushtimargi readers in their dual roles as authors, translators, editors, or commentators to reauthorize their vernacular texts for contemporary audiences and in light of contemporary circumstances. Such reauthorization happened most explicitly through new styles of commentarial writing, which emphasized the texts' historicity,

[1] Richard Bauman and Charles L. Briggs, *Voices of Modernity: Language Ideologies and the Politics of Inequality* (Cambridge: Cambridge University Press, 2003), 16. My use of the term "modern" aligns with the work of Bauman and Briggs (2003). That is, it does not correspond to "sweeping generalizations about the nature of [a single] modernity," or to rigidly defined periods of precolonial and independent India but, rather, to what Baumann and Briggs have suggested are "modernities": "social categories, texts, contexts, forms of knowledge, and social relations" that are "produced and reproduced, legitimized, denigrated, challenged, superseded, and often revived in discourse-oriented terms" (17).

[2] Bauman and Briggs, *Voices of Modernity*, 17.

Religious Reading and Everyday Lives in Devotional Hinduism. Emilia Bachrach, Oxford University Press. © Oxford University Press 2022. DOI: 10.1093/oso/9780197648599.003.0003

authenticity, and, perhaps most importantly, their enduring relevance for 19th- and 20th-century readers.

According to scholar Paul J. Griffiths, commentaries (a term I will complicate later in this chapter) are the "principal means by which communities of religious readers have expressed themselves discursively."[3] While certain Pushtimargi texts, such as Vallabhacharya's 16th-century Sanskrit *Subodhinī*, have consistently accumulated written commentaries since the time of their composition, other than Hariray's *Bhāvprakāś* (which is accepted as inherent to the *84VV* and *252VV* for most Pushtimargis today), there are no other substantial written commentaries on the hagiographies that predate the 1860s.[4] In part, this is because the written *vārtā*s had, before this period, likely been read aloud primarily in community settings where a hereditary leader or knowledgeable devotee would provide oral commentary on the stories for fellow devotees. As future chapters show, such community gatherings remain the most common context in which the *vārtā*s are read. However, the shift from manuscript to book culture in the late 19th century enabled a growing number of literate Pushtimargis to read independently and to therefore engage discursively—in print—with the *vārtā*s beyond prescribed community settings. It was due to these changes in reading practices that the *vārtā*s became popular sites for various forms of written commentary. Today, Pushtimargis continue to author *vārtā* commentaries of various sorts, which are printed in an unabated flow. These commentaries often circulate with printed versions of the canonical *vārtā*s (see Chapter 1) and are therefore widely available to devotees, many of whom have printed copies of these texts in their personal collections. As Dwarkadas Parikh—a 20th-century devotee-commentator and the editor of enduringly popular versions of the *84VV* and *252VV*—wrote in a 1971 essay (with only slight hyperbole), "there would hardly be a single place where [Pushtimargi] Vaishnavas are found in India where there is not at least one copy [of the *84VV*]."[5] In this way, the late 19th-century emergence of print culture paved the way for 20th- and 21st-century Pushtimargis to participate in this "principal means" of expressing themselves as religious readers, but also as "modern" readers.

[3] Griffiths, *Religious Reading*, 77.

[4] Ulrike Stark, *An Empire of Books: The Naval Kishore Press and the Diffusion of the Printed Word in Colonial India* (Ranikhet, India: Permanent Black, 2007), 399–401.

[5] I have used Barz's translation of this statement (Barz, "The *Caurāsī Vaiṣṇavan kī Vārtā* and the Theology of the Puṣṭimārg," 49) as it is found in Parīkh's text: Dvārkādās Puruṣottamdās Parīkh, ed., *Caurāsī Vaiṣṇavan kī Vārtā* (*Tīn Janma kī Līlā Bhāvnā Vālī*) (Mathura, India: Śrī Govarddhan Granthmālā, 1971), *kha*.

In responding to their socio-historical circumstances, commentators—both devotees and hereditary leaders—added new and distinct layers of written exegesis to Pushtimargi texts in their forms as published books.

In what follows, I first flesh out some of the nuances of the social and historical circumstances that corresponded to the emergence of print in northwest India and to the growing popularity of Pushtimargi book culture. Key to this moment is the widely known Bombay Supreme Court case, known as the Maḥaraja Libel Case, which ultimately led to a public shaming of the Pushtimarg as an "illegitimate" Hindu community. During the trial's hearings, the British judges and lawyers invoked *Vārtā Sāhitya* repeatedly to show how the Pushtimarg was in contradiction to the "ancient Hindu religion" based on the Sanskrit *Veda*s. The first part of the chapter demonstrates how British judges and lawyers during the Maharaja Libel Case read and questioned the *vārtā*s publicly, perhaps for the first time, in ways likely foreign to most Pushtimargi readers. Those who questioned the *vārtā*s in this context were not questioning them as religious readers might. Rather, those who questioned the hagiographies in the court of law were interrogating them as textual representations of the Pushtimarg in order to determine whether or not the tradition was "authentically Hindu." The context of putting an Indian religious community and its vernacular literary traditions under legal scrutiny in British Colonial–era Bombay courts "testifies to the emergence of an Orientalist legal apparatus that displaced traditional structures of religious authority in the process of asserting its own ability to adjudicate Hindu orthodoxy."[6] I then move on to unpack the social climate that followed the Maharaja Libel Case, connecting it to how Pushtimargis as readers, but also as authors and commentators, of the late 19th century took advantage of new technologies of print to reauthorize their devotional

[6] J. Barton Scott, *Spiritual Despots: Modern Hinduism and the Genealogies of Self-Rule* (Chicago: University of Chicago Press, 2016), 126. For more on the Orientalist legal apparatus and the "construction" of Hinduism, see Brian K. Pennington, *Was Hinduism Invented?: Britons, Indians, and the Colonial Construction of Religion* (Oxford: Oxford University Press, 2005). In 1866, another community—the Ismaili Muslim Khojas—also went to court to defend their status as "authentically Muslim." Just as Pushtimargi hagiographies were interrogated during the hearings in the Maharaja Libel Case, so too were the *ginān*s, the Khojas' Gujarati devotional texts, scrutinized during the Aga Khan Case hearings. For further information, see Teena Purohit, *The Aga Khan Case: Religion and Identity in Colonial India* (Cambridge, MA: Harvard University Press, 2013), 29. For further references to sectarian disputes that went to court among Gujarat-based religious communities, see Mitra Sharafi's *Law and Identity in Colonial South Asia: Parsi Legal Culture, 1772–1947* (Cambridge: Cambridge University Press, 2014) and John E. Cort's "The Jain Knowledge Warehouses: Traditional Libraries in India," *Journal of the American Oriental Society* 115, no. 1 (1995): 77–87.

literature. The final portion of the chapter offers several close readings of commentaries and reworkings of *vārtā* texts to provide examples of how devotees of the late 19th and 20th centuries analyzed the hagiographies in response to their specific social and historical contexts. Ultimately, I suggest, these examples demonstrate how "commentarial reading" is one significant mode by which Pushtimargis read: "commentarial reading," which here is connected to commentarial *writing*, is meant to guide fellow readers in the practice of textual interpretation, which in turn aids devotees in the process of articulating community identity in light of contemporary circumstances—even, or especially, particularly difficult ones.

Reading *Vārtā Sāhitya* During the Maharaja Libel Case

In 1861, Pushtimargi hereditary leader Jadunath Brijratanji Maharaj filed a suit for libel against Karsandas Mulji, a prominent journalist, for publishing an article in which Mulji had written that "the sect of Vallabhacharya" was heterodox and immoral.[7] Mulji's article, which notably mentioned Jadunath Maharaj by name, went on to state that "no other sectaries have ever perpetrated such shamelessness, subtility, immodesty, rascality, and deceit as have the sect of the Maharajas."[8] Jadunath Maharaj's suit for libel went to trial and ended up making its way to Bombay's Supreme Court. The trial, which came to be known as the Maharaja Libel Case, was dubbed at the time as the "greatest trial of modern times since the trial of Warren Hastings."[9] The hearing was sensationalized in Indian and foreign newspapers and filled twenty-four days in court, spanning nearly three months. While Mulji was found guilty of libel based on legal technicalities, the case resulted in a caricature of the Pushtimarg as a tradition presided over by deviant gurus and based on "heterodox" vernacular texts—specifically, *Vārtā Sāhitya*.[10] Sir Matthew Sausse, one of the two British judges who presided over the hearings, concluded that the Pushtimarg's "doctrines and principles" were

[7] Karsondas Mulji, *History of the Sect of Maharajas, or Vallabhacharyas in Western India* (London: Trübner & Co., 1865), 172–175. The article "The Primitive Religion of the Hindus and the Present Heterodox Opinions" was first published in 1860 in the Gujarati-language newspaper, the *Satya Prakāś* ("The Illumination of the Truth").

[8] Mulji, *History of the Sect of Maharajas*, 174.

[9] B.N. Motiwala, *Karsondas Mulji: A Biographical Study* (Bombay: Karsondas Mulji Centenary Celebration Committee, 1935) 33; cf. Scott, "How to Defame a God," 184.

[10] Shandip Saha, "Creating a Community of Grace: A History of the Puṣṭi Mārga in Northern and Western India: 1493–1905" (PhD diss., University of Ottawa, 2004), 301.

"opposed to what we know of the original principles of the ancient Hindu religion which are said to be found in the Veds. [. . .]" and were therefore "contrary to those of the ancient Hindu religion."[11] While hereditary leaders had taken community conflicts to colonial (and precolonial) courts in previous decades (and would continue to do so well after 1862), this case was unique in that it led to a public, legal definition of the Pushtimarg that directly minimized the ways in which a majority of devotees understood their own religious community, and significantly the ways in which a majority of devotees *read* and interpreted their devotional literature.[12]

One reason that the Maharaja Libel Case received so much press was that its hearing was carried out in Bombay, the then-capital of the Bombay Presidency (a region that included some parts of today's state of Gujarat) and the seat of British administration and intellectual exchange in western India. By the late 19th century, Bombay also had a sizable Pushtimargi community, in part because it was a growing center for commercial trade, which was attractive to devotees hailing from merchant communities.[13] This period also marked a time of mounting disputes over authority between what historian Christine E. Dobbin has called the "Bombay Intelligentsia," of which journalist Karsandas Mulji was a prominent figure, and the so-called merchant aristocracy—that is, those who had inherited authority in both their caste-based and religious communities.[14] Karsandas Mulji was not the first (or the last) to attack the Pushtimarg as indicative of what he and other self-proclaimed reformers felt to be the "unchecked authority" of "despotic" gurus who were seen as threats to the power of the "Bombay Intelligentsia" and their British counterparts.[15] Mulji's condemnation of the Pushtimarg in general, and eventually of Jadunath Maharaj by name, was also grounded in widespread efforts across India during the 19th century to sanitize so-called folk religious traditions.[16]

[11] Mulji, *History of the Sect of Maharajas*, 82. For further information, see Shandip Saha, "From Vaiṣṇavas to Hindus: The Redefinition of the Vallabha Sampradaya in the Late Nineteenth and Early Twentieth Centuries" (paper presented at the International Conference for Early Modern Literature in North India, Shimla, India, August 3–5, 2012).

[12] For more on court cases that involved members of the *sampradāy*, see Saha, "Creating a Community of Grace," 220–257, 257–316.

[13] These merchant groups included *bāniyas*, among others (Shodhan, "Legal Representations," 156).

[14] This is Christine E. Dobbin's term. See *Urban Leadership in Western India: Politics and Communities in Bombay City 1840–1885* (London: Oxford University Press, 1972).

[15] For further information on this, see Scott, *Spiritual Despots*.

[16] Festivals still celebrated by Pushtimargis, such as Holi, Annakut, and Janmashtami, were seen as superstitious by socio-religious "reformers" and to encourage unsavory displays of "uncontrolled" affective devotion (Shodhan, "Legal Representations," 174–175. See also Amrita Shodhan,

In arguing that the Pushtimarg was a debased tradition during the hearings, Mulji and his lawyers relied on the testimonies of seven witnesses and of Jadunath Maharaj himself and presented a selection of Pushtimargi literature—namely, the *84VV* and *252VV*—in English translation, which was read aloud in court. The hagiographies, which are mentioned over a dozen times in the hearing's transcripts, were essentially determined by the legal authorities to exemplify the Pushtimarg's institutionalized immorality and to epitomize all that was corrupt about Krishna-centered *bhakti* and Vaishnavism in general.

The first extended mention of the *vārtā*s occurred on the third day of the hearings (Tuesday, January 28, 1862), when Pushtimargi devotee Runchor Munjee was questioned as a witness. In an account of his travels and pilgrimages, meetings with hereditary leaders, and understanding of "Brahmanism" and "gooroos," Munjee states that he has read the "story of the 84 Vyshnavs, also the story of the 252" (referring to the *84VV* and *252VV*), including the "story of Krishnadass carrying his wife on his shoulders for the purpose of her fulfilling an adulterous engagement which she had made with another Bania."[17] At this point, nothing more is explained about the details of the "story of Krishnadass," which refers to a hagiography from the *84VV* about Krishnadas and his wife, two disciples of Vallabhacharya.[18] In most versions of the story, Krishnadas departs for a business trip, leaving his wife alone at home for several days. While he is gone, fellow devotees stop by their home. Feeding fellow devotees is of paramount importance in Pushtimargi tradition, and so Krishnadas' wife becomes distressed when she realizes that she has no extra food or money to buy provisions. When she visits the local grocer, he tells her that she can take what she needs if she returns at a later date to spend the night with him. Krishnadas' wife agrees and goes home to feed her visitors. When Krishnadas returns from his travels and learns what has transpired, he is pleased because his wife has followed through on their mutual dedication to serving fellow *bhakta*s. Since staying true to one's

"Women in the Maharaj Libel Case: A Re-examination," *Indian Journal of Gender Studies* 4, no. 2 [1997]: 123–239).

[17] *Report of the Maharaj Libel Case and of the Bhattia Conspiracy Case, Connected with It* (Bombay: Bombay Gazette Press, 1862), 70. The trial's transcript was also printed in the following source: *Maharaja Libel Case Including Bhattia Conspiracy Case, No. 12047 of 1861, Supreme Court Plea Side: Jadunathjee Bizrattanjee Maharaj vs. Karsondass Mooljee and Nandabhai Rustamji* (Bombay: D. Lukhmidass, 1911).

[18] This episode is traditionally the *84VV*'s seventy-fifth narrative (*Kṛṣṇadās strī puruṣ kī vārtā*).

word is also of paramount importance, Krishnadas gladly helps his wife to ready herself for her promised rendezvous with the shopkeeper. Krishnadas even carries his wife to the grocer's doorstep on his own shoulders so that her feet do not become muddied in the street. When she arrives, the grocer asks the woman how her feet have stayed so clean. When she explains, he throws himself at her feet proclaiming that she and her husband are great souls. He apologizes for his crude request, gifts her a new sari, walks her home, and tells her that she has inspired him to join the Pushtimargi fold.

Even this abbreviated account of the *vārtā*'s basic storyline (which excludes all of the conversational textures of the narratives discussed in the previous chapter) was not shared during the trial, though presumably others in the courtroom, including the judges, were familiar with at least some telling of Krishnadas' hagiography. After Munjee refers to the story, Mr. Anstey, Mulji's lawyer, interrupts the witness to ask the following: "Is the conduct of the husband approved or censured in the book?" According to the trial's transcript, the following exchange unfolds:

> Mr. Bayley [the plaintiff's lawyer] objects to the question being put; his learned friend might as well examine the witness on the contents of the Bible.
>
> The objection was overruled. The conduct of the husband, the wife and the third party in the story is praised. The good faith of the wife to her promise [to meet the grocer] is particularly praised.[19]

Munjee goes on to admit that "not being acquainted with the Shastras, I cannot say whether or not these stories are repugnant to religion or morality in one sense."[20] When Munjee then tries to explain more accurately the devotional and moral intentions of the narrative, saying, "the moral of the story is that all three parties were true to their faith," Judge Sir Joseph Arnould interjects, saying, "I don't think it is worth following it up. It is a story without a moral after all!"[21]

Krishnadas' *vārtā* and other seemingly provocative hagiographies are openly questioned and debated by Pushtimargis in contemporary contexts, but they are never, in my experience, omitted from community discourse

19 *Report of the Maharaj Libel Case*, 70.
20 Ibid.
21 *Report of the Maharaj Libel Case*, 71.

or flatly dismissed as immoral. In fact, this particular story is often analyzed with ease among Pushtimargi readers I spend time with, in part due to Hariray's commentary, which emphasizes the significance of serving fellow devotees. Hariray also suggests that the narrative is difficult to comprehend and should therefore be read only by those with firm faith. The British judge, however, abruptly brushes off any analysis of the *vārtā*, and the self-deprecating witness is pressured to agree with the legal authorities by claiming that he himself is not familiar with the "Shastras"—that is, the body of (mostly ancient) Sanskrit treatise literature that was increasingly favored by British administrators as definitive on Hindu law and moral codes.[22]

Toward the end of the trial Mr. Anstey, addressing the court on behalf of Mulji, summarized the witnesses' presentations of Pushtimargi literature during the hearings:

> Some of the witnesses have clearly stated that the old Shastras have been *pro tanto* superseded by the doctrines of stories such as those of the 252 and 84 [Vaishnavas]. Whether they are allegorical or not, is a matter of little moment: the plaintiff himself did not dare call them allegorical, but said they were given as examples. [Therefore,] according to him, adulterine love is the most appropriate where with to approach the Almighty.[23]

The complexity of *vārtā* literature—the theological and devotional positions it promotes, its humor, the dialogical relationship between text and commentary, and the intertextual connections between the *vārtās* and other Pushtimargi texts (including *śāstrik* discourse itself!)—were never acknowledged during the trial. Moreover, the distinct hermeneutical practices that devotees like the witness Munjee would have likely brought to readings of the hagiographies in devotional settings were never given recognition: the texts were used as mere "factual," "material" evidence. "The old Shastras," the court had determined, had been replaced with the *vārtās*—texts that demonstrated the Pushtimarg's heterodoxy and immorality. Thus, it was under the colonial legal system that the multiple, albeit sometimes contested, sources of Pushtimargi authority were rendered

[22] The transcript of the trial also reveals, however, that Jadunath Maharaj said, "our faith is not opposed to the doctrines of the Veds and the Shastras [. . .] Krishna occurs in the portion of the Veds" (*Report of the Maharaj Libel Case*, 168–170). He also implied that Braj Bhasha literature was not "philosophical or theological" (*Report of the Maharaj Libel Case*, 170).

[23] *Report of the Maharaj Libel Case*, 182. The judge also stated that "if the Shastras enjoined the offering of women, I would believe in the doctrine!" (ibid).

irrelevant in the public eye. Moreover, the "Hindu-ness" of Pushtimargi vernacular texts, and of the *sampradāy* itself, was the main issue at stake and could now be defined based on the knowledge of Orientalist scholars, self-proclaimed reformers, and colonial judges.[24]

The Emergence of Vernacular Book Culture in the Trial's Aftermath

In the decades following the Maharaja Libel Case, the religious, historical, and moral authenticity of the Pushtimarg would continue to be challenged by those who sought to define "Hinduism" in terms of specific texts and practices.[25] In light of these attacks and within the broader context of late 19th-century British Colonial India, hereditary leaders and devotees felt compelled to reassess and reassert what constituted their literary canon and their interpretations of religious texts more broadly. The *vārtās*, which were directly attacked in the Maharaja Libel Case, were claimed by some within the community to be inaccurate representations of Vallabhacharya's "original teachings."[26] Both Jadunath Maharaj and Govardhanlal Maharaj (Nathdwara's leading member of the Vallabha Kul beginning in 1877), for instance, responded to so-called reformers' accusations by conceding that some hereditary leaders and their devotees had "turned away from proper conduct," which had disabled them from properly following or teaching the primary tenets of the Pushtimarg.[27] In response, they proposed that members of the Vallabha Kul actively remake their image by giving "proper spiritual advice" to devotees, and by opening religious schools that would educate the community on Vallabhacharya's Sanskrit teachings and the

[24] For more on this, see Haberman, "On Trial."

[25] In 1875, for instance, Dayanand Saraswati, a self-proclaimed *ṛṣi* of Vedic revival and founder of the Arya Samaj, launched an attack against the community, outlined in his pamphlet *Vallabhācārya Mat Khaṇḍan* ("The Denouncement of the Doctrine of Vallabhacharya"). For further on Saraswati, see K.C. Yadav, ed., *The Autobiography of Dayanand Saraswati* (New Delhi: Manohar, 1987). For more on such attacks against the Pushtimarg, see Charlotte Vaudeville, "Multiple Approaches to a Living Hindu Myth: The Lord of the Govardhan Hill," in *Hinduism Reconsidered*, ed. Gunther D. Sontheimer and Hermann Kulke (Delhi: Manohar, 1989), 221; Catherine Clémentin-Ojha, "A Mid-nineteenth-century Controversy over Religious Authority," in *Charisma and Canon*, ed. Vasudha Dalmia, Angelika Malinar, and Martin Christof. (Oxford: Oxford University Press, 2001), 187.

[26] Shodhan, "Legal Representations," 245.

[27] Recall that Jadunath Maharaj had implied that vernacular texts lacked philosophical authority during the trial of the Maharaja Libel Case (*Report of the Maharaja Libel Case*, 168–170).

Bhāgavatapurāṇa (that is, texts that were claimed by some to be in "direct accordance with Vedic scripture").[28] Other hereditary leaders, such as Pandit Gattulalji and Devakinandacharya, engaged in public lectures on proper guru-*śiṣyā* (teacher–student) relationships. Devakinandacharya also gave a series of lectures on "Vaishnava *dharma*" and *sanātana-dharma* (or eternal-*dharma*, a "modern" articulation of Hinduism), during which he told devotees to avoid vernacular texts that might be misread as condoning morally transgressive behavior.[29]

Assessments of Pushtimargi texts and practices made by the Supreme Court during the Maharaja Libel Case and in its immediate aftermath were, however, not definitive. As in the past, community identity would continue to be negotiated through ongoing debate, particularly debate specific to religious literature. Interlocutors in such debates did, however, at least for some time, find it necessary to respond directly or indirectly to the court's and others' public accusations, and to broader issues that these accusations had raised. Moreover, the timing of the trial during the late 19th century coincided with the rise of commercial printing in urban India and the increasingly wider distribution of religious literature as printed, published books. Although devotees participated in the Pushtimarg's institutional growth in multiple ways during this period, contributing to the production of books—as patrons, commentators, or authors—was seen as an especially popular means by which to influence the terms of community (re-)education.[30] The types of books made available to devotees, and to the public, began to frame Pushtimargi literature in new ways, in turn influencing both what and also how people read. Specifically, the *vārtā*s, presented in novel forms and through new mediums, were recognized again as authoritative, canonical texts. This in turn provided renewed interest in using the hagiographies as platforms from which to discuss community identity and devotional practice.

Bharatendu Harishchandra (1850–1885), a leading Hindi literary figure, publicist, patron of the arts, and follower of the Pushtimarg, was a key player in the reauthorization of *Vārtā Sāhitya* and in the process of shaping people's reading practices during the 19th century and

[28] Saha, "Creating a Community of Grace," 311.

[29] Shital Sharma, "Middle-class Modernities," 102.

[30] Shital Sharma offers a summary of one particular devotee-author of the 19th century, Lallubhai Pranvallabhdas Parekh (1850–1911), who established a Pushtimargi library and was cofounder of the Gujarat Vaishya Sabha and Vaishnava Parishad. His own Gujarati publications focused on Vallabhacharya's works (Sharma, "Middle-class Modernities," 104).

beyond.[31] While Harishchandra, like other Vaishnava reformers of his time, was critical of what he saw as a decline in the Pushtimarg's moral leadership, his methods of addressing needed change did not participate in the "Sanskritization" of the tradition or the erasure of vernacular literature. Instead, Harishchandra used Hindi literature to champion a brand of a "nationalized Vaishnavism" from "within the ranks."[32] Though he participated in Banaras' Dharma Sabha and at one point formed a trans-sectarian movement called the Tadiya Samaj (1873), which positioned itself with principles of *sanātana-dharma*, Harishchandra remained loyal to the Pushtimarg and found direct inspiration from the tradition's devotional literature in his own writing. Take, for example, Harishchandra's *Uttarārdha Bhaktamāl* ("The Addendum to the Garland of Devotees"), which was published in the magazine *Hariścandra Candrikā* ("Harishchandra's Moonlight") in 1876. This Hindi composition draws both on the trans-sectarian hagiographical text the *Bhaktamāl* ("A Garland of Devotees") and the *84VV*, and it asserts that the Pushtimargi hagiographies are chief among all Vaishnava texts.[33] Further, in his 1877 drama *Candrāvalī*, Harishchandra recounts the divine love between Krishna and one of the Braj *gopīs*/*sakhīs*, Chandravali. While the play's central motif is *viraha*, a common theme of Krishna *bhakti*, the drama "also furnishes an excellent example of a writer recasting traditional material to meet his own artistic needs."[34] The character of Chandravali in Harishchandra's drama mimics the actions of the same figure in 17th-century author Hariray's *Bhāvprakāś* commentaries on the *84VV* and *252VV*, where Chandravali is the otherworldly form of Vallabhacharya's son Vitthalnath.

Harishchandra's open engagement with the Pushtimargi hagiographies helped to make a "strong ideological link" between Vaishnava *bhakti* and what became identified as the core texts of the Hindi literary canon. Crucial to the establishment and maintenance of this emerging vernacular canon was the newly commercialized printing press. In her monograph, *An Empire of Books*, Ulrike Stark outlines how the commercialization of printed books

[31] Harishchandra belonged to the Naupatti Mahajans, Varanasi's commercial aristocracy (Vasudha Dalmia, "'The Only Real Religion of the Hindus': Vaiṣṇava Self-representation in the Late Nineteenth Century," in *Representing Hinduism: The Construction of Religious Traditions and National Identity*, ed. Vasudha Dalmia and Heinrich von Stietencron [New Delhi: Sage Publications, 1995], 178).

[32] Vasudha Dalmia, *The Nationalization of Hindu Traditions*: Bhāratendu Hariśchandra and Nineteenth-century Banaras (Delhi: Oxford University Press, 1997), 366.

[33] James P. Hare, "Garland of Devotees: Nābhādās' Bhaktamāl and Modern Hinduism" (PhD dissertation, Columbia University, 2011), 205.

[34] W. Garlington, "Candrāvalī and the *Caurāsī Vaiṣṇavan kī Vārtā*," in *Bhakti Studies*, ed. Greg M. Bailey and Ian Kesarcodi-Watson (New Delhi: Sterling, 1992), 252.

in India during the 19th century, specifically with respect to the pioneering Naval Kishore Press of Lucknow (est. 1858), led to a new level of mass production, transmission, and canonization of books in Hindi and Urdu.[35] As this chapter noted in its introduction, many of these Hindi texts were Vaishnava specific, and by the 1880s, the press's small collection of Vaishnava titles quickly expanded to include key vernacular works associated with the Pushtimarg.[36] During 1883–1884 alone, in association with the Mumbai ul-Ulum Press in Mathura, Naval Kishore printed four Pushtimargi texts in Hindi, including versions of the *84VV*.[37]

Although several collections of Pushtimargi hagiographies had been previously published in the late 1860s at the Vyaghrapad Press (an enterprise owned by Thakur Giriprasad Varma at Beswan in Aligarh), Naval Kishore's publications of the *vārtās* allowed the texts to reach a wider readership than they ever had before. This development, along with Harishchandra's own efforts to publicize Vaishnava literature, points to the larger and longer process of reclaiming distinct Vaishnava identities through Hindi (and other vernacular) literature that would continue for several decades.[38] Historian William Pinch speaks to this process when he writes that the popularization of print within Hindu sectarian groups, such as the Pushtimarg, led to an "increasing doctrinal self-consciousness" in bringing to light and juxtaposing the multiple, and sometimes inconsistent, exegeses of religious texts.[39] As the forthcoming examples exhibit, this was very much the case for 19th- and 20th-century Pushtimargi readers-cum-commentators and their engagement with the vernacular literature of their tradition.

[35] Stark writes, "Commercialization describes the transformation of the printed text from artifact and cultural asset into a cheap and easily available consumer commodity" (Stark, *An Empire of Books*, 4).

[36] Stark speculates that the Naval Kishore's emphasis on the textual traditions of Vaishnava *bhakti* was connected to Harishchandra's cultural authorization of these texts, but also to "Naval Kishore's own religious grounding in Vaishnavism [. . .]" (Stark, *An Empire of Books*, 394).

[37] These texts included the *Caurāsī Bārttā* ("Eighty-Four Chronicles"), a version of *84VV* based on the manuscript tradition that excludes Hariray's *Bhāvprakāś*. The Naval Kishore Press also promoted writings of a Pushtimargi poet named Govardhandas Dhusar. Dhusar's works include the *Dohāvalī: Do Sau Bāvan kī Nāmāvalī* (1884), the *Brajvilās Sārāvalī* (1884), and the *Mohanmālā: Saurāsī kī Nāmāvalī*—all of which appear to be minor reworkings of the *84VV* and *252VV* (Stark, *An Empire of Books*, 394). The Mumbai ul-Ulum Press in Mathura was run by Naval Kishore's caste-fellow, Kanhaiyalal Bhargava (Stark, *An Empire of Books*, 395–451).

[38] The *vārtās'* place in the Hindi literary canon would continue to be established by publications such as Sir George Abraham Grierson, *The Modern Vernacular History of Hindustan* (Calcutta: The Asiatic Society, 1889), and Rāmcandra Śuklā, *Hindī Sāhitya kā Itihās* (Varanasi, India: Nāgari Pracāriṇī Sabha, 1957). Shukla's book was first published in 1929.

[39] William R. Pinch, *Peasants and Monks in British India* (Berkeley: University of California Press, 1996), 54. See also Stark, *An Empire of Books*, 22–23.

In terms of form and content, the earliest printed editions of the Braj Bhasha hagiographies followed rather seamlessly from the manuscript tradition(s) that preceded them. Within several decades, however, the *vārtās* as published books had several distinct features that significantly shifted how Pushtimargis received their devotional literature. Many late 19th- and early 20th-century editions of *vārtā* texts differ from their manuscript counterparts mainly by including ornate title pages, publication information, advertisements for other books from the same publisher, and tables of contents. Other versions of the texts, however, also began to include more elaborate forms of "paratext," including lengthy introductions by the books' editors (or others), glossaries, topical essays, study guides, footnotes, and various other types of commentary.[40] More broadly, "paratext" refers to elements of a book that mediate the book to the reader.[41] Paratextual elements of *vārtās* in book form are significant to consider here because they impart how publishers, printers, translators, and editors—all readers themselves—felt about how the texts should ideally be consumed. While different from the oral commentary that emerges from community and public readings of the *vārtās* (see Chapters 3–5), written commentary that appears in the *84VV* and *252VV* as published books is especially meant to guide readers as they explore the world of the *vārtās*, situated as it is within a distinctly sectarian and also premodern milieu. Nearly all popular versions of the *84VV* and *252VV* that are in circulation today have multiple layers of paratext, which today's readers expect to find in their copies of these texts. Devotee Megha Choksi (whom we met in Chapter 1), for instance, told me in response to my inquiry about why there were so many introductory essays, lists of historical places, and intertextual references, etc., in her well-loved copy of the *84VV*,

> All of this is based on a lot of research, just like you [Emilia] do research. These *granths* are like an ocean and all of this [essays, commentaries, etc.] helps Vaishnavas to understand better. It is difficult to read alone. Everyone

[40] The narratives also garnered attention in the Hindi literary world as early examples of Hindi prose. For further on the *vārtās*' place in Hindi literary traditions, see Ṭaṇḍan, *Vārtā Sāhitya*; Harimohandās Ṭaṇḍan, *Vraj ke Vaiṣṇav Sampradāya aur Hindī Sāhitya* (Allahabad, India: Sāhitya Bhavan, 1997).

[41] In Gérard Genette's (translated) words, paratext refers to "literary and printerly" conventions that "mediate between the world of publishing and the world of the text, and which determine how texts are formed into books, circulated, and received by the reader" (*Paratexts: Thresholds of Interpretation*, trans. Jane E. Lewin [Cambridge: Cambridge University Press, 1997], 1).

needs some guidance, so there are these essays and also Vaishnavas ask questions and discuss things in *satsaṅg* so we can understand things better.

In other words, in concert with textual exegesis and discussion during *satsaṅg*, Megha feels that these paratextual elements of her *84VV* in book form help to orient her and her fellow devotees when they read the hagiographies. In this way, when these textual features of the *vārtā*s as published books first appeared during the late 19th century, they marked a shift in the culture not only of writing and publishing religious texts, but also of reading them. Stark speaks to this phenomenon when she writes,

> Print culture had brought with it the transition gradual [*sic*] from practices of collective oral exposition to silent individual reading, entailing the need for a new type of textual explanation. This was particularly evident in the case of religious texts, which traditionally relied on oral exposition in the form of public readings (*kathā*). Whereas such oral practices centered on the Brahmin priest or learned pandit as the sole exegete of the text, in a private reading situation this interpretive function had to be assumed by the text itself. What was needed were commentaries that would facilitate contemporary readers' understanding of the classics with regard to both their archaic and dialectical language and their subject matter.[42]

Though the print revolution certainly made Pushtimargi religious literature available to the independent devotee-reader in new ways, community readings of the hagiographies, as Megha's comment indicates, were never replaced by printed versions of the hagiographies with modern commentaries.[43] *Vārtā Sāhitya* is one of innumerable Hindi literary genres of the 17th century that has roots in oral culture (although many such genres were composed in verse, rather than in prose). As Stark notes, the printed book entered and came to flourish in "a world deeply imbued with oral traditions: it coexisted and interacted with old and strong oral cultures."[44]

[42] Stark, *An Empire of Books*, 397.

[43] Anindita Gosh writes that the situation was similar in Bengal during the same period: "Availability of multiple copies of the same work did not inevitably prompt the demise of communal reading" ("An Uncertain 'Coming of the Book:' Early Print Cultures in Colonial India," *Book History* 6 [2003]: 36). For more on Indian book culture between the 18th and 20th centuries, see Ghosh's book, *Power in Print: Popular Publishing and the Politics of Language and Culture in a Colonial Society, 1778–1905* (New York: Oxford University Press, 2006).

[44] Stark, *An Empire of Books*, 13.

So, too, did printed books emerge in a culture with deep respect for manuscript culture. Even to the illiterate, the written (or printed) word could constitute an object of devotion.[45] Because there are few reliable statistics on the rates of literacy in North and West India during the 19th century, it is difficult to estimate the number of Pushtimargi devotees who continued to engage with the *vārtā*s in primarily oral settings and how many were reading the narratives in gatherings with multiple copies of texts, or on their own. It is likely that then, as now, temples and certain families kept copies of major Pushtimargi texts—as manuscripts or as books—from which hereditary leaders or devotees could read aloud to the community in *satsaṅg*. Silent, private reading of written religious texts was likely a relatively rare practice for a majority of Pushtimargis well into the early 20th century. As Anindita Ghosh suggests, in the context of urban Bengal during the same period, "access to the written word was thus a process much more broadly defined than simply the silent reading of an individual in isolation, literacy in its classic sense."[46] That is to say, many regional reading cultures in the new "print era" were rather immersed in preprint practices of reading aloud and *listening* to the printed word read aloud. Wider access to (printed) texts, however, did change the "plural uses and interpretations" of religious literature and therefore "broadened the possibilities and patterns" of print consumption.[47] Also, community readings in the absence of hereditary leaders (indeed "Brahmin priests" as Stark notes) *did* become more popular with the increasing availability of books in the late 19th and early 20th centuries and are now, in the 21st century, among the most familiar contexts in which the *vārtā*s and other Pushtimargi texts are read (Chapters 4 and 5 address this further).

During the same time that the *vārtā*s became widely available in print, they also began to be regularly translated from Braj Bhasha into Gujarati. Based on my review of early *vārtā* publications, it appears that among the first printed Gujarati versions of any *vārtā* text was the *Corāśī Vaiṣṇavnī Vārttā*, a translation of the *84VV* without Hariray's *Bhāvprakāś*, which was published by the Rajnagar Type Foundry Printing Press of Ahmedabad in 1899.[48] Like other late 19th- and early 20th-century publications of the *84VV*, this particular version of the text includes a decorated title page, a

[45] Ibid.

[46] Ghosh, "An Uncertain 'Coming of the Book,'" 46.

[47] Ibid.

[48] Purṇacandra Śarmā, ed., *Corāśī Vaiṣṇavnī Vārttā* (Ahmedabad, India: Hargovinddās Harjīvandās Pustakvāḷā; Rājnagar Ṭāip Fāūnḍrī Prinṭiṅg Pres, 1899).

brief note by the editor, a table of contents, and a list of other texts by the same publisher. Early translators not only referred to Braj Bhasha texts as a basis for their translations but also stay extremely close to the original language. Sometimes a word that is believed to be esoteric or dated will be glossed with a more contemporary Gujarati word. However, even such relatively minor glosses are kept to a minimum. By the middle of the 20th century there were as many versions of the *84VV* and *252VV* published in Gujarati as in Braj Bhasha. While according to some commentators (as we will see in forthcoming examples), translating the *vārtā*s into Gujarati made the texts more accessible to readers in their mother tongue, such changes from Braj Bhasha to Modern Gujarati (which share as many similarities as do Braj Bhasha and Modern Hindi) primarily reflect a translation between historical periods and social and geographical context (much like commentaries themselves, as we will explore) rather than a translation between two radically different languages, per se.[49]

There are various types of modern "commentaries" on the *vārtās*, many of which are inspired by or are in direct conversation with Hariray's prestigious *Bhāvprakāś*. Some of these commentaries share the more formal features of what is normally recognized as "traditional" scholarly commentary, including a partial or full reproduction of a *vārtā* text along with an embedded or separate set of written comments that explain, describe, add to, gloss, alter, question, or in some other way critically engage with the narratives.[50] In Hindi or Gujarati these types of commentaries are referred to as *ṭīkā*, *bhāṣya* (commentary), or *sār* (essence).[51] I also, however, consider written "commentary" that comes in the form of *paricāy*, *prastāvnā*, or *be bol* (introductory essays or prefaces) to devotional texts. Still other sources that I have examined—both here and in Chapter 3—are *nibandh*s (freestanding essays) or transcribed *pravacan*s, which assume prior knowledge of the hagiographies and may only refer to the *vārtā*s or rely on the narratives' idioms or themes in order to advance particular arguments or teachings.

[49] Gujarati of the 19th century was closer to the Braj Bhasha of the *vārtās* than was Khari Boli (current speech) Hindi. Some argue that it was not until Mohandas K. Gandhi took the initiative in the 1920s that Gujarati became standardized (V. Sebastian, "Gandhi and the Standardisation of Gujarati," *Economic and Political Weekly* 44, no. 31 [2009]: 94). For more on language formation during this period, see Riho Isaka, *Language, Identity, and Power in Modern India: Gujarat, c. 1850–1960* (London: Routledge, 2022).

[50] For a useful typology of religious commentary, see Griffiths, *Religious Reading*, 109–148.

[51] *Ṭīkā* can also refer to a "sub-commentary," that is, a commentary on a commentary (e.g., a *bhāṣyā*). See McGregor, *The Oxford Hindi-English Dictionary*, 404.

In what follows, I consider several examples of late 19th- and 20th-century written commentaries on and reworkings of the *vārtās*, the contents of which represent broader trends in how the narratives were read during and after major 19th-century moments described in the beginning of this chapter—that is, the Maharaja Libel Case and its aftermath, and the increasing popularization of vernacular literature through print. Each example reveals the efforts of Pushtimargi reader-commentators to culturally reauthorize the hagiographies by emphasizing their authenticity and historicity as well as their enduring applicability to 19th- and 20th-century readers' lives. These cultural reauthorizations of the narratives thereby helped Pushtimargis to defend the significance of their devotional literature and its relevance to the contemporary moment.

Four Examples of *Vārtā Sāhitya* Reauthorized Through Written Commentary

The Śrīnāthjī kī Prākaṭya Vārtā: To Be Read by "Historians" and "Archeologists"

This first example shows one way the *vārtās* were historicized, and, by extension, how the growth of the Pushtimargi community was placed into a historical timeline that aligned with modern historiographical expectations. However, this example is also a peculiar place to begin, given my emphasis on commentaries: it is mostly the existence of a particular written *vārtā* itself that is of interest here, though I do analyze some telling introductory commentary in one version of the text in question.

The Braj Bhasha *Śrīnāthjī kī Prākaṭya Vārtā* is a relatively short, standalone hagiographical text generally recognized by contemporary devotees as central to *Vārtā Sāhitya* and to a broader canon of written Pushtimargi texts. The narrative traces the manifestation of Krishna as Shrinathji at Mount Govardhan in Braj during the 15th century, the establishment of the deity's *sevā* by Vallabhacharya and his first disciples in the mid-16th century, and the deity's subsequent movement in the late 17th century to Nathdwara, Rajasthan. While there is little doubt that certain episodes familiar to most versions of this narrative circulated orally and in manuscript form prior to the 19th century (for instance, some parts of the narrative appear in 17th-century manuscripts of *84VV*), all evidence suggests that the whole text as it is commonly received today was only committed to writing in the 1860s—the very period in which the Pushtimarg was in the national spotlight for its so-called degenerate expressions of Hinduism in the Maharaja Libel Case.

Contemporary Pushtimargi readers generally accept that the *Prākaṭya Vārtā* was authored by Hariray, the illustrious descendant of Vallabhacharya to whom the *Bhāvprakāś* and other vernacular texts of the tradition are also attributed. However, as Heidi Pauwels and I have addressed elsewhere, if this attribution holds true, we would have to accept that Hariray's lifespan was in fact an unlikely one hundred and twenty-five years, between 1590 and 1715, and that his account was therefore in part an eyewitness one, as the bulk of the events in the *vārtā* play out during the 17th century.[52] Beyond this, however, manuscript records do not place the text's composition before the 19th century. In my archival research, I located and studied three manuscripts of the text, which either bear colophons dating transcription to the mid-19th century or appear in all manners to be of this time period.[53] Other extant manuscripts, which I have not studied, but which are listed in the catalogs of the Vrindavan Research Institute and the Rajasthan Oriental Research Institute, also date the text to the 1860s.[54] Moreover, the available printed editions from the 19th and 20th centuries never specify their sources, nor do they mention any manuscript traditions (a practice that was regularly followed by Pushtimargi editors of the time).

Published versions of Shrinathji's emergence story also point to the text's commitment to writing in the 19th century. One 1986 edition, for instance, which was published at the request of Govindlal Maharaj (1928–1994), Nathdwara's then leading member of the Vallabha Kul, emphasizes the *vārtā*'s modern provenance in its paratext. This edition is nearly identical in

[52] For further information on this, see Heidi Pauwels and Emilia Bachrach, "Aurangzeb as Iconoclast? Vaishnava Accounts of the Krishna Images' Exodus from Braj," *Journal of the Royal Asiatic Society* 28, no. 3 (2018): 485–508.

[53] The first *Prākaṭya Vārtā* manuscript I examined claims to come from Bhadrapur (Bhavnagar District, Gujarat, India). Now kept in a private collection in Ahmedabad, it contains no colophon or date but appears from the quality of the paper to be no older than the late 19th century. The text has ninety folios, of which the first fourteen and last six are *kīrtan* lyrics. The second manuscript (seventy-five folios, which are badly damaged and incomplete) is dated 1855 CE (1912 Vikram Samvat "*caitra sudi* 13") and is kept in a private temple library in Ahmedabad. Its colophon specifies that "Pārekh Māyācand Kuśaldās" wrote it for "Ācārya Abhirām Mahāśaṅkar." The third manuscript, found in the same temple library (one hundred and six folios), contains no colophon or date but is likely from the 19th century based on the quality of the paper and its similarity to other 19th-century texts. All three texts are similar to each other (the varying number of folios is due to inclusion of non-*vārtā* material, such as *kīrtan*) and nearly identical to 19th-century published editions. For more on printed editions of the *Prākaṭya Vārtā*, see Ṭaṇḍan, *Vārtā Sāhitya*, 107.

[54] For more on the text's manuscript history, see Pauwels and Bachrach, "Aurangzeb as Iconoclast?"

content and form to an earlier publication, which was edited by Mohanlal Vishnulal Pandya and printed at Lakshmi Venkateshwar Steam Press in 1905.[55] Although both editions are close to the 19th-century manuscripts that I examined, in his introduction to the text Pandya specifically refers to two of the oldest published editions: first, a lithograph published in 1884 by the request of Munshi Naval Kishore, and second, an 1886 printing by the Vyaghrapad Press at Beswan, which was based on the 1884 text.[56] In his *Prastāvnā* ("Introduction") to the 1905 edition, Mohanlal Vishnulal Pandya does not cite the 1884–1886 editions as references but, rather, asserts that they are full of *aśuddhatā* (infelicities).[57] He calls his own project a restoration that he hopes to present before *itihās lekhak* (historians) and *prācīn padārthān ke shodhak* (archeologists).[58] Pandya also claims that he received assistance in the research for his edition from Shri Gattu Lalji.[59] This mention of Gattu Lalji (1844–1897) is particularly significant because he was one of the more prominent Pushtimargi leaders to have publicly defended the *sampradāy* and other Vaishnava groups during the 1860s when Ram Singh II, a local Rajasthani ruler, famously accused Pushtimargis and other Vaishnava *sampradāy*s of heterodoxy in Jaipur.[60]

While Pandya never says how his version of the *vārtā* actually differs in content from the 1884–1886 versions (and there are no apparent ways in which it does), his introduction to the text makes it clear that part of the reason for publishing the *vārtā* had to do with the desire to defend a clear and accurate presentation of Pushtimargi history. Whatever its actual date of composition or commitment to writing, the *Prākaṭya Vārtā*'s publication and circulation in book form during the 19th and 20th centuries contributed to assertions of the *sampradāy*'s historicity, and therefore authenticity.

[55] Pandya was an English-educated Brahmin from the "Gangetic heartland of British India" (Cynthia Talbot, "Contesting Knowledges in Colonial India: The Question of Prithviraj Raso's Historicity," in *Knowing India: Colonial and Modern Constructions of the Past: Essays in Honor of Thomas R. Trautmann*, ed. Cynthia Talbot [New Delhi: Yoda Press, 2011], 174).

[56] Ṭaṇḍan, *Vārtā Sāhitya*, 107; Stark, *An Empire of Books*, 394–395.

[57] Viṣṇulāl Paṇḍyā, ed., *Śrī Govardhannāthjī ke Prākaṭya kī Vārtā* (Bombay: Śrī Veṅkaṭeśvar, 1905), 5.

[58] Paṇḍyā, *Śrī Govardhannāthjī ke Prākaṭya kī Vārtā*, 2–3.

[59] This individual was also known as Shri Govardhanlalji and was the son of Ghanshyam Bhatt and Ladobetiji (Paṇḍyā, *Śrī Govardhannāthjī ke Prākaṭya kī Vārtā*, 6).

[60] This is discussed at greater length in Pauwels and Bachrach, "Aurangzeb as Iconoclast?" For more on Ram Singh II's accusations, see Catherine Clémentin-Ojha, "A Mid-nineteenth-century Controversy over Religious Authority."

Pandya is clear that his imagined audience of readers not only includes the faithful but also "historians and archeologists."[61]

Beyond its questionable provenance as a written text, the *Prākaṭya Vārtā*'s form and content stand out as distinct from other *vārtā* texts. First, while the narrative does include records of direct speech—a key feature of the *84VV* and *252VV* as discussed in Chapter 1—a majority of the story is told from a third-person omniscient point of view. Second, while duly filled with narratives about Krishna's playful and divine interventions in the *laukik* world, the *Prākaṭya Vārtā* also includes a detailed record of dates, which punctuate the storyline as it unfolds over centuries. This feature, which gives Shrinathji's emergence story a distinctly "historiographic texture," is unique in the larger corpus of Pushtimargi hagiography and, I argue, a distinctly modern phenomenon.[62] Handwritten copies and early print versions of the *84VV*, for instance, rarely and inconsistently mention dates of any kind. Today, however, alongside the *Prākaṭya Vārtā* (which is widely read in book form by contemporary Pushtimargis), most versions of the *84VV* and *252VV* also include references to specific dates, which help commentators ground the narratives in an externally "verifiable" historical timeline (later in this chapter I discuss some of the ways dates appear in modern versions of the *84VV* and *252VV*). These distinctions between what may be modern and premodern iterations of devotional texts remind us of how the purpose of the texts has been interpreted in different ways, and often in ways that emphasize multiple, overlapping functions. As one Pushtimargi reader told me, "Our *vārtā*s are like *purāṇa* (legend) and *itihās* (history) combined: they tell us what has happened, that is, history, what will happen, and what continues

[61] Similarly, other Pushtimargi texts also claim early modern provenance but were likely committed to writing in the 19th / early 20th centuries. The Sanskrit *Vallabhadigvijaya* ("Vallabh's Victory Tour"), for instance, claims composition in Samvat 1658 (1601 CE). According to John S. Hawley, no prior manuscript history of the *Vallabhadigvijaya* has been located and there are no extant references to it prior to 1900 (the Rajnagar Type Foundry Press of Ahmedabad first published the text in 1906). The *Vallabhadigvijaya*—which describes Vallabhacharya's inheritance of spiritual authority from the Vishnuswami Sampraday after winning theological debates at Vijayanagar court—wants to persuade its readers that the "victory in Vidyānagar" was a "definitive harbinger of subsequent victories in many other places" (John S. Hawley, "How Vallabhācārya Met Kṛṣṇadevarāya" [paper presented in Mumbai, K. R. Cama Oriental Institute, January 7, 2012]). Historical veracity aside, the narrative is designed to link Vallabhacharya with a preexisting Vaishnava *sampradāy* according to a linear historical narrative, thereby providing the Pushtimarg with spiritual and historical authenticity that some feared was lacking in the Maharaja Libel Case's aftermath.

[62] Christian Lee Novetzke, "The Theographic and the Historiographic in an Indian Sacred Life Story," *Sikh Formations* 3, no. 2 (2007): 169–184. Novetzke's article uses life stories of the 13th-century Maharashtrian poet-saint Namdev to argue that the genre of hagiography should be read for its historical "texture" as much as for its theological and devotional content.

to happen."[63] What this statement shows us is that some Pushtimargi readers understand the narratives to be "historical" yet also to transcend "history." This should come as no surprise: it is often the case that the theographic and the historiographic (theological and historical textures) coexist in religious readers' reception of their beloved premodern (and modern!) texts, even as contemporary commentators might feel the need to highlight certain aspects of the narrative over others.[64]

Lallubhai Chaganlal Desai's "Factual Footnote" Commentary and Dwarkadas Parikh's "Reflection on *Vārtā* Literature"

While different readers have perceived the so-called objective historicity of Pushtimargi hagiography in multiple ways, after the Maharaja Libel Case it became quite common for commentators to write specifically about the "factual" nature of Pushtimargi *vārtās*. Among the most popular editions of these texts to include such notes are those first published in the early 20th century in Gujarati by a devotee named Lallubhai Chaganlal Desai. On the decorated title page of his 1917 publication, directly below the title, *Śrī Ācāryajī Mahāprabhu (Śrī Vallabhācāryajī) nā 84 Vaiṣṇav nī Vārtā*, appears the following: "Based on countless *prācīn* (ancient) texts, numerous *ṭippaṇī* (commentaries), and both ancient and contemporary *aitihāsik* (historical) data, Lallubhai Chaganlal Desai has specially edited this text with his [added] philosophical and doctrinal comments."[65]

Desai's versions of the *84VV* and *252VV* contain relatively standard accounts of the texts' protagonists but omit the *Bhāvprakāś*.[66] However,

[63] Sumit Sharma, personal communication, March 18, 2012.

[64] Though toward different ends than I have discussed here, Vasudha Dalmia also discusses *vārtā* texts composed in the 19th century in her article "The Establishment of the Sixth *Gaddī* of the Vallabha Sampradāy: Narrative Structure and the Use of Authority in a *Vārtā* of the Nineteenth Century" (in *Studies in South Asian Devotional Literature*, ed. Alan W. Entwistle and Françoise Mallison [New Delhi: Manohar, 1994], 94–117). For further information on the role of historiographical thinking and cultural production in modern Vaishnava traditions, see Shruti Patel's forthcoming monograph, "The Play of History: The Making of the Svaminarayan Community in Modern India."

[65] The title for the 1917 edition, which does not list full publication information but specifies printing in Chaganlal's own neighborhood (Chaganpol, Khatripol, in Ahmedabad, India), has a different title than the editions from the 1970s and later. These later editions simply use the title *84 Vaiṣṇavnī Vāto*.

[66] I have primarily referred to these editions: Lallubhāī Chaganlāl Desāī, *84 Vaiṣṇavnī Vāto* (Ahmedabad, India: Koṭhārī Prakāśan Ghar, 1970); *252 Vaiṣṇavnī Vāto* (Ahmedabad, India: Śrī Lakṣmī Pustak Bhandar, 1976); Lallubhāī Chaganlāl Desāī, *Śrī Ācāryajī Mahāprabhu (Śrī Vallabhācāryajī) nā 84 Vaiṣṇav nī Vārtā* (Ahmedabad, India: Śrī Lakṣmī Pustak Bhandar, 1917).

almost as if to replace the role of Hariray's commentary, Desai includes two types of comments throughout the narratives. The first type, which Desai labels as *sār*, is provided so that the narrative's "aim is clearly grasped."[67] Desai's *sār* comments, even with reference to publicly debated episodes (such as those scrutinized in the Maharaja Libel Case), are not in fact radically different from the explanatory comments of Hariray's *Bhāvprakāś*. However, the portion of the *Bhāvprakāś* that describes the three layers of each devotee's *laukik* and *alaukik* existence (see Chapter 1) are notably absent. Rather than glorifying, explaining, and justifying the actions of the lauded figures by naming them as participants in Krishna's *alaukik nitya līlā*, Desai limits his *sār* comments to theological and practical explanations that expand upon the relationships that devotees cultivate with Krishna in the *laukik* world alone.[68] While Desai's text continues to recognize the protagonists of the *84VV* and *252VV* as *daivī jīvs*, we rarely get a glimpse of Krishna's otherworldly *līlā* or a sense of causal connections between the *alaukik* and *laukik* worlds.

The significance of omitting the *Bhāvprakāś*' "three lives" narrative is highlighted not only by Desai's additional *sār* comments, but also by what he calls *hakikat fūṭnot* (factual footnotes), which he includes throughout the text. These notes stand out from the *sār* comments because they focus almost exclusively on providing information about devotees' this-worldly social and geographical location, notes that were not always included in pre-19th-century versions of the *vārtās* (in recensions of the narratives both with and without the *Bhāvprakāś*). Sometimes this information is related to the contemporary early 20th-century location of Krishna icons and the names of their current Vallabha Kul caretakers. Other times, however, Desai's footnotes clearly assert the "objective" historical accuracy of the narratives. In the first *vārtā* of the *84VV* for instance, Desai includes a footnote (occupying half of the page), which contains detailed information about the protagonist Damodardas Harsani's caste (Kshatriya) and family history, occupation, and place and date of birth (Vikram Samvat 1531).[69]

Before the publication of Desai's 1917 *84VV*, the type of detail we see in his "factual footnotes" is notably absent from manuscript and printed editions

[67] Desāī, *84 Vaiṣṇavnī Vāto*, 5.

[68] An example of this can be found in protagonist Parvati's *vārtā* in the *84VV*. As discussed in Chapter 1, Parvati's leprosy condition is linked to her otherworldly role in *līlā*. In Desai's version, however, there is no *alaukik* explanation for Parvati's ailment. Instead, Desai writes, "by having firm faith in the words of Vitthalnath, even a serious disease can be eliminated [. . .]."

[69] Desāī, *84 Vaiṣṇavnī Vāto*, 3; Desāī, *Śrī Ācāryajī Mahāprabhu (Śrī Vallabhācāryajī) nā 84 Vaiṣṇav nī Vārtā*, 5.

of the *vārtās*. From the 1940s onward, however, printed versions of the *84VV* and *252VV* generally include the same types of details Desai puts in his footnotes—though more often than not, such information appears in the form of appendices or introductory notes that precede the *vārtā* narratives (Desai's versions of the *84VV* and *252VV* are still in circulation, although they have gradually been replaced by more contemporary Gujarati translations or Braj Bhasha reproductions). Do these assertions of "worldly" matters significantly impact today's religious reader and show that the modern commentator wishes to heighten the historiographic texture (the historical credibility) of the *vārtās*? Contemporary readers of the *vārtās* in Gujarat often encourage me to notice paratext that highlights the *vārtās*' historicity. However, once it is clear that my personal and academic interests in the texts as a foreign researcher have little to do with ascertaining a so-called objective history or authenticity, Pushtimargi readers quickly draw my attention to other matters, as we will see in the following chapters. In a sense, then, some forms of commentary and other paratextual elements of the texts that focus on the *vārtās*' historicity function as a defense against accusations by "outsider" readers. And, of course, "outsider" readers seemed to be increasing in number after the 19th-century print revolution. Some Pushtimargi commentators speak directly to such audiences in their writing.

Chief among such commentators was Dwarkadas Parikh, a prominent Gujarati devotee associated with hereditary leaders based in Kankroli, Rajasthan, but with contemporary leadership in Baroda, Gujarat. While numerous versions of the *84VV* and *252VV* continue to be published in Braj Bhasha and in Modern Hindi and Gujarati, Dwarkadas Parikh's 1948 Braj Bhasha edition of the *84VV* and 1953 edition of the *252VV* are highly regarded and continue to be extremely popular, even among devotees whose mother tongue is Gujarati. These versions of the texts continue to be reprinted every decade or so and are also the basis for numerous other versions of the texts (including Gujarati and English translations). University students and scholars who have worked with the *vārtās*, both in India and abroad, almost exclusively refer to Parikh's editions (when drawing from non-manuscript versions of the hagiographies), many of which include a large amount of paratext and introductory commentaries—which other scholars have not, to my knowledge, previously analyzed. Such paratext includes glossaries of Braj Bhasha terms and statements related to the numerous manuscripts that were consulted in the production of both editions. With each newly printed edition of Parikh's texts come new layers of commentary by devotees and hereditary leaders.

Parikh's own most explicit statement about the *vārtās*' historical authenticity is found in a Gujarati essay titled *Vārtā Sāhitya Mīmāṃsā* ("A Reflection on *Vārtā* Literature"), which is included among several introductory essays in the early editions of his *84VV*. In his opening to the essay, Parikh claims to address the *aitihasiktā* (historicity) and *pramāṇiktā* (authenticity) of *Vārtā Sāhitya*. The devotional sentiments of these texts, Parikh writes, do not diverge in even the slightest way from Vallabhacharya's *siddhānt*. Hence, Parikh claims, the texts are authentic representations of the tradition. While *ādhunik vidvāno* (contemporary scholars) have claimed that the texts are not historically accurate, Parikh asserts that any seeming incidents of *virodhabhās* (contradiction) in the texts have been misread—a point that he aims to prove in his essay. His hope, he writes, is that his essay will be proof enough for "all scholars" to accept the veracity of the hagiographies, and therefore the authenticity of the Pushtimarg.

Parikh has several methods of proving the accuracy and authenticity of the *vārtās* as historically and theologically sound texts. His first argument is based entirely on the undoubted veracity of Vallabhacharya and Vitthalnath's *vacanāmṛt*—a central feature of the *84VV* and *252VV*, as we recall from Chapter 1. This *vacanāmṛt*, which in essence holds the truth of the Pushtimarg, Parikh claims, was passed down directly and accurately from Vallabhacharya to his son Vitthalnath, and also to his first disciple Damodardas Harsani. Vitthalnath's disciples Govardhandas and Krishna Bhatt were the scribes who wrote down the narratives of Vallabhacharya's disciples, which they had heard told again and again by Vitthalnath's fourth son, Gokulnath. Gokulnath was the one to have orally dictated to the *vārtās*' scribes which figures should be included as the chosen eighty-four and two hundred and fifty-two Vaishnavas of the *84VV* and *252VV* (of course, he notes, there are many more disciples who are worthy of praise!). And finally, Gokulnath's grandnephew, Hariray, was the *ṭīkākār* (the commentator) who is credited with authoring the widely circulated *Bhāvprakāś* commentaries, which appear in all versions of Parikh's *84VV* and *252VV*. Parikh even visually maps out the way in which Vallabhacharya's nectarous speech was passed on through each generation by including a *rekhācitra* (line diagram), which includes key dates (e.g., Vallabhacharya's lifespan).[70]

[70] Dvārkādās Puruṣottamdās Parīkh, *Vārtā Sāhitya-Mīmāṃsā* (n.p.: Sandeś Prakāśan, 1949), 2.

Parikh then goes on to cite a selection of Vallabhacharya's and Vitthalnath's *vacanāmṛt*, which he reads against Sanskrit treatises written by both preceptors. The written (transcribed) *vacanāmṛt* from the *vārtā*s matches the written (and unquestioned) truths from Vallabhacharya's treatises. Hence, the *vārtā*s must be accurate, both historically and also theologically.[71] Parikh then moves on to read the *vārtā*s against other kinds of texts. Figures and incidents that appear in the *vārtā*s, he claims, are mentioned in a wide variety of "historical" sources including Nabhadas' *Bhaktamāl* and the memoirs of two Mughal emperors: the *Akbarnāmā* ("Akbar's Memoirs") and *Jahāṃgīrnāmā* ("Jahangir's Memoirs").[72] Furthermore, Parikh reasons, Mughal emperors themselves appear in the *vārtā*s, as do many members of their royal courts (e.g., Tansen, one of Akbar's court poet-musicians). All of these points, Parikh suggests, show how the *vārtā*s are themselves reliable historical sources.

Parikh also responds to specific "doubts" and "criticisms" that have been made by modern scholars about the *vārtā*s and their authors. For instance, Parikh highlights the work of one Hindi literary critic, Dr. Dhirendra Varma. Parikh claims that Dr. Varma questions whether or not the *252VV* is truly the work of Gokulnath in a text called *Vicārdhārā* ("Ideology").[73] One of the reasons for Varma's question, Parikh explains, is that the language in this text is different from the style of language in the older *84VV*.[74] This is a moot point, writes Parikh in defense, because "at that time so many styles of Braj Bhasha were prevalent."[75]

In response to doubts raised in another book, *Ādhunik Puṣṭimārgīy Bhāṣā Sāhityanī Śoc Stithi* ("The Deplorable State of Modern Pushtimargi Vernacular Literature"), Parikh specifically defends not only the historicity of the *vārtā*s, but also the moral and theological grounding of specific characters.[76] Amid other examples of "questioned" narratives, Parikh

[71] D. Parīkh, *Vārtā Sāhitya-Mīmāṃsā*, 14–15.

[72] D. Parīkh, *Vārtā Sāhitya-Mīmāṃsā*, 10.

[73] The Hindi reads, "*kyā 252 Vaiṣṇavoṁ kī Vārtā Gokulnāth kṛt hai?*" I have not found record of any publication by this title authored by Dhirendra Varma. In other texts, however, Varma addresses similar matters. See Dhirendra Varma, *La Langue Braj* (Paris: Adrien-Maisonneuve, 1935), 31–32.

[74] Contemporary scholars have corroborated Varma's alleged comments about language in the *252VV*. Shandip Saha, for example, claims that "the use of Gujarātī and Persian words in the texts again also points to the [*252VV*] being redacted in the cultural milieu of Western India" (Saha, "A Community of Grace," 231, fn. 22). R.S. McGregor simply notes that the text has a "latter type of language [when compared with the *84VV*]" (*A History of Indian Literature*, 209).

[75] The Gujarati reads, "*vrajbhaṣānī keṭlīy śailīo te samaye pracalit hatī.*"

[76] Parikh does not mention any author of this title, and I was not able to find record of such a publication.

defends the *vārtā* about Krishnadas and his wife—the very same narrative that was highlighted in the Maharaja Libel Case. Parikh directly dismisses any claim by the *pablik* (public) that the wife of Krishnadas was a heretic or that she was anything but a "simple woman whose devotional sentiments were *pūjya* (venerable)."[77] If you read the text with the wrong "perspective," then of course you will misinterpret the narrative, Parikh explains. The final point of this particular *vārtā* narrative, according to Parikh, is one of faith—both of keeping one's faith and of spreading the Faith: "Krishnadas' wife spontaneously and guilelessly promised the shopkeeper [to spend the night with him] . . . but if she had not given her word in this way then there never would have been an opportunity for pure devotional sentiments to have arisen in the shopkeeper."[78] Just as Hariray suggests in his *Bhāvprakāś* comments on the episode, Parikh also concludes that anyone who reads the *vārtās* with no intimate knowledge of Pushtimargi theology will clearly come to disastrous misinterpretations. Such is the fate of "modern scholars." Thus, Parikh asserts both that his essay will convince such "modern scholars" of the *vārtās*' authenticity and morally and theologically sound teachings and that in order to avoid misinterpretation the reader will have to essentially become an "insider" by assuming the correct *dṛṣṭi* (perspective). While Parikh does not go as far as to say that only initiated members of the Pushtimarg can properly read and interpret the narratives, his final comments do have this implication.

Parikh's *Vārtā Sāhitya Mīmāṃsā*, perhaps more than any of the other texts and commentaries I discuss in this chapter, typifies the kind of historicizing response that *vārtā* commentators had to the various 19th- and 20th-century accusations by readers of the hagiographies who were not familiar with or sympathetic to Pushtimargi literature or theologies. Parikh's response and the form of his response (a written, commentarial essay attached to the *84VV* in book form) also remind us of the changing ways in which Pushtimargi readers were able to engage with and contextualize their religious texts in order to defend them against "outside" criticisms—but *also* in order to express devotion to the texts themselves.

77 D. Parīkh, *Vārtā Sāhitya-Mīmāṃsā*, 34–39.
78 D. Parīkh, *Vārtā Sāhitya-Mīmāṃsā*, 39.

The *Puṣṭimārgīy Patrācār* and Self-Study Reading

Essays like Parikh's and the types of details that Desai includes in his "factual footnotes" are not *merely* defensive or meant to orient "outsider" readers on how to "properly" read *Vārtā Sāhitya*. Devotee Megha Choksi's suggestion that paratext is included in *vārtās* as books because "everyone needs some guidance" so that they "can understand things better" shows how such elements of the printed texts are also considered significant for Pushtimargi readers themselves. This was precisely what Kashika Bhatt-Rawat, a devotee in her mid-twenties and a recent graduate of a program in business management, told me when I asked about how she first started to read Pushtimargi books. She explained that her first encounters with the *vārtās* were in the context of *satsaṅgs* in a small Ahmedabad temple where she used to visit weekly with her family. Before finally getting her own copy of the *84VV* (a Braj Bhasha version of Parikh's text) upon receiving her *brahmasambandha* initiation mantra at age nineteen, Kashika had only heard the *vārtās* read aloud and discussed by hereditary leaders and older family and community members at her temple. When she first began to "study" her own copy of the *84VV*, she told me that she was surprised and excited see all of the "research and historical facts" in the opening pages of her book. This made her say to herself, "Wow! there is so much I need learn about *sevā* from Shri Harirayji and *vārtājī*, but I also need to learn all of these [other] things, like where all the *svarūps* are located today, when all the *gosvāmī bālaks* [male descendants of Vallabhacharya] were born . . . " This type of categorizing and listing that we see in contemporary versions of the *vārtās* shows how Pushtimargis continue to use the hagiographies to map out the contours of their literary canon and sectarian landscape. This is an extension of the early modern *vārtā* genre itself, which, like other genres of hagiography, is keen to articulate a "grammar" of sectarian tradition. Categorizing and listing in commentaries is therefore by no means a modern phenomenon. What is distinctly modern, however, is the *type* of lists (e.g., certain types of references to dates and places) that we see in book versions of the *84VV* and other *vārtās* as printed texts. Even though "everything in *vārtājī* is accurate," as Kashika explained, the paratextual information that was included in her copy of the *84VV* prompted her to seek out further details about the *sampradāy*'s history. These "extra details and guides," she said, also help her to appreciate more deeply the devotional and theological teachings that she and her fellow Pushtimargis discuss when they gather together to read from their respective copies of the *84VV* in *satsaṅg* (Kashika attends a weekly *satsaṅg* held by a woman named Gita who lives in the neighborhood where Kashika moved to after marriage).

As Kashika's remarks indicate, paratextual comments and essays in devotional books may provide readerly direction to the average devotee—direction that is meant to supplement the guidance readers also receive in understanding and interpreting the *vārtā*s from their fellow devotees and gurus. Some publications, however, aim to give readers an education on and experience of Pushtimargi literature that, by design, does not rely on the contexts of in-person *satsaṅg* or other community gatherings. Take, for instance, the Gujarati language *Puṣṭimārgīy Patrācār* ("Pushtimargi Correspondence"), a lengthy book (over five hundred pages) specific to the eighth year of a ten-year correspondence course through the Vallabha Vidyapith (aka, the Vallabha University). The course promises to offer a comprehensive guide to Pushtimargi history and literature, theology, and ritual practice.[79] This particular book is considered to be advanced ("PhD Level").[80] It contains four sections and various subsections under the broad category of *sevā bhūṣaṇ*, which refers to the ritual practices of Krishna's loving service and all related trappings. The eighth-year *Patrācār*, and all other nine books that accompany the course of study, are authored primarily by devotee Ramesh Parikh and published through the Shree Vakpati Foundation, a community-run trust in collaboration with Vallabha Kul leadership based out of Kankroli, Rajasthan, and Baroda, Gujarat.

According to an English-language webpage dedicated to the course of study at www.vallabhkankroli.org, the Vakpati Foundation established "Pushtimargiya Open University" because it,

> . . . enabled the common people to acquire the knowledge of pushtimarg by reading the materials provided by the university itself. [. . .] Also, this medium is the best for the modern youths to get acquainted with this path. [. . .] vaishnavas do not know the principles of pushtimarg. We are ignorant about the do's and don'ts of pushtimarg. To acquire this knowledge, we need to do "Satsang" daily. But in this modern age, the "Satsang" is generally not practiced in the houses of pushtimargiya vaishnavas. In this situation, there is always a danger to get distracted and diverted from the main path

[79] The course is also available in Hindi and English.
[80] "Shree Vallabh Vidyapeeth (Pushtimargiya Open University)," http://www.vallabhkankroli.org/activities_shree%20vallabh%20vidhyapith.htm, accessed August 16, 2018.

> of pushtimarg. In lieu of this situation, we impart the genuine knowledge of principles of pushtimarg, the pushtimargiya course syllabus was designed and started in 1996 A.D.

As this description indicates, the materials for the course are designed specifically for devotees for whom more "traditional" modes of learning—namely, community reading and discussion during *satsaṅg*—are not viable (such devotees may include those living in the diaspora without fellow Pushtimargis nearby). While few of the people I speak with who have taken part in the correspondence course read these course materials in total isolation from others, many do find the layout and organization of the provided materials to be "user-friendly" and accessible to individual study. As devotee and avid reader Dr. Yojana Mahajan told me of the course, "it [the course] is not necessary for those who find time for weekly *satsaṅg*, but, yes, it is helpful for some devotees who are just starting to become acquainted with the literature and do not have all of the original *granth*s themselves." Though she may not find the course itself necessary for those who attend *satsaṅg*, Yojana does read aloud from selections of the *Patrācār* during a *satsaṅg* that she leads in her home (see Chapter 4). Another devotee, Mona Desai, found the course essential to maintaining her regular reading practices while she was temporarily separated from her Ahmedabad-based Pushtimargi community and regular *satsaṅg* gatherings. In addition to taking the correspondence course, she also tuned in for *satsaṅg* via phone calls while she was living for a time in Toronto, Canada (other devotees do the same through various virtual platforms).

The majority of the eighth-year *Patrācār* toggles back and forth between selections of primary source devotional texts translated into Gujarati from Braj Bhasha or Sanskrit, and exegesis or commentarial essays written by Ramesh Parikh and hereditary leaders. The *vārtā*s are referred to throughout the entire text. For example, one section includes a list of "golden nuggets" that can be gleaned from each of the narratives in the *84VV*. In other sections, specific *vārtā* narratives are referred to as examples of particular types of ritual conduct (e.g., how to practice *sevā* when there is discord in the home). About three hundred pages through the *Patrācār*, however, the text is entirely devoted to the eighty-four lauded figures of the *84VV*. This final, hefty section of the text bears the subtitle *Tum Bīn Tatva Kuch Nahīṃ Jagmeṃ*, or "Without You There Is Nothing in This World." This section begins with the *Caurāsī Ḍhol*, a Gujarati devotional song authored by 19th-century poet

Dayaram (1777–1853) and is followed by an eighteen-page introduction to Parikh's translations and commentaries on the *84VV*.[81]

Like the description of the ten-year course and its purpose at www.vallabhkankroli.org, Ramesh Parikh's introduction to his *vārtā* translations and commentary picks up on the theme of accessibility and the needs of contemporary devotee-readers. It also speaks of language and aesthetics. As he writes, generations of Pushtimargis have read *vārtā* literature during *satsaṅg*. The current generation, however, has lost a connection to the literature and finds extracting meaning from the original Braj Bhasha prose extremely difficult.[82] These statements, embedded in the introductory essay, clearly assert a shift in the status of Braj Bhasha: the language is no longer easily legible and in fact slightly obscure.

In addition to the updated style of these "modern" Gujarati translations, this section of the *Patrācār* is also distinct because of its commentarial statements, which come at the end of each *vārtā*. The first section of the commentary is called the *Bhāv Darśan* ("The Divine Vision of the Inner Meaning") and is notably written by one of most erudite and prolific living hereditary leaders, Shyam Manohar Goswami of Kishangarh-Mumbai (about whom we will learn more in the following chapter). As the *gosvāmī* writes in his commentary that follows the *vārtā* of Vallabhacharya's first disciple Damodardas Harsani, "each *vārtā* of the 84 Vaishnavas requires extremely elaborate consideration, such that it would take one year for each and every *vārtā*. Therefore, to consider the 84 *vārtā*s would take 84 years!"[83] This caveat aside, Shyam Manohar Goswami offers a succinct essay (he says much more in his own *pravacan*s dedicated to the *vārtā*s, as we will explore in the following chapter) that unpacks the significance of the narratives vis-à-vis Sanskrit philosophical treatises attributed to Vallabhacharya (e.g., the *Navaratna*, or "Nine Jewels" from the *Ṣoḍaśagrantha*). Following Shyam Manohar Goswami's exegesis is a two-page summary of the *mahatvapurṇ vāto* (important points) gleaned from Hariray's *Bhāvprakāś*.

While Shyam Manohar's commentary is not included in each of the *Patracār*'s featured *vārtā*s, Ramesh Parikh is consistent in giving his own exegesis after each translation by listing what he calls the *siddhānt navnīt*,

81 For more on this 19th-century Pushtimargi poet, see Rachel Dwyer, *The Poetics of Devotion: The Gujarati lyrics of Dayaram* (Richmond, UK: Curzon Press, 2001).

82 Rameśbhāī V. Parīkh, ed., *Puṣṭimārgīy Patrācār: Śuddhādvait Sevābhūṣaṇ* (Vadodara, India: Śrī Vākpati Foundation, 2002), 292.

83 Rameśbhāī V. Parīkh, ed., *Puṣṭimārgīy Patrācār: Śuddhādvait Sevābhūṣaṇ* (Vadodara, India: Śrī Vākpati Foundation, 2002), 318.

or the "essence" of the narrative's "doctrine." Similar to some of the earlier printed editions and commentaries examined in this chapter, Ramesh Parikh and Shyam Manohar Goswami make lucid certain historical details but do not omit the "otherworldly" details of each *vārtā* figure's experience in Krishna's *līlā*. Likewise, this relatively recent translation and commentary (first published in the 1990s and still in wide circulation in 2021) seems little concerned with matters of social propriety that may have been highlighted in the aftermath of the 19th-century Maharaja Libel Case. That is, the type of direct and sometimes defensive responses to the (de)moralizing attacks against the Pushtimarg of the late 19th century are no longer clearly detected. Rather, there is consistent concern with ensuring that the vernacular *vārtā*s are clearly aligned with the writing of Vallabhacharya himself (something even Hariray's *Bhāvprakāś* strives for) and, perhaps most importantly, that the narratives are presented in a fashion that appeals to a wide audience, including youth.[84]

The *Patrācār* shows that anxieties about the Pushtimarg's authenticity and moral character that dominated both public and intra-sectarian discourse during the late 19th and early 20th centuries are no longer primary concerns for the community today. Nonetheless, the significance of Pushtimargi literature as printed, published books has steadily remained important to both the continuing practices of religious reading and also to the sometimes-heated debates within the community about Pushtimargi identity and practice. As the *Patrācār* makes clear, contemporary Pushtimargis maintain a distinct concern for how to make their tradition accessible and appealing to an ever-shifting demographic of devotee-readers while still maintaining "authentic" presentations of literature and sectarian teachings that mark their tradition as cohesive and authoritative.

Final Thoughts on Commentarial Reading

The 19th-century print revolution had long-lasting effects on the Pushtimargi community—both by making written devotional texts more widely available, and by providing devotee-readers with new technologies through which to contribute to textual exegesis. In turn, these new layers of exegesis in the form of written, printed commentaries have been

[84] Despite this aim, I have not found that youth are primary participants in the course.

significant for Pushtimargis, who, when reading *vārtā* texts as books, enter not only into dialogical relationships with fellow readers and with the hagiographies themselves, but also with the layers of commentary left by previous generations—generations who were responding to their own distinct sociohistorical circumstances. While the Maharaja Libel Case may no longer be at the forefront of readers' minds when they engage with their devotional literature today, the way Pushtimargi commentarial practices developed alongside the birth of the book during the 19th and 20th centuries is inextricably linked to how devotees reauthorized their vernacular literature in response to the Libel Case and its aftermath.

The material I have presented here also shows that written commentaries and various paratextual framings are distinct features of religious reading that enable devotees to debate not only the terms of what it means to be a religious reader to begin with, but also the terms of religious and social belonging more broadly. In the following chapters, I further examine the nuances of how contemporary Pushtimargis negotiate between precept and practice and cultivate devotional relationships with each other and with Krishna through reading and discussing (and indeed writing about) their devotional literature, particularly the *84VV* and *252VV*. Finally, the birth of the book as an accessible mode for engaging with religious texts during the late 19th and 20th centuries also paved the way for reading and textual exegesis via ever-emergent dialogical platforms, including the Internet. Whether in print or on virtual platforms, practices of commentarial reading have continued to characterize Pushtimargis' roles as religious readers and Krishna devotees.

3

Public Reading

Debating Text, Temple, and Religious Authority

In September 2013, several Pushtimargi acquaintances sent me multiple email, text, and Facebook messages, urging me to visit a Facebook page called "Shreenathji v/s Rajasthan Congress Government." The subtext of this social media community page was embedded in the sentence "*ShreeNathji ki sampati par Rajasthan congress ki buri nazar*," or "The evil eye of Rajasthan Congress [-led government] on Shrinathji's property (or "wealth")," which appeared on a banner as the Facebook page's cover photograph.[1] As I began to explore the page, reading the ever-growing number of posts and comments in English, Hindi, and Gujarati, the issue in question became clear: local government officials had allegedly nominated three non-Pushtimargi individuals to the temple board at Shrinathji's *havelī* in Nathdwara, Rajasthan. According to many Facebook commentators, by placing such individuals on the temple board against the terms of the 1959 and 1973 temple acts, which state that all board members must also be initiated members of the Pushtimarg, the government was not only showing open disregard for community leadership in Nathdwara and its legal agreement with the state but was also revealing its efforts to gain further economic control over Shrinathji's notoriously well-endowed temple, which attracts thousands of pilgrims and tourists on a regular basis.[2] As one

[1] "Shreenathji v/s Rajasthan Congress Government," accessed March 1st, 2014, https://www.facebook.com/pages/Shreenathji-vs-Rajasthan-Congress-Government/522192447862408. This content is no longer available at the URL accessed in 2014. "Sampati" (*sampattī*) means "property" or "wealth."

[2] The temple acts suggest that members of the board are to attend to the temple's "secular affairs" ("The Nathdwara Temple Act, 1973," accessed October 30, 2013, http://devasthan.rajasthan.gov.in/Files/Upload/6262007105849AM%20NathdwaraTempleRules1973.pdf, 9; "The Nathdwara Temple Act, 1959," accessed October 30, 2013, http://www.devasthan.rajasthan.gov.in/Files/Upload/1003201164910PM%20Nathdwara%20Temple%20Act%201959.pdf, 8). When I speak of tourism I am thinking specifically about the fact that Nathdwara is now listed as a "place to visit" in guidebooks and on Internet sites that appeal to a transnational audience. For example, "Things to Do In Nathdwara," accessed April 9, 2022, https://www.tripadvisor.com/Attractions-g1162444-Activities-Nathdwara_Rajsamand_District_Rajasthan.html. For a discussion of "religious" vs. "secular" tourism, see Shalini Singh, "Secular Pilgrimages and Sacred Tourism in the Indian Himalayas," *GeoJournal* 64,

Religious Reading and Everyday Lives in Devotional Hinduism. Emilia Bachrach, Oxford University Press. © Oxford University Press 2022. DOI: 10.1093/oso/9780197648599.003.0004

commentator wrote, "Vaishnavs, you must be aware that Rajasthan congress govt. has forcefully inducted 3 politicians in the Nathdwara temple board for their greed and vested interest."[3]

In addition to spreading the news about the local government's alleged interference with temple management in Nathdwara—a complicated issue that I will explain over the course of this chapter—the "Shreenathji v/s Rajasthan Congress Government" Facebook page also quickly became one of many venues in which ongoing questions about contemporary Pushtimargi practices, particularly vis-à-vis *sevā*, could be debated openly. While many interlocutors on the Facebook site similarly referred to Pushtimargi literature as informative and authoritative on the debates in question, there was little consensus on particular modes of textual interpretation or on how, in the end, hereditary leaders and devotees should practically respond to the larger questions that the temple-board dispute had elicited.[4] Who should be permitted to perform Shrinathji's *havelī sevā* and how? How, according to both state-based legal and Pushtimargi community norms, should management at the Nathdwara *havelī*—and at other temples—function? And finally, what can readings of Pushtimargi devotional literature reveal about how temple *and* domestic *sevā* functioned in the past, and how it should function in the present and future?

Building on the previous chapter, which described how Pushtimargi readers composed written commentaries on devotional texts to culturally reauthorize their *sampradāy* and its vernacular literature after a turbulent 19th-century moment, this chapter considers how public readings and interpretations of the same texts influence widespread contemporary debates over Pushtimargi *havelī sevā* and devotional practices more broadly. I argue that "public readings"—a term I use to refer to several genres of reading and oral

no. 3 (2005): 205–223; Doron Bar and Kobi Cohen-Hattab, "A New Kind of Pilgrimage: The Modern Tourist Pilgrim of Nineteenth-Century and Early Twentieth-Century Palestine," *Middle Eastern Studies* 39, no. 2 (2003): 131–148; Claudia Bell and J. Lyall, *The Accelerated Sublime—Landscape Tourism and Identity* (London: Praeger, 2001).

[3] Rajeev Baheti, December 10, 2013 (7:21 p.m.), comment on "Shrinathji Temple," accessed December 25, 2013, https://www.facebook.com/shrinathjitemple/posts/379186805517553.

[4] Unlike Daniel Miller's (2011) monograph, in which he argues that one of Facebook's primary functions is to provide users with a space in which to express themselves when "offline sociality" is difficult, I suggest that in the Pushtimargi context Facebook is one of many interconnected modes by which individuals contribute to community debates (*Tales from Facebook* [London: Polity, 2011], 183–184). For Pushtimargi Facebook users in the diaspora, of course, the social media platform provides an otherwise difficult-to-access space in which one can immediately contribute to conversations and debates based in India (or anywhere, for that matter).

exegesis, but primarily *pravacans*—as well as virtual spaces like Facebook, have become important platforms for Pushtimargi reader-exegetes to negotiate such community-wide concerns.[5] In addition to formal interviews and more casual discussions with various members of the Pushtimargi community, my primary sources here include audio-video recordings and printed transcriptions of *pravacans* and conversation threads found on social media. In looking at competing textual interpretations and homiletic practices employed by different exegetes, we begin to see a broader narrative concerning competing visions for the Pushtimarg's future and its identity as a Hindu devotional community in the contemporary world. On the one hand, some assert that their community must develop, structurally and theologically, to accommodate the perceived needs of modern devotees and Krishna alike. On the other hand, some feel that such plans for "development" are based on a blatant misreading of Pushtimargi written text-based doctrine and that the community should "return" to a more "authentic" mode of devotional living. Those on both sides of this dispute feel that their own positions are justified by specific modes of reading and analyzing devotional texts as well as their direct communication with Krishna. In this way, Pushtimargis' public readings are analytically grounded, as exegetes advance their positions through careful interpretations of selected textual materials. Their public readings are also performatively distinct, in that exegetes read and discuss written texts as illustrative of various teachings before an audience in both public virtual and in-person settings.[6] While exegetes' interpretations of Pushtimargi literature vis-à-vis *havelī sevā* are principally concerned with maintaining Krishna's loving care, what I present here also shows how religious texts are embedded in the very human effort to confront *social* change, in turn helping devotees and hereditary leaders as a community to bridge the *laukik* and the *alaukik*, the worldly and the otherworldly.

[5] I have also addressed Pushtimargis' use of social media elsewhere: Emilia Bachrach, "Is Guruji Online?: Internet Advice Forums and Transnational Encounters in a Vaishnav Sampraday," in *Indian Transnationalism Online: New Perspectives on Diaspora*, ed. Ajaya K. Sahoo and Johannes G. de Kruijf (London: Ashgate, 2014), 163–176.

[6] James W. Watts discusses what he calls "dimensions" of scripture in analogous ways. Scripture, he suggests, has three dimensions: performative, semantic, and iconic. For further on these "dimensions," see James W. Watts, "The Three Dimensions of Scriptures," *Postscripts: The Journal of Sacred Texts and Contemporary Worlds* 2 (2006): 135–159.

Temple Board Controversies and Nathdwara *Havelī* Renovations

As the discussion on the "Shreenathji v/s Rajasthan Congress Government" Facebook page unfolded, various commentators began to post citations from devotional texts, which were intended to offer perspective on the ongoing dispute between members of the Pushtimargi community and the local government. Several such references included on the Facebook page were drawn from the *Śrīnāthjī kī Prākaṭya Vārtā*, the text that describes Shrinathji's emergence and subsequent journey from Braj to Nathdwara in the late 17th century. Some commentators compared the local Rajasthan government to the Mughal emperor Aurangzeb, who in the *Prākaṭya Vārtā* is said to have followed Shrinathji on his westward journey in hopes that the deity would take up residence at the imperial headquarters, rather than in a Rajput kingdom. According to the *vārtā*'s logic, Shrinathji had orchestrated the entire situation so that he could use Aurangzeb's pursuit (among other incidents) as a pretext for moving to Nathdwara, where the deity wished to be relocated for various *alaukik* reasons. In the same way, contemporary Facebook commentators noted, Shrinathji must have purposefully caused the current controversy over temple management in order to make his caretakers aware of his own *śram* (exertion). But what did Shrinathji desire now? Maybe he wanted to be moved to Gujarat, where a majority of his followers now reside, or back to Braj, some reasoned. Or perhaps he was trying to communicate special instructions about how to renovate his own *havelī*.

Other Facebook commentators focused on how *vārtā* narratives warned against the dangers of looking greedily upon *devadravya* (God's wealth), or the material belongings of Krishna deities like Shrinathji. One episode from the *84VV* was posted multiple times in Hindi in direct response to this issue. My translation of this passage is as follows:

> Arriving, the Vaishnava said to Shri Acharyaji, "My Lord! The Shri Dwarkanathji *svarūp* has arrived with wealth." [. . .] then Shri Acharyaji said, "Has seeing Shri Thakurji's wealth pleased you?" Shri Gopinathji responded, saying, "According to your teaching, he whose mind becomes fixated on Shri Thakurji's wealth becomes impure." Shri Acharyaji heard this and replied, "Indeed, this is our path." —*84 Vārtājī*."[7]

[7] September 29, 2013, comment on "Shreenathji v/s Rajasthan Congress Government," accessed on October 16, 2013.

The cited text refers to an account about Damodardas Sambhalvare, whose hagiography appears in the *84VV*. The background to this brief and oft-cited *vārtā* episode is that Damodardas and his wife, both disciples of Vallabhacharya, have just passed away. After the couple's passing, their maid, who is also a devotee, gathers all the family's belongings, including their household *svarūp* Dwarkanathji, and sets off in a boat across the Yamuna River to offer all the possessions and the deity to Vallabhacharya. When Vallabhacharya's elder son Gopinath sees Dwarkanathji in the boat with all these possessions he jokes that, "Lakshmi, the goddess of wealth, arrives with Narayan [another name for Krishna as the deity Vishnu]." As cited by the Facebook commentator, Vallabhacharya replies to Gopinath's statement as a way to assert the message that having worldly desires for material wealth (which ultimately belongs to Krishna) is against Pushtimargi teachings. To further articulate his point, the *vārtā* reports that Vallabhacharya offers (through submersion) all of the material possessions to the Yamuna River (a goddess) because he knows that "Damodardas' wayward and greedy son will eventually come after the wealth and try to claim it for himself."[8]

Facebook commentators strategically cited this *vārtā* episode as a way to argue that the local government's alleged move to place non-Pushtimargi individuals on the temple board is akin to looking greedily upon the wealth of Shrinathji (recall the subtext to the page's title: "*ShreeNathji ki sampati par Rajasthan congress ki buri nazar*"). In other words, the *vārtā* narrative was read as offering a direct commentary on—or way of interpreting—the contemporary issue in question. In addition to being a sectarian offense, the government's move is also seen by Pushtimargis as going against the legal terms of the Nathdwara 1959 and 1973 temple acts, which state that all board members must be initiated Pushtimargis who have been recommended by Nathdwara's leading hereditary leader, known as the *tilkāyat*.[9] The current *tilkāyat*, Rakesh Maharaj, is therefore generally accepted as Shrinathji's primary caretaker. He is also the president of the Nathdwara *havelī* board.

[8] D. Parīkh, *Caurāsī Vaiṣṇavan kī Vārtā*, 39.

[9] *Tilkāyat* refers to the eldest living hereditary leader of a particular branch of Vallabhacharya's lineage—a branch descending from the first of seven sons born to Vallabhacharya's son and successor Vitthalnath (1515–1585). The history of legal mandates on places of worship by state and federal authorities in India is complex and does not reflect the familiar separation of "church and state" as it does in certain countries (e.g., the United States—though, of course, such matters are complex and debated in the United States as well). For more on these mandates, see Deonnie Moodie's *The Making of a Modern Temple and a Hindu City: Kalighat and Kolkata* (New York: Oxford University Press, 2018).

Since the 1959 Temple Act, it has been customary for local government officials to choose new board members every three years in accordance with the *tilkāyat*'s recommendations.[10] According to both the temple acts, members of the board are to "do all such things as may be incidental and conducive to the efficient management of the secular affairs of the temple,"[11] including the allocation of temple funds for renovation and development projects, as well as the payment of all temple employees, referred to as *sevak*s (of which there are hundreds). All matters "connected with the conduct of seva and puja and other ceremonies and of festivals of the temple according to the customs and usages of the Pushti Margiya Vallabhi Sampradaya shall be under the direct control of the Goswami [that is, the *tilkāyat*]."[12]

In 2013, a devotee named Sanjay, one of the commentators on the "Shreenathji v/s Rajasthan Congress Government" Facebook page, told me that in addition to suspecting that Rajasthani politicians wished to use temple funds for personal or state benefit (namely, to boost tourism in the region), he also feared that the government would interfere with the board's plans for renovations (it remains unclear to me if this was a legitimate threat, as renovations seem to have continued without apparent obstruction).[13] Recent statements made by the board on the temple's official website assert that in "Phase One" of the "Temple Extension Plan," which is now well underway, various additions to the original 17th-century complex will be constructed, including: an "Exhibition Hall, Restaurants, Waiting Space for 25,000 persons" as well as "Public Utility Services [public toilets], Temple Board Offices," and "28 Donor Cottages."[14] The *tilkāyat*'s son, Vishal Goswami, who will inherit the role of Shrinathji's primary custodian from his father, provides regular updates on the ongoing renovations via his social media platforms, including Instagram, Facebook, and YouTube. As of July 2021, Vishal Goswami's Instagram account suggests that the temple renovations (not to mention greater measures for cleanliness and sanitization due to the COVID-19 pandemic) are ongoing. There are also countless projects for expanding pilgrim-centered facilities, such as guarded parking lots and

[10] A current list of members can be found at the official Nathdwara *havelī* website: "Member Board Info," accessed October 21, 2013, http://www.nathdwaratemple.org/Management/BoardMemberInfo.aspx.

[11] "The Nathdwara Temple Act, 1973," 9; "The Nathdwara Temple Act, 1959," 8.

[12] "The Nathdwara Temple Act, 1973," 9; "The Nathdwara Temple Act, 1959," 8.

[13] Personal communication, October 21, 2013.

[14] "Temple Extension Plan," accessed October 21, 2013, http://www.nathdwaratemple.org/Development/TempleExtensionPhaseI.aspx.

"five-star" hotels and cottages for pilgrims in Nathdwara. As Vishal Goswami writes in the text of an August 2020 Instagram post, "The Shrinathji Mandir in Nathdwara is not only devalaya (the house of god) but also Nandalay (the house of Nand [Krishna's adoptive father in Braj]). That is why when innovations like electricity hadn't been accepted in temples elsewhere, they had been welcomed" in Shrinathji's *havelī*. "After all," he continues, citing one of Vallabhacharya's treatises, " 'yatha dehe tatha deve.' What we find comfortable ourselves we must preserve to offer to Prabhu [God]."[15] In other words these projects are, according to Vishal Goswami, both innovative and scripturally sound achievements that directly benefit the ability of the community to best serve Shrinathji.

For Sanjay and other Facebook commentators I correspond with, these renovation projects led by hereditary leaders and the Nathdwara temple board are welcome for precisely the reasons Vishal Goswami indicates in the aforementioned Instagram post: they are pioneering, but also grounded in "tradition." According to another devotee, Deepa Shah—a resident of Baroda, Gujarat, and a generous donor to Shrinathji's *havelī* and to a neighboring *havelī* in Kankroli, Rajasthan—temple renovations are also just as necessary for the comfort of a *havelī*'s resident deity as they are for his human caretakers. "We feel transported to another time when we visit Kankroli and take Shri Dwarkadhishji's *darśan*," she said, referring to the *svarūp* housed there. "But just as Shri Vallabhacharya's disciple Damodardas only offered Shri Dwarkadhishji the finest items," she continued, citing a *vārtā* about the deity and his first caretaker, "we too should keep His *havelī* in the best condition. Otherwise He will not be pleased and He will not want us to visit."[16] Deepa's comments again reinforce how Pushtimargis use devotional texts to support their positions on temple renovation for Krishna's comfort, which is inherently linked to their ability to cultivate a relationship with the deity.

[15] "Our Pushti Siddhant Says," accessed August 29, 2020, https://www.instagram.com/p/CEbZOlaBu9l/.

[16] In desiring improved comfort for Krishna *svarūps* and for devotees, the vision for temple renovations shared by devotees like Deepa is also similar to what some of Joanne Waghorne's interlocutors shared in the case of the renovated Mundaka Kanni Amman temple in a middle-class Chennai neighborhood. Joanne Punzo Waghorne, *Diaspora of the Gods: Modern Hindu Temples in an Urban Middle-Class World* (New York: Oxford University Press, 2004). For further information, see Joanne Punzo Waghorne, "The Gentrification of the Goddess," *International Journal of Hindu Studies* 5, no. 3 (2001): 227–267. As Waghorne suggests, renovations including fans, porches, and parlors reflect (certain middle-class) devotees' own class-specific urban surroundings and sensibilities, as well as their concern that the goddess receive the best possible care (Waghorne, *Diaspora of the Gods*, 227–267).

Thus, for devotees like Sanjay and Deepa, the essential problem with the government's recent attempt to place non-Pushtimargi individuals on Nathdwara's temple board lies in the fact that so-called outsiders have attempted to interfere with sectarian management and, by extension, with the wealth and renovation plans at Shrinathji's temple.[17] Conversely, it seems entirely appropriate that Shrinathji's *havelī* is well endowed through community members' donations and has continued to grow as a major site of pilgrimage, which requires a formal system of temple management and an increasing number of facilities. "Our Shriji (Shrinathji) draws devotees from all over the world," an elderly pilgrim once announced to me as we were waiting in line to enter the *havelī* for an evening *darśan*. "Everyone who comes here, rich and poor, wants to offer something. We all want to contribute to Shriji's *vaibhav* (majesty)."

Shrinathji's regal *havelī* complex is especially known for its long-established tradition of *sevā*, which enacts Krishna's *līlā* through rituals of feeding, dressing, and singing to the deity at prescribed times of day and according to the season. These *sevā* rituals require scores of temple *sevaks*, including professional cooks, painters, and musicians.[18] The Nathdwara *havelī* was designed and built with these elaborate *sevā* performances in mind. Some temple rooms, for instance, are strictly reserved for the preparation of dairy products, while others are used for crafting Shrinathji's clothing.[19] While the system of temple patronage has changed and the number of pilgrims has

[17] While it is not this chapter's focus, it should be noted that one prominent justification for government involvement in temple management has often been that religious leaders, like those in Nathdwara, are not able to manage temple finances without seeking personal financial gains (I am grateful to Deonnie Moodie for suggesting that I note this trend). This is taken up, for instance, in a Rajasthan High Court Case titled "Tilkayat Govindlalji and Ors. v. State and Ors."

[18] One of the most prominent features of ritual worship in Pushtimargi temples (and homes) is the system of *aṣṭayām sevā*, which refers to eight specific periods of the day within the round-the-clock *sevā* of Krishna. Most temples have slightly distinct systems, but many are related to a publication called the *Tippanī* ("The Observation"), published monthly by the Nathdwara *havelī*'s temple board and circulated widely. For further information on temple calendars and seasonal observances, see Bennett, *The Path of Grace*, 101–141.

[19] Modern temples, particularly those built during the late 20th and 21st centuries, bear little resemblance to Shrinathji's *havelī*. For instance, fewer new temples have the kind of intricately constructed space for the ritual preparation of food and clothing for *sevā*. Furthermore, very few new temples include a separate *nij mandir*, or private inner sanctum, in which the *svarūp* is generally kept in older *havelīs*. As Amit Ambalal has described, Shrinathji's sprawling *havelī*, which ultimately is supposed to represent Krishna's "original home in the land of Vraja [Braj]," was traditionally only open to the "public" in restricted areas on the ground floor (Ambalal, *Krishna as Shrinathji*, 19). Though not specific to Nathdwara, Peter Bennett addresses modes of *havelī sevā* here: Peter Bennett, "Krishna's Own Form: Image Worship and the Pushti Marga," *Journal of Vaishnava Studies* 1, no. 4 (1993): 109–134; Peter Bennett, "In Nanda Baba's House: The Devotional Experience in Pushti Marg Temples," in *Divine Passions: The Social Construction of Emotion in India*, ed. Owen M. Lynch (Berkeley: University of California Press, 1990), 182–211.

significantly increased since the 17th century, pilgrims' donations have always been a primary means of supporting the temple's dynamic ritual life. In this way, community donations are seen to support inevitably and justifiably what the temple board and many devotees articulate as the ongoing and necessary growth of Shrinathji's *vaibhav*, namely, through increasingly elaborate performances of *sevā* and the Temple Extension Plan.

Pushtimargis with whom I speak are generally unified in their opposition to so-called outsiders being placed on Nathdwara's temple board. Where they are *not* in agreement is on plans for renovation, which many feel will cause both pilgrims *and* Shrinathji to suffer. Much like those who support renovations, those who oppose them rely on specific modes of reading Pushtimargi literature and on direct communication with Krishna himself to articulate their positions. In her online diary, a Mumbai-based devotee named Abha Shahra Shyama describes (in Romanized Hindi and in her own English translation) her position on the matter. In one entry she narrates her experience of visiting Nathdwara during the winter of 2012, when she claims to have communicated directly with Shrinathji about how he himself was being affected by temple reconstruction. Apart from my bracketed comments, the following text is verbatim from the online diary:[20]

> As there is the construction work going on around the Haveli; a truck was being loaded with the stone debris from the inside of the left side area right inside the Lal Darvaza [one of several main entrances into the *havelī*]. It caused immense noise as the workers did not have any instructions from the temple board to work silently. We were astonished as to how the mandir board allows this much noise all through the night. We realised why we were called here so early when Shreeji's melodious voice echoed, in which Shreeji told us, "*Dekho puri raat kitni awaz karte hain. Yeh koi sochta nahi ki main andar sou raha hun, itne aawaz meinn mai kaise sau sakte hu. Kissse ko kuch bhao hi nahi hai ki Shreeji andar sau rahe honge. Tum logon ko iseliye jaldi bulaya tha, ye dikhane ke liye. Main yaha kiyon rahu? Main yaha se bhaag jaata hun.*" ("Entire night they make so much noise. See there is no bhau [that is, *bhāv*]. They do not even consider that Shreeji is sleeping

[20] Abha's diary entry uses nonstandard spelling in Romanized Hindi. Her English translations do not always match the order of her Hindi sentences or provide literal meaning (e.g., Abha glosses the Hindi phrase, "Main yah se bhaag jaata hun," with "Why should I stay here?" rather than "I am going to run away from this place").

inside and would be disturbed. I called you'll early to show this, no one cares. Why should I stay here? All are selfish.")[21]

In the same entry, Abha goes on to write about how the "entire mandir board, as well as the Tilkayatji is responsible for this lack of proper planning and supervision [. . .]." Justifying her open criticism of temple management and the authority of the *tilkāyat*, Abha explains that Shrinathji himself communicated with her and directed her to share these experiences—just as he had communicated with and directed the actions of those "84 and 252 great Vaishnavas" whose lives are extolled in the *vārtās*. As we know from Chapter 1, direct verbal communication with Krishna is integral to how the written *vārtās* indicate intimacy between devotee and deity, and it is therefore something that contemporary devotees like Abha yearn for and report experiencing themselves. Elsewhere in her blog, Abha elaborates on this point, suggesting that intimate knowledge of the "historical" *vārtās* helps the devotee to cultivate both piety and intimacy with Krishna but also permits the modern devotee to live in the same devotional mode of the *vārtās*' lauded protagonists. Abha in fact designates many of her own blog entries as "live vaartas," which she glosses as "stories of direct interaction [with Krishna] in today's time period."[22] In this way, the canonical written *vārtā* narratives offer clear models for Pushtimargis like Abha as they engage with Krishna and participate in contemporary community debates.

Devotees such as Abha are not the only ones to use devotional literature to justify their critique of the temple board and *havelī* renovations. The most vocal opposition, in fact, comes from Shyam Manohar Goswami of Mumbai, one of the Pushtimarg's most widely respected hereditary leaders, but also a contentious figure whose public readings and exegesis of Pushtimargi literature circulate widely in print and on virtual platforms. Shyam Manohar Goswami's opposition to temple renovation in Nathdwara lies specifically in his belief that Vallabhacharya's 16th-century teachings, and Pushtimargi devotional literature more broadly, do not support the *jāher* (public) worship of Krishna deities. "One cannot," he has written, even "speak of a 'sectarian temple.' "[23] Therefore, according to Shyam Manohar Goswami, Pushtimargi

[21] Abha Shahra Shyama. "Happenings Around the Mandir," accessed November 30, 2013, http://www.shreenathjibhakti.org/shreenathji_mandir.htm. This content is no longer available at the URL accessed in 2013.

[22] "Live Vaartas" (accessed September 14, 2021, https://www.shreenathjibhakti.org/post/shreenathji-live-vartaas).

[23] The Hindi reads, "*sampradāyik mandir nahīṃ kahā jā sakta*" (Śyām Manohar Gosvāmī, *Puṣṭividhānam: Pāṭhāvalī* [Mumbai: Sahayog-Prakāśan, 2002], 9).

"temples" such as the one in Nathdwara are fundamentally illegitimate institutions that have been built to support what he sees as the money-powered religious observances and preferences of many of his hereditary-leader counterparts and their affluent devotees. Those who see matters otherwise are, according to him, "misinterpreting," intentionally or not, "authoritative" texts. "Reading properly," the *gosvāmī* suggests, "would solve such misinterpretations."

Now that we have established what is at stake in the controversies around *havelī* renovations in Nathdwara, I turn more pointedly to how Shyam Manohar Goswami—as one significant hereditary leader of the community—reads and analyzes Pushtimargi literature, particularly in relationship to his perspectives on temples and *sevā*. The ways in which Shyam Manohar Goswami delivers *pravacans* on "authoritative texts" provides a distinct example of how Pushtimargis read *Vārtā Sāhitya* and related literature to promote their positions on contemporary community thought and practice.

Public Reading and Homiletics with Shyam Manohar Goswami

Shyam Manohar Goswami's frequent discourse on Pushtimargi devotional literature, including *Vārtā Sāhitya*, is often streamed live on social media platforms, attracting thousands of online viewers and dozens of devotees at the in-person events.[24] His public readings—primarily in the form of *pravacans*—are typically formal affairs, featuring only Shyam Manohar Goswami himself as an exegete.[25] Occasionally, however, he will hold collaborative readings and lectures with fellow hereditary leaders or devotees

[24] Many of these *pravacans* are recorded and posted to YouTube. They are also frequently transcribed (and sometimes translated from Hindi or Braj Bhasha to Gujarati) and published as printed books. Video recordings and published transcriptions of Shyam Manohar Goswami's *pravacans* can be found at Pushtimarg.net.

[25] The term *pravacan* generally refers to public lectures and often those with distinctly religious content. While there are multiple genres for oral teachings and public readings in the Pushtimarg (including *kathā*, which can include more formal recitations of a text such as the *Bhāgavatapurāṇa*), *pravacans* are the most ubiquitous. In the case of widely respected leaders like Shyam Manohar Goswami, *pravacans* draw at least several dozen people, depending on the venue. In the case of Shyam Manohar Goswami, these sermons take place in Pushtimargi meeting halls or other rented spaces, but not in temples per se. Other hereditary leaders deliver *pravacans* in temple spaces. The perceived need for increasingly large venues for these events is a primary reason devotees cite for expansion plans at many temples.

with whom he agrees on matters of textual interpretation and Pushtimargi doctrine.[26] He also teaches public university classes as well as privately organized ones and holds various types of seminars and theological debates with fellow hereditary leaders (with whom he may or may not agree on theological matters; we will learn more about these contexts as this chapter progresses). Though Shyam Manohar Goswami's *pravacan*s are unique in many ways, he does share some common practices with his counterparts. For instance, like many of his fellow Pushtimagi *pravacankār*s (exegetes), Shyam Manohar Goswami typically begins his lectures with a Pushtimargi Sanskrit prayer (of five verses), called the *maṅgalācaraṇ* (benediction), and concludes with a popular Braj Bhasha *kīrtan* attributed to the 16th-century poet Surdas (one of the *aṣṭachāp* poets whose hagiography is featured in the *84VV*).[27] Also familiar to the *pravacan*s of other exegetes, Shyam Manohar Goswami's *pravacan* "stage" (often an actual elevated stage or podium) does not usually feature an image or form of Krishna himself but, rather, displays paintings or statues of Vallabhacharya and his early descendants (which often hang or sit behind the exegete), as well as the texts that are read from or referred to during a given *pravacan* session (the texts sit elevated on a stand in front of the exegete unless the exegete is actually reading directly from them).

These familiar practices aside, Shyam Manohar Goswami's homiletic style stands out in various way. As he says himself, "My *vārtā pravacan*s are radically different than those of the other *gosvāmī bālaks*."[28] For instance, unlike other hereditary leaders (such as the female leader Goswami Indirabetiji, whom we will meet in Chapter 5), Shyam Manohar Goswami does not embellish his *pravacan*s with the intermittent singing of devotional songs alongside musical accompaniment performed by singers and musicians. Such semiprofessional performances, for which there is increasing demand in recent years, are today fairly standard fare in other hereditary leaders' (and devotees') *pravacan*s. In addition to eschewing the types of musical accompaniment used by his Vallabha Kul counterparts, the content and form of Shyam Manohar Goswami's *pravacan*s, too, are distinct. While other exegetes will often read a paragraph or narrate an account from a *vārtā* (or recite a verse from a Sanskrit text) and then follow with a detailed, though sometimes

[26] See, for example, "Pushtiswadhyay," accessed December 22, 2020, https://www.youtube.com/watch?v=xKbyzEf5v60&t=2241s&ab_channel=Pushtiswadhyay-GoswamyShriShyammanoharji.

[27] For more on Surdas, his poetry, and the ways in which he was adopted as a sectarian poet by Pushtimargis through hagiography, see John S. Hawley, *The Memory of Love: Surdas Sings to Krishna* (New York: Oxford University Press, 2009).

[28] Personal communication, July 2017.

repetitive, spoken exegesis that stays close to the text and is interspersed with the performance of related devotional singing, Shyam Manohar Goswami presumes that his audience will—and *should*—have already read the narratives in question. Shyam Manohar Goswami does, however, read aloud from portions of the *vārtā*s that feature Vallabhacharya's *vacanāmṛt* (even more so than portions of the texts featuring Krishna's speech). It is specifically from these dialogical portions of the hagiographies that Shyam Manohar Goswami's *pravacan*s arise, bringing him out of specific *vārtā* stories themselves and into various layers of analysis that are meant to align the narratives with Vallabhacharya's teachings, such as those recorded in Vallabhacharya's *Ṣoḍaśagrantha*.[29] Inspired by the centrality of Vallabhacharya's *vacanāmṛt* in his *vārtā pravacan*s, Shyam Manohar Goswami has also published separate collections of this "nectarous speech" as it is recorded in the *vārtā*s (e.g., the *Vacanāmṛtsaṃkalan*, or "Collection of Nectarous Speech," which can be found in PDF format on Pushtimarg.net).

Even when speaking in a distinct style of Braj Bhasha-inflected Hindi—rather than in Gujarati, the first language of most contemporary devotees—Shyam Manohar Goswami unpacks dialogue from the *vārtā*s and sometimes opaque Sanskrit verses in ways that seem to break down potential barriers between the premodern texts and his contemporary audiences effectively. As one avid follower of his *vārtā pravacan*s commented,

> Shyambava's speech is also *vacanāmṛt*, though he doesn't call it that—each word is full of *amṛt* [nectar]. But he is also humorous and not at all pretentious. He shows us how to read and understand why the *vārtā*s teach us about Shri Mahaprabhuji's *siddhānt*.

Shyam Manohar Goswami seems to generate this affect both by referring to straightforward examples of devotional behavior as depicted in the *vārtā*s themselves and by explicitly stating that the hagiographies' protagonists are "speaking" directly to his contemporary audience members: "this *vārtā* is a bit distinct, but it is ultimately about you," as he said during a 2017 *vārtā pravacan* inspired by devotee Rana Vyas, whose hagiography appears in the *84VV*. A longer excerpt from the first minutes of the *pravacan* inspired by

[29] As with nearly every Pushtimargi canonical text, Shyam Manohar Goswami has written on Vallabhacharya's sixteen treatises. See, for example, Śyām Manohar Gosvāmī, ed., *Ṣoḍaśagranthāḥ* (Bombay: Sṭuḍio Bahār, 1980).

Rana Vyas' *vārtā* shows further how Shyam Manohar Goswami speaks to devotees and initiates his *pravacans*:

> Here, from our Rana Vyas' *vārtā* come these instructions via Vallabhacharya's *vacanāmṛt*: "Though you have defeated these scholars [in scriptural debate] you should not be prideful. Pride destroys any accomplishment." Each *vārtā* has episodes. Just like all the different episodes that appear in a TV serial, Rana Vyas' *vārtā* has such episodes. His problems and the solution to these problems are just like your own problems and your own solutions to said problems. These problems are not unique to Rana Vyas—they are also yours. [Vallabhacharya's] *vacanāmṛt* explains this: "you should not be prideful. Pride destroys accomplishments."

As this example makes clear, Shyam Manohar Goswami does not, at the outset, provide any context for the part of Rana Vyas' *vārtā* that describes Vyas defeating scholars in scriptural debate. Rather, he only reads aloud from a small portion of the text that he feels represents the narrative's primary teachings as they are embedded in Vallabhacharya's spoken directions to practice humility. In the following hours of the *pravacan* (which spanned eleven days and generated over three hundred pages of transcribed text), Shyam Manohar Goswami regularly toggles back and forth between modern psychoanalysis, a wide range of references to (and direct readings from) Pushtimarg-specific and other religious texts, and lighthearted everyday-life examples intended to make Vallabhacharya's teachings on humility inviting and applicable for the listener living in the here and now.[30] As devotee Dr. Yojana Mahajan said of the *gosvāmī* in response to my question about how she experiences his public readings, "Shyambava's *vārtā kathā*s go on for hours and hours, but it doesn't *feel* like hours of sitting there in one place because his teachings lift [us] up." In other words, Shyam Manohar Goswami—like many of his Vallabha Kul counterparts—is perceived to be a charismatic, inspiring teacher and skilled exegete.

While not all of Shyam Manohar Goswami's *pravacans* explicitly focus on debates surrounding *havelī* reconstruction and *sevā*, his convictions

[30] While distinct, other hereditary leaders do apply similar rhetorical strategies. I discuss those of Goswami Indirabetiji in the next chapter, but other *gosvāmīs*, too, such as Goswami Anandbava, discuss texts similarly. See Goswami Anandbava, "The Ego in Pushtimarg: The Slip Between the Cup and the Lip," accessed August 13, 2012, http://pushtimarg.com/anandbava/2011/the-ego-in-pushtimarg-the-slip-between-the-cup-and-the-lip/.

on these topics do manage to seep into nearly every one of his lectures and written commentaries that I have encountered. For instance, in the same aforementioned *pravacan* on Rana Vyas' *vārtā*, which has no specific reference to temple-based *sevā* practices, Shyam Manohar Goswami mentions the tensions around the Nathdwara *havelī* multiple times, including in the following statement: "If you [the devotee] do not have time to practice *sevā* yourself, then what's the use? Don't have someone else do it—then it's no longer *sevā*. We have this very same problem in Nathdwara today [where paid *sevak*s are responsible for Shrinathji's daily care]."[31] This statement comes in the context of an extended discussion on ego and social attachments—the primary theme throughout Rana Vyas' *vārtā*.

In addition to having ever-ready comments on Shrinathji's *sevā*, Shyam Manohar Goswami also organizes some of his *pravacan*s and writings to focus specifically on questions of Pushtimargi places of worship. One of the ways in which he organizes such *pravacan*s is by curating historical timelines of sectarian development, highlighting select episodes from a wide variety of texts, including the *84VV* and the *Śrīnāthjī kī Prākaṭya Vārtā*. Organizing *vārtā* narratives in this manner is a conscious "editorial" choice as most *vārtā* texts, especially the *84VV* and *252VV*, do not follow linear historical logic. By strategically organizing *vārtā* episodes in this way, Shyam Manohar Goswami—like his 19th- and 20th-century counterparts as discussed in Chapter 2—is also able to emphasize particular trajectories of ritual development, such as the growth of the Pushtimargi temple in the first place.

One type of repeated historical reference that Shyam Manohar Goswami makes is meant to show that while Shrinathji's first temple in the region of Braj *was* "public"—that is, was open to more than just the hereditary leaders who directly cared for the deity—the death of Vallabhacharya's son Vitthalnath marked a shift in the deity's intended worship: "In the beginning Shrinathji's *devālaya* (God's abode; temple) was public, we cannot deny this fact, but after [the death of Vitthalnath] it became *khānagī* (a family matter)—this too is an *aitihāsik tathya* (historical fact) that we often forget."[32] According to Shyam Manohar Goswami, the *vārtā*s report that just before Shrinathji was moved to Rajasthan in the 17th century there was a familial dispute over which of Vallabhacharya's descendants were to be Shrinathji's primary caretakers

[31] "Shri Vallabh vachanamrut Rana vyas Ki varta," accessed August 29, 2019, http://pushtimarg.net/video-pravachana/?post_id=4739.

[32] Ṣyām Manohar Gosvāmī, *Ādhunak Nyāyapraṇālī no Āpasī Ṭakarāv* (Kacch, India: Śrī Vallabhācārya Ṭrasṭ, 2006), 12.

and therefore which lineage holders were to preside in Nathdwara with the Pushtimarg's most prestigious deity. Ultimately, *vārtā*s report that Shrinathji himself, with the help of the Mughal emperor, intervened and decreed that the descendants of Vitthalnath's first son were to perform *sevā* during sixty-five days of the year, but that each of the six other lineages (recall that Vitthalnath had seven sons) were to have the right to perform *sevā* during the remaining three hundred days.[33] When speaking and writing about this matter, Shyam Manohar Goswami cites both the *Śrīnāthjī kī Prākaṭya Vārtā* and an imperial *farmān* (edict), which describes and dates the Vallabha Kul's dispute and decided outcome.[34] The reason for these events, Shyam Manohar Goswami claims, had as much to do with the perceived threat of the then Mughal emperor Aurangzeb (1618–1707) destroying temples as it did with Vallabhacharya's primary teachings and Shrinathji's own preferences.[35] Once Vallabhacharya and Vitthalnath had passed away, Shrinathji himself knew that the "purity" of his *sevā* could be compromised. The deity thus determined that his own care should be kept in the hands of hereditary leaders who were to serve him *privately*. The average devotee could have full access to Shrinathji (that is, to Krishna) through his or her own private *sevā* of a consecrated *svarūp*. This narrative is clearly told in the *vārtā*s, argues Shyam Manohar Goswami, who notably approaches both imperial *farmān*s and Pushtimargi hagiographies as equally valid sources of historical narrative during his *pravacans*. Furthermore, he notes, Shrinathji was the only Pushtimargi *svarūp* to have ever expressed the desire for any kind of public place of worship (a temple) to begin with: each of the other *svarūp*s whose accounts appear in the *vārtā*s are only described as having been cared for in the private homes of hereditary leaders or of devotees. In these ways, Shyam Manohar Goswami actively continues the legacy of historicizing the *vārtā*s, as discussed in Chapter 2 with reference to 19th- and 20th-century written commentaries, but explicitly uses them to speak to contemporary issues.[36]

[33] Gosvāmī, *Ādhunak Nyāyapraṇālī no Āpasī Ṭakarāv*, 21; Paṇḍyā, ed., *Śrī Govardhannāthjī kī Prākaṭya Vārtā*, 39–40.

[34] See, for example, Gosvāmī, *Ādhunak Nyāyapraṇālī no Āpasī Ṭakarāv*, 21.

[35] Gosvāmī, *Ādhunak Nyāyapraṇālī no Āpasī Ṭakarāv*, 25. For more on the perception of Aurangzeb in Braj, see Pauwels and Bachrach, "Aurangzeb as Iconoclast?"

[36] When Pushtimargi literature does not align with extra-sectarian sources, however, or when literature does not illuminate Vallabhacharya's teachings, Shyam Manohar Goswami suggests that there is reason to be suspicious. In other words, he is not willing to read hagiography as an accurate account with a blind eye to other narratives. He told me that he has doubts, for instance, about hagiographic accounts of certain *baiṭhak*s (shrines that commemorate sites where Vallabhacharya recited the *Bhāgavatapurāṇa*), which he believes were written to serve the purposes of competing lineages within the Vallabha Kul (personal communication, July 18, 2012).

As with Pushtimargis who oppose his readings of devotional texts, Shyam Manohar Goswami's ultimate aim as a textual exegete vis-à-vis the topic of *havelī sevā* is to ensure that Shrinathji receives "proper" care. Beyond his insistence that "public" temple worship goes against Pushtimargi text-based teachings—a matter that he has taken beyond the *pravacan* stage and into the legal system—Shyam Manohar Goswami's concern for Krishna's care also extends to his teachings on domestic *sevā*.[37] After all, as he explained to me in a conversation at his Mumbai residence, Vallabhacharya's treatises and *Vārtā Sāhitya* are "focused on domestic *sevā*, not on *havelī* [worship]." Although Vallabhacharya's own writings do not provide a lucid step-by-step "practical guide" for domestic *sevā* practices, the very "foundation" of Vallabhacharya's philosophical system, Shyam Manohar Goswami explained, is the devotee's personal, and hence private, performance of *sevā* for a Krishna *svarūp*. "*Gṛhe sthithvā svadharmataḥ*," he said, reciting a verse from one of Vallabhacharya's Sanskrit philosophical treatises, the *Bhaktivardhinī* ("The Strengthening of Devotion").[38] Translating into Hindi from the Sanskrit, Shyam Manohar Goswami explained that Vallabhacharya's statement demands that the devotee "remain a householder, follow his own *dharma*, and perform Krishna's *sevā* in the home." Shyam Manohar Goswami believes that contemporary devotees—namely, urban affluent residents of Gujarat and of Mumbai—have begun to abandon this fundamental practice because they fear that the responsibility of *sevā* will interfere with their "modern lifestyles." Instead, he claims, devotees increasingly prefer to visit temples where they can participate in *vittajā sevā*, or service in the form of financial donation. *Vittajā sevā* in and of itself is not the problem, Shyam Manohar Goswami suggests. With the *brahmasambandha* initiation mantra, Vallabhacharya instructs the devotee to dedicate all aspects of life, including material wealth, to Krishna. However, the physical performance of *sevā* for one's own personal *svarūp*, bestowed upon a devotee by his or her guru after initiation, is an important part of devotional practice in the Pushtimarg and should not be abandoned

[37] In 2005, when the Nathdwara temple board appealed to Rajasthan's High Court for compliance with proposed *havelī* renovations, Shyam Manohar Goswami filed a petition, which is recorded in the state's legal record. In the petition he argues that Nathdwara's *havelī* was constructed to exclude people from seeing its essence, namely, the "'Rasalila' [that] is being played by Lord Shri Natha Ji during night" (N. Mathur, "Dhirendra Manharbhai (Shri) and . . . vs. State Anr. on 6 May, 2005," accessed October 13, 2013, http://indiankanoon.org/doc/977892/?type=print). Furthermore, he argues, since the *havelī* was intended to be a "personal house" for Shrinathji and his designated caretakers, the *havelī* should not be subjected to the protocols of other major Hindu places of worship, such as the renowned Minakshi and Kashi Vishwanath temples.

[38] Personal communication, July 15, 2012. The *Bhaktivardhinī* appears in the *Ṣoḍaśagrantha*.

in favor of *vittajā sevā* alone. Furthermore, one should only dedicate material wealth to one's personal Krishna *svarūp*, not to the *svarūp* of one's guru or of any other devotee. Thus, donating to *havelīs* and supporting a system that separates the deity from the personal care of his or her devotional caretaker, is, according to Shyam Manohar Goswami, against the primary—and what he understands to be the text-based, and thus "authentic"—teachings of the Pushtimarg. In this way, Nathdwara's system of temple management as well as its reliance on devotees' *vittajā sevā* (donations for Shrinathji's *sevā*) is, according to Shyam Manohar Goswami, against the Pushtimarg's fundamental precepts.

The reason things have come to this, Shyam Manohar Goswami continued to explain, crossing and uncrossing his white *dhotī*-clad legs and raising his hand emphatically, is that hereditary leaders have long since forgotten that "it is their duty, just as it is the duty for the disciples they initiate into our *sampradāy*, to perform *sevā* in private homes."[39] Indeed, many members of the Vallabha Kul who have inherited authority to care for prestigious Krishna *svarūps* like Shrinathji do not perform daily *sevā* or live permanently in the (often) rural towns where these deities have been housed in *havelīs* for decades, and sometimes centuries. Nathdwara's *gosvāmīs*, for instance, live most of the year in Mumbai, traveling back to Nathdwara only on certain occasions in the seasonal ritual calendar. "If you let another man care for your wife and pay to see her, then who are you, and what is she?" Shyam Manohar Goswami said provocatively, referring to the ways in which most temples are run by community donations and paid temple *sevaks*. "If you ask me," he said, concluding our discussion on the matter, "Shriji has long since left Nathdwara and returned to Braj. An icon may remain, but Shrinathji Himself has gone." Shyam Manohar Goswami's use of the word *mūrtī* (icon) re-emphasizes his belief that Shrinathji, the essential *svarūp*, or self-manifested form of Krishna, is no longer present in the Nathdwara.[40]

[39] A *dhotī* is a single long piece of cloth tied as pants. *Dhotīs* are often considered "traditional" attire for Indian men.

[40] Shyam Manohar Goswami thus discourages pilgrimage to Nathdwara—a once sacred place "sullied" by "money-powered development." Braj, however, he considers the "pure and eternal" home of Shrinathji. See his comments on pilgrimage here: "Pilgrimage," accessed March 1, 2014, http://www.pushtimarg.net/pushti/history/pilgrimage/. Yet Braj, too, has become a site for pilgrim-oriented development, and debates over its "purity" are becoming commonplace. For more on contemporary development in Braj, see John S. Hawley, *Krishna's Playground: Vrindavan in the 21st Century* (New York: Oxford University Press, 2020). For more on Braj pilgrimage, see Haberman's *Journey Through the Twelve Forests*.

As these examples demonstrate, Shyam Manohar Goswami's positions on *sevā* are connected to how he reads and interprets the *vārtās* in conversation with Vallabhacharya's own writings. When read in this way, he suggests, the *vārtās* provide contemporary devotees with a "timeless guideline" that should ultimately lead to divine intimacy with Krishna. In light of his particular emphasis on aligning the *vārtās* with Vallabhacharya's "primary tenets"—which, we might note, is a clear *re*-emphasis of what Hariray's *Bhāvprakāś* and other commentaries also aim to accomplish—Shyam Manohar Goswami has developed an entire series of *vārtā pravacan*s that analyze the hagiographies' written prose narratives in terms of Pushtimargi *siddhānt* as it is written in Vallabhacharya's treatises. *Vārtānkī Saiddhāntik Saṅgati*, for example, is one collection of his transcribed *pravacan*s, which can be downloaded for free in PDF format from Pushtimarg.net.[41]

In addition to highlighting portions of the *vārtās* that he feels illuminate Vallabhacharya's teachings on *sevā* (e.g., the aforementioned citation from the *Bhaktivardhinī*), Shyam Manohar Goswami is insistent that "*śāstra bhagvān nī ājñā che*" (God's command is the manual).[42] In other words, while *sevā* should be informed by text-based teachings and should generally include the ritual elements understood to be essential to the care of Krishna *svarūp*s—*bhog-rāg-śṛṅgār*, or the offering of food, the singing of devotional songs, and the adornment of the deity—appropriate performances of *sevā* are ultimately dependent on the desire of each individual's Krishna *svarūp* and on each devotee's personal circumstances.[43] Connecting his analysis explicitly to Pushtimargi hagiographies, Shyam Manohar Goswami points out that some *vārtā* protagonists only offer their *svarūps fakaṭ rotlī* (plain bread), *khīr* (rice pudding), or even water alone because "this is all they had in their

[41] In addition to Vallabhacharya's writing and the *vārtās* themselves, Shyam Manohar Goswami and other Pushtimargis also refer to the Sanskrit *Sādhanadīpikā*—a "commentary" on the *sādhan*, or the "mode" or "practice" (of *sevā*)—which is attributed to Vallabhacharya's first son Gopinath (1512–1543). The *Baḍe Śikṣāpatra* is also referred to in contemporary *sevā* commentaries and manuals and considered by some to be a *sevā* guide. Like Shyam Manohar Goswami, other Pushtimargi leaders have also written their own manuals on *sevā*. For example, see: Sumit Madhukarjī Śarmā, *Śrī Vallabhīy Puṣṭi Sevā* (Ahmedabad, India: Pushtimargi Vaiṣṇav Pariṣad, 2010).

[42] Śyām Manohar Gosvāmī, *Sevā: Ṛtu, Utsav, Manorath* (Mandvi-Kacch, India: Śrī Vallabhācārya Ṭrasṭ, n.d.), 24.

[43] Gosvāmī, *Sevā: Ṛtu, Utsav, Manorath*, 52–53. According to *sevā* manuals dating back to the 17th century, the three common elements of Pushtimargi *sevā*—*bhog-rāg-śṛṅgār*—were connected to *aṣṭayām sevā* (eight traditionally appointed times for worship), and therefore to Krishna's *nitya līlā* as described in the *Bhāgavatapurāṇa*, to Pushtimargi *utsavs* (festivals; e.g., Holi), and to *ṛtū* (season). In contemporary *sevā* manuals these elements of ritual are often codified, and hereditary leaders and devotees alike continue to produce didactic, although often conflicting, accounts of how worship should be performed according to teachings of different Vallabha Kul lineages.

homes."[44] These offerings, made out of *prem-lakṣaṇ bhakti* (devotion characterized by love), are always accepted by Krishna, whereas decadent offerings made egotistically are rejected.[45] The ultimate *phal* (spiritual fruit) of *sevā* is therefore Krishna's own satisfaction—*sevā* can never be performed with any thought of reward, favors, or consolations on the part of the devotee.[46] And further, "devotion may arise anytime or anywhere, with or without the *sādhan* (ritual practice) or *nīyam* (rules) associated with the performance of *sevā*."[47] Likewise, Shyam Manohar Goswami warns, simply reading the written *vārtā*s does not mean that one has understood the narratives in terms of Vallabhacharya's *siddhānt* or the historical development of the *sampradāy*.[48] Therefore, he reminds his devotees repeatedly, ongoing, careful, and dedicated study of Pushtimargi texts in relationship to one another is required to fulfill the obligations of the modern devotee.

This consideration of Shyam Manohar Goswami's homiletics emphasizes his distinct modes of religious reading and teaching. In providing his audiences with accessible, albeit philosophically complex and sometimes controversial, guides to devotional living in the contemporary world, Shyam Manohar Goswami's style of exegesis is reminiscent of other commentarial traditions within the Pushtimarg (e.g., Hariray's *Bhāvprakāś* and the 19th- and 20th-century commentaries examined in the previous chapter). However, his particular positions on *sevā*—not to mention his way of unpacking the *vārtā*s in light of Vallabhacharya's theological treatises, historical records, real-life examples, and even modern psychological theory—stand out as unique among many of his counterparts.

[44] Gosvāmī, *Sevā: Ṛtu, Utsav, Manorath*, 21. Another popular narrative depicting this sentiment is found in the *vārtā* of Padmanabhadas, where Thakurji states his preference for the simple chickpea offerings from his impoverished devotee over the lavish food items offered by the wealthy and prideful. Verse eleven from the *Baḍe Śikṣāpatra* notes this *vārtā* as primary when learning about *sevā*. See Harirāy and Gopeśvar, *Śrī Harirāy kṛt Baḍe Śikṣāpatra: Śrī Gopeśvar kṛt Vrajbhāṣāṭikāsahit*, ed. Śrī Subodhinī Sabha (Lucknow, India: Janakprasād Agravāl, 1972).

[45] In an oft-cited *vārtā* from the *84VV*, Thakurji kicks over a plate of *bhog* because the devotee who has offered the food has been mentally preoccupied with his own observances of purity and pollution (the devotee was afraid that his dirty clothes would touch Thakurji's plate, thereby polluting the offering). The account is traditionally found in the thirty-first *vārtā* of the *84VV* (the account of Jagannath Joshi).

[46] See Paul Arney's discussion on this aspect of *sevā* as described in the *Baḍe Śikṣāpatra*: "The *Bade Shikshapatra*: A Vallabhite Guide to the Worship of Krishna's Divine Images," in *Krishna: A Sourcebook*, ed. Edwin F. Bryant (Oxford: Oxford University Press, 2007), 505–536.

[47] Gosvāmī, *Vārtānkī Saiddhāntik Saṅgati*, 221.

[48] Gosvāmī, *Vārtānkī Saiddhāntik Saṅgati*, 268.

The *Puṣṭi Siddhānt Carcā Sabhā* and Defending the Benefits of Collective, Temple *Sevā*

While many of his fellow hereditary leaders are quick to agree with Shyam Manohar Goswami that the devotee's focus should be on cultivating an intimate relationship with Krishna through emotionally attentive and philosophically informed rather than formulaic *sevā* practices, a majority of the *gosvāmīs* with whom I speak suggest that Shyam Manohar Goswami's interpretations of devotional texts vis-à-vis *havelī sevā* and the "public" use of temples are unfounded. Individuals opposing Shyam Manohar Goswami also use *pravacans* and virtual platforms as venues for reading devotional literature and showing how it supports *their* positions on *sevā* and temple management/patronage. Over the last several decades, formal scriptural debates between Shyam Manohar Goswami and his opponents have further polarized such divergences. One of these events, the *Puṣṭi Siddhānt Carcā Sabhā* ("The Pushti Doctrine Colloquium"), took place in Mumbai in 1992 and featured debates between Shyam Manohar Goswami and hereditary leader Hariray Goswami of Jamnagar, Gujarat.[49]

The 1992 Doctrine Colloquium was attended by dozens of hereditary leaders. The debate was structured in such a way that Shyam Manohar Goswami essentially questioned Hariray Goswami on a number of predetermined doctrinal points, including *sevā-prayojan* (*sevā*'s purpose) and *sevā-sthal* (*sevā*'s location). According to the transcribed publication of the event, the length of each exchange varied, as did the degree to which the two hereditary leaders disagreed on Pushtimargi doctrine and textual interpretations. One of the most contentious issues was, not surprisingly, the nature of the *sevā-sthal*. At the end of the debate Hariray Goswami had articulated that according to his readings of Pushtimargi literature, he *did* believe that a "Pushtimargi *mandir* [temple]" could exist, but that it must exist within the context of a *ghar* (home). Therefore, the "traditional" Pushtimargi *havelī*, he argued, as a home to both descendants of Vallabhacharya and also to Krishna *svarūps*, is a perfectly legitimate location for *sevā* in the ways that it is performed today. In other words, the status quo need *not* be challenged.[50]

[49] The *Carcā Sabhā* was held in a mix of Hindi and Gujarati. For the transcribed debate, see *Saṃyukt Prakāśan* ["Joint Publication"], Śyām Manohar Gosvāmī and Gosvāmī Viṭṭhalnāthjī, *Puṣṭi Siddhānt Carcā Sabhā: Saṅkṣipt Vivaraṇ* (Mumbai: Narottam Bhāṭīyā, 1992).
[50] Gosvāmī and Gosvāmī Viṭṭhalnāthjī, *Puṣṭi Siddhānt Carcā Sabhā*, 5–8.

While Hariray Goswami did not specifically articulate his position on *vittajā sevā* during the debate, other members of the Vallabha Kul who were present at the *Carcā Sabhā* or who sent in their written comments to be published along with the transcribed publication of the event spoke very clearly on the matter. Vrajraman Goswami of Mathura, for instance, stated in a letter that Shyam Manohar Goswami's use of scripture was *anargal* (incoherent; uninhibited) and in fact showed little understanding of Vallabhacharya's teachings on *sevā*, or of the *vārtās*' explanation of these teachings through narrative examples.[51] In his comments, hereditary leader Vrajraman Goswami referred to several *vārtā* episodes, which he claims show how Pushtimargi devotees of the 16th century donated their wealth to *jāher mandirs* (e.g., Purnimal Kshatri's *vārtā*, which recounts the building of Shrinathji's first temple in the region of Braj).[52] In some cases, Vrajraman Goswami noted, the *vārtās*' protagonists are in fact told directly by Vallabhacharya to *only* perform *sevā* through financial donation (e.g., Govinddas Bhalla's *vārtā*).[53] The *vārtā* of Vasudevdas Chakda of the *84VV*, he also pointed out, includes both a narrative about how to avoid misusing Shrinathji's wealth (e.g., a warning not to trade the deity's belongings for food supplies that would be used to feed devotees), and also a clear example of how devotees who had pure devotional sentiments were praised for using worldly gains in the service of Shrinathji *and* of other *svarūps*.[54] Just as with any type of *sevā*—mental or physical—Vrajraman Goswami suggested, the devotee should have pure devotional sentiments when offering material wealth to support the performance of *havelī sevā*.[55] "How," Goswami Vrajraman writes, "could Shrinathji's *havelī*, or any *havelī* for that matter, have been maintained without the [donated] *sāmagrī* (ritual materials) of Vaishnavas?"[56]

[51] Yogeśkumār Gosvāmī, ed., *Puṣṭi Siddhānt Carcā Sabhā: Vistṛt Vivaraṇ* (Mumbai: Saṃvād Sthāpak Maṇḍal, 1992), 14–16.

[52] This is normally the twenty-fourth account in the *84VV*. See D. Parīkh, ed., *Caurāsī Vaiṣṇavan kī Vārtā*, 161–165.

[53] This is typically the eleventh account in the *84VV*. See D. Parīkh, ed., *Caurāsī Vaiṣṇavan kī Vārtā*, 105–110.

[54] Gosvāmī, *Puṣṭi Siddhānt Carcā Sabhā: Vistṛt Vivaraṇ*, 17.

[55] Gopeshvar's commentary on Hariray's ninth and tenth verses of the *Śikṣāpatra* addresses this: "The money that is put to use in *sevā* should be considered *puṣṭi*, whereas money outlaid on the *karma mārg*—on such things as gifts [to Brahmins or mendicants], fire sacrifices, or offerings to the ancestors—should be considered *maryādā*. However, if money is spent on luxury items, it is stolen, or it goes in a tax or a fine, it should be deemed *āsurī*" [and therefore not be used in *sevā*] (Arney, "The Bade Shikshapatra," 522).

[56] Gosvāmī, *Puṣṭi Siddhānt Carcā Sabhā: Vistṛt Vivaraṇ*, 17. *Sāmagrī* in the context of ritual worship (not only specific to the Pushtimarg) is a technical term referring to the food, clothing, and ornaments offered to a Krishna *svarūp* during *sevā*.

Shyam Manohar Goswami consistently argues that Pushtimargi devotional literature reveals a shift in the practice of community contributions to Shrinathji's *sevā* after the death of Vitthalnath. In contrast, most hereditary leaders and devotees vehemently defend the same positions that Vrajraman Goswami and Hariray Goswami expressed as part of the *Carcā Sabhā* and therefore oppose any move to halt construction in Nathdwara or to significantly alter current forms of temple administration and *sevā* (at Shrinathji's *havelī* or elsewhere). Moreover, Shyam Manohar Goswami's detractors assert that Pushtimargi *havelī*s not only have always functioned as homes for both Krishna deities and their Vallabha Kul caretakers, but also as places where devotees come to participate collectively in *sevā* of *havelī svarūp*s, and to meet with fellow devotees and gurus who offer advice on the performance of domestic worship, often via *vārtā*-specific *pravacan* or *satsaṅg*. Although all larger temples, both new and old, have hired *sevak*s to perform certain temple rituals, even the smallest of *havelī*s rely on the fully voluntary services of devotees—not only in the form of financial offerings, but also in the form of specific *sevā* ritual preparations. While direct physical access to a temple *svarūp* and the deity's cooked food is commonly restricted to either hereditary leaders or to initiated and specially trained Brahmin *sevak*s, all devotees who have received Pushtimargi initiation are typically eligible to participate in the preparation of uncooked food items.[57] This can include measuring rice and lentils, cutting up fruits and vegetables, or milking cows and straining the milk.[58] All of these acts of *sevā* go toward the preparation of a temple *svarūp*'s daily meals, which in turn are consumed as *mahāprasād* (the consecrated food offering) by whoever cares for the deity, including hereditary leaders and their families, temple *sevak*s and their families, and sometimes devotees (namely, on special occasions, such as the celebration of Krishna's birthday).[59]

[57] For more on ritual food preparation, see Paul M. Toomey, "Food from the Mouth of Krishna: Socio-Religious Aspects of Sacred Food in Two Krishnaite Sects," in *Food Society, and Culture: Aspects in South Asian Food Systems*, ed. R.S. Khare and M.S.A. Rao (Durham, NC: Carolina Academic, 1986); Paul M. Toomey, "Krishna's Consuming Passions: Food as Metaphor and Metonym for Emotion at Mount Govardhan," in *Divine Passions: The Social Construction of Emotion in India*, ed. Owen M. Lynch (Berkeley: University of California Press, 1990); and Paul M. Toomey, "Mountain of Food, Mountain of Love: Ritual Inversion in the Annakuta Feast at Mount Govardhan," in *The Eternal Food: Gastronomic Ideas and Experiences of Hindus and Buddhists*, ed. R.S. Khare (Albany: State University of New York Press, 1992).

[58] This is the case in temples that have an onsite *gauśāḷā* (dairy), which many larger and more traditionally designed temples do.

[59] Select items from *mahāprasād*, such as pieces of fruit, are distributed on a daily basis to crowds of devotees who come to certain *havelī*s (e.g., the Goswami Haveli in Ahmedabad's old city), while more substantial consecrated food offerings, such as cooked sweet items, can be obtained in a "take-away"

Krishna *svarūps* in Pushtimargi homes and temples are also traditionally offered fresh *pān* (betel leaf) and flower garlands. Devotees often name the collective preparation of food, *pān*, and garlands as among the most fulfilling ways in which they participate in collective *sevā*, and, as many community members point out to me in response to my questions about Shyam Manohar Goswami's teachings, such activities are "absolutely permitted in our *sampradāy* because you can read about this *sevā* among those great Vaishnavas [in the *84VV* and *252VV*]." This type of collective *sevā* is particularly significant for older devotees who are either retired from professional careers or have few familial and domestic duties. As Manjula, an elderly woman in Ahmedabad told me, "I have been coming daily at four o'clock in the afternoon to the Goswami Haveli to string flower garlands for Shri Natvarlalji [one of the Krishna *svarūps* housed at the temple] for the past thirty-five years. This is my greatest *sevā*." Manjula also performs daily *sevā* for a Krishna *svarūp* in her home but asserts that this practice can only be enhanced, not inhibited, by participating in community *sevā* practices in her local temple. Manjula, who attends weekly *vārtā satsaṅgs* at the Goswami Haveli (see more on this in the following chapter), explained that both the "texts themselves" as well as hereditary leaders' interpretations of the hagiographies support her ritual practices at the temple: "*vārtājī* shows these very things [collective *sevā*]! There are so many lessons about how it is very good to be in the company of other Vaishnavas. Those righteous ones [the *vārtā* protagonists] are always stringing flower garlands together and speaking of God," she explained. Shyam Manohar Goswami's detractors argue that if hereditary leaders attempt to restrict this kind of community *sevā* in so-called public *havelīs* and prohibit the renovation of such spaces according to the changing expectations of contemporary devotees, the community would not only be denying an essential aspect of its unique past and present but would also be less likely to have a vibrant future.

The question of the Pushtimarg's "vibrancy" (an English word devotees use often) and its future, in addition to concerns with Krishna's general comfort through *sevā* practices, undergirds my interlocutors' positions on all sides of *havelī sevā* and renovation debates. Physical temple spaces are at the heart of these debates not only because temples are homes for Krishna *svarūps*, but also, as devotees like Manjula discussed, because they are centers

box by paying a small donation. For a useful article on *prasād* in general, see Andrea Marion Pinkney, "*Prasāda*," in *Brill Encyclopedia of Hinduism*, ed. Knut A. Jacobsen, 103–111. (Leiden: Brill, 2014).

for community growth and fellowship. According to Bhavesh Shukla, a head administrator at a recently built temple in Ahmedabad, new or newly renovated temples provide spaces that are appealing to devotees, particularly to youth. New temples, for instance, are more hygienic than older *havelīs* in their preparation of the deities' *bhog* and the distribution of *prasād*, he told me, reflecting a growing community concern, particularly during major festivals (such as Annakut) when large amounts of food are prepared and offered to *svarūps*. Newer temples also have more space for devotees to come together for *darśan*, as well as facilities that accommodate large community gatherings and youth and women's programs. Because of this, Bhavesh noted, "our newly built temples are similar to Swaminarayan temples," referring to the temples of one of the most visible and rapidly growing forms of transnational Hinduism, which also has roots in Gujarat. "And because of this [similarity]," Bhavesh continued, "Pushtimargi Vaishnavas prefer to come to new temples. See for yourself," he continued, "you will only find older folks at those older *havelīs*, while here you will find families and men and women of all ages coming together in one place."[60]

Bhavesh's reference to Swaminarayan temples is particularly significant because it reflects a widely voiced concern that the Gujarat-based Swaminarayan community, particularly the branch known as the "Bochasanwasi Shri Akshar Purushottam Swaminarayan Sanstha" (BAPS), is "more vibrant" than the Pushtimarg because it is better at attracting youth and garnering community support by way of monetary donations and volunteer work. The reason Pushtimargis give for this is that BAPS temples, which have continued to grow in number in India and abroad since the early 20th century, are "extremely inviting." When devotees clarify what is meant by "inviting," they note that BAPS temples not only have space for a significant number of devotees to take *darśan* of temple deities but are also fully equipped with facilities such as *pravacan* halls, spaces for large-scale festivals and cultural programs, libraries, guest houses, and, often, museum-like exhibitions.[61] Indeed, anthropologist Hanna Kim's conversation partners in BAPS confirm that the dynamic nature of BAPS temples has a direct impact

[60] In my own experience, these distinctions are not always clear. That is, families, including children and youth, do seem to visit older temples.

[61] According to Hanna Kim, BAPS achieved Guinness World Records in 2007 for having the largest number of temples worldwide—some 713 at the end of 2007—and for having the world's largest "comprehensive Hindu Temple" (Hanna Kim, "A Fine Balance: Adaptation and Accommodation in the Swaminarayan Sanstha," in *Gujarati Communities Across the Globe: Memory, Identity and Continuity*, ed. S. Mawani and A. Mukadam [London: Trentham Books, 2012], 147).

on youth engagement. "Young *satsangis*," Kim writes, "are in unanimous agreement that the temple and temple related activities have played a significant role in helping them to embrace 'Swaminarayan religion' and to speak with confidence about 'my religion.' "[62]

Kim also suggests that BAPS has successfully grown as a community because its leaders consistently realize the need to "address the shifting particularities of its membership within a given social and political context, within the dimensions of gender, age, variations in degree of *satsaṅg* commitment, and even language preferences."[63] While the Pushtimargi community has similarly managed to address shifting particularities of its membership, often through innovative practices of religious teaching (e.g., online streaming of *pravacans*), the lack of fully centralized authority (there are multiple branches of hereditary leaders) and the related tensions over the legitimacy of temple spaces are reasons that devotees like Bhavesh express anxiety about the future of the tradition, especially when compared with BAPS.[64] According to Bhavesh, the best way to ensure that Pushtimargis remain active in the community is by keeping temples well funded and equipped with facilities that allow for a variety of activities and collective worship. If movements—what some call "fundamentalist" movements—like the one led by Shyam Manohar Goswami take hold, he fears, youth will lose interest not only in *sevā*, but also in the tradition altogether. Although Shyam Manohar Goswami has countered this view of his "movement"—in part by establishing his own non-temple-based *sansthāns* (institutes) and keeping his teachings accessible through a strong online presence—newly built Pushtimargi temples, which continue to grow in number and size, remain far more popular than such institutes and indeed than many older, unrenovated *havelīs*.[65]

[62] Hanna Kim, "Public Engagement and Personal Desires: BAPS Swaminarayan Temples and Their Contribution to the Discourses on Religion," *International Journal of Hindu Studies*, 13 (2010): 377.

[63] Kim, "A Fine Balance," 154.

[64] E. Allen Richardson discusses how the development of Pushtimargi temples in the United States must also be distinguished from parallel developments among BAPS and other Hindu communities (e.g., ISKCON) because (at least in part) of the Pushtimarg's lack of centralized authority. See E. Allen Richardson, *Seeing Krishna in America: The Hindu Bhakti Tradition of Vallabhacharya in India and Its Movement to the West* (Jefferson, NC: McFarland, 2014), 153–154, 160–165.

[65] Shyam Manohar Goswami's founding of the Vallabhacharya Vidyapith in Halol, Gujarat, is one example of such an institute. Funding for the Vallabhacharya Vidyapith comes through the "Vallabhacharya Trust," a trust run like any other, but that only supports *non*-temple-related activities, such as educational institutions, youth programs, and the preservation and publication of texts. *Havelī*/temple trusts became popular in the 19th century, in part because so-called reformers within the Pushtimargi community wished to manage places of worship independent from hereditary leaders. Today such temple trusts are generally managed by both nonhereditary devotees and hereditary leaders who work together to run temple programs (as in Nathdwara).

Despite the divergent perspectives on temple renovations and *sevā* that I have highlighted here, Pushtimargis seem to consistently agree that it is vital to cultivate environments in which all members of the community—including young people, and more generally people with commitments to the conveniences of contemporary, affluent lifestyles—may find their tradition, including devotional literature itself, accessible, accommodating, and inclusive. By arguing that Pushtimargis should "return" to what he sees as a scripturally informed devotional lifestyle, Shyam Manohar Goswami is *not*, he emphasizes, suggesting that devotees relinquish the "comforts of modern living." As one of his followers suggested, "you can still read properly all of the *granth*s and live a modern lifestyle."[66] In other words, the so-called conveniences of modern life themselves are not the issue for Shyam Manohar Goswami *or* for those who fall on the opposing side of Pusthimargi temple and *sevā* debates. Rather, the root of the perceived "problem" for all seems to be tied to practices of reading and interpretation themselves. The same devotional texts, including the *vārtā*s, engender various modes of public reading that in turn yield distinct interpretations of "tradition" in relationship to the ever-shifting realities of the Pushtimargi community.

Public Reading in the Pushtimarg's Performative Canon

This chapter has focused on how widely debated controversies in the contemporary Pushtimargi community are taken up formally by specific reader-exegetes, namely, through *pravacan*s, and more informally on virtual spaces like Facebook. Although never streamed live or featured on social media platforms, the 1992 *Puṣṭi Siddhānt Carcā Sabhā*—during which hereditary leaders formally squared off about the nature of Pushtimargi text-based teachings in relationship to modern *sevā* practices—directly corresponds to the other types of reading discussed in this chapter. Both virtually staged or accessed *pravacan*s and debates, as well as those that are accessed primarily

[66] Shyam Manohar Goswami's own use of the phrase "modern lifestyle" refers to many ways of contemporary living, including the way in which many devotees work long hours outside of the home and travel for leisure and to visit family in India and abroad. As discussed in Chapters 4 and 5, some devotees feel that it is difficult to balance their occupational and familial lives with what is ideally the round-the-clock *sevā* for Krishna *svarūp*s. In several oral and written commentaries and on the website, Pushtimarg.net, Shyam Manohar Goswami writes about what he sees to be the misguided assumption that a "modern lifestyle" cannot accommodate loving *sevā*. See, for example, "Pushti Sahitya Seva," accessed August 29, 2020, https://pushtimarg.net/seva/.

in person, are part of a common and distinct facet of the Pushtimarg's performative canon. All of these modes of "public reading" rely on reciting aloud or citing from and carefully unpacking selected excerpts of devotional literature to support individual exegetes' positions on contemporary issues. Therefore, exegetes and more casual devotee-readers who read "publicly"—before virtual and in-person audiences—are engaging with texts in ways that are both analytically and performatively distinct. In some ways these modes of reading are well established, growing out of the written textual traditions themselves. Yet they are also innovative. For instance, in his *pravacan*s, Shyam Manohar Goswami analyzes the *vārtā*s in novel ways by discussing them in light of contemporary media (e.g., television programming) but also maintains the well-established practice of authenticating the hagiographies by centering Vallabhacharya's *vacanāmṛt* as it appears embedded in the written *vārtā*s. Likewise, devotee-blogger Abha Shahra Shyama of Mumbai innovates the common practice of reporting Krishna's direct speech by blogging about it in her "live vaartas" to support her claims that Shrinathji's Nathdwara *havelī* should not be renovated.

In considering public reading as part of the Pushtimarg's performative canon, it becomes clear that what is ultimately at stake for hereditary leaders and devotees is how these modes of reading are used to navigate community identity, ritual practice, and visions for the future. This envisioning of the future, and of the present, has significant material consequences for the physical landscape of the tradition: despite how different Pushtimargis feel about the result of temple renovations and construction, places of worship are structurally in flux. As new types of physical spaces are opened up, they accommodate some and clearly work to alienate others. Alongside structural changes in temples, virtual spaces, too, are (re)constructed, allowing Pushtimargis the world over to participate in community conversations and devotional practices in new ways. Though not discussed in this chapter, social media spaces have also made *more* "public" so-called *jāher mandir*s, inviting viewers, regardless of their status as initiated devotees, to engage affectively through *darśan* with Pushtimargi Krishna *svarūp*s (I have only seen this practiced at newly constructed temples). On all sides of the *havelī* renovation and *sevā* debates Pushtimargis seem to commonly acknowledge that these physical and structural changes to places of worship have significant consequences for Krishna—himself and in relationship to his devotees. Thus, while Krishna's well-being, alongside that of his caretakers, remains primary in negotiations over text-based precept and practice, devotional narratives, and the deity himself, are pulled into a "worldly" register as devotees navigate the ever-shifting landscape of their tradition.

As we turn now from public readings as discussed in this chapter to more intimate spaces of community reading and dialogue, which focus more on individuals' daily lives as Krishna's caretakers, we are reminded of the radical plurality of sectarian discourse, even in scripturally specific settings.

4

Community Reading

Learning Affective Piety

The heavy rains have slowed things down considerably across Ahmedabad on this August monsoon evening in 2011. In the narrow lanes of Kalupur, a densely populated district in the old walled city, the showers have caused flash flooding, and everything has come to a standstill. At one of Kalupur's primary Hindu temples, the Goswami Haveli, nearly a hundred devotees have arrived to take *darśan*—that is, to see and be seen by Shri Natvarlalji, the primary Krishna *svarūp* housed there. The large wooden doors of the temple remain closed, as preparations for *darśan* are still underway, and everyone huddles in the covered areas outside the old stone building to wait, watching the rain. "Just look at it come down," a woman named Kishori says, as she smiles and claps her hands, letting out a whoop of joy. "The monsoons bring so much joy." When the doors finally open, signaled by the ringing of a bell, those gathered rush inside, sliding on the wet marble floors as they make their way to the front of the red gate that separates the deity from the crowd of devotees. One of the temple's hereditary leaders, Tilak Goswami, flings open the curtain to reveal the image of Shri Natvarlalji.[1] A mere five inches in height, the large-eyed Krishna deity wears a turquoise outfit, fashioned by devotees, and matching crown, and is seated on a large human-sized swing decorated in turquoise, bead-encrusted cloth. Tilak Goswami wears a turquoise sash over his white garments. His wife, mother, and two young sons, who have joined him to serve Shri Natvarlalji ceremoniously, are also clad in the color. The two boys dart about as their parents and grandmother perform the service by gently rocking the deity on the swing and offering him flowers and a variety of food items—sweets, finely chopped pieces of fruit, and saffron milk—all served in miniature silver bowls. The women's turquoise saris

[1] Tilak Goswami also goes by Tilak Bava and more formally by Madhusudanlal Goswami. His father Vrajnath Maharaj currently presides over the Goswami Haveli—a role that Tilak Goswami, and his eldest son after him, will inherit.

Religious Reading and Everyday Lives in Devotional Hinduism. Emilia Bachrach, Oxford University Press. © Oxford University Press 2022. DOI: 10.1093/oso/9780197648599.003.0005

shine with silver embroidery. The devotees, also wearing various shades of blue and green to match the deity and his caretakers, feast their eyes on the scene. A small group of men and women sit to the side of the crowd on the marble floor, performing *kīrtan* that corresponds to the occasion, with harmonium and symbols as accompaniment. The songs' Braj Bhasha lyrics, many composed several centuries ago, tell of Lord Krishna's divine pastimes during the monsoons, when he teased, charmed, and romanced the beautiful cowherd maidens of his earthly home in the bucolic region of Braj. On this day, however, the sound of the rain nearly drowns out the voices, drums, and harmonium. Everything is just rain and turquoise.

When the fifteen-minute *darśan* period has ended, Tilak Goswami and his family close the curtain, putting Natvarlalji to sleep for the night. They then exit the temple and seat themselves in the adjacent meeting hall. Just as he has done most Sunday evenings for over a decade, Tilak Goswami will lead his congregation in a community reading of *Vārtā Sāhitya*. For many hereditary leaders like Tilak Goswami, reading the *vārtā*s means reading hagiographic accounts not only of one's own ancestors and their disciples, but also of their *havelī svarūp*s, the "self-manifested forms" of Krishna like Shri Natvarlalji and Shrinathji, who reside in many long-standing temples across northwest India. Perching himself on a decorated cushioned chair in front of those gathered, Tilak Goswami begins to read. The atmosphere is celebratory, yet relaxed. Many devotees read along with their own copies of the text. Some of those gathered chime in to ask questions and to discuss and debate the meaning of the mutually cherished stories. Others lean against the wall and close their eyes, while still others run after young children, who race in and out of the temple, tracking in mud and screeching with delight. The reading and discussion go on for several hours—far longer than usual, due to the heavy rain. When Tilak Goswami finally closes the large yellow and red book from which he has been reading, wrapping it carefully in gold-colored cloth, it is nearly midnight. Members of the congregation put away their own copies of the text and conclude the gathering in a collective prayer, honoring each other as fellow devotees, the figures about whom they have just read, their gurus, and Krishna. Auto rickshaws are finally running again, and so people say departing farewells—"*Jāī Shri Krishna*! Hail to Lord Krishna!"—and head home, ending their turquoise monsoon evening.

What I have described here is somewhat distinct to my observations of *vārtā* readings at the Goswami Haveli, but the devotional atmosphere and collective learning that I witnessed in this Kalupur temple are familiar to many types of gatherings across Ahmedabad city in which Pushtimargis assemble to read and discuss the hagiographies. This chapter draws on an ethnographic archive collected between 2010 and 2017 to analyze how devotees use these contexts of community reading to cultivate Pushtimarg-specific, though highly personalized, modes of affective piety and, more broadly, to learn how to navigate between being devotional caretakers of Krishna on the one hand, and fulfilling various roles in social, but particularly familial, contexts on the other. As with the written commentaries and on- and off-line modes of "public reading" considered in Chapters 2 and 3, discussions of devotional literature during these gatherings may address matters of community-wide concern, such as propriety in *havelī sevā* and temple management. More frequently, however, these discussions attend to the more intimate and private negotiations of individual devotees' everyday lives and devotional practices: how to live with family members who do not follow the Pushtimarg, what kinds of clothing to wear during home *sevā*, or what kinds of food to prepare for one's household Krishna *svarūp*. The learning that takes place during these gatherings therefore includes not only learning how to read and interpret devotional literature in the first place, but also learning how to apply Pushtimargi precepts attended to in the *vārtā*s to the everyday circumstances of individuals' lives. Although there are various public forums and written text-based guides for interpreting Pushtimargi literature with respect to performing *sevā*, such as those discussed in Chapters 2 and 3, community readings like those I describe at the Goswami Haveli continue to be the primary settings in which devotees feel that devotional precepts and practices can be learned and nurtured.

Although community readings are somewhat idiosyncratic within and across different gatherings, what occurs in these spaces is also ritualized: each gathering that I observed over a seven-year period unfolded according to certain shared patterns of behavior and with many shared expectations. For example, most gatherings regularly begin and end with a common set of collectively recited prayers or songs. However, as *rituals* of reading whose participants are focused on cultivating devotion and religious learning, these gatherings stand out. Community readings are not, to use Clifford Geertz's notorious phrase, a "model of and for something other than itself."[2] These

[2] Anna M. Gade, "Taste, Talent, and the Problem of Internalization: A Qur'ānic Study in Religious Musicality from Southeast Asia," *History of Religions* 41, no. 4 (2002): 342. Gade is, in part, drawing here on Clifford Geertz's discussion of ritual (specific to recitations of the Qur'an and Arabic aesthetics) in "Art as a Cultural System," in *Local Knowledge: Further Essays in Interpretive Anthropology* (New York: Basic Books, 1983), 94–120, reprinted from *Modern Language Notes* 91 (1976): 1473–1499.

gatherings are spaces in which the knowledge gained is meant to deepen and change over time and likewise to be questioned in light of one's changing life circumstances. Studies of ritual learning, however, have tended to focus on the knowledge gained in a ritual setting as a "one-time affair."[3] That is, once the ritual has been successfully completed, it is understood to have changed "knowledge" into "action." While devotees do certainly take knowledge gained in the contexts of community reading into various activities (e.g., a devotee may learn to perform Krishna's *sevā* in new ways), readers of the *vārtā*s understand the devotional stories to promote learning that is emergent, namely, toward the ever-changing and indeed challenging process of caring for Krishna as a divine being.

As we saw in Chapter 3 and will again see repeatedly in this and in the following chapter, *vārtā* protagonists become potentially imitable figures who "teach" contemporary readers how to nourish devotional and social relationships through their example. In this way, Pushtimargis' engagement with the *vārtā*s reflects what other scholars working on the contemporary reception of hagiographic texts have noted about their interlocutors. As Karen Ruffle writes in her study of Shiʿi women in Hyderabad, Shiʿism is taught (and Shi'i are therefore socialized) through hagiographies. Hagiography, she writes, "plays a vital role in teaching important religious lessons. Hagiography is a dynamic genre of religious literature that makes accessible to everyday Shi'a traditions of theology and law."[4] The *vārtā*s also present today's readers with avenues for challenging devotional paradigms of the past and for weaving their own contemporary experiences into the narration of their early modern counterparts' life stories. Paul Ricoeur speaks to this phenomenon when he describes how readers naturally "appropriate" texts as they seek to interpret and make sense of them: "interpretation brings together, equalizes, renders contemporary and similar, thus genuinely making one's own what was initially alien."[5] In the case of Pushtimargis' readings of *Vārtā Sāhitya*, the process of "making one's own" extends beyond the act of reading and identifying with the narratives and their protagonists to include the process of learning intimacy with Krishna who, through ritual practice and with divine grace, slowly reveals his presence to those who care for him. In this way, as my

[3] Gade, *Perfection Makes Perfect*, 122.

[4] Karen G. Ruffle, *Gender, Sainthood, and Everyday Practice in South Asian Shiʿism* (Chapel Hill: University of North Carolina Press, 2011), 4.

[5] Paul Ricoeur, *From Text to Action: Essays in Hermeneutics II*, translated by Kathleen Blamey and John B. Thompson (Evanston, IL: Northwestern University Press, 1986), 119.

conversation partners repeatedly explained, Thakurji becomes "a member of the family." Therefore, distinct from the goals of reading to historicize or to debate matters of sectarian propriety around more public issues like the use of temples, the goals of community reading are inherently linked to devotees' cultivation of *bhāv*—a difficult-to-translate term that often means something akin to "devotional sentiments" and "affective piety"—and therefore to the ways in which Krishna becomes "a constant feature of the heart-mind."[6] In this way, *Vārtā Sāhitya*, as a body of devotional literature, is not merely appropriated by readers who make the texts "their own" by identifying the "possible" from imitable protagonists. Instead, reading the narratives also projects and donates "the infinite power of possibility itself, apart from any effort [the reader] might make to project a possibility" of their own.[7] As understood by Pushtimargi readers, the "infinite power of possibility" that hovers, always present, above a reader's own efforts—efforts to cultivate devotion and to learn—is Krishna himself, whose grace-bestowing divinity resonates in the pages of devotional books and among those who read them.

Community Reading as *Satsaṅg*

> *puṣṭimārgīy janoṁ ke liye vārtājī kā mahatva* [*sic*]
> *dainik satsaṅg ke rūp meṁ sarvopari rahā hai.*
> For Pushtimargi folks, the importance of our revered *vārtā*s has remained paramount in the form of daily *satsaṅg*.[8]
>
> —Goswami Rukmini Bahuji, 2009

Gatherings in which community readings of the *vārtā*s are featured are most commonly referred to as *satsaṅg*s.[9] The term itself—which I gloss as

[6] While "devotional sentiments" is a fairly common gloss for the word *bhāv*, the term carries various meanings in different text-based and conversational contexts. In many contexts *bhāv* is used by Pushtimargis to describe not only the sentiments of *bhakti* (loving devotion), but also the emotional and social ways of being in relationships with fellow devotees and Krishna. People often describe other devotees in terms of the *quality* of their *bhāv* (good, bad, pure, etc.), which refers specifically to their piety vis-à-vis ritual behavior and their general affect within Pushtimargi and even broader social spaces.

[7] David E. Klemm, "Ricoeur, Theology, and the Rhetoric of Overturning," *Literature and Theology* 3, no. 3 (1989): 278.

[8] Gosvāmī Rukmiṇī Bahūjī, "Śubhāśīrvād," in *Do Sau Bāvan Vaiṣṇavan kī Vārtā* (*Tīn Janma kī Līlā Bhāvnā Vālī*): *Dvitīya Bhāg*, ed. Dvārkādās Parīkh (Indore, India: Vaiṣṇav Mitra Maṇḍal, 2009), 3.

[9] Another term used along with *satsaṅg* is *bhagavadvārtā* (godly discourse). The term *bhagavadvārtā*, like the term *kathā*, can also refer to the *Bhāgavatapurāṇa*, both to the text itself

"gathering of the faithful"—is used repeatedly in written *vārtā* narratives as well as in other Pushtimargi texts, including Vallabhacharya's *Bhaktivardhinī* treatise.[10] Devotees experience intense joy from participating in such *satsaṅg*, *vārtā* narratives tell us, and both the guru and Krishna himself gain deep satisfaction from the meeting of fellow devotees.[11] Moreover, throughout *vārtā* narratives we see images of *satsaṅg*—of community singing, reading, and discussion—as a practice that both confirms and recreates religious commitments. As we recall from Chapter 1, Hariray opens his *Bhāvprakāś* in the *84VV* by telling his readers to receive the narratives in the context of "discussion" among and about fellow Vaishnavas. As Hariray writes, recounting a setting in which Gokulnath is orally recounting the stories of Vallabhacharya's disciples, "Today the fruits of my recitation [of Vallabhacharya's *Subodhinī*] will be known through a discussion of the eighty-four Vaishnavas."[12] Discourse on the *84VV*'s protagonists is here understood to be supreme. Or, as one modern commentator suggests in a "compilation of Pushti Truths" to be "emulated and venerated" by *vārtā* readers, "from *satsaṅg* even the dried up heart becomes moist [with devotion]."[13]

"Moistening the heart" with devotion and thereby readying the devotee to deepen their connection to Krishna through *sevā* is a common, underlying goal of Pushtimargi *satsaṅg*, but it is also more broadly connected to the nine traditionally recognized ways in which to advance along the path of Vaishnava *bhakti*. These nine modes of *bhakti* are famously outlined in the *Bhāgavatapurāṇa* and are regularly recalled by contemporary devotees as follows: (1) *śravaṇa* or "listening" to the narratives of Krishna, (2) *kīrtana* "singing the praises" of Krishna, (3) *smaraṇa* "remembering" or focusing the mind on Krishna, (4) *pāda-sevana* or ritual "service," (5) *arcana* "worship" of Krishna's form, (6) *vandana* "praising" Krishna, (7) *dāsya* or approaching Krishna with an attitude of "servitude," (8) *sakhya* or approaching Krishna with an attitude of divine "companionship," and (9) *ātma-nivedana* or

and to discussion or exegesis of it. Though addressing a very different time period and social context, David F. Pocock also addresses Pushtimargi *satsaṅg* in his ethnographic study, *Mind, Body, and Wealth: A Study of Belief and Practice in an Indian Village* (Oxford: Basil Blackwell, 1973).

[10] Redington, *The Grace of Lord Krishna*, 127 (verses 7b–8).

[11] For example, see the *vārtā* of Santdas Chopra, traditionally the seventy-sixth *vārtā* in the *Caurāsī Vaiṣṇavan kī Vārtā*.

[12] D. Parīkh, *Caurāsī Vaiṣṇavan kī Vārtā*, 1–2.

[13] Dvārkādās Parīkh, "Granth meṁ Prāpt Puṣṭi ke Anukāraṇīy aur Mānanīy Tathyoṁ kā Saṃkalan," in D. Parīkh, *Caurāsī Vaiṣṇavan kī Vārtā*, 37. The Hindi terms I have translated as "emulated" and "venerated" are *anukāraṇīy* and *mānanīy*.

"self-surrender."[14] Pushtimargi *satsaṅg* especially incorporates the first three of these nine modes (*śravaṇa*, *kīrtana*, and *smaraṇa*), which are enacted through singing devotional songs and reading and discussing devotional literature, including *Vārtā Sāhitya*.[15]

All of the *satsaṅg* gatherings that I observed over the course of seven years in Ahmedabad took place in people's private homes or in temple spaces. While these two types of spaces do not attract mutually exclusive demographics, temple and home-based *satsaṅg*s are often oriented in distinct ways. Gatherings in temples, for instance, are frequently led by male hereditary leaders like Tilak Goswami and tend to be quite large, ranging from twenty-five to over one hundred participants. Those led by *beṭījī*s or *bahūjī*s (male hereditary leaders' daughters or wives, respectively), whether in temples or in private homes, are smaller, ranging from ten to thirty devotees. There are exceptions to this norm, however, especially in the case of the now late female leader Goswami Indirabetiji (d. 2016) and a small number of other *beṭījī*s and *bahūjī*s who have recently taken her lead in appearing publicly as authoritative exegetes who attract large crowds. *Satsaṅg*s led by community members who are not hereditary leaders vary in size, with an average of ten participants. Some community-led *satsaṅg*s convene in temple spaces, such as Ahmedabad's popular Vallabh Sadan temple, which has a robust library and other easily accessible amenities for textual learning. More commonly, though, community-led gatherings take place in devotees' private homes.

Community *satsaṅg* leaders are often avid readers of Pushtimargi literature who are deemed by fellow devotees and hereditary leaders alike to be role models in the practice of *sevā*. Such devotees, like Dr. Yojana Mahajan, a doctor of obstetrics and gynecology, may be inspired to initiate a *satsaṅg* of their own accord.[16] Dr. Mahajan, for instance, was inspired to begin hosting her *satsaṅg* in 2000 after she was the attending doctor at the birth of her

[14] *Bhāgavatapurāṇa*: 7.5.23–24.

[15] The terms *kīrtan maṇḍaḷ* or *maṇḍaḷī* (circle; assembly) are used to refer to gatherings that emphasize devotional singing over reading. Even in the case of gatherings that focus specifically on the *vārtā*s, devotional songs are typically performed as a way to formally commence or conclude readings and discussion.

[16] As previously stated, all of the people I discuss in this book (with the exception of certain public figures and published authors) are given pseudonyms. I had previously given Dr. Mahajan a different pseudonym (Kashmira Sharma) in this published article: Emilia Bachrach, "Religious Reading and Everyday Lives," in *Text and Tradition in Early Modern India*, ed. Tyler A. Williams et al. (New Delhi: Oxford University Press), 413–433. My reasons for changing this pseudonym here are two-fold: first, the surname Mahajan is a closer match vis-à-vis caste and community affiliation for this person than is Sharma; second, after first assigning the name Kashmira I became acquainted with two people by this name, who do not appear in my book, and wish to avoid any confusion.

guru and his wife's son. Alternatively, a well-respected and knowledgeable community member may be asked by their fellow devotees or by hereditary leaders to initiate a *satsaṅg*. In either case, the reason for starting a *satsaṅg* often relates to the desire or request to give selflessly to the community and to educate fellow Vaishnavas as an act of *sevā*. To lovingly serve fellow devotees, the *vārtā*s themselves tell us, can be just as important as the *sevā* of Krishna. Several devotees with whom I spoke told me that they had been given specific instruction by their gurus or by Krishna himself to initiate a *satsaṅg*. As we saw in Chapter 1 with Shalini Goswami Bahuji, it is also common for hereditary leaders to encourage recent initiates, or *brahmasambandhī*s, to join *satsaṅg*s as a way to learn about *siddhānt* and *sevā*.[17]

During my time in Ahmedabad I was never aware of any sense of explicit competition, in terms of attendance or even function, between gatherings led by community members and those led by their hereditary leader counterparts. While some devotees openly disagree with the teachings of their gurus, most of the people I speak with maintain that community members' commentary on the *vārtā*s could never contend with the *vacanāmṛt* or *divyā vāṇī* (divine words) of Vallabhacharya's descendants. Hereditary leaders' exegesis is thus understood by many to be inherently beneficial to listen to, but also to be more "correct" than the commentary offered by fellow devotees. This said, other devotees explicitly express preference for gatherings led by and for devotees because of the absence of formal sectarian authority. Indeed, occasionally devotees' discussions during *satsaṅg* relate to the behaviors and qualities (positive or negative) of hereditary leaders themselves. Moreover, both types of *satsaṅg*s may be seen as serving different purposes. As one woman named Kamala told me,

> Of course, I go to the temple for *vacanāmṛt*, too. Bava [referring to a hereditary leader] has so much knowledge, all [members of the] Vallabha Kul are very intelligent.[18] But it's such a big crowd and I sit in the back with my son, he comes with me, and we can't hear the *vacanāmṛt* well. We don't ask our questions there in front of everyone. But I am fortunate to hear Bava, aren't I? I should go there. I am so fortunate. In Gitaben's *satsaṅg* I also learn so

[17] Likewise, as discussed in Chapter 1, many of the hereditary leaders and senior devotees with whom I have conversations suggested that I join *satsaṅg* gatherings as a way to learn about the Pushtimarg and about *Vārtā Sāhitya* specifically.

[18] Bava (*bāvā* or *bābā*) in this context is a term of respectful endearment reserved for male hereditary leaders who are not the eldest direct descendants of their particular Vallabha Kul lineage.

> much: what to do here and there, and about *sevā*.[19] In [her] *satsaṅg* I don't feel shy to ask any questions even though I really don't know anything. Some women and men sit in front with Bava and talk all the time, but I don't want to ask him anything directly. It doesn't look good, so I also go to the smaller *satsaṅg* and ask questions and talk a lot with the other Vaishnavas.[20]

Kamala's statement reveals that her reasons for going to a *satsaṅg* led by fellow devotee Gita have to do with the comfort and ease of asking questions and speaking uninhibitedly, without the embarrassment of not "knowing anything," as she says. In Gita's *satsaṅg* Kamala feels comfortable speaking about the performance of *sevā*. Kamala also expresses, however, that while other devotees engage vocally in meetings where a religious leader is present, her own reason for listening to a hereditary leader's textual exegesis at her local temple has as much to do with hearing "Bava's knowledge" as it does with fulfilling a perceived obligation: "I should go there. I am so fortunate," she says. While in this chapter I will be highlighting dynamic verbal exchanges in which devotees are actively engaged with each other and with hereditary leaders in discussion and debate about devotional literature and what it is perceived to teach, Kamala's comment about attending her guru's *satsaṅg* (she refers to it as *vacanāmṛt*, which is common when referring to a hereditary leader's exegesis during *satsaṅg*), simply because she "should" and is "fortunate" enough to do so, also reflects the sentiments of many of her fellow devotees. Sometimes, in addition to a desire to learn and to "moisten the heart with devotion," attending *satsaṅg*s or *pravacan*s can be about performing a perceived duty or about the comfort of listening to religious literature being read aloud in the company of one's fellow *bhakta*s. That is to say, seemingly passive participation should not be overlooked as disengaged or meaningless.

A majority of the people I interviewed during my research on community reading claimed that all initiated Pushtimargi devotees could freely join any type of *satsaṅg*. However, in practice, the membership of such gatherings is rather more specific. In the case of *satsaṅg*s led by community members, this specificity is often due to preexisting social (often temple-based) or familial connections, as well as to the relationship known as guru-*bahen* or guru-*bhāī*—that is, being a "sister" or "brother" of a fellow devotee by virtue

[19] The suffix "ben" on "Gitaben" is a term of respect meaning "sister" (*bahen* in Gujarati) and is used widely among Gujarati speakers. *Bhāī* (brother) is used in a similar way for men.

[20] Personal communication, February 16, 2012.

of having been initiated into the Pushtimarg by the same guru or immediate family of hereditary leaders. Simply put, devotees often learn about or decide to start their own *satsaṅg*s based on certain preexisting relationships. Larger gatherings, especially those led by prominent hereditary leaders, may be advertised on temple websites, in newsletters, or in pamphlets mailed to devotees or distributed or displayed in temple spaces. However, it is more common that individuals learn about community readings by word of mouth. Indeed, this is how I learned of all of the *satsaṅg*s that I attend. Many of the smaller gatherings I attend in Ahmedabad, two of which I discuss in this chapter, are truly intimate affairs, where hosts act as gatekeepers, making sure that those who join are "ready for a deep commitment to textual study," as one *satsaṅg* leader explained it to me. Nonetheless, if my own inclusion in these groups points to anything, it shows that a rather blatant "outsider" to the Pushtimarg—a white foreigner explicitly marked as a researcher and not a devotee—may join and partake in the "deepness" of group readings without overtly interrupting the devotional nature of the *satsaṅg* environment.

As my forthcoming description of several specific gatherings will illustrate, the gender and age of *satsaṅg* participants, as much as the gender and assumed authority of *satsaṅg* leaders, is significant. When in Ahmedabad I attend nine *satsaṅg* gatherings on a regular basis. Except for gatherings at the Goswami Haveli, where families attend with children, these *satsaṅg*s are attended by adults between the ages of twenty and eighty, with an overwhelming majority of middle-aged participants.[21] The reason for the prominence of this demographic seems to be related to both professional and domestic commitments. Men and women who have grown children and either have retired or work less frequently outside of the home than their younger counterparts simply have more time to devote to religious activities than they did in earlier years.[22]

[21] Asking directly about someone's age can be considered rude (especially when asking women). Furthermore, acquiring accurate details about individuals' ages has not been important for the purposes of this study.

[22] This issue of gender and life stage is similarly discussed here: Mary E. Hancock, "The Dilemmas of Domesticity: Possession and Devotional Experience Among Urban Smārta Women," in *From the Margins of Hindu Marriage: Essays on Gender, Religion, and Culture*, ed. Lindsey Harlan and Paul B. Courtright (New York: Oxford University Press, 1995), 61. It should also be noted that children and youth, who occasionally join *satsaṅg* gatherings, are more actively engaged with devotional literature through classes and activities specifically tailored for them. Summer camps, weekend classes, and other youth networks are common. The "Vallabh Youth Organization" is one such network and can be found online here: "Vallabh Youth Organization," accessed January 12, 2020, https://vyoworld.org/.

Five of the nine gatherings I attend are frequented only by women.[23] A women-only *satsaṅg* has the potential to cultivate an environment in which issues that women feel most comfortable discussing in the company of other women—including discord in the home, especially with spouses and in-laws, and issues of "purity" and "pollution" around menstruation—can be raised. Also, as one devotee told me, "I am a woman, so I naturally learn more from other women [than from men] about how to do *sevā* correctly and how to make my home a Pushtimargi home."[24] Even beyond women-only gatherings, however, women dominate *satsaṅg*s and temple events. Women likewise spend more time attending to domestic *sevā* performances than men do. Women's primacy as ritual practitioners and religious readers in *satsaṅg* is often explained to me (by men and women alike) in terms of women's "inherent qualities" of devotional nurturing and, as one interlocutor Kishori put it: the ability to "balance multiple commitments at once. We [women] can balance *sevā* with work." Another devotee Kumud explained to me that women do not necessarily have more time than men do for *satsaṅg*. "In fact," she continued,

> women are busier than men. Many of us work professionally and also do work in the home even if we have a *kām vāḷī* (female domestic worker). Women always get up earlier and go to bed later. But it's true that men go to work at jobs located farther away [from the home].

"The real reason that women go to *satsaṅg* more and do *sevā* more frequently," Kumud continued, "is that women have more devotional sentiments than men. We're more attached [to Krishna]." When asked to clarify this claim, which I have heard from multiple female and male devotees, Kumud pointed to protagonists from the *vārtā*s, but mostly to non-Pushtimarg-specific female role models in Krishna narratives, such as the Braj *gopī*s or Krishna's foster mother Yashoda, as examples of how female figures had more devotional sentiments than men.[25] "Women have more devotional sentiments

[23] I never learned of any men-only *satsaṅg*s. Both male and female hereditary leaders, however, meet informally with devotees, often in gender-segregated groups, after formal temple events. I was told by Tilak Goswami, for instance, that many men regularly approach him with personal questions, asking for advice on how to read Pushtimargi texts in relationship to *sevā*, family, occupation, etc. As a woman, I could not comfortably join these gatherings, though I often joined such informal gatherings with women and male or female hereditary leaders.

[24] Personal communication, January 4, 2012.

[25] Personal communication, November 22, 2011.

because we naturally are enamored, like the *gopīs*, and we naturally know how to care for Thakurji. He is a child in our own homes and we are like his mother, like Mother Yashoda," another woman Neha explained.[26] "Men can do this too, but for women it is more natural." This sentiment is common to other *bhakti* traditions, and specifically to classical *bhakti* literature, where even male devotees may take on the form or voice of a woman in order to more successfully gain intimacy with the divine. The reader may recall from Chapter 1 that in Pushtimargi literature and memory Vallabhacharya himself is associated with Radha, Krishna's most intimate counterpart in *līlā*.[27] During one *satsaṅg* gathering I attended, I noticed that only one of fifteen regular participants was a man. When I asked this male participant about his presence, he explained that during *satsaṅg* "we're all *gopīs*, we're all the same." Therefore, in some cases, male Pushtimargi devotees understand their participation in *sevā* and *satsaṅg* to be connected to their own feminine qualities vis-à-vis Krishna devotion.

Devotees' abilities and desires to join *satsaṅgs* are also influenced by the venue, timing, and frequency of these gatherings. Larger gatherings tend to meet once a week in temples where hereditary leaders maintain affiliation or keep their primary residence.[28] *Satsaṅgs* that meet regularly in temple spaces are normally scheduled directly after a temple's penultimate or final *darśan* period in the evening and last between one and three hours. While most temples administer the standard eight daily performances of *sevā* associated with the Pushtimarg and other Vaishnava traditions, they are generally only open for public *darśan* four to five times during the day—starting early in the morning and, depending on the season and other events in the religious calendar, ending around seven o'clock in the evening when the temple's resident *svarūps* are put to sleep for the night. Final *darśan* periods of the day attract large crowds, as evenings best accommodate devotees of various demographics: professional people are returning home from work, students have been dismissed from school, and those who attend to domestic matters, such as preparing meals, normally feel free to leave home during this time.

[26] Personal communication, November 29, 2011.

[27] It is worth noting that even in traditions where the divine is female, men impersonating women—or female impersonation—is common. See, for example, Joyce Burkhalter Flueckiger, *When the World Becomes Female: Guises of a South Indian Goddess* (Bloomington: Indiana University Press, 2013).

[28] Some temples have designated spaces for such events, which are called *dīvān-e-āms* (public meeting halls) in more traditional *havelīs*, and *sabhā hols* (meeting halls) in more recently established temples. See Chapter 3 for a description of different kinds of temples.

Sundays, which are typically nonworking days for economically privileged residents of Ahmedabad, are especially busy times at Pushtimargi temples. Larger *satsaṅg*s held in temple spaces are therefore frequently scheduled on Sunday evenings.

While smaller *satsaṅg*s led by community members may also convene at local temples, such gatherings are more commonly held in people's private homes. The individuals who host and sometimes lead *satsaṅg*s are often, though not exclusively, among the more affluent members of the community who have spacious homes that can accommodate such gatherings. Accordingly, the homes of many *satsaṅg* hosts are situated in the wealthier neighborhoods of Ahmedabad's "new-city," to the west of the Sabarmati River. This can mean that *satsaṅg* participants who live in parts of the "old-city," to the east of the Sabarmati, or in more distant suburbs, must travel quite a distance in order to reach a *satsaṅg* gathering. As the city's demographics continue to shift and more and more affluent Pushtimargi families relocate to both urban areas of Ahmedabad's "new-city" and into the suburbs, the demand for new local gatherings, and likewise for new temples, continues to grow. Even during the years that I was actively involved in language study and research in and around Ahmedabad (2009–2017), I was introduced to six distinct gatherings that had only just taken shape within the preceding few years.[29] These gatherings seem to successfully accommodate devotees living in discrete and sometimes far-flung regions of the city's suburbs, as well as those who have specific scheduling conflicts with other preexisting *satsaṅg*s. According to one *satsaṅg* leader,

> There is more and more interest for *satsaṅg*s to be established in each and every "society" [an Indian housing scheme], but people keep moving out, farther and farther away. Three women have left my group this year because they live with their sons and daughters-in-law who have taken larger homes in the suburbs.[30]

Even with Ahmedabad's recently built and ever-expanding citywide rapid-transit bus system, not everyone can easily travel such a distance.

[29] Likewise, countless small-scale temples funded by trusts or directly by local community members were established during my time in Ahmedabad. These matters are discussed in greater detail in Chapter 3.

[30] Personal communication, November 12, 2011.

While gatherings led by hereditary leaders often meet on Sunday evenings in order to accommodate the maximum number of devotees, many smaller *satsaṅg*s are planned according to individual participants' schedules. Dr. Yojana Mahajan, for instance, hosts her *satsaṅg* on Wednesday and Friday evenings because these are the days that she is on call for walk-in appointments at her gynecology clinic, which is located on the first floor of her large home.[31] This schedule also suits Yojana's regular *satsaṅg* participants—all women who are able to leave their respective places of employment or homes in time to meet with fellow devotees for nearly three hours twice a week. Yojana's *satsaṅg* schedule, which has participants meeting for five to six hours weekly, is only slightly out of the ordinary: most home-based *satsaṅg*s meet for an average of three hours weekly throughout the entire year.

In most of the temple and home-based *satsaṅg*s that I attend, participants read *vārtā* as well as other Pushtimargi texts, as books, from start to finish, skipping few if any episodes, and without any particular emphasis on which time of year or in which season they should commence or conclude their readings. "We start at the beginning and we read until we are finished," Yojana once told me straightforwardly. "We have been reading like this for twelve whole years," Yojana tells me of her *satsaṅg*, "so we have read through all of the *vārtā*s, and other *granth*s, too, over twelve times." In one *satsaṅg* meeting, participants will read and discuss anywhere from one to four *vārtā*s and, depending on the gathering, other selections of literature. As discussed at greater length in the following chapter, Yojana and other avid readers also read small selections from the *vārtā*s outside of the context of *satsaṅg*, often each night before sleep:

> If we read every day, just one *prasaṅg*, we are reminded of so many things. Each and every *prasaṅg* will give us support daily. Sometimes we might return to an episode for some particular reason, to remember some *siddhānt*—or maybe we just recall an episode and smile and then sleep more easily that night.

The comfort found in the regularity of reading devotional literature as a practice that occurs both during *satsaṅg* and as part of the individual devotee's more private daily routine highlights not only the deeply ritualized quality of

[31] Yojana tries to avoid interruptions during her three-hour-long *satsaṅg* but occasionally does step out to take phone calls or to attend to urgent matters in her clinic.

religious reading, but also the ways in which the *vārtās* mark the emotional and practical lives of readers in subtle but profound ways.

Previous chapters have already established that *Vārtā Sāhitya* does much more than report didactic accounts of Pushtimargi orthodoxy and sectarian history: the *vārtās* are primarily devotional texts with aesthetically distinct ways of teaching about theology, devotional practice, and religious identity through intertextually and dialogically rich narratives of devotees' lives. These aspects of the texts, however, become especially apparent during community readings where affective piety is cultivated and religious precepts and doctrines are learned, questioned, and challenged—even by those without inherited authority.

Three Ahmedabadi *Satsaṅgs*: Family Dynamics and Questioning Texts

Negotiating Family Dynamics I

At 5.30 on a humid June evening, a three-hour-long *satsaṅg* session begins with the performance of a *dhoḷ* (Gujarati-style devotional song) by the 19th-century Gujarati poet, Dayaram:

> Taking a vow, I bow daily to the dust of my Guru's lotus feet;
> Remover of sorrow, Treasure of joy, Giver of the fruit of devotion and love.
> Here I describe by name those eighty-four great devotees
> Who fulfilled the purpose of Shri Vallabha, Shri Vitthal, and Shri Krishna.[32]

These lines, which commence Dayaram's praise-poem called the *Caurāsī Dhoḷ* ("Eighty-four Dhol"), are sung at the start of each *satsaṅg* hosted by Dr. Yojana Mahajan in her Ahmedabad home. The rest of the *dhoḷ* offers the names and signifying qualities of the eighty-four devotees who are remembered for their devotional attributes and for having been most dear to Vallabhacharya as recorded in the *84VV*. Once Yojana's *satsaṅg* is initiated with the performance of the *dhoḷ* and other Pushtimargi prayers, the

[32] I thank Goswami Anandabava for graciously assisting me in my translation of the *Caurāsī Dhoḷ*. All mistakes are my own. The song was sung in Yojana's *satsaṅg* on June 22, 2012.

thirteen women who have gathered open their respective copies of the *Coryāsī Vaiṣṇavo nī Vārtāo*—a Gujarati translation of the *84VV*.[33] I also open my copy of the text, but Dipa, seated to my left, snatches the book from my lap and opens it to a different page: "we're starting here," she says in her booming voice, with a big grin on her face.[34] Dipa, like many of the devotees I spend time with in *satsaṅg*, seems to take pleasure in assuming a teacher's role—and not just with me, the often fumbling ethnographer, but also with others who may be new to the context of *satsaṅg*. Yojana signals to Dipa to begin reading aloud. Dipa repositions herself in the white plastic chair she is seated in, tucks the end of her green and white *bāndhaṇī* (tie-dyed) sari behind her copy of the *Coryāsī Vaiṣṇavo nī Vārtāo*, and brings her glasses to her face. She clears her throat and begins to read aloud with great gusto. The *prasaṅg* that Dipa reads comes from the *vārtā* concerning Purushottamdas and his wife, two "Kshatriya devotees from Agra." The episode can be summarized as follows:

> When Purushottamdas and his wife meet Shri Acharyaji, they prostrate themselves and ask for initiation. Shri Acharyaji initiates the couple, giving man and wife *mālā*s (religious necklaces) to wear around their necks as markers of their new Vaishnava identities. However, when Purushottamdas asks to perform the Lord's *sevā*, Shri Acharyaji tells the couple that their mothers are *āsurī jīv*s (wicked beings), and so they must wait some time before beginning *sevā*. Indeed, when the couple's mothers discover that man and wife are wearing *mālā*s they become upset, thinking, "Our children have become ascetics!" Purushottamdas explains that wearing the *mālā*s does not mean that they have become ascetics and that the mothers may still share the family home. "However," Purushottamdas clarifies, "unless you also receive initiation from Shri Acharyaji, we will not accept food and water from your hands." Hearing this, the mothers become enraged: "Do you wish to disgrace us and our community? We might as well die!" Indeed, during the night the mothers drown themselves in the household well.

33 R. Parīkh, trans., "*Coryāsī Vaiṣṇavo nī Vārtāo*: Tūm Bīn Tattva kachu nahī Jagmeṃ (84 Bhagavadīya tatva Vicār)," in *Puṣṭimārgīy Patrācār: Śuddhādvait Sevābhūṣaṇ*, ed. Rameśbhāī V. Parīkh (Vadodara, India: Śrī Vākpati Foundation, 2002), 291–448.

34 All translated dialogue during this and subsequent *satsaṅg*s described in this chapter was originally spoken in Gujarati unless otherwise noted. Code-switching (between Gujarati, Hindi, and English) is common.

> After completing the last rites, the couple goes to Shri Acharyaji who tells them that now they can perform *sevā*.[35]

Dipa finishes reading the episode and lowers her reading glasses to hang around her neck. Another *satsaṅg* participant, Neha, gets up from where she is seated across the room and fills a glass with water from a clear glass pitcher that Yojana's cook Swapna has provided for the group. We pass the water around the room to Dipa, who takes a long drink. "It's warm, isn't it?" Yojana says and gets up to turn on the air conditioner. Everyone readjusts themselves and turns to focus on Yojana, who, as this *satsaṅg*'s leader, is always the first to initiate discussion. Yojana nods her head a few times, furrows her eyebrows, and begins her commentary: "This *vārtā* poignantly describes the anguish experienced when families of Vaishnavas do not understand the *puṣṭi* lifestyle." Yojana continues,

> But I was also deluded once—I was also thinking that my husband and in-laws must be some sort of ascetics. They wouldn't even let me in the kitchen after marriage until they had taken me to get initiation. Even after my *brahmasambandha*, I was completely ignorant: I didn't know anything, not even how to say *Jāī Shri Krishna* [a standard greeting between most Pushtimargis].

Yojana explains that while at first she neither understood nor felt compelled to follow the religious observances of her husband's family, it was natural in her position as new *bahū* (daughter-in-law) to appease her spouse and in-laws. "Don't misunderstand," Yojana says adamantly. "I am not saying that you should force your *bahū*s to become Vaishnavas. I naturally felt compelled to follow along . . . and before long," Yojana says, placing her hands to her heart, "I had replaced the *Hanumān Cālīsā* ('Forty Praises to Hanuman')[36] with the *Yamunāṣṭaka* ('Yamuna's Octet')!"

At this point Yojana begins to recite the first verse of the *Yamunāṣṭaka*, Vallabhacharya's Sanskrit praise poem about the river goddess Yamuna Devi

[35] My English synopsis is based on the narrative as it was being read aloud in Gujarati from R. Parīkh, "*Coryāsī Vaiṣṇavo nī Vārtāo*," 399. A full translation of this *vārtā* as it appears in Dwarkadas Parikh's 2011 edition of the *84VV* can be found in this book's Appendix.

[36] This is a non-Pushtimargi poem about the monkey-god Hanuman as the ideal devotee of Lord Rama.

and her singular devotion to Lord Krishna. "But let's return to Purushottamdas and his wife," Yojana says, wrapping up her own observations,

> The reason Shri Acharyaji called their mothers wicked was that they tried to take away the *mālās*. But according to me, they were merely ignorant. *Baheno* (sisters): Shri Acharyaji would never permit us to disrespect our mothers and fathers. We are not to understand from this account that we are permitted to remove ourselves from our families . . . even if they are, as I was once, ignorant of the *puṣṭi* lifestyle. As long as Thakurji doesn't suffer we must show some patience.

Yojana concludes with a quotation from the *Vivekadhairyāśraya* ("Discretion, Patience, and Refuge"), another of Vallabhacharya's sixteen short Sanskrit treatises, which takes its place alongside the *Yamunāṣṭaka* in the *Ṣoḍaśagrantha*. The verse Yojana quotes is frequently cited in many versions of the *84VV*: *pratīkāro yaddṛcchātaḥ siddhaścennāgrahī bhavet/bhāryādīnāṁ tathānyeṣāmasataścākramaṁ sahte//*. To translate, "But if a remedy of [one's suffering] should chance to occur, one should not stubbornly insist [on continuing to suffer]. One should, however, patiently endure the wrongs committed [against oneself] by wife and children, household, and others."[37] Hearing this, the other women nod in agreement, seemingly impressed with Yojana's ability to recall and recite the Sanskrit verse with apparent ease.

Yojana wipes her forehead with her purple and white cotton *dupatta* and relaxes into the corner of the sofa where she is seated. Waving her hands in a familiar gesture, she finally opens the floor for whatever further reflections, questions, and discussion may be stimulated by the reading of Purushottamdas' *vārtā*. During the next hour many women ask questions and share personal experiences and reactions. Most of those gathered take careful notes in journals specially designated for their weekly readings. Some write meticulously in the margins of their copies of the *Coryāsī Vaiṣṇavo nī Vārtāo*. "I never thought to do this," Neha tells me in the rickshaw we share back to our adjacent neighborhoods. "But Yojanaben really knows how to teach us, and keeping notes—just like you [Emilia] do—is very helpful. I learn so much every week and when I'm away [from *satsaṅg*] I can continue to study on my own."

[37] Redington, trans., *The Grace of Lord Krishna*, 96.

While much is shared during this particular gathering, one remark from Dipa nicely demonstrates the way that contemporary readers make sense of the stories with respect to their own lived realities. "In my home, I'm alone in my *sevā*," explains Dipa. "I found Shrinathji on my own and nobody in my family is sympathetic." Dipa goes on to describe how it feels to be the only practicing Pushtimargi devotee in her family and how she frequently experiences criticism from her husband and two teenaged sons, in part because they do not follow the widely recognized food restrictions of the community. Such restrictions include abstaining from garlic, onions, alcohol, eggs, and meat (Pusthimargis' shorthand for this diet is "pure vegetarian"), as well as routine and seasonal fasting. For many, these restrictions also include only accepting food that has first been offered to one's household Krishna *svarūp*.[38] These prescriptions preclude some observant members of the community, like Dipa and Yojana, from eating in other people's homes or in restaurants—leisure activities that are otherwise considered common for many middle-class and affluent residents of Ahmedabad. "But I don't complain," Dipa continues, "I make the food that my family asks for and then ritually purify myself. It is not suitable behavior for a Vaishnava to make complaints."

Dipa's remarks highlight the ways in which readers learn from the *vārtā*s by weaving the narratives into the everyday fabric of their own family dynamics, social exchanges, religious thought, and ritual practice. Just as Purushottamdas and his wife are shown to struggle with explaining their new faith commitments to uninitiated family members, *satsaṅg* participants discuss the challenges they experience in learning to balance Pushtimargi prescriptions and what is often referred to as *kautumbik mūlyo* (family values)—that is, familial and social obligations.[39] Moreover, domestic stability and the successful performance of *sevā* are often considered to be interdependent. "If Thakurji [Krishna] is unhappy, the Vaishnava is unhappy; and if the Vaishnava is unhappy, then Thakurji cannot endure it," one of my interlocutors explained to me in a private interview.[40]

These kinds of devotional relationships between a devotee and their household deity are central to many of the *vārtā* narratives and continue to be articulated both by individual devotees in *satsaṅg* and during public readings (e.g., *pravacans*). As one contemporary *vārtā* exegete explains,

[38] After offered to the deity, the devotee receives the food offerings as consecrated (*mahāprasād*).
[39] The Gujarati phrase *kautumbik mūlyo* is likely a calque of the English phrase "family values."
[40] Interview with female interlocutor in Ahmedabad (March 3, 2012).

> Shri Thakurji will slowly begin to take shape according to you and will begin to identify with each and every member of your family. God's involvement will increase as He becomes a family member and becomes woven into your family's *kathā* (tale).[41] [As it is written in the *Bhaktivardhinī*:] *gṛhe sthitvā svadharmataḥ*.[42]

The brief excerpt quoted from Vallabhacharya's *Bhaktivardhinī* means "remain a householder and follow one's own *dharma*." The larger context for this frequently cited teaching is Vallabhacharya's instruction to remain, whenever possible, within the social network of one's family: while everything should be *samarpit* (dedicated) to Krishna, the devotee is not encouraged to live removed from the social world.[43] The *vārtā* of Purushottamdas and his wife playfully engages with this Pushtimargi precept when the two "wicked" mothers mistake their children's new Vaishnava identities, represented by the *mālā*s, for a choice to leave their particular caste community and shun their families. Purushottamdas and his wife are, of course, *not* to be taken as ascetics, and their attempt to explain this to their indignant mothers is highlighted in the narrative. While the rather histrionic end to the two mothers is found to be somewhat objectionable to Yojana and her *satsaṅg* participants ("Vallabhacharya would never permit us to disrespect our mothers and fathers," Yojana told her gathering), reading Purushottamdas' narrative opened the floor for discussion on how devotees should harmonize their roles as devotional caretakers of Thakurji with their roles as mothers and wives. The ease with which devotees identify with and critique *vārtā* protagonists in this way appears to be distinct when compared with certain European hagiographical traditions. For instance, in her study of medieval Christian women's religiosity, Caroline Walker Bynum writes that:

> Indeed, medieval hagiographers pointed out repeatedly that saints are not even primarily "models" for ordinary mortals; the saints are far too dangerous for that. Like Christ himself, they could not and should not be imitated in their full extravagance and power. Rather (so their admirers say),

[41] As noted previously, the word *kathā* can sometimes be used interchangeably with the term *satsaṅg*, though it more frequently refers to ritualized recitations and exegesis of the *Bhāgavatapurāṇa*. The word itself has multiple meanings in different contexts, including tale, story, storytelling, and exegesis.

[42] Bhūpendra Bhāṭiyā, *Ṣoḍaśagranthāgat Upadeś ane tem-nī 28 Vārtāo (Bhāg 2)* (Rajkot, India: Purvī Press, 2008),13.

[43] See more on Vallabhacharya's views on renunciation in Chapter 1.

> they should be loved, venerated, and meditated upon as moments in which the other that is God breaks through into the mundane world, saturating it with meaning.[44]

While some *vārtā* figures may be approached as too "full of extravagance and power" to be imitated, they seem to be open to some degree of criticism and are considered at least *potentially* imitable. Recall, as discussed in the previous chapter, how hereditary leader Shyam Manohar Goswami described the *vārtā* of Rana Vyas as being "ultimately about you," as he spoke to his *pravacan* audience.

Negotiating Family Dynamics II

Across the city from Yojana's house, another *satsaṅg* gathering similarly attends to the issue of harmonizing *kautumbik mūlyo* and commitments to Pushtimargi precepts and Krishna's care. Rajabetiji, a female descendant of Vallabhacharya and Tilak Goswami's paternal aunt, is the host of this gathering of thirty men and women in her suburban home each Thursday afternoon. Like Dr. Yojana Mahajan, Rajabetiji lives in an affluent suburb of Ahmedabad and has her *satsaṅg* participants gather in a spacious basement room. Unlike in Yojana's living room, where everyone sits on chairs or sofas together, the men and women who gather in Rajabetiji's basement sit on mats on the floor, as they might in a temple setting. A few older participants sit on low plastic chairs in the back of the room, but Rajabetiji, who is seated in a well-cushioned seat, is visibly elevated above those gathered, signaling her authority as a member of the Vallabha Kul. When I asked Rajabetiji to describe the nature of the gatherings she hosts, she explained that the most important thing about all contexts of community reading—not just her weekly *satsaṅg*—is that such contexts provide participants with opportunities to learn about Pushtimargi precepts, particularly vis-à-vis "proper" *sevā* practices. She also suggested, however, that discussing the *vārtā*s can lead to what she called "healthy *puṣṭi* debate." Indeed, "healthy debate," as Rajabetiji explained, is a key mode by which *satsaṅg* participants feel that they can learn

[44] Caroline Walker Bynum, *Holy Feast and Holy Fast: The Religious Significance of Food to Medieval Women* (Berkeley: University of California Press, 1988), 7.

and deepen their devotional sentiments—whether with hereditary leaders or only among fellow devotees.

One such debate in Rajabetiji's *satsaṅg* sprang from reading the *vārtā* of Damodardas Sambhalvale, a figure from the *84VV* who was said to have lived in the town of Kanauj, in today's Uttar Pradesh.[45] In one episode, which Rajabetiji reads aloud to *satsaṅg* participants, Vallabhacharya asks his disciple Damodardas if there is anything that he desires. Damodardas replies, "Aside from your grace, there is nothing that I desire." Vallabhacharya then tells his disciple, "Ask your wife if she desires anything." When Damodardas' wife says that she wishes to have a son, Vallabhacharya tells her, "a son will come." Several days later Damodardas' wife becomes pregnant. However, to confirm her pregnancy, she consults a fortune teller who happens to be passing through town.[46] "Yes," the fortune teller reassures the mother-to-be, "a son will come." When Damodardas again meets with his guru, Vallabhacharya tells him, "Don't touch me! By consulting someone other than myself on this matter, your wife has committed the offence of *anyāśray* (taking refuge in another)!"[47] Before departing for his home in Adel, Vallabhacharya tells Damodardas, "There will still be a son, but he will be a *mlecch* [a vile-outsider; non-believer]."[48] When Damodardas' wife hears what has been prophesied, she stops performing *sevā* for fear that she will pollute Thakurji and tells her mother, "If I do have such a son, take him away from me immediately. I never want to see his face!" At this point the narrative pauses for Hariray's explanatory comments, which include the teaching that

[45] The *vārtā* was read aloud from D. Parīkh, *Caurāsī Vaiṣṇavan kī Vārtā*, 24–39. Some participants followed along from R. Parīkh, *Coryāsī Vaiṣṇavo nī Vārtāo*, 131–132.

[46] The term I have translated as "fortune teller" is *ḍākotiyā* in most Braj Bhasha versions of the *vārtā* and *teliyo rājā* in Gujarati versions. The Gujarati term is explained as "a Tantrik who bathes in oil, or puts on clothes dripping with oil and pretends to tell future events by looking into the oil": P.G. Deśpāṇḍe, *Gujarātī-Angrejī Koś* (Ahmedabad, India: University Granth-nirmāṇ Board, 2002), 459.

[47] The actions of Damodardas' wife are determined to result in *anyāśray* not because she consulted a fortune teller but, rather, because she consulted *any* person other than her own guru. *Vārtā* commentator Hariray discusses the dangers of *anyāśray* in detail in the *Baḍe Śikṣāpatra* (a text he also refers to when discussing *anyāśray* in his *Bhāvprakāś* commentaries in the *vārtās*). The *vārtās*' emphasis on the term is also addressed here: John S. Hawley, "The Four Sampradāyas: Ordering the Religious Past in Mughal North India," *South Asian History and Culture* 2, no. 2 (2001): 169.

[48] The term *mlecch* is generally used in the *vārtās* to refer to Muslim characters along with the term *yavan*, which can mean "a foreigner (by origin); a Muslim; a European; a barbarian" (McGregor, *The Oxford Hindi-English Dictionary*, 839). In most instances *mlecch* is inherently pejorative, but not always to the same degree. My conversation partners and contemporary translators have interpreted the word in several ways—sometimes glossing or replacing it with the more ambiguous *adharmī* (immoral), and sometimes even explicitly stating that the term does *not* refer to Muslims. As discussed in Chapter 1, several Muslim figures are shown in the hagiographies to have become ardent Pushtimargi devotees.

"there is no greater perversion than taking refuge in another. It is just like the woman who loses all her *dharma* by leaving her husband to be with another man."[49]

When Rajabetiji finishes reading the episode and Hariray's commentary, she opens the floor for immediate responses from those gathered. "This one has lots to teach us," she says. "What do we learn here?" A woman named Surekha, who is seated in one of the plastic chairs in the back of the room, expresses the following sentiment:

> I don't speak to anyone who isn't Vaishnava. When the woman comes for the trash, I leave it there and I don't even look at her. I buy my vegetables from a Vaishnava only. . . . I come here, to Raja's *satsaṅg*, but otherwise, I keep so few social relations. Now, imagine how Damodaras' wife must have been feeling—giving birth to a *mlecch*!

Around the room several *satsaṅg* participants are shaking their heads and clicking their tongues in agreement, but most of those gathered make clear faces of disapproval. "You surely have firm faith, Surekhaben," Rajabetiji says, "but your situation in life allows you to take so much time for your *sevā* . . . and one should perform *sevā* free from pride." Surekha fidgets in her chair. Rajabetiji smiles at Surekha and then indicates that another woman named Lila may have something to share with the group. Lila, a middle-aged school-teacher, often confronts the sharp-tongued Surekha in weekly *satsaṅg*. Just as Yojana had emphasized in her commentary on the *vārtā* of Purushottamdas, Lila explains that she cannot comprehend how Vallabhacharya would endorse turning away family members—especially children. On the matter of *anyāśray* she states that, indeed, "Damodardas' wife had no reason to consult the fortune teller." It was her *aparādh* (transgression) to do so. Yet Lila goes on to explain that she does not endorse the kinds of exclusive sectarian behavior that prohibits interactions with "others." "I too have firm faith," she says, "but this I cannot endure."

Lila's commentary reflects her own life situation and is a corrective to the statement given by Surekha. In a private conversation, Lila explained her particular familial circumstances to me. Like Dipa from Yojana's *satsaṅg*, Lila struggles with family members who are not adherents of the Pushtimarg. Her only son, who lives abroad in Florida, is openly apathetic

[49] D. Parīkh, *Caurāsī Vaiṣṇavan kī Vārtā*, 37.

about the "*puṣṭi* lifestyle" and is also married to a German woman, who, as Lila explains, "understands nothing about Indian culture—let alone *sevā* and Thakurji. She also eats meat in the house and feeds it to the kids. It's a difficult thing for me and it gives me sorrow." Regardless, Lila has a close relationship with family: "It's my task to bear the burden, not theirs," she explains, again echoing sentiments shared by Dipa in Yojana's *satsaṅg*. "But the problem is this: when I go to Florida to visit them how can I bring my Thakurji?" Instead of bringing her Krishna *svarūp* with her when she travels to visit family in the United States, as many Gujarat-based devotees frequently do, Lila entrusts a close friend to care for the deity. "Shobha takes my Thakurji when I'm in Jacksonville but allows me to sing to him on the phone each night. In Ahmedabad it's morning and he's just waking up." Lila's sentiment wonderfully expresses the attachment she has for her personal Krishna deity as well as her ability to effectively satisfy both familial commitments and what she considers to be her obligations as Thakurji's caretaker.

Lila's personal account and the exchanges from Raja's *satsaṅg* further highlight the distinct ways community readings of the *vārtā*s function: reading the hagiographies in *satsaṅg* provides a platform for devotees to share everyday experiences and the ways in which these experiences follow or challenge certain models for Pushtimargi thought and practice. The example of Rajabetiji's group also indicates that devotees do not have predictable or uniformly shared reactions to the texts that they read together. Rather, readers are actively engaged in negotiating between what the narratives are perceived to teach and their own individual interpretations. To again invoke Paul Ricoeur on the matter, this phenomenon points to how readers "appropriate" texts as they seek to interpret and make sense of them.[50] However, this type of engagement is also specifically reminiscent of certain structures in the *vārtā*s themselves, particularly Hariray's *Bhāvprakāś*: just as the commentary raises doubts and glosses the actions of *vārtā* characters in terms of *siddhānt*, contemporary readers also entertain questions—not only questions about the *vārtā*s, but also questions that challenge interpretations heard from fellow readers and even established religious authorities.

[50] Ricoeur, *From Text to Action: Essays in Hermeneutics II*, 11.

Questioning the *Vārtās*

A telling example of this particular "questioning" feature of Pushtimargi *satsaṅg* occurred at the tail end of a gathering hosted by Tilak Goswami at the Goswami Haveli.[51] The discussion in question focused on issues of "purity and pollution" during *sevā* and was triggered by Tilak Goswami's reading of an episode about a devotee named Virbai. Here is a summary of the episode that Tilak Goswami read aloud in Braj Bhasha:

> When Virbai gave birth to a son she was distressed because, due to her impure state, she could not perform *sevā*. "Who will awaken Shri Thakurji?" she thought to herself. After several days she began to cry over the matter and felt great *viraha*: "What shall I do?" Then Shri Thakurji spoke to her, "What does it matter that there is nobody else to wake me? You alone should wake me!" Surprised, Virbai replied, "My Lord! I've fallen into *aghor narak* (fearsome hell). How can I touch you?" Then Shri Thakurji told Virbai that she could return to *sevā*: "Bathe and put on fresh *kāch* (garments). I will not have anyone else perform my *sevā*. This is my order, there will be no transgression."[52]

After reading the episode, Tilak Goswami begins by offering those assembled a simple gloss: "Our Virbai was such a dedicated devotee . . . that Shri Thakurji said, 'don't cry like this, perform my *sevā*. It is no transgression.'" However, Tilak Goswami quickly goes on to comment on the broader theme of ritual purity and the ways in which devotees should dress when performing *sevā*:

> See, Shri Thakurji told Virbai: wear your *kāch*, that is, sari.[53] Today the situation is such that so many ladies are wearing . . . what do you say, those things called "maxi" [a woman's nightgown or housedress]. They don't put on the sari and according to me . . . this is not right.

[51] I attended this reading session on December 1, 2011.

[52] Tilak Goswami reads from D. Parīkh, *Caurāsī Vaiṣṇavan kī Vārtā*, 339–344.

[53] The word *kāch* is defined as "*dhotī*, esp. the end of the *dhotī* tucked in at the waist behind" (McGregor, *Oxford Hindi-English Dictionary*, 186). My conversation partner Sumit Sharma, who is well read in *Vārtā Sāhitya*, confirmed that here *kāch* refers to a sari tied in a "*dhotī* style" as per the aforementioned definition (personal communication, March 31, 2012).

At this point Tilak Goswami's wife, Vrajbhamini Goswami, who often joins her husband and their congregation for weekly *vārtā* readings, interjects, "But isn't it okay if the maxi that a lady uses is *only* used during *sevā*?" Vrajbhamini Goswami goes on to explain that many women tell her that they prefer such maxi garments to the sari even while observing all normative measures of ritual purity. "Because of this," she continues, "I tell them that it is acceptable." Tilak Goswami grimaces, "A *sevā* maxi!" The discussion soon spreads into the crowd of nearly seventy devotees:

> "Of course, ladies must wear a sari in *sevā*—we can't be so lazy!"
> "If ladies wear sari then men must wear *dhotīs*!"
> "My daughter doesn't even know how to tie a sari—let alone do *sevā*!"

While the issue of how to perform and prepare oneself properly for *sevā* is a sincere and serious matter, the debate sparked by Virbai's *vārtā* is also lighthearted and filled with laughter. One teenage boy makes a face like Tilak Goswami and repeats his guru's complaint, "*sevā* maxi!," and then bursts into laughter. Tilak Goswami finally brings the laughter and discussion to a close by returning to the reading—but not before he and Vrajbhamini Goswami come to the conclusion that the appropriate clothing to wear during *sevā* depends on the devotee's individual relationship with his or her guru and with Thakurji himself. Although both Tilak Goswami and Vrajbhamini Goswami frequently offer less ambiguous advice about *sevā*, the suggestion that normative behavior depends on personal circumstances and relationships is quite common during *satsaṅg* debates about the *vārtā*s. Furthermore, as an exegetical strategy, the suggestion that propriety around "purity and pollution" during *sevā* is situational emerges from the *vārtā*s themselves, as is evident from the narrative about Virbai and her directive from Krishna to override societal concerns for suspending *sevā* after childbirth.

The element of humor, just as it arose during the Virbai discussion, often finds its way into *satsaṅg*, particularly when devotees draw attention to seeming incongruence between elements of contemporary life and the ritual practice of *sevā* as described in the hagiographies. During *satsaṅg* at a different temple, I recorded a similar conversation—with which I introduce this book—in which one participant joked about ordering Thakurji a pizza rather than preparing him more traditional food offerings, such as milk-based sweets. While many found the comment immediately humorous, others seriously questioned why Thakurji could not be fed such food items ("Isn't He supposed to eat what we eat? Isn't He a part of the family?"). Like the debate about sartorial propriety during *sevā*, the debate about whether or not to feed Thakurji pizza yet again points to the kind of questioning that occurs when devotees discuss the relationship between textual models and real-life practices. Humor during *satsaṅg*, I suggest, also reveals a certain sense of intimacy between devotees and their religious leaders and helps to facilitate (perhaps by diffusing potential tensions) the kinds of serious questions that are so integral to such *vārtā* readings.[54]

In a separate discussion with Tilak Goswami he reinforced the significance of this type of questioning:

> We [hereditary leaders] should also emphasize the importance of reading and learning in this way. If you seek to know more and strengthen your *bhāv*, then it is okay to even have religious debate with your guru. These are positive Vaishnava qualities . . . we can see such behavior modeled by characters from the *vārtās*.[55]

While I did not ask Tilak Goswami specifically about the conversation he and his wife had during *satsaṅg* in response to reading Virbai's *vārtā*, he suggested that both men and women should be equally encouraged to participate in such negotiations. Pointing again to the hagiographies themselves, he reminded me that female *vārtā* characters, as much as their male counterparts, exhibit such behavior and therefore men and women equally should engage in "healthy *puṣṭi* debate" (here he used the same phrase as Rajabetiji). "Every devotee will find his own stream that will lead him to that ocean [of *bhakti*]," he continued. "It depends on one's guru, own nature, life circumstance, but ultimately it is all *Bhagvān nī kṛpā* (God's grace)."[56] Of course, not all hereditary leaders share these sentiments or Tilak Goswami's relaxed and inviting demeanor. His sentiments are, however, echoed by other hereditary leaders, including Shyam Manohar Goswami, who said the following during a *pravacan* about this type of dialogue: "What's the use of being

[54] For further reading on "ritual levity," see Selva J. Raj and Corinne G. Dempsey, eds., *Ritual Levity and Humor in South Asian Religions* (Albany: State University of New York Press, 2010).

[55] Personal communication, February 21, 2012.

[56] Personal communication, October 16, 2012.

like a bird in a cage? One has to leave that cage and engage in discussion—this is how you learn."[57]

Paul J. Griffiths has suggested that reading "religiously" shapes one's role as an interpreter, and that the primary aim of religious readers is to "come closer to texts"—even if by challenging and questioning them.[58] Similarly, Linda Hess, in her work on the practice of *śaṅkā* (raising doubts) about the *Rāmāyaṇa*, eloquently describes this aspect of religious reading:

> But the questioning process is not just a means of getting answers. Those who question are already assumed to be lovers [of the *Rāmāyaṇa*], and the process enacts the love that exists. It is a way of lingering in the text, enjoying *satsang*, savoring the endless possibilities of wisdom and pleasure that text and community afford.[59]

The context of Pushtimargi *satsaṅg* similarly reminds us of these distinct features of religious reading. Here reading is inherently a collective and dynamic practice that inspires community dialogue, learning, and debate on matters specific to the everyday, familial, and gendered realities of contemporary readers. This way of reading is also a natural extension of the *vārtā* genre itself. The *vārtā*s, along with Hariray's *Bhāvprakāś* commentaries, are inherently conversational texts, which themselves seek to interpret and validate Pushtimargi doctrine through narrative examples of devotees' idiosyncratic lives.

Ultimately, as *vārtā* readers repeatedly point out, *satsaṅg* provides a space in which to cultivate devotional sentiments, which allows Pushtimargis to strengthen their relationships with each other, and with Thakurji. This network of relationships, as historian of religions Robert Orsi has argued, is a defining feature of any religious tradition. Religion, Orsi writes, is not only a "medium for explaining, understanding, and modeling reality"; it is also a "network of relationships between heaven and earth involving humans of all ages and many different sacred figures together."[60] These relationships have

[57] This *pravacan* was given in Mumbai in February 2013. See "Seminar," accessed March 1, 2013, http://72.167.35.235/ongoing/fal_seminar_2013/01_upkaram/. This content is no longer available at the link accessed in 2013.

[58] Griffiths, *Religious Reading*, 42–43. While aspects of Griffiths' framework are useful, he does not account for the ways in which religious readers continuously manipulate and alter the vocabulary and conceptual tools used to read texts in terms of contemporary circumstances.

[59] Linda Hess, "Lovers' Doubts: Questioning the Tulsi Rāmāyaṇ," in *Questioning Ramayanas*, ed. Richman, 28.

[60] Robert A. Orsi, *Between Heaven and Earth: The Religious Worlds People Make and the Scholars Who Study Them* (Princeton, NJ: Princeton University Press, 2005), 2.

"all the complexities—all the hopes, evasions, love, fear, denial, projections, misunderstandings, and so on—of relationships between humans."[61] Above all else, community readings offer a forum for learning how to nurture these complex relationships.

Unpacking the nuances of community reading during *satsaṅg*s has shown that religious readers read not only with the ambition to "come closer to texts," but also with the aim of becoming active interlocutors with each other and their beloved hagiographies—retelling and questioning well-known narratives in light of everyday experiences and personal convictions. Recognizing this aspect of community reading again reveals the diversity of scriptural interpretation and moral discourse. It also provides us with a direct way to consider a diversity of interpretive voices, often not recorded, including the voices of women. As for the modeling of behavior, this seems the particular province of hagiography.[62] Although textual prescriptions and (mostly) male hereditary leaders continue to assert their authority in creating and maintaining the status quo, *satsaṅg*s demonstrate that negotiations of normative behavior can be fluid—situated in particular socio-historical moments and influenced by intersubjective relationships, both human and divine.[63]

[61] Ibid.

[62] For further reading on this particular function of hagiography in South Asia and beyond, see John S. Hawley, ed., *Saints and Virtues* (Berkeley: University of California Press, 1987); Rupert Snell and Winand M. Callwaert, eds., *According to Tradition: Hagiographical Writing in India* (Wiesbaden: Harrassowitz, 1994); Ruffle, *Gender, Sainthood, and Everyday Practice in South Asian Shi'ism*; and Stewart, *The Final Word*.

[63] Here we might think of "status quo" in terms of Pierre Bourdieu's theory of "habitus," or social practice more broadly—namely, that social phenomena influence and are influenced by social practice. See Pierre Bourdieu, *Outline of a Theory of Practice* (Cambridge: Cambridge University Press, 1977).

5

Women's Reading

Navigating Family, Gender, and Devotion

"Come, come—let's move before the traffic gets even worse," Mona shouts as she climbs into a taxi with Sonali. I dodge vehicles, crossing the street to join the two women who are now sitting in the idling car. We are headed for what promises to be an especially festive evening *darśan* of Shri Natvarlalji at the Goswami Haveli in Kalupur. It is Diwali, a Hindu festival celebrated in much of India and all corners of Ahmedabad, and the roads are becoming increasingly congested as we head the nearly three kilometers from Law Garden toward Nehru Bridge, where we will cross the Sabarmati River into the old city. The taxi driver turns off the car while we sit at a busy intersection, and Sonali and I take advantage of the time to get to know each other. While I have known Mona for several years, I have only just been introduced to Sonali, who lives in an apartment a few buildings away from Mona's house in a posh Ahmedabad neighborhood. I tell Sonali about my research on Pushtimargi literature and reading practices, which she has already heard about from Mona. "Come over next week," she says, giving me a "visiting card," which features her name and mobile number alongside an image of Shrinathji's face with a peacock feather in his crown and the greeting "*Jāī Shri Krishna*" in Gujarati script.

The conversation then turns to our families. "Do you have any children?" Sonali asks, squinting her eyes and putting her hand on mine. "No, I do not," I answer. "Why not?" Sonali queries, trying, I presume, to guess my age. "Well," I answer automatically, "I'm still working on my PhD. Once I complete the degree, then my husband and I would like to have children." This type of answer always seems to be met with quick affirmations from members of the Pushtimargi community, both men and women: "Yes, finish school first, studies are very important," I often hear. Sonali, however, does not reply as I anticipate. Instead, she says, "You know I do not have any children either," looking quizzically back and forth and at me and at Mona, the older of the two women, who has two grown children and several grandchildren. "Oh?"

Religious Reading and Everyday Lives in Devotional Hinduism. Emilia Bachrach, Oxford University Press. © Oxford University Press 2022. DOI: 10.1093/oso/9780197648599.003.0006

I answer carefully. Mona looks reassuringly at us both, remaining silent. "I'm in *sevā* and *satsaṅg* all day," says Sonali confidently, taking out a small, pocket-sized book of devotional songs—Braj Bhasha *kīrtan* and Gujarati *dhoḷ*. She flips to a marked page in the book and starts to sing a Diwali *dhoḷ*, directing us to join her in song, evidently ending the discussion about children.

Family dynamics are an ever-present part of conversations that I witness and am invited to participate in with Pushtimargis in Ahmedabad. While such discussions unfold among all types of company, and among strangers as among friends, in my experience women are most vocal about intimate family matters and related social struggles in the company of other women. While these types of conversations happen casually, as they did with Sonali while sitting in a taxi, they are also prominent in the context of women-only *satsaṅg*s, as we saw them described in the previous chapter, where devotees gather to read and discuss devotional literature. Sonali, however, does not attend any of the *satsaṅg*s that most of her friends and fellow devotees attend weekly, nor does she attend temple events except on a select number of annual celebrations like Diwali.[1] Rather, as she shared with me over tea in her living room the week after we met on Diwali, she prefers to read with her closest women friends and, she continued, patting the cushion of her newly reupholstered brown velour sofa, "with my husband when he is in the mood for *satsaṅg*, right here in my own apartment." Sonali went on to describe how she primarily reads and discusses devotional literature with her friends over the phone and through WhatsApp messages. "I am here for *satsaṅg* twenty-four seven. Well, not twenty-four seven," she said correcting herself. "Basically, I'm available whenever I'm not in *sevā*. Thakurji comes first, then Vaishnavas. They [Vaishnavas] are like my family."

Sonali went on to recount a story about a Pushtimargi friend whom she counseled through her husband's death by sharing quotes from the *84VV* and the *Baḍe Śikṣāpatra* via daily WhatsApp messages and phone conversations. "She was really suffering, but I am telling you this: each and every day I would send her one bit from the *granth*s and her mood would slowly improve. This saved her, I am telling you." Sonali has many such stories about offering

[1] In her research on class, gender, and Pushtimargi social history, Shital Sharma found that her affluent female interlocutors favored home-based over temple-based worship. Sharma speculates that part of this preference is connected to the cultivation of privileged class and caste identities among some women (Sharma, "A Prestigious Path to Grace"). While my research with affluent Pushtimargi women has not always confirmed this speculation, Sharma's theory certainly lines up with certain concerns that I heard women (affluent and otherwise) voice during my time in Ahmedabad, as discussed further throughout this chapter.

emotional support to her friends, mostly fellow Pushtimargi women. Key to how she counsels others, and key to her own "mental health" (an English term she used herself), is devotional literature. "Without daily reading I myself feel truly lost. When I read, sing, and talk with other Vaishnavas in *satsaṅg*, then I feel I can manage anything. Krishna is *here* in our *satsaṅg*," Sonali said emphatically, placing her hand on an open page of her copy of the *84VV*. Although Sonali's experiences as a devotee-reader are distinct, as are the experiences of each of the devotees I spend time with in Ahmedabad, her engagement with Pushtimargi literature aligns with that of many women in the community. Sonali reads as a way to deepen devotional ties to Krishna while also navigating, and helping others to navigate, the challenges of everyday life or even sometimes more acute challenges, like the passing of a loved one, a grandchild's illness, or tensions with a spouse. As Sonali's example also makes clear, women's practices of reading—whether with female friends, with family members, or on their own—are affective and embodied practices.[2] Reading, that is, directly impacts women's well-being. This chapter foregrounds these affective and embodied modes of women's religious reading by following the lives and reading practices of Sonali Dogra, Mona Desai, and Dr. Yojana Mahajan. In doing so, I argue that these and other Pushtimargi women use devotional literature as a forum in which to nurture their social and devotional relationships, as well as their own and their family members' mental and emotional health. In emphasizing the affective and embodied elements of reading here, I am not suggesting that analytic reading constitutes a separate practice or that *only* women's reading is affective and embodied. Rather, given my emphasis on more analytic modes of oral and written commentary in previous chapters, this chapter is meant to highlight the ways in which religious reading can also be a more intimate practice that is affectively charged in distinct ways. I draw on my ethnographic archive at large but focus on experiences with Sonali, Mona, and Yojana because their social positions and devotional lives provide an accurate snapshot of the wider community of Ahmedabad-based observant

[2] Two authors who attend to affective and embodied practices of reading include Anna Gade and Tamara Bhalla. Gade's *Perfection Makes Practice* considers, in part, the technical ways in which readers of the Qur'an have emotional and embodied responses to recitation that lead to "a permanent change of the moral state" (40). Bhalla's *Reading Together, Reading Apart* stresses how readers read "critically" and affectively as they identify with and also judge the narratives (namely, novels in Bhalla's study) that they engage with. Neither attend specifically, as I do here, to well-being or mental health more broadly.

Pushtimargis—both men and women (though especially women, for reasons I further describe in this chapter).[3]

Although I spend time with a wide range of devotees when in Ahmedabad for research, Sonali, Mona, and Yojana have become particularly important interlocutors because they represent observant members of the community in terms of typical demographics and devotional practices. First, a majority of observant Pushtimargis who practice domestic *sevā*, visit temples, or engage in regular practices of reading are married women, particularly middle-aged or elderly women. Sonali, Mona, and Yojana are all married and were all born between 1945 and 1975. As with many of their female and male counterparts, all three women are professionally employed: Sonali does bookkeeping from home for the work she and her husband conduct together in paper product sales, Mona and her husband own and run a small jewelry store, and Yojana is an obstetrician and gynecologist (her husband is a surgeon). Finally, representing the caste and class status of their community at large, Mona, Sonali, and Yojana all hail from *baniyā* (traditionally merchant caste) communities and are relatively affluent: they are homeowners, travel regularly in and beyond India for leisure and to visit family abroad (especially in North America), and pay others to help them with domestic tasks (e.g., house cleaning, shopping for provisions, cooking, gardening, commuting to work, etc.).[4]

In addition to what they describe as demanding domestic and professional lives, Sonali, Mona, and Yojana are committed to the daily, round-the-clock performance of Krishna's *sevā*. While some of these women's family members, including their husbands, participate in daily *sevā* rituals, Sonali, Mona, and Yojana, as with most of the other Pushtimargi women I spend time with in Ahmedabad, tell me repeatedly that they are Krishna's primary

[3] My use of the term "observant" is not meant to indicate a binary between observant and non-observant. I use the term "observant" to refer to devotees who practice domestic *sevā* in some fashion and regularly engage in other devotional practices with fellow devotees (e.g., visiting temples or participating in *satsaṅgs*). There are certainly many initiated Pushtimargis who do not represent this type of devotee and who still understand themselves to be observant in other ways.

[4] While Sonali, Mona, and Yojana all have hired men and women to help with domestic work, they tell me that "housework," which includes being caretakers for family members, is demanding and time-consuming. For further information on how these lifestyles, particularly regarding paid domestic workers, reflect what is typically considered middle-class status, see Steven Derné's *Globalization on the Ground: New Media and the Transformation of Culture, Class, and Gender in India* (New Delhi: Sage Publications, 2008) and William Mazzarella's essay, "Middle Class" ("Middle Class," accessed October 3, 2020, https://www.soas.ac.uk/south-asia-institute/keywords/file24808.pdf. Finally, John S. Hawley discusses Hindu middle classes here: "Modern India and the Question of Middle-Class Religion," *International Journal of Hindu Studies* 5, no. 3 (2001): 217–225.

caretakers—a role that often requires hours of daily ritual labor, such as specialized food preparation and keeping up with the changing needs of the deity based on seasonal lunisolar calendars. While neither men nor women point to Pushtimargi teachings, textual or otherwise, to explain why women "do more *sevā* than men," most devotees I speak with suggest that women are simply better suited than their male counterparts to being caretakers and to balancing professional, familial, and devotional demands. "Women have more devotional sentiments because we naturally are enamored [with Krishna], like the *gopīs*, and we naturally know how to care for Thakurji," one woman explained. "Men can do this too, but for women it is more natural."[5] Whether or not women feel it is more "natural" for them to be Krishna's caretakers, some feel that their commitments to *sevā* are infringed upon by the demands associated with their roles as caretakers for their *human* family members and as working professionals. In other words, for some women, their relationship with Krishna is a chief priority—a priority they demonstrate during *satsaṅg* when they discuss the ways that certain familial responsibilities distract them from the deity's care.

Observant Pushtimargi women emphasize that practices of religious reading help them to accomplish the devotional labor involved in both Krishna's *sevā* as well as the types of everyday "work" that their class-specific professional and domestic commitments present. Additionally, religious reading can contribute to how women assert distinct types of authority in their families and in their broader community. As Kashika Bhatt-Rawat, a newly married Pushtimargi woman in her mid-twenties, explained,

> Being someone who reads [devotional literature] gives me freedom. My mother-in-law does not question me so much because [I read and attend *satsaṅg*]. I can move around as I please and she doesn't expect me to work [in the house] when I am fatigued. My girlfriends don't do *sevā* or go to *satsaṅg* and they are not so lucky.

This assertion about devotional practices (in this case, reading and caring for Krishna) being associated not only with female piety and emotional-mental health, but also with a distinct kind of agency in familial contexts, resonates with what other ethnographers have reported in their research on women's devotional practices in India. For instance, as Antoinette E. DeNapoli

[5] Personal communication, November 29, 2011.

shows in her study of female ascetics and their householder counterparts in Rajasthan, female storytellers see their own devotional performances as having the power to "right the wrongs" against religious women.[6] However, as with many of the women DeNapoli works with, the vast majority of Pushtimargi women generally do not see their own devotional practices as a form of protest or resistance that "pushes back at or reinterprets normative patriarchal constructions of womanhood."[7] In fact, when asked directly about the possibility of challenging the status quo vis-à-vis gender norms, Pushtimargi women often tell me that "God's grace" is the real reason for any social, emotional, or economic comfort they experience in their lives. As Kashika explained to me emphatically, "The real reason I am treated well [by husband and in-laws] is because Krishna has bestowed His blessings on me. This is all Shri Thakurji *nī icchā* (the wishes of Thakurji)."

Although I do approach some women's devotional practices in terms of what DeNapoli, citing Patricia Sawin, has called "coded protests,"[8] many of the women I spend time with fashion themselves to be relatively socially and religiously conservative, specifically when it comes to marriage. Women often cite marriage as a nonnegotiable social milestone in their lives, one that at once may complicate their pre-marriage *sevā* practices, but also one that cultivates the "householder lifestyle" atmosphere they believe Thakurji will thrive in. Women also suggest that their *sevā* and reading practices directly contribute to their *strī dharma*, or their socio-religious roles as "dutiful women," specifically as wives, but also as mothers, daughters-in-law, etc.[9] Linking *sevā* to the performance of *strī dharma* is further connected

[6] Antoinette E. DeNapoli, *Real Sadhus Sing to God: Gender, Asceticism, and Vernacular Religion in Rajasthan* (New York: Oxford University Press, 2014), 87. Joyce B. Flueckiger, in the article "Wandering from 'Hills to Valleys' with the Goddess: Protection and Freedom in the Matamma Tradition of Andhra," also writes about the idea of women's "freedoms" due to religious practices vis-à-vis women's relationship to the goddess Gangamma (in *Women's Lives, Women's Rituals in the Hindu Tradition*, ed. Tracy Pitchman [New York: Oxford University Press, 2007]).

[7] DeNapoli, *Real Sadhus Sing to God*, 87. For more discussions in this vein, see Smita Jassal, *Unearthing Gender: Folksongs of North India* (Durham, NC: Duke University Press, 2012); Lisa Knight, *Contradictory Lives: Baul Women in India and Bangladesh* (New York: Oxford University Press, 2011); Pintchman, *Guests at God's Wedding: Celebrating Kartik Among the Women of Benares* (Albany: State University of New York Press, 2005), esp. 179–194; Meena Khandelwal, *Women in Ochre Robes: Gendering Hindu Renunciation* (Albany: State University of New York Press, 2004); Ann Grodzins Gold and Gloria Goodwin Raheja, *Listen to the Heron's Words: Reimagining Gender and Kinship in North India* (Berkeley: University of California Press, 1994); and Saba Mahmood, *Politics of Piety: The Islamic Revival and the Feminist Subject* (Princeton, NJ: Princeton University Press, 2005).

[8] Patricia Sawin, *Listening for a Life: A Dialogic Ethnography of Bessie Eldreth Through Her Songs and Stories* (Logan: Utah State University Press, 2004), 98–134.

[9] In addition to rituals specific to Krishna's *sevā*, all married Pushtimargi women I spend time with in Ahmedabad also observe common north and northwest Indian Hindu rituals associated with

to how Pushtimargi women see their ritual practices as supporting both the well-being as well as the *ābrū* (status) of their entire family. This is common among Hindu, but also Jain, women in South Asia, as exhibited in the work of M. Whitney Kelting. In her book, *Heroic Wives: Rituals, Stories and the Virtues of Jain Wifehood* (2009), Kelting shows how the Gujarati Jain women she works with understand their own ritual practices as wives to transfer well-being and merit to other family members, particularly husbands.[10] Therefore, like many of their Jain and other Hindu counterparts, Pushtimargi women practice a kind of "creative conformity" in their devotional performances and in their participation with authoritative discourses.[11] Pushtimargi women at once affirm and transform certain social and religious norms, innovating practices of religious reading and *sevā* to navigate everyday challenges and to assert distinct kinds of agency in their lives.

Women seek out well-being through their roles as readers of devotional literature, from being in *satsaṅg* with fellow devotees, and also from being in conversation with Pushtimargi hereditary leaders. Sonali, Mona, and Yojana all have close relationships with their gurus as well as with their gurus' wives and other family members. As Yojana explained,

> They [gurus and their families] are not like other Vaishnavas, of course. They are the Vallabha Kul, but we feel for them like they are a special kind of family. When we celebrate the birth of a *lālan* (son of a hereditary leader) or *beṭījī* we are celebrating like [they are] family. We would do anything for them and we also feel they support us every day.

Even Sonali, who rarely meets with her guru in person, has regular phone conversations with the *gosvāmī* and his wife, who are based in Baroda.

One Pushtimargi hereditary leader, however, stands out as a distinct type of guru and role model for these women: Goswami Indirabetiji (1939–2016), the first and only female descendant of Vallabhacharya to have gained a

maintaining *strī dharma* (e.g., Karva Chauth). For a rich and detailed study of women's *dharma* as a socio-religious category in contemporary India, see Jennifer Ortegren's monograph, *Middle-Class Dharma: Gender, Aspiration, and the Making of Contemporary Hinduism*, forthcoming with Oxford University Press.

[10] M. Whitney Kelting, *Heroic Wives: Rituals, Stories and the Virtues of Jain Wifehood* (New York, Oxford University Press: 2009), 36.

[11] Elizabeth M. Bucar, *Creative Conformity: The Feminist Politics of U.S. Catholic and Iranian Shi'i Women* (Washington, DC: Georgetown University Press, 2011).

global following, and the only *beṭījī* to have initiated her own followers into the Pushtimarg. While Sonali is one of just a handful of Pushtimargis I know personally to have received initiation from Goswami Indirabetiji, the female leader has been deeply influential in the lives of countless women and men across the community. Soon after initiation by the *beṭījī*, Sonali was initiated again by her current guru, a male *gosvāmī*. Sonali's reasoning for this was that she wanted to avoid association with a conflict that had arisen around the *beṭījī*'s leadership—a conflict, as I discuss in greater detail later in this chapter, between those who feel that only direct *male* descendants of Vallabhacharya should initiate new devotees into the fold, and those who feel the role of the guru should be extended to descendants irrespective of gender. One of the ways that Goswami Indirabetiji has been especially influential for women, including her fellow female members of the Vallabha Kul, is through her legacy as a public reader-exegete. This role, as women like Sonali have explained it to me, continues to be—even after the *beṭījī*'s death—a significant motivating factor in how and why they themselves read. In what follows, I show how Pushtimargi women, including Goswami Indirabetiji herself, have affectively and creatively engaged with long-established techniques of ritual practice and textual exegesis as mediums for maintaining, but also subtly altering, the structure of their social and devotional relationships—and in the case of the *beṭījī*, the very structure of community leadership and the public image of the Pushtimarg. Before turning to Goswami Indirabetiji as an inspirational figure, however, we must first consider the nuances of how Sonali, Mona, and Yojana use religious reading to cultivate well-being for themselves, their families, and Krishna.

Reading with Sonali Dogra: *Satsaṅg* and Women's "Mental Health"

"*Vārtā* number thirty-two: this is from the *vārtā* about Ranaji. Now listen," Sonali says, looking at me and speaking loudly toward her cell phone, which is propped up against a pink glass figure of a dancing couple in ballet costumes on her living room coffee table. Her fellow devotee, Bhavika, who lives in Mumbai, is on the other end of the call, on speakerphone. "*I* didn't pick this one, this is where we left off," Sonali continues, explaining to me how she and Bhavika had been reading together from the *84VV* during previous long-distance *satsaṅg* discussions. "It's fate that we're reading this one today. It's always up to Shri Thakurji Himself. The Vaishnavas in this story were right *here* near Ahmedabad, when it was still called Rajnagar. So, listen." Sonali goes on to read the following *vārtā* aloud in Braj Bhasha, which I translate and summarize here:

> Episode 2: . . . Once, after Rana Vyas and his fellow devotee Jagannath Joshi had taken a purifying bath in the Saraswati River, they seated themselves in preparation for their evening rituals. There, they saw a Rajputani (a Rajput woman) whose husband had died come to commit *satī*.[12] Jagannath Joshi asked Rana Vyas, "How are *satī*s reincarnated?" Rana Vyas shook his head and replied, "It is in vain that they burn their human bodies with ghosts. If such a beautiful body attached herself to the Lord's *sevā* then she would be saved. But there she goes, burning herself with a ghost," he said, still shaking his head. Just as he was shaking his head the Rajput women saw Rana Vyas and her resolve for committing *satī* totally fell away. Then the woman said to the people with whom she was gathered, "My resolve has fallen away. The people told her that they wouldn't let her back into the house. "We will burn you here and now." But the woman said that she wouldn't come home. "Build me a hut right here on the bank of the river, I shall reside here," she said. "If you forcefully burn me, then the curse of my death is on you." The next day, when Rana Vyas and Jagannath Joshi returned to bathe in the Saraswati River, the Rajput woman asked Rana Vyas: "Why did you shake your head when you saw me yesterday?" "We were speaking to each other and laughing. How is it your business?" Rana Vyas told the Rajput woman. The woman asked why he was hiding things from her. "You shook your head while you were speaking and because of that my resolve fell away and I didn't commit *satī*. So, tell me the truth now. Tell me what my duty is and I'll do what you say. You saved me from burning, so do me a favor and tell me what I should do." The woman continued to strongly insist like this, so Rana Vyas told her what he had said: that even though she had been given a beautiful human body she was burning herself with a ghost. "A body that has not chosen to remember the name of the Lord is corrupt and needs to be corrected," he explained. "I now seek refuge with you," the Rajput woman said. "I will sing devotional songs and remember the Lord's

[12] *Satī* literally means "virtuous" or "chaste" but refers to so-called faithful wives who burn themselves (or are made to burn themselves) with the corpses of their husband. It can also be an epithet of the goddess Parvati, as well as a more common name for an earlier incarnation of the goddess.

> name, just as you tell me, so that my hereafter improves. Therefore, grant me grace." Rana Vyas replied, saying, "You are now in a state of ritual impurity [because of your husband's recent passing]. Come back when it has worn off and then I'll instruct you." Then the Rajput woman prostrated herself and went to her hut. But the pangs of separation from the Lord grew and the hours seemed to stretch on. "When will the impurity be removed, when will Rana Vyas give me instructions so that I can remember the Lord's name and devote myself to Him. . . ?!" She thought to herself. After her period of ritual impurity ended, Rana Vyas, while keeping Shri Acharyaji in mind, gave her the eight-syllable initiation mantra and her passion for Shri Thakurji swelled. From that day forward she recited *Shri Krishna śaranaṃ mama* (the "Shri Krishna is my refuge" initiation mantra) and engaged in service to her fellow devotees, which helped her ego melt away. She took *prasād* daily in the home of Rana Vyas. Later, Shri Acharyaji formalized her initiation, knowing her to be a godly being. Association with such devout Vaishnavas as Rana Vyas is an expedient way to become a recipient of Shri Thakurji's divine grace.

This was one of the few times I had heard this particular *vārtā* read aloud among Pushtimargis in Ahmedabad, and I was eager to hear how Sonali and Bhavika would discuss the narrative. In my own reading of the story I have been struck—as other scholars have been—by the figure of the "Rajputani" widow who refuses *satī* and ultimately uses the pretext of becoming devoted to Krishna to escape death by fire.[13] She also rejects the wishes of the "people with whom she was gathered," presumably the kith and kin of her deceased husband. As often is the case, however, the parts of the narrative that I find to be most provocative were not those that my interlocutors chose to explicitly focus on. Sonali's first remark in response to the *vārtā* was rather conventional, essentially glossing the story itself: "See," Sonali said in a teaching voice, "the Rajputani came to realize that her human form was beautiful and that she could serve Krishna. So, she didn't become a *satī*. She left that place and she found refuge with Ranaji—he was a devout Vaishnava. Do you understand?" She looked at me and I nodded "yes." "Bhavikaben, did you

[13] See, for example, Vasudha Dalmia, "Women, Duty, and Sanctified Space in a Vaishnava Hagiography of the Seventeenth Century," in *Constructions Hagiographiques dans le Monde Indien: Entre Myth et Histoire*, ed. Françoise Mallison (Paris: Champion, 2001), 205–219. As Dalmia notes, it would be a mistake to read this and other *vārtā* narratives that depict figures pushing back against real or hyperbolized social norms as an indication that the early Pushtimargi community was in fact built around uplifting the downtrodden.

understand?" Bhavika answered that she did, and I nodded again, waiting for Sonali to continue.

Sonali continued, still using the teaching that the human body was "a vessel for Krishna's *sevā*" as a jumping off point to address Bhavika's familial situation, which Bhavika had apparently shared with Sonali in their previous *satsaṅg* conversations. "If your Dinesh [Bhavika's husband] doesn't like how much time you are spending in *sevā* you *must* explain to him, 'This is what my body is made for, this [*sevā*] isn't time I spend going to some "kitty party" or something like it. This is Shri Thakurji's *sevā*, this will benefit the entire family.'"[14] In their subsequent conversation about Rana Vyas' *vārtā*, Sonali and Bhavika stayed on the topic of tensions that Bhavika seemed to be having with her husband around how much time she was dedicating to *sevā* and *satsaṅg*. Bhavika lamented that her husband Dinesh had recently said to her, "You love that god [Krishna] more than you love me," when she had announced her preference for staying home while the rest of her family traveled to Delhi to spend the weekend with Dinesh's brother. Sonali listened to and consoled Bhavika, explaining that Bhavika had done nothing wrong by reasoning with Dinesh about staying home in Mumbai, and that her ultimate purpose as a Pushtimargi was to serve Krishna.[15] However, just as the *vārtā* itself seems to suggest, Sonali's use of the "human body is a vessel for Krishna's *sevā*" teaching also served as a pretext to discuss Bhavika's "right" to take time away from what seemed to be a demanding spouse and two teenaged children so that she could keep Krishna away from "family tensions." In this way, while suggesting that Krishna's own well-being was at stake, Sonali was also suggesting that Bhavika take time for herself.

This type of conversation, which in the case of Sonali and Bhavika became rather personal and emotionally charged, is not uncommon among my

[14] Kitty parties refer to women-only social gatherings popular among middle-class and affluent Indian women. Anne Waldrop discusses kitty parties in "Kitty-parties and Middle-class Femininity in New Delhi," from the edited volume *Being Middle-Class in India: A Way of Life*, ed. Henrike Donner (New York: Routledge, 2011), 162–183. Shital Sharma also discusses kitty parties in Pushtimargi communities in her article, "Consuming Krishna."

[15] The way that Bhavika and Sonali discuss marital tensions is suggestive of how tensions between spouses and women's objects of devotion are depicted in the *vārtās*. Such tensions are also discussed more broadly in narratives about saintly Hindu female figures, and by contemporary communities of Hindu women. Amy Allocco suggests this as well. As she writes, "alongside more well-known examples from textual traditions (e.g., Mirabai), several resonant examples from vernacular contexts exist in the academic literature where deities and spirits are implicated in the deaths and/or marital troubles of their devotees." ("Vernacular Practice, Gendered Tensions, and Interpretive Ambivalence in Hindu Death, Deification, and Domestication Narratives," in *The Journal of Hindu Studies* 13, no. 2 [2020]: 27, n. 5. Allocco gives several examples [Allocco, "Vernacular Practice," 28, n. 5]).

female conversation partners in Ahmedabad and shows again how women's reading of *Vārtā Sāhitya* and other devotional literature can function as a way to directly address gender-specific familial tensions. As Sonali told me later, her meetings with Bhavika help improve her friend's "mental health," which is ultimately important for Krishna's own well-being, but also for the well-being of Bhavika's entire family. "The *bhakta* desires for nothing more than to keep Shri Thakurji happy and free from worries," Sonali reminded me. This sentiment about Thakurji's needs being met in ways that also correspond to the well-being of his caretakers resonates with the ways that some Pushtimargis speak about renovating Shrinathji's 17th-century *havelī* in Nathdwara: updating the temple is meant to serve both deity and devotees (see Chapter 3). In fact, many women tell me that decision-making about daily life, and even about especially significant events or issues, directly correlates to Krishna's own needs. Sonali, for instance, once told me that she had decided not to have children (and had convinced her husband that this was a wise choice) because of her own "intentions to work alongside" her husband, but also because she intended to be a "fulltime *sevak* so that Shri Thakurji would never suffer from discomfort or solitude." While perhaps there were other reasons for not having children that Sonali did not share with me, her assertion about her own life decisions vis-à-vis her relationship with Krishna was at the center of how she herself understood the matter. Though Sonali has never told me explicitly that she considers herself a "mother" to Krishna, it is widely accepted among Pushtimargis that Thakurji is indeed to be cared for *like a child* in that he needs constant tending to and unwavering love and affection.[16] Centering Krishna's well-being in making decisions about family and professional work also reflects how many protagonists from *Vārtā Sāhitya* are embroiled in trying family circumstances. Like Sonali and Bhavika themselves, *vārtā* protagonists are often depicted as having to find creative ways to maintain relationships with difficult family members so that *sevā* might continue undisturbed, and so that Thakurji does not experience stress.[17] In this way, women like Sonali and

[16] Anthropologist Anishka Gheewala-Lohiya's forthcoming dissertation, "Everyday Play in Mothering Krishna; Rethinking Devotional *Seva* (Service) and Prayer in the Pushtimarg" (London School of Economics), will attend in detail to women's practices of *sevā* in terms of this concept of mothering the deity.

[17] See, for example, the *vārtā* about Purushottamdas and his wife that was discussed during Yojana's *satsaṅg* (Yojana's group read the *vārtā* from: R. Parīkh, trans., "*Coryāsī Vaiṣṇavo nī Vārtāo*," 399). The Rajputani narrative offers a slightly different type of example where it is only after completely giving up all familial attachments that a potential devotee finally finds Krishna's grace.

Bhavika seem to be using the well-known grammar of the written *vārtā*s in their practices of reading and exegesis, and in the ways in which they understand their devotional lives more broadly (for further on the *vārtā*s' literary grammar, see Chapter 1).

Sonali's example also shows how women's *satsaṅg* fosters not only "female hermeneutic agency"[18] as we saw exhibited in Chapter 4, but also friendships and emotional support among women. Tracy Pintchman, in her work on women's ritual practices in Banaras, has also discussed the way women form and foster friendships in relation to Krishna devotion—specifically during the month of Kartik (October–November). Pintchman describes how, during their month-long ritual performances, Banarasi women meet each morning to build their own version of Krishna's storied world by fashioning clay figures from the Ganges River, singing devotional songs, and telling stories that narrate the deity's life from birth to marriage. Toward the end of the month, the Banarasi female ritual practitioners are explicit in their storytelling about how the *gopī*s, who are also called *sakhī*s as they are in the *vārtā*s, become the "model for ritually based human female friendships."[19] For many women who practice these rituals, suggests Pintchman, "the *sakhi* relationship represents a female–female union that imitates the marital bond but may surpass blood or marital kinship bonds in terms of its professed meaningfulness in women's lives."[20] The way women appropriate the figure of the *sakhī* also shows how women have "adapted Krishna traditions in ways that engage their own interpersonal concerns and values."[21] Indeed, whether in *satsaṅg* or *sevā*, Pushtimargi women (and men) often think of themselves as *sakhī*s/*gopī*s, in relationship to one another and in relationship to Krishna. While due to their affluence, literacy, and professional lives, my interlocutors represent a rather different demographic than those with whom Pintchman worked, both groups of Krishna devotees similarly use ritual time (reading or telling stories) to cultivate and foster female friendships and networks of emotional support vis-à-vis their relationships with Krishna. Such

[18] In *Women and the Bible in Early Modern England*, Femke Molekamp discusses how women "not only participated in, but (depending on status) could also organize, devotional reading at home." These practices of community reading among women, Femke notes, "fostered the growth of female hermeneutic agency and can be connected to developments in female religious literary culture" (Molekamp, *Women and the Bible in Early Modern England*, 85).

[19] Tracy Pintchman, ed., *Women's Lives, Women's Rituals in the Hindu Tradition* (New York: Oxford University Press, 2007), 9. Pintchman discusses the *sakhī* relationship between women in Banaras during Kartik rituals at greater length in her monograph, *Guests at God's Wedding*.

[20] Pintchman, ed., *Women's Lives, Women's Rituals*, 9.

[21] Ibid.

friendships are integral to how women use religious reading to nurture family dynamics and cultivate their own, and others', well-being.

In the following example we can discern how reading helps women to cope with familial tensions, but with a more pointed focus on how women promote their own well-being through the embodied, ritual act of reading itself, rather than through textual analysis and identification with particular narratives or protagonists per se.

Dr. Yojana Mahajan: Devotional Reading for a "Meditative State"

Each time I meet with Yojana in her home she insists that I eat—not just a snack with tea, but a full meal. Because all of the food prepared in Yojana's house is first offered to her beloved Krishna *svarūp*, the meals she serves are always considered *prasād*, or Krishna's consecrated leftovers. It is difficult to decline Yojana's offers because of this, and likewise because I know that anything I am given will have been lovingly prepared by Swapna, the masterful cook (also a Pushtimargi devotee) who comes daily to do much of the cooking in Yojana's home. "You see, Thakurji always finds a way to nourish those who seek Him out," Yojana told me when I finally gave in to a second plate of lunch one afternoon when I was visiting her in July 2017. Yojana knows that I do not consider myself a Krishna devotee, but, as with many of my Pushtimargi interlocutors, she suggests with unwavering certainty that even if I do not know it to be the case, my academic inquiries are in some way linked to my search for devotional fulfillment (specifically through forming a relationship with Krishna).

Unsurprisingly, food is understood by Yojana and by many Pushtimargis to be an important vehicle for receiving Krishna's grace in physical form. Or, as Yojana put it herself, "When we accept *prasād* it is as if we are consuming Krishna's grace." Books, too, can become *prasādī* (sanctified) items if they have first been offered to Krishna. "How exactly do the books become, *prasād*?" I asked Yojana, "Does Krishna read the books that he is offered?" "What kind of question is that?" Yojana asked, perplexed. "Well if Krishna first consumes the food you prepare as *bhog*, I thought that perhaps *prasādī* books were *prasādī* because Krishna reads them first," I tried to clarify. "Shri Thakurji *enjoys* the books, He sees them and accepts them first. He takes so much pleasure in them. He listens, He is always listening when we read,"

Yojana explained, "and when we read, we're always reading for Him, and about Him. That's the way it works," Yojana said, making a clear distinction between how food and books become blessed.

Yet, Yojana then went on to describe her own practices of devotional reading in the same way that she describes her consumption of *prasādī* food items. "When I am reading," she explained, stretching her arms out in front of her, "I feel that I am imbibing Krishna's grace. I can feel it throughout my body. It is like I am drinking nectar and it puts me into a meditative state." This rather distinct assertion about how it *feels* to read seems to explain Yojana's dedication to her highly ritualized reading practices: she reads devotional texts daily upon waking (*after* bathing and just before commencing her morning rituals of Krishna's *sevā*) and before sleep (just before putting her Krishna *svarūp* to sleep for the night), with her husband or alone before going to work, before embarking on any trip outside her home, and twice a week for up to three hours with the women who join her for *satsaṅg* in her living room (see Chapter 4). In addition to the ways in which reading helps Yojana to learn "about Pushtimargi philosophy, history, and *sevā*," her reading practices help her to enter into what she describes in English as "a meditative state" in which she can "feel Krishna's grace" in her body. As Yojana detailed, this specific bodily experience helps her to manage her extremely busy, and sometimes stressful, professional life as an obstetrician and gynecologist and her relationship to her spouse Damodar, a surgeon, to whom she has been married for nearly forty years.

One particular example of how Yojana described her reading in terms of coping with work and her marriage stands out. Yojana had just recently opened her own home-based clinic, which occupies the first story of her large house in an affluent suburb of Ahmedabad. As we sat in her clinic office during a break one afternoon, she recalled with pride and satisfaction how she had walked downstairs from her home into her new workspace in order to, as she explained wistfully, "help my first patient in my very own clinic. A woman was there with gestational diabetes, I remember that first patient very clearly." But she also remembers that this first week at her home clinic had caused a lot of stress, namely, because her husband Damodar had not been particularly supportive of the project to build the clinic and was therefore "in a very bad mood for days and days." She continued, "He was concerned that there wouldn't be enough privacy between our home, our *sevā*, and our family, and my clinic work. But I really desired the [home] clinic *because* I wanted to be able to be with Suraj and Raksha [her son and daughter]—they were still living with us—and I had been feeling so much *viraha* from being away from *sevā* all day." Yojana explained that it was after this first day, filled with both excitement about her new work arrangement and also tension with her husband, that she had initiated her practice of reading before starting work each morning (her pre-work reading sessions take place before going downstairs around 8.30 am, while her pre-*sevā* readings begin at around 5.30 am). Damodar had joined her to read before she walked downstairs for the clinic on that first day, she told me, and continued to do so on most days afterward. On that first day, they read one short episode from a *vārtā* (she couldn't recall which one), and on subsequent mornings they would similarly read small selections from the *84VV*, the *Baḍe Śikṣāpatra*, or the *Ṣoḍaśagrantha*. This practice offered them a time to be in *satsaṅg* together and to *feel* "calm" before entering their mutually hectic days as medical professionals. "That's it," she said. "That's how it [reading] helped. Everything is Shri Thakurji's *līlā*. There, now you've recorded my entire *jīvan caritrā* (life story)," Yojana joked.

This particular anecdote about Yojana's reading practices is straightforward: stopping to read devotional texts helped her to diffuse tensions with her spouse in a particularly charged moment. Although daily and weekly ritualized reading had already been an important part of her life, Yojana's use of *satsaṅg* with her husband Damodar on the day she opened her home clinic inspired her to add before-work readings as a new dimension to her ritual schedule. She noted that, as with reading, Thakurji's *sevā* itself also put her into a "meditative state": "*Sevā*, too, makes me feel as if I am imbibing Shri Thakurji's grace," she said. But she also added that she dare not initiate *sevā* if she is already feeling tense because she does not want to bring her tensions to Thakurji directly. As I hear from my Pushtimargi conversation partners regularly, and as we learned from Sonali, Thakurji is influenced by his caretaker's emotions. If they are upset, Thakurji will also be upset. If there is discord in the home, Thakurji will feel and suffer from familial tensions. Yojana asserts, however, that reading devotional texts, reciting prayers, or singing devotional songs are important practices that she can engage in even—or *especially*—during moments of anxiety.[22] She knows that such devotional practices will

22 "It even works when a woman is in labor," Yojana also remarked. "Reading?" I asked. "No! I can't imagine reading in labor, but I was with my Raksha [her daughter] when she had her first baby, and it was a very long and painful labor. I told her, 'recite the *Śrī Yamunāṣṭaka*, again and again,' and she did. She knew it by heart because we used to read it with her daily. Then the baby was born vaginally and they were both healthy."

overtake her "almost immediately" and soothe her. "This is why we sing and read at the start of *sevā*," she explained.

The women who join Yojana's weekly *satsaṅg* gatherings tell me that she is an expert or "specialist" reader from whom they learn to better interpret devotional literature in relationship to their own lives.[23] I, too, have witnessed Yojana's expertise as a reader-exegete during *satsaṅg*: she, like many of her hereditary leader counterparts, is adept at unpacking the significance of *vārtā* narratives vis-à-vis other texts, namely, Vallabhacharya's treatises and the *Bhāgavatapurāṇa*, and at facilitating conversations that invite her fellow devotees to engage affectively with the stories (see Chapter 4). Therefore, while I am familiar with Yojana's expertise as a *satsaṅg* leader and her analytical engagement with texts, in my one-on-one conversations with her she rarely mentions specific narratives in connection to her own devotional practices or personal experiences. Rather, it is the more affective and embodied qualities of reading itself that she generally chooses to reflect on. This is an important reminder that even storytelling texts like the *vārtā*s can become part of devotees' daily, ritual practices of devotional reading—specifically, in Yojana's own words, for entering "a meditative state" in which they can begin to feel emotionally grounded. Yojana's example is also important because it disrupts my own ethnographic desires to find and analyze the nuances of women's exegetical practices. Despite my emphasis in this book on how reading goes hand in hand with dialogue and debate, in my conversations with Yojana, and through my observations of her and others' reading practices, it is clear that there is no patent distinction between more analytical and affective-and-embodied modes of reading. That is, women (and men) do not see a major distinction between more conversationally motivated (exegetical) *satsaṅg* and intimate, more introspective types of reading. During her morning readings with her husband, Yojana explained, there is little time for discussion: "We just read in the morning. There is no time to discuss anything. We just have five minutes most days." Religious reading, then—both as an affective and analytical process—nourishes the devotee, and by extension immediate family members and Krishna himself.

23 For more on the role of the "specialist" reader, see Griffiths, *Religious Reading*, 61–71.

Mona Desai: Reading Through "Joys and Sorrows"

"Do I remember the first time I read *Vārtā Sāhitya*?" Mona chuckled after repeating the question I had posed during our first extended conversation about her life as a Pushtimargi devotee and reader. "I would have to think a little bit carefully about that," she said, tapping the well-manicured nails of her right hand on her glass kitchen table, and pushing a plate of nuts and dried fruits toward me with her left. "I don't think it's so significant when I first started to read [Pushtimargi literature]," Mona continued, "but I do have a memory I would like to share with you." Mona stood up and took a photograph from its magnetic frame on the refrigerator: "My granddaughter and my grandson," Mona said, pointing with affection to the two young children in the photograph. Mona had spoken to me before of her grandchildren, who lived with the older of her two sons and his wife in Toronto, Canada. Mona and her husband Parimal (along with their Krishna *svarūp*) visit their Canadian family for several months every year in the early spring. They had just returned from their annual visit the week before I visited Mona in her Ahmedabad home in July 2017. "This year Ani's health is a bit better," Mona said. She sat down again, still holding the photograph between her thumb and forefinger. Anand (Ani), who had turned eight in April, has a set of neurological disorders and epilepsy, which remain severe but have, according to Mona, become less difficult to manage in recent years—in part, as she went on to explain, because of her own relationship to devotional texts. In discussing her family in this way, Mona's sentiments reveal how reading can be interpreted not only as promoting the well-being of women and their immediate family members, but also vicariously the welfare of faraway kin who are perceived to need special types of support.

The memory Mona shared with me in response to my question about when she had first read *Vārtā Sāhitya* was about her grandson's birth: "It was the very same day—he was born on the *very same day* as Shri Mahaprabhuji's *prākaṭya* (emergence).[24] This was truly a divine moment for me," Mona recalled emotionally. She went on to explain that she knew as soon as she learned the news of her grandson's birth that he would have a special connection to Krishna, and that this feeling was confirmed when, in the evening after Anand's birth, she had opened her copy of the *84VV* to seek comfort.

[24] Since Vallabhacharya's birthday is celebrated according to a lunisolar calendar, the date of its celebration shifts annually in the Gregorian calendar. In 2009, the year Mona's grandson was born, it was on April 20.

The *prasaṅg* that Mona remembers reading that night comes from what is traditionally the twelfth *vārtā*, which tells the story of a woman referred to as Amma, or "Mother." I have summarized the episode in English as follows:

> Upon the birth of her second son, Amma's husband and other kin unexplainably passed away. She was alone responsible to raise her sons. Shri Thakurji appeared to Amma in a dream and told her to seek out Shri Acharyaji and become his disciple. "Worship me as one of your own sons," Shri Thakurji also told the woman. When Shri Acharyaji came to Amma's town, she took initiation from the teacher, who shone brilliantly like a thousand suns. Shri Acharyaji bestowed upon Amma a small child *svarūp* of Shri Krishna and she began His *sevā*. Amma was in bliss watching her own two sons play and share food with Shri Thakurji. Then one day her eldest son died. Soon after her younger son, too, passed away. Amma was plunged into a state of grief. She mourned the loss of her children and the loss of Shri Thakurji's playmates. Krishna Himself noticed Amma's sorrow and asked Shri Gusainji to come and comfort His grieving caretaker. When Shri Gusainji arrived, he witnessed Shri Thakurji drinking a cup of milk with His own two hands. Shri Gusainji was so impressed that he requested that Amma bring the leftover milk to him as *prasād*. In this way Amma was blessed.

After telling me an abbreviated version of Amma's *vārtā*, Mona explained why the hagiography moved her so much in relationship to her grandson. "Nothing can take away the grief of losing a child," Mona said.

> But you see, Shri Thakurji was so attached to her [Amma's] sons and the Lord Himself was like her own child. This is how I felt about Ani: he was not well and he was suffering, I knew that, but I also took comfort in knowing that everything was according to Shri Thakurji's wishes.

In the months after Anand's birth, Mona and Parimal had traveled to Toronto to help her son and daughter-in-law as they managed life with two full-time jobs, a "*tufānī*" (stormy; rambunctious) toddler, and now an infant with disabilities who was in and out of the hospital. When describing her feelings about her experience living with her son's family for four months in the aftermath of Anand's birth, Mona used the phrase "*sukh ane duḥkh*" (happiness and sorrow) several times. The bitter sweetness she experienced was two-fold: she was physically near to her son's family, but during a difficult time, and she felt both personally helpless and also comforted by knowing all was according to "Shri Krishna wishes."

It was during this period, when Mona could not attend in-person *satsaṅg* gatherings with her fellow devotees in Ahmedabad, that she began her studies as part of the "correspondence course" in Pushtimārgi philosophy with the Vakpati Foundation's Pushtimargiya Open University (also called the Vallabha Vidyapith, as discussed in Chapter 2). Mona began to move quickly through the course materials, completing what was intended to take seven years of study in just four. She felt that with each set of course materials she read she felt her "knowledge and love" for Pushtimargi philosophy deepening, but she also felt with increasing certainty that her grandson Anand was blessed by Krishna and by Vallabhacharya. Using words similar to those Yojana had used when describing how her own body and mind responded positively to reading, Mona explained that she could *feel* "Shri Thakurji's grace" when she read for the Vallabha Vidyapith's correspondence course, and she could *feel* that Anand, too, was a recipient of Krishna's grace. While Mona would not make a direct correlation between her own reading practices or *sevā* and the improvement of her grandson's health—namely, because she maintained that everything was up to Krishna's own design—it is clear that both her interpretation of *vārtā* narratives as well as her advancement as a reader-student have helped her to emotionally cope with her grandson's condition.

This particular example also shows how religious reading as a devotional practice helps Mona to reaffirm her belief that her grandson's disabilities are part of Krishna's own way of offering grace. As with Sonali's and Yojana's experiences of reading as a way to foster well-being and mental health, reading Pushtimargi literature provides Mona with examples of devotional living (e.g., as shown in Amma's *vārtā*), which she feels positively influence her own welfare and vicariously that of her grandson. Again, Mona's example shows how religious reading is an embodied and affective practice that transforms women's ways of being in the world, particularly as they are in relationship with family and with Krishna. Finally, the ways that all three women—Sonali, Yojana, and Mona—engage with devotional texts as readers show their creative conformity, that is, their ability to tailor long-standing practices of Pushtimargi reading to suit their own fluid needs as women.

As a way to segue into the final portion of this chapter, it is also noteworthy that Mona's inspiration to enroll in the correspondence course came from Goswami Indirabetiji, whose promotion for the Pushtimargiya Open University during her live-streamed *pravacan*s on YouTube were "*jabardast* (terrific)," as Mona explained. "She was special and unique—the only woman *ācārya* (preceptor; teacher) of our Pushtimarg." Indeed, Goswami Indirabetiji was unique as a female guru of the Pushtimarg, but her consideration here is especially significant because she inspired women like Mona through her innovative role as public exegete.

Goswami Indirabetiji as Public Reader-Exegete

When I first met Goswami Indirabetiji in 2012, four years before her death, she was seated beneath a wall-sized painting of the river goddess Yamuna Devi. Yamuna Devi—one of several significant female counterparts to Lord Krishna in Pushtimargi theology—was depicted in familiar tones of blue and purple, wearing a red sari and holding, with outstretched hands toward Krishna, a garland of pink and white lotuses. Goswami Indirabetiji was clad in a crisply ironed white sari with thin gold trim and had around her neck a garland of red flowers, which had just been bestowed upon her by a group of devotees who were departing when I arrived. As I was seating myself on the floor in front of Goswami Indirabetiji, her attendant and friend Sejal invited me to view the female leader in a very particular way: "you see, our Pujya Shri Jiji [an affectionate name for the *beṭījī*] is just like this, sitting here like the Goddess Yamuna." Many living devotees and hereditary leaders alike assert that Pushtimargi teachings, including those found in the *vārtā*s, make it clear that Vallabhacharya and his descendants are not "supposed" to be revered *as* incarnations of Krishna (or in this case, the Goddess Yamuna) but, rather, as divinely inspired in the earthly realm and with divine counterparts in the eternal world of Krishna's Braj *līlā* (as told in Hariray's *Bhāvprakāś*). What is also clear to many Pushtimargis, even to those with deep respect and love for Goswami Indirabetiji, is that women are not "supposed to" assume the mantel of guru who initiates new devotees into Pushtimargi Hinduism. As established in previous chapters, Pushtimargi hereditary leadership is based on a system of male primogeniture descending from Vallabhacharya himself. Nonetheless, those who follow Goswami Indirabetiji, who is sixteen generations removed from her illustrious ancestor, repeatedly challenge both of those norms, not only by having followed the female leader as a primary guru during her lifetime, but also by approaching her as an embodiment of divinity. Some suggest that she was actually an incarnation of Goddess Yamuna (Shri Yamuna *svarūp*), while others spoke more broadly of the *beṭījī* as divinely maternal. As one devotee put it, she was "not a mother to human children, but a divine mother to everyone. She was *puṣṭi-avatār* (the embodiment of *puṣṭi*)." However, what I heard most commonly from my conversation partners—particularly women, including Mona, Sonali, and Yojana—was that Goswami Indirabetiji's defining characteristics were her charisma as a public speaker who was deeply knowledgeable about Pushtimargi philosophy, and her compassion as a teacher who cared about the everyday realities, and emotional struggles, of her followers.

In 1962, at the age of twenty-four, Goswami Indirabetiji began her studies at the Women's College of Baroda, becoming the first female member of the Vallabha Kul (*bahūjī* or *beṭījī*) to attend an educational institution.[25] By 1971 she had completed her BA, an MA in Sanskrit literature, as well as "traditional" forms of education in Pushtimargi philosophy. Like fellow Pushtimargi hereditary leader Shyam Manohar Goswami, whose textual exegesis was considered in the previous chapter, Goswami Indirabetiji was widely respected as particularly erudite, having received both Pushtimargi as well as more academic training. As one *gosvāmī*'s wife suggested to scholar Shital Sharma, "whether a guru is a woman or a man is irrelevant. Only that person who has the '*yogyitā*' [the qualifications] should be a guru."[26] Goswami Indirabetiji was understood by many in the community to have had these qualifications. She also lived up to the "job," as Mona explained to me,

> Not all *gosvāmī bālak*s want to have the responsibilities of guru. Some just want to do a normal job—business or something. And there are those who only do the things they are forced to do, but they do not live for Shri Thakurji or serve the *kūl* [dynasty; Vallabha Kul] or Vaishnavas.

Pushtimargis do not, therefore, necessarily accept the inherited authority of the Vallabha Kul as always and inevitably linked to sound leadership. Religious leaders should fulfill certain duties: they should "serve" the community, not only by performing *havelī sevā* and hosting temple events, but

[25] Before Goswami Indirabetiji, female members of the Vallabha Kul who received formal schooling were taught privately in their homes (Kānti R. Gāndhi, *Bhaktiras Calke, Jīvan Madhurū Malke: Param Viḍuṣī Pūjya Gosvāmī Indirābeṭījī* [Mumbai: Paramount Printing Press, 2000], 11–12).

[26] Sharma, "A Prestigious Path to Grace," 272.

also by teaching Pushtimargi philosophy through public religious lectures (e.g., *pravacans*) and written publications.

Before Goswami Indirabetiji herself, one of the few *beṭījī*s remembered for her public leadership was Yamunabetiji (c. 1669–1730; also known as Yamunesh Prabhuji) from Dungarpur, Rajasthan. According to Hindi hagiographies written about her, Yamunabetiji claimed the authority held by her late father Gopendra Prabhuji when he passed away in 1684 without a male heir.[27] While her male cousin was also a contender for the position of head *gosvāmī* in Dungarpur, Yamunabetiji seems to have succeeded in assuming leadership because of her superior mastery over Pushtimargi theology and literature, which she lectured on during several pilgrimage tours of western India. Yamunabetiji never married—thus breaking "tradition"—but also retaining a certain authority as a daughter of the Vallabha Kul. Several centuries later, Goswami Indirabetiji used similar strategies: she never married, and she used her role as a public reader-exegete to gain authority in a male-dominated tradition.[28]

Throughout her life Goswami Indirabetiji was prolific as a writer-author and a reader-exegete. She wrote devotional poetry in Gujarati and published several collections under the pen name Shravani.[29] She also published Gujarati translations of *vārtā* and other popular genres of Pushtimargi devotional literature. With the support of her grandfather in 1971, Goswami Indirabetiji became one of the first female descendants of Vallabhacharya to give *pravacan*s. In addition to performing *pravacan*s on vernacular devotional literature, she also became well known for her *kathā*s, or public recitations of and lectures on the Sanskrit *Bhāgavatapurāṇa* (by all accounts, she is the first and only woman in the tradition to perform *kathā*). As discussed in Chapter 1, the *Bhāgavatapurāṇa* holds a special place in Pushtimargi collective memory because of how Vallabhacharya and his early descendants are said to have used the text to spread their devotional teachings. Multiple *vārtā*s, for instance, recount how Vallabhacharya's and his son's exegeses of the *Bhāgavatapurāṇa* were so powerful that they had

[27] Printed versions of Yamuneśprabhujī's hagiography are found in several contemporary Gujarati and Hindi reprints, including Gosvāmī Karamśībhāī Vastabhāī Diyorā's *Śrī Jamuneś Mahāprabhujīnā Jīvan Caritāmṛt* (Surat, India: Gosvāmī Vastabhāī Naraśībhāī Diyorā, 2002). Shital Sharma discusses Yamunabetiji's hagiographies in her dissertation. See Sharma, "A Prestigious Path to Grace," 175.

[28] Unlike Yamunabetiji, however, Goswami Indirabetiji assumed authority of her own accord, rather than to fill the "seat" of a deceased father or brother.

[29] See, for example, Śrāvaṇī, *Gāvalḍī Māre Banvuṃ Che* (Baroda, India: Vraj Dham Adhyatmik Kendra, 2003). The poems in this collection are written in a mix of Gujarati and Hindi.

to sit beneath the shade of sacred Shami trees so as not to burn the earth beneath them.[30] Emphasizing her reverence for the position of *kathākār*, or exegete of the *Bhāgavatapurāṇa*, Goswami Indirabetiji often positioned herself seated just below life-size statues of her male ancestors Vallabhacharya and Vitthalnath during her *kathās* (other *gosvāmīs* do this as well). Many of her followers have also pointed out that the female leader never accepted "a single penny" for her "personal purpose" in delivering exegesis on the *Bhāgavatapurāṇa*. This is significant because *Vārtā Sāhitya* and other Pushtimargi texts seem to prohibit using public readings and exegesis of the *Bhāgavatapurāṇa* as a source of income (although some *gosvāmīs* are accused of doing just this today).[31]

Just as her forefathers are remembered for having used exegesis of the *Bhāgavatapurāṇa* to spread Pushtimargi teachings, Goswami Indirabetiji's public readings gave her a platform to offer her own interpretation of Pushtimargi texts. Goswami Indirabetiji's interpretations of texts were creatively conformist: in many ways her teachings and her affect as an exegete did not radically diverge from those of her male counterparts, who themselves often claim to be passing on Vallabhacharya's "original teachings" through their public readings (see Chapter 3 for examples of this). When I met with Goswami Indirabetiji in 2012, she explained that "every time I give a lesson, I am passing on the message of Shri Acharyaji himself." Raising her right hand in the air, she continued, "*His* message was revolutionary! I am not saying anything new." At the same time, however, as with many of her male counterparts, Goswami Indirabetiji's *pravacans* and *kathās* frequently reflect on how to apply Pushtimargi teachings (most frequently as they are understood through vernacular texts like the *vārtās*) to the emotional well-being of her followers and to the realities in which a majority of contemporary Pushtimargis live. During one 2012 *pravacan*, for instance, Goswami Indirabetiji read aloud from a *vārtā* about one of Vallabhacharya's disciples who traveled professionally as a merchant as a way to teach her audience a lesson on *sevā*. "Just as the merchant carried Shri Thakurji around in his turban so that he could practice *sevā* throughout the day as he traveled," she explained, "so too can the modern Vaishnava carry on with

[30] Scholar Priya Kothari's forthcoming doctoral dissertation, "Preaching and Public Memory: Storytellers of Krishna in the Vallabha Tradition of Western India" (University of California, Berkeley), will focus on professional Pushtimargi *kathākārs*, or preachers of the *Bhāgavatapurāṇa*.

[31] "Pushti Satsang," accessed August 8, 2020, https://www.facebook.com/427657920746929/posts/goswami-108-shri-indira-betiji-mahodayashreeit-is-15-days-since-aapshris-nitya-l/630939863752066/. This content is no longer available at the link accessed in 2020.

business and even fly by airplane here and there with Shri Thakurji safely in tow." The ability to travel with Thakurji, she emphasized, would reduce stress and "mental anguish" for both deity and devotee. Goswami Indirabetiji went on to encourage audience members who performed Thakurji's *sevā* to acquire what she called *jhāpījī*s, or portable homes designed specifically for Krishna *svarūp*s.[32] These handcrafted boxes come equipped with specialized compartments to safely store all of the specialty items that devotees use in their daily care of *svarūp*s, including clothing and ornaments, bedding, food and water, and miniature toys. Flying in and out of the Ahmedabad airport I have often seen these *jhāpījī*s as devotees carefully place them on the security conveyor belts, watching anxiously to see that they arrive undisturbed on the other side. When I spoke to Goswami Indirabetiji after the *pravacan* during which she discussed *jhāpījī*s, she again emphasized that by lecturing on the "meaning" of the *vārtā*s in ways that help contemporary devotees live practically she was only doing what her forefathers did before her: "I am speaking only what Shri Acharyaji and Shri Gusainji taught. It is the nature of things to change, so we change with the times, but this behavior doesn't change Shri Krishna. God is immutable."

While she was not alone in her emphasis on interpreting Pushtimargi literature in terms of the realities of contemporary living, Goswami Indirabetiji's followers have repeatedly explained to me that one of the reasons they were so attracted to the female leader as a guru was because of, as Sonali once said, the "forward thinking attitude" with which she delivered her teachings and her emphasis on well-being. According to another Pushtimargi woman, named Preetha, who struck up a conversation with me after she saw me reading Goswami Indirabetiji's biography during a layover in Chicago's O'Hare Airport in 2018,

> I know because she was a woman she was controversial, but I think really it was because she was so forward thinking [. . .] If you listen to her lectures on all of the *granth*s she was basically saying, go on and live and let live, just do it, you know, for God, and for humanity. Now that she has entered *nitya līlā* there are so many stories about all the people she really inspired, especially women. And she was really giving to society with her humanitarian efforts.

[32] One can find images of these "travel systems" online. See, for instance, "Travel Systems," accessed September 27, 2020, https://hindureligiousitems.com/products/wooden-jhapiji-travel-system.

Goswami Indirabetiji demonstrably broadened the scope of how contemporary hereditary leaders engage charitably with communities within and beyond the *sampradāy*. Although there is a long and well-documented record of Vaishnava devotees engaged in philanthropy for, as Sonali said, the "common good," as a hereditary leader Goswami Indirabetiji emphasized acts of charitable giving beyond the *sampradāy* in new ways.[33] For example, she established various trusts through which she oversaw and managed efforts to subsidize the building of hospitals, eye clinics, and relief in the wake of natural disasters (primarily in Gujarat, but elsewhere in India and overseas as well).[34] While other *gosvāmī*s also engaged in philanthropic efforts before and during Goswami Indirabetiji's lifetime, multiple devotees and hereditary leaders suggested to me that it was her example, particularly beginning in the 1980s when she began traveling abroad, that re-inspired a new generation of *gosvāmī*s to "encourage humanitarian aid from the *gaddī* [throne; that is, position of authority]." So common was the association of philanthropy with the female leader that she would often be introduced as a "humanitarian" in brochures announcing her upcoming *pravacan*s, and in commemorations after her passing in 2016. As was written on the cover of a Pushtimargi magazine the month after her death, Goswami Indirabetiji was the "Pushti Bhakti Marg's Founder-Guru Shrimad Vallabhacharya's Truthful Descendent, Krishna-Devotee, Yamuna-Swaroop, Beloved of Vaishnavas, Humanitarian, Vaishnavacharya."[35] Likewise, in an online tribute to the leader on Facebook, one of her followers wrote in English that "Pujiya Jiji is the best answer to such people" who think that the Pushtimarg is "just for Krushna [Krishna] seva" and that "we don't believe in helping anyone" or that "we are not part of the society."[36] She was a "perfect example of a divine personality who balanced Shri Krushna Seva and service to mankind" and worked for "women's empowerment."[37]

Goswami Indirabetiji was remarkable to her followers, and in the broader community, but her status as a *woman* hereditary leader makes her legacy all the more notable. When I met with Goswami Indirabetiji, I asked her

[33] For further information on the modern history of philanthropy among merchant Pushtimargi communities, see Aarti Bhalodia, "Princes, Diwans and Merchants: Education and Reform in Colonial India" (The University of Texas at Austin, 2012).

[34] Shital Sharma also discusses Goswami Indirabetiji's philanthropic work: Sharma, "A Prestigious Path to Grace," 269.

[35] Pramod Amin, ed., *Vraj Venu* 1, no. 4 (Sept.–Dec., 2016): 1–36.

[36] Gujarati speakers often pronounce "Kṛṣṇa" as "Krushna." This is not uncommon, as the Sanskritik *ṛ* is/has been pronounced variously across different linguistic regions of South Asia.

[37] "Pushti Satsang."

directly about her role as a female leader: "What challenges have you faced as a woman guru in the Pushtimarg?" I queried. Before answering me she confidently rattled off not only her achievements as reader-exegete (she had given "hundreds and hundreds of *pravacans* and *kathās*," she asserted), but also her position as the primary caretaker for the Krishna *svarūps* that resided in the temple that she herself presided over. The temple that the *beṭījī* established is part of a much larger complex in Baroda, Gujarat, where we had our meeting. She noted that one of her greatest achievements was the temple complex itself, which she named Vraj Dham Haveli and had been built in 1999.[38] Her attendant Sejal elaborated on the details of the *havelī*: "Here we have meeting halls and a visitors' guesthouse," Sejal said, gesturing out the window to one of the three buildings in the complex. She then continued, speaking triumphantly about her guru,

> Jiji [an affectionate name for Goswami Indirabetiji] has established classes [both specific to *sevā* and also vocational] for women, and women's *satsaṅgs*. You'll stay for Shri Dwarkanathji's *darśan* and for *mahāprasād*. And who will perform *āratī* (a lamp ritual)?[39] Jiji does this, she does *everything* here.

As in other temples, where paid and unpaid volunteers help in and around the temple, Vraj Dham Haveli has a host of *sevaks*. What is distinct here, however, is that both male *and* female temple officiants help not only with Krishna's food preparations, but also more directly with the performance of *havelī sevā* itself. This in and of itself is remarkable in the Pushtimargi context where the *sevā* rituals that happen in the innermost rooms of traditionally designed *havelī*s (feeding and clothing Krishna, as described in Chapter 3) are generally reserved for male hereditary leaders and other Brahmin men specially trained in Krishna's *sevā*.[40]

After reinforcing her achievements, Goswami Indirabetiji finally answered my question about how she was received as a Pushtimargi female guru: "I am simply living according to Shri Acharyaji's teachings," she said, "Nowhere is there a teaching from Shri Acharyaji that marriage is required: what *is*

[38] Prior to 1999 Goswami Indirabetiji lived with her older brother Shri Mathureshji Maharaj and his family, also in Baroda.

[39] *Āratī* is a ritual performed by circularly moving a five-wicked lamp before a deity. It also refers to devotional songs associated with the *āratī* ritual.

[40] While the matter did not arise in our conversation, Shital Sharma's discussions with Goswami Indirabetiji confirm that women temple officiants and *sevaks* observe menstrual restrictions while engaged in ritual work around the *havelī* (Sharma, "A Prestigious Path to Grace," 269).

required is that the Vaishnava does not renounce the world." I had not asked her directly about her unmarried status but was well aware that her decision not to marry along with her decision to administer initiations had made her especially controversial among some members of the community, particularly many of her male Vallabha Kul counterparts. The point of Vallabhacharya's distinct teaching on non-renunciation, she asserted, was specifically to avoid egotistical behavior. According to her, "Family helps to ward off the growth of ego. And look, I have always served Shri Krishna and my family. I have always served Vaishnavas and humanity."[41] As a householder tradition, both the sons and daughters of hereditary leaders are expected to marry (men and women alike marry into prescribed Brahmin caste groups). Historically both *bahūjī*s and *beṭījī*s, especially after marriage, lived somewhat guarded lives in accordance with ideals for the preservation of women's "modesty." Until somewhat recently, as one *bahūjī* from Ahmedabad told me, "all *bahūjī*s were in full *pardo* (seclusion from unwanted male gaze) all of the time. The veils they wore went all the way down to the floor: total coverage."

Goswami Indirabetiji's life as a female leader who rose to prominence through her presence as a charismatic and learned reader-exegete inspired both other *beṭījī*s and *bahūjī*s as well as women devotees like Sonali, Yojana, and Mona to assume roles as readers and writers—and more broadly as learners and teachers.[42] According to Yojana, after Goswami Indirabetiji paved the way, women today are even *more* engaged in religious learning than their male counterparts—not "just" with respect to the ritual practices of *sevā*, but also with respect to Pushtimargi philosophy, which is "best learned through studying the original *granths*." In addition to emphasizing how influential Goswami Indirabetiji was in her lifetime, Yojana also suggested that another reason for women's growing interest in textual study is that

[41] I did not ask Goswami Indirabetiji about her choice to have administered Pushtimargi initiation (a practice she stopped after controversy over the matter became heated). Her biographer, however, asked her directly about her choice, and about her role as an exegete. In response she suggested that her identity is not fixed by gender (Gāndhi, *Bhaktiras Calke, Jīvan Madhurū Malke*, 37–38). Vallabhacharya and Vitthalnath, she went on, understood Krishna's *gopī*s to be teachers and role models: "Why, then, can't women be gurus today?" (38).

[42] For instance, Brajlata Bahuji, who is married to Goswami Indirabetiji's brother Chandragopalji Goswami, was inspired by her sister-in-law to pursue an MA in Sanskrit (Sharma, "A Prestigious Path to Grace," 176). Brajlata Bahuji is also an author (Sharma, "A Prestigious Path to Grace," 272). Brajlata Bahuji shared with Shital Sharma that it was also because of Goswami Indirabetiji's "progressive and at times even rebellious attitude towards male Mahārāj authority" that it was conceivable for Brajlata to "'step-outside' the Mahārāj household and offer public lectures on various texts ranging from the Bhāgavata Purāṇa, the vārtās, and Vallabha's philosophical treatises" (Sharma, "A Prestigious Path to Grace," 177).

Vallabhacharya's philosophical system is "basically focused on helping the devotee balance life. Shri Vallabhacharya teaches this: that Krishna should be the center of our lives, but that we cannot renounce all the duties of our lives." Yojana's comment suggests that Pushtimargi philosophy, like the practice of reading itself, is especially helpful for women because it helps them balance social and devotional demands.

This chapter has shown that women's practices of religious reading, whether alone or in *satsaṅg*, not only provide models for devotional living but also help women to cultivate emotional and social well-being as they navigate family dilemmas and more acutely distressing situations. In doing so, women innovate long-standing practices of reading and of ritual behavior—often in creatively conformist ways. Goswami Indirabetiji, for instance, used her status as an erudite reader, writer, and public exegete to assume a fairly "traditional" role as Pushtimargi guru. Yet she also innovated that role, both by virtue of being a woman to begin with (not to mention an unmarried woman), but also by expanding expectations for her fellow *gosvāmīs* to lead the community in new ways (e.g., through humanitarian projects and supporting devotees, practically *and* emotionally). Goswami Indirabetiji therefore subtly challenged traditional Pushtimargi boundaries in ways that were specifically meant to support her devotees'—particularly women's—well-being. Both because of Goswami Indirabetiji's direct inspiration and because of their own intimate networks of female friendship, other Pushtimargi women, too, read in ways that sustain their own, their families', and Krishna's well-being. Mona, Yojana, and Sonali's reading practices all emphasize these affective "benefits" of reading: reading allows Yojana to feel Krishna's grace in her body, reaching a "meditative state," Mona to find emotional comfort as she copes with her grandson's illness, and Sonali to achieve "mental health" for herself and for her conversation partners.

In many ways it is difficult to gauge how contemporary nonhereditary Pushtimargi women's practices of reading are "new," or different from those of their counterparts in the past. As Chapter 2 outlined, there is little accurate data on literacy and practices of reading among different demographics of readers prior to the 20th century. Much of what I have been able to learn about Pushtimargis' reading practices of previous decades and centuries come from written commentaries—none of which are authored by women—or from the *vārtā* narratives themselves. However, what clearly makes women's practices of the contemporary moment distinct is that their interactions with their families and with Krishna require them to negotiate between what is prescribed and described in 17th-century texts and their own everyday-life experiences in the 21st century. The "here and now" is indeed always situated within a distinct set of social and historical circumstances. Although these negotiations are not unique to women alone, women's practices as discussed here distinctly reveal the ways in which religious reading both guides ritual-devotional behavior and also influences networks of care and individual and familial "mental health," to return to Sonali's use of this phrase.

Conclusion: Religious Reading and Everyday Lives

During the bleakest early months of the COVID-19 pandemic in 2020, when my interlocutors in Gujarat were experiencing various degrees of stress and social isolation, virtual *satsaṅg* gatherings became a vital way to maintain devotional networks. Although my interlocutors tell me that meeting virtually cannot fully replace *all* styles of in-person gatherings, technologically mediated *satsaṅg*s and *pravacan*s are increasingly fulfilling many of the functions of religious reading that I have discussed in this book. Reading devotional literature during the pandemic continues to be a dialogical, embodied, and affective practice—one that helps devotees to orient themselves in relationship to each other and to Krishna during an especially difficult social moment. Even when they shift from the physical, communal spaces of temples and devotees' living rooms, both the public and more intimate styles of reading Pushtimargi texts that I have analyzed in this book persist. "*Satsaṅg* has changed during this time, but we still convene. Prabhu [God] does not look badly upon this moment: it is a purposeful challenge He is making us endure," Yojana told me during a WhatsApp phone call just before the new year in 2021. In emphasizing that such practices of religious reading endure through very different socio-historical moments, including the one in which we find ourselves now, I am not suggesting that Pushtimargis' relationships to their devotional texts are timeless. On the contrary, by showing how Pushtimargis continuously, and consciously, turn to religious literature to help them cultivate devotion and to navigate precept and practice, this book has suggested that neither texts themselves, nor the ways in which readers interpret them, are immutable. These relationships are marked by innovation and demonstrate that self-conscious adaptations in reading practices do not diminish their sanctity. Texts and readers, returning again to Edward W. Said's suggestion, are worldly, even as Pushtimargis engage with their religious texts as embodiments of Krishna that help them to bridge the *laukik* and *alaukik*—the worldly and the otherworldly.

Religious Reading and Everyday Lives in Devotional Hinduism. Emilia Bachrach, Oxford University Press. © Oxford University Press 2022. DOI: 10.1093/oso/9780197648599.003.0007

Pushtimargi hagiographies, as discussed in this book's first chapter, are designed in part to facilitate just this type of "bridging"—not only between Krishna's *līlā* and devotees' everyday lives, but also between *vārtā* narratives themselves and the broader landscape of Pushtimargi devotional literature, ritual practices, and community networks. As dialogical texts that inspire ongoing discussion, Pushtimargi *vārtā*s support contemporary readers in how they cope with personal and community challenges, affectively and through different modes of exegesis. That is to say, the worldliness of written texts points more broadly to the ways in which texts, like readers and reading practices themselves, are always situated in specific social and historical contexts. For instance, in the aftermath of the Maharaja Libel case during the late 19th and early 20th centuries, Pushtimargi readers strove to reauthorize their vernacular literature by emphasizing its "authenticity," showing both the elasticity of the *vārtā*s in relationship to their readers *and* devotees' perceived need to change modes of receiving premodern texts to suit their present circumstances. In changing the physical texts themselves through the medium of print and the addition of new written commentaries, practices of reading inevitably changed, too. Commentarial reading—the theme of this book's second chapter—is a primary way in which we can learn about hermeneutical approaches to particular text traditions and more broadly about past and present interpretive communities. In addition to being telling examples of how commentarial writing functioned during a transformative moment in the Pushtimargi community, the written texts considered in Chapter 2 also illuminate the performative process by which readers re-establish their vernacular literature as canonical. It is not as if written commentaries that predate this period (though there are few extant) "operated under a precanonical consciousness," to borrow a phrase from scholar Deven Patel.[1] Rather, during this particular historical moment Pushtimargi vernacular texts became subjects of a "tense debate around which an audience of readers and scholars competed for hermeneutic control."[2] Of course, in the context of the Maharaja Libel Case and its aftermath, it was not only "readers and scholars" who debated the *vārtā*s within the context of sectarian history and philosophy, but also colonial judges and self-proclaimed reformers like Karsandas Mulji, who used the hagiographies as fodder to argue that the Pushtimarg was representative of "heterodox" Hinduism. Just as Patel suggests that

[1] Patel, *Text to Tradition*, 50. As I suggest in Chapter 2, aside from Hariray's *Bhāvprakāś*, there are few written commentaries on *Vārtā Sāhitya* that predate the 19th century.

[2] Patel, *Text to Tradition*, 50.

late-medieval commentaries on the *Naiṣadhīya* show how the popular Sanskrit poem that he considers became the "locus" for debates about the "very *norms* of good poetry,"[3] late 19th- and early 20th-century *vārtā* commentaries reveal how the *vārtā*s had become—in a very specific historical moment—a locus for debates about the very *norms* of modern Hinduism. Even after the intensity of this late 19th-century moment had passed, reading practices were forever changed with the popularity of book culture, which allowed Pushtimargis to read more independently and to contribute discursively in print to their literary traditions. My own study of Pushtimargi readers and texts in this book has hewn closely to the ways in which the community itself has worked to continuously redefine Pushtimargi identity and practice through reading religiously. Yet, Patel's work on the *Naiṣadhīya* reminds us that studying reading practices (religious or otherwise) can illuminate how "norms" are established between communities and beyond sectarian boundaries.

This book's third chapter hints at the ways in which public readings during contemporary *pravacan*s and via discourse on social media platforms look beyond the Pushtimarg itself as devotee-readers debate community-wide concerns over *havelī sevā* and temple reconstruction projects of the 21st century. Even those who are fully immersed in reading Pushtimargi texts as sectarian texts, like hereditary leader Shyam Manohar Goswami, often compare Pushtimarg-specific practice to that of other religious traditions (e.g., the Swaminarayan Sampraday), and to daily-life practices and modes of self-perception not explicitly marked as "religious" to begin with (e.g., Shyam Manohar Goswami's use of psychoanalysis when analyzing the *vārtā*s). Though South Asia studies scholars attend to multiple interpretations of texts that have canonical status in and beyond Pushtimargi Hinduism (including the *Bhāgavatapurāṇa*, which is revered, if not debated, across Vaishnava traditions as well as in other sectarian/Hindu communities),[4] religious reading as a topic of comparative study has drawn little scholarly attention. One reason for this may be that many—perhaps a majority—of South Asians, past and present, may not read or engage with *written* texts at all. Through decades of research, religious studies scholars working in South Asia and beyond have repeatedly shown that the academic overreliance

[3] Ibid.
[4] See, for instance, Ravi Gupta and Kenneth Valpey's edited volume *The Bhāgavata Purāṇa: Sacred Text and Living Tradition* (New York: Cambridge University Press, 2013).

on textual study in teaching about and researching religion is myopic. As scholars Megan Goodwin and Ilyse Morgenstein Fuerst say pointedly in their podcast, "people's practices tell us more about religions than texts . . . for a whole host of reasons."[5] However, engaging analytically and affectively with *narratives*—whether oral or written—is undoubtedly a central way in which many religious people in South Asia and beyond traverse their everyday lives. Recognizing that narratives in one form or another are central to religious peoples' lives is not new. However, this book invites students and scholars of canonical religious texts to consider anew that reading is always a cultural practice and therefore one that requires the same degree of attention as written texts "themselves." It is not *merely* that reading as a cultural practice deserves the same attention scholars give to texts: what I am suggesting here is that relationships *between* texts and readers deserve careful scholarly attention. To fully appreciate the intrinsic dynamism of religious texts we must consider the ways that people relate to and interpret their religious literature—that is, we must approach religious texts as part of their broader performative canons.

Pushtimargis debate the ways in which their texts should be read and analyzed to guide contemporary practice. That they *should* be read, however, is not contested. Indeed, according to one of my first Pushtimargi conversation partners in Jaipur, the *vārtās* are read ". . . by everyone. Even if people don't read daily in this way, they will know these stories. They are primary for followers of the Pushtimarg and they put us in a devotional mood each time [we read/hear them]. They are an ocean for us." As shown in this book's Introduction and in Chapters 3–5, devotees' conversations that arise from reading the *vārtās*—often in close relationship to the *Bhāgavatapurāṇa* and Vallabhacharya's treatises—touch on all matters of daily individual and community life, from sectarian leadership to gendered ways of fulfilling familial roles. These conversations, whether formalized through *pravacan* or specific types of discourse during *satsaṅg*, are often affectively charged. The emotional quality of these discussions, and of the narratives themselves, are influenced both by people's intense love for their Krishna *svarūp*s and by their relationships with family members. As shown in Chapters 4 and 5, Pushtimargis, particularly women, regularly discuss the challenges they face in balancing the needs of their family members with the demanding

[5] Megan Goodwin and Ilyse Morgenstein Fuerst, "Episode 102: Who Gets Left out of 'Religion'?," accessed January 29, 2020, in *Keeping 101: A Killjoy's Introduction to Religion*, podcast, audio, 01:16, https://keepingit101.com/e102.

round-the-clock care they provide for Thakurji. Particular hagiographies, and certainly the context of *satsaṅg* itself, help devotees to mitigate these challenges. Occasionally, though, as we learned from Dr. Yojana Mahajan in Chapter 5, it is not solely the content of the stories or discussion about texts that animate reading as a religious practice: sometimes *reading itself* as a practice is what cultivates devotees' well-being, putting the devotee into a "meditative state."

Pushtimargis as religious readers tend to take up what we might think of as a type of permanent "residence" in the "habitats" built (at least in part) by their beloved texts. These habitats—cultural environments—need constant care and maintenance. Texts themselves need to be refurbished on occasion by being translated, reframed, or analyzed in innovative ways to suit the reader's present. Physical texts, too, need repair, as evidenced by the patched-up, well-loved, and well-worn copies of religious texts many of my conversation partners read from during *satsaṅg*. And just as Pushtimargis understand Krishna himself to be manifest in texts and in their readings, the *svarūps* that devotees care for, too, are sensitive to change. Such change can come about unexpectedly, as it has during the COVID-19 pandemic. For instance, certain *sevā* supplies, such as specialized ingredients for the preparation of Krishna's food, have suddenly become difficult to obtain. But Thakurji requires his caretakers to change their ways of attending to him based on more expected, daily, and seasonal changes as well. For example, Thakurji prefers cooling foods and liquids on long summer days, and warming ones during the winter. In this way, my interlocutors repeatedly remind me, a certain kind of context sensitivity is called for in the way one lives in this world, including the ways one reads and cares for family and for Krishna. Examples of such context sensitivity and creative continuity have punctuated this study, beginning with this book's opening anecdote, which showcased women coming to the conclusion that Thakurji could be fed pizza as long as the "untraditional" meal was prepared with loving care so that the deity would not burn his lips. In part, the ability to recognize and act upon this constant need to "change with the times" is how hereditary leaders and devotees alike seem to judge their own (and others') success as reader-exegetes and as ritual practitioners of *sevā*. We might remember this sentiment in Goswami Indirabetiji's proclamation that "it is the nature of things to change, so we change with the times, but this behavior doesn't change Shri Krishna. God is immutable." This sentiment is likewise apparent in any number of ways I have described devotees' innovations in their *sevā* practices based on how daily routines are altered because of social or professional requirements. Recall, for example, how Lila, from Rajabetiji's *satsaṅg* (Chapter 4), told me that when traveling to visit family in Florida she still finds time to sing to Thakurji over the telephone as he is waking up each morning back in Ahmedabad, in her friend's care.

In bringing my account of religious reading and everyday lives in devotional Hinduism to a close, I turn to a very straightforward question Mona Desai asked me one afternoon when I had come to her house to say goodbye after a brief visit to Ahmedabad in 2015. "In the end what did you learn from your research on our Pushtimarg?" Mona queried. Pushtimargis often ask me these types of direct "what did you learn" questions in order to confirm that I have "properly" understood whatever it is they feel I should have gleaned from any given event (a *pravacan*, a *satsaṅg* gathering, a specific text, etc.). In response to such inquiries, I often provide what I believe to be well-established and neutral accounts of Pushtimargi teachings relative to whatever specific issue is being analyzed. I tend to respond to questions in this way even when Pushtimargis ask me about contentious topics, such as Goswami Indirabetiji's practice of initiating devotees as a female descendant of Vallabhacharya, or the renovation of *havelī*s and the public-facing changes to temples more broadly. "Well," as I once responded to such a question posed to me by one of Shyam Manohar Goswami's followers about whether or not *I* (a non-Pushtimargi) should be permitted to donate money to Shrinathji's *havelī*, "this is not up to me to decide, is it? I have been told that *gosvāmī*s and Vaishnavas themselves must determine such matters, but that Krishna makes the final decision." In this case, my conversation partner did not accept my attempt to dodge his question. "No, tell me what you think," he said, "you're a researcher, aren't you?" Somewhat embarrassed, I explained that I simply did not have a good answer, nor did I feel it was my place to make any conclusive statements about what Pushtimargis should or should not be doing. Mona, too, was dissatisfied with my similarly vague answer to her question: "I've learned so much." I went on, explaining (though she already knew) that I had written a doctoral thesis on the topic of *Vārtā Sāhitya* and hoped one day to complete a book. "I will give you a copy of my book," I said, hoping to get away with not saying more. "Emilia," Mona said, concluding our conversation on the matter, "whatever you have understood is very good, but it is only what *you* have understood."

With this comment, Mona cautions me to acknowledge my own subjectivity as a scholar—something I have grappled with throughout my research for this book. In prompting me to consider myself in this way, Mona's comment also echoes a popular South Asian parable about a group of blind people examining a creature unknown to them—an elephant. One, touching the elephant's trunk determines it is like a large snake, while another, feeling one of the animal's ears, suggests it must be like a fan. While this parable has been narrated and interpreted in various ways, its ultimate teaching is that one person's perception of any given thing is subjective: something can only begin to be understood from multiple perspectives. My evocation of this parable and of Mona's parallel suggestion that my ability to "know" will always be limited exemplifies one of the broadest arguments of this book: no study of how people read religiously can claim to be final because, much like the practice of religious reading itself, it is an ongoing process. I end, therefore, with an invitation to others to further explore the topic of religious reading—among and between multiple communities, and from various perspectives—and of texts as therefore inherently linked to various repertoires of performance and to daily life. We might draw inspiration from the way my conversation partners commonly conclude their readings of Pushtimargi hagiographies from the *84VV* during *satsaṅg*: "a telling of this story can have no end."

Appendix: Select Translations of Key Texts

What follows are three translations of complete *vārtās* as they appear in Dwarkadas Parikh's edited versions of the *84VV* (2011) and *252VV* (2009). These translations are meant to serve as examples of the general structure of the written narratives as they appear in most modern versions of the *84VV* and *252VV* that contain Hariray's *Bhāvprakāś* commentaries. I have selected these particular narratives because they are average in length and likewise have an average number of *prasaṅgs*. My translations stay close to Parikh's text. However, in aiming to convey the unique literary flavor of the hagiographies, I have also omitted certain redundancies and have added certain clarifications. Comments in footnotes provide further information about theological, social, and linguistic details of the narratives.

Example A: The Vārtā *of Tulsa (from the* 84VV*)*

NB: The following *vārtā* describes events in the life of a devotee named Tulsa (Tulsāṃ), whose *vārtā* appears in a sequence of narratives that also describe her family members, including her father Padmanabhadas.

Now is told the *bhāv* of the *vārtā* of Tulsa, the daughter of Shri Acharyaji's *sevak* Padmanabhadas.[1]

> ***Bhāvprakāś***: In *līlā*, Tulsa is a *sakhī* named Manikundala and her father Padmanabhadas is Champaklata, one of Svamini's eight *sakhīs*. Just as the *jyotī* (aura) of a *maṇī* (gem) in a *kuṇḍālī* (earring), Manikundala spreads light in four directions. Tulsa is a *sāttvik* (virtuous) devotee.[2] She is attentive to the command of Padmanabhadas.

Episode 1: One day a Vaishnava, a *sevak* of Shri Acharyaji, came to Tulsa's house. He took *darśan* of Shri Mathuranathji (Tulsa's Krishna *svarūp*) at *rājbhog āratī* (Krishna's midday food ritual).[3] Then Tulsa said to this Vaishnava: "Rise and take a bath. Take *mahāprasād*." "I'll go home to take my bath," the Vaishnava responded. Tulsa remained silent. Then the Vaishnava got up and left for his home, leaving Tulsa feeling a bit mournful. "That Vaishnava has left my house hungry," she thought to herself.

[1] Here I take *bhāv* to mean the "mood" or "meaning" of the *vārtā*. The translated text appears in D. Parīkh, ed., *Caurāsī Vaiṣṇavan kī Vārtā*, 53–58

[2] As discussed in Chapter 1, *sāttvik* refers to one of the three *guṇs* (qualities) that Hariray applies to each of the protagonists in the *84VV* and *252VV*. This is the "highest" quality that Hariray applies to the *vārtās*' protagonists.

[3] Mathuranathji is the Krishna *svarūp* that Tulsa and her family care for in the *84VV*. This *svarūp* continues to be worshiped by descendants of one branch of the *sampradāy* in Kota, Rajasthan. *Rājbhog* refers to one of eight established periods of *sevā*—the time, usually before noon, when Krishna *svarūps* are offered a full meal.

> ***Bhāvprakāś***: The Vaishnava, a *gauḍ* (Bengali) Brahmin, did not take Shri Mathuranathji's *mahāprasād* because of his caste convention.[4] Tulsa understood this and therefore did not insist that he take the *prasād*. In *līlā*, this Vaishnava is the *sakhī* of Lalitaji, Saurbha by name. Tulsa as Manikundala is a *sakhī* of Padmanabhadas as Champaklatahas. Shri Mathuranathji is under her power. Therefore, the Vaishnava did not eat the *mahāprasād*—without the command of Lalitaji how could he take it? This is why the Vaishnava went to his own home, which caused Tulsa to feel mournful.

Then Tulsa thought to herself, "It must be due to his caste conventions that he did not take the *sakhaṛī* (cooked in water) food items.[5] Alright then, tomorrow morning I will serve *prasād* of fried bread." Later she prepared and set aside some sieved flour. Then she went to sleep. That day Tulsa did not take *mahāprasād*. Then, that night, Shri Mathuranathji said to Tulsa in a dream, "In the morning serve *mahāprasād* to that Vaishnava. He will not eat *mahāprasād* at his own home."

> ***Bhāvprakāś***: From this it should be understood that Shri Thakurji meant: "Tomorrow the Vaishnava will take the *mahāprasād*. Do not worry." Later, after the first incident at Tulsa's home, Shri Thakurji had questioned the Vaishnava: "Why did you not take the *mahāprasād* from Tulsa's place? Take it in the morning. This is also the command of Lalitaji." Indeed, Lalitaji also said: "Take the *mahāprasād* from Tulsa's place. There is no distinction between her and our own *bhāv* for Shri Thakurji."[6]

Episode 2: Then, at dawn Tulsa prepared fried bread, woke Shri Thakurji, and began to perform *śṛṅgār sevā*.[7] In the meantime, the Vaishnava took his morning bath and arrived at Tulsa's house ready to perform Shri Thakurji's *sevā*. Tulsa prepared the *bhog* and came outside, saying to the Vaishnava, "*Jāī Shri Krishna*. Get up, go bathe, and remember the Lord." The Vaishnava responded, saying, "I have come, bathed and am in a ritually pure state." When the time came, Tulsa completed the *rājbhog* and performed *āratī*. The Vaishnava took *darśan*. Then Tulsa prepared Shri Thakurji for rest, came outside, and placed *prasād* in a leaf plate for the Vaishnava. On the plate she placed fried bread, sugar balls, chickpea dumplings in curd, and pickles.[8] "Take the *prasād*," she said. Then the

[4] The Braj Bhasha reads, "*jñānt vyauhār*." Here *jñānt* seems to refer to a *gotra* or a particular lineage, rather than to caste as such. Both parties are Brahmin—one *gauḍ* (Bengali) and the other unspecified.

[5] *Sakhaṛī* refers to grains that have been cooked in water but can also include certain kinds of bread and various kinds of cooked, raw, or pickled fruits and vegetables. *Ansakhaṛī* refers to sweets, dairy products (milk, butter, curd, etc.), fried breads, and certain kinds of dried fruits and nuts. For further information on types of food and food preparation, see Bennett, "In Nanda Baba's House: The Devotional Experience in Pushti Marg Temples," 197.

[6] This is a fine example of how Hariray explains or justifies characters' behaviors in the *laukik* world by referring to *līlā*. On the one hand, the Vaishnava does not accept certain food items due to "caste conventions" in the *laukik* world—he is a Bengali Brahmin, and Tulsa's family is from a different (unspecified) Brahmin community. On the other hand, Hariray explains that the *real* reason that the Vaishnava does not accept the food is because he is in a different group of *sakhīs* in *līlā* and therefore needs to receive permission from his head *sakhī* before accepting food from a *sakhī* of a different group.

[7] *Śṛṅgār sevā* refers to one of the eight established periods of *sevā*, but also more generally to ritually dressing and decorating a Krishna *svarūp*.

[8] In the Braj Bhasha text, these items are listed as *pūrī*, *būrā*, *dahītharā*, and *sandhāno*. In other versions of the *84VV*, *dahītharā* reads *dahībara*, which is likely the correct form of the word.

Vaishnava said, "I will not take this. Put out *sakharī prasād*—that I will take." Then Tulsa said, "do not feel concerned about not taking it—this is after all the way of your caste conventions." The Vaishnava responded with "This is indeed true. At first I had it that way, but now I have been given the command to accept what you have offered. Therefore, I'll take the *mahāprasād*." Tulsa put out both *sakharī* and *ansakharī prasād* before the Vaishnava and he took the *sakharī prasād*. Afterward, when the Vaishnava returned to his own house Tulsa felt very pleased.

> ***Bhāvprakāś***: From this it should be understood that if a Vaishnava comes to your home, you should show him all the respect in your power. Why? It is said in *Śrī Bhāgavat* (*Bhāgavatapurāṇa*) that the house in which you do not even get offered water, etc., is considered to be the hole of a snake. So, Tulsa showed the Vaishnava such affection.

Episode 3: Once Shri Gusainji came to Tulsa's house. Thinking him to be greater than even Shri Thakurji, Tulsa performed *sevā* very well for her *guru* and Shri Gusainji was very pleased. One day Shri Gusainji was resting after his meal. Tulsa pleased Shri Gusainji by reciting accounts of the Lord. Then, Shri Gusainji, who was in a state of great satisfaction from hearing the *Bhāgavatapurāṇa*, said to Tulsa, "Of course the child of such a great devotee as Padmanabhadas should be just like this."

> ***Bhāvprakāś***: The meaning of this is that, if Tulsa is a *sakhī* in *līlā*, then why would she not be like this? In *līlā* Shri Gusainji has the form of Chandravaliji. He relates to Shri Thakurji through the romantic sentiment of *parakīyā bhāv* (the devotional sentiments of one who belongs to another). Therefore, the comic sentiment is also very dear to him. He asks saucily: "Does Shri Thakurji make you experience the bliss of his physical form? You are too a *sakhī* after all. Doing the *sevā* of Shri Thakurji you also gain some power over Him. Therefore, you are also involved in our partnership." He speaks with this manner of sarcasm. But Tulsa is a pure, *sāttvik* devotee. She is not very saucy. She is refined.

Later, Shri Gusainji asked Tulsa, "Does Shri Thakurji make you share in the depths of devotional feeling?" In reply Tulsa said, "My Lord. I eat my fill and sleep comfortably. But recitation of Shri Acharyaji's scriptures should be performed constantly." Shri Gusainji was very pleased by her reply:

> ***Bhāvprakāś***: "I eat my fill and sleep easily" can mean: as though we were receptacles, Shri Thakurji makes us share in that experience to the extent that our stomachs may contain the *rasa*. Therefore, in the company of Shri Thakurji we are allowed to sleep comfortably. We maintain *svakīyā bhāv* (the sentiment of a woman who is faithful to her husband), are happy, and there is no reason to worry: this is the primary sense. From the perspective of focusing one's *bhāv* on the guru, then the meaning of what Tulsa said to Shri Gusainji is as follows: "My Lord! Torn away from Shri Thakurji; I have taken numerous births, but in no birth have I filled my belly. I have not slept happily. Now, you give me grace and have taken me into your refuge. Now, in this birth, my stomach is filled and I have also slept in the sole refuge of Shri Thakurji. I endured sadness in each birth due to ignorance." This is one meaning of Tulsa's statement.
>
> And from the *dainya pakṣ* (perspective of humility), the statement, "what devotional feelings does Thakurji make us feel?" can be taken to mean the following: "My stomach is filled. I sleep easily. Just as an animal simply eats and sleeps. Any further

functions come about because they are imposed by the will of others: hit the animal and then it will perform an action. Similar is our fondness for eating and drinking." Some people perform *sevā* because of the fear of others' condemnation, but this is not how the children of Padmanabhadas perform *sevā*. In this way it is done for the sake of public prestige. Therefore, we can take Tulsa's answer to the statement, "What does He make me experience?" in the sense of what the poet Surdas has sung: "Who can manage the lowly, they simply fill their bellies and sleep." That is, "These base people should not even be spoken to. They merely desire comfort of the body. I am also such a type. However, the lessons of Shri Acharyaji's scriptures should always be recited." The sense of this statement is that even though the base may not understand the meaning of Shri Acharyaji's scriptures, through the mere act of recitation Shri Acharyaji still shows all of his power. Therefore, Tulsa's readings of Shri Acharyaji's works do not indicate her own *puruṣārth* (human accomplishments). Rather, the beauty of reciting Shri Acharyaji's works is that by simply reciting them the Lord shows His grace. In this way, having heard the love-wrapped words of Tulsa, Shri Gusainji's heart was heavy with pleasure.[9]

Such was Tulsa as a devotee that Shri Gusainji always remained pleased with her. Therefore, there is no limit to the extent of her *vārtā*; how much can the essence of it be revealed?[10]

Example B: The Vārtā *of Purushottamdas (from the* 84VV*)*

Now is told the *bhāv* of the *vārtā* of Purushottamdas and his wife, Kshatriyas, who lived in Agra at Rajghat:[11]

Bhāvprakāś: In *līlā*, Purushottamdas is the *sakhī* of Shri Chandravali who goes by the name of Madhavi. His wife's name in *līlā* is Malati. The worldly homes of these two Kshatriyas were situated near to each other in Agra at Rajghat. It was into these homes that Purushottamdas and his wife were born. As the two Kshatriya families were very friendly with one another the men of both families said to one another: "It would be good if our son and daughter got married." So, the two families united and the marriage took place. Within a year both fathers passed away. Once, when Shri Acharyaji arrived in Agra, Purushottamdas and his wife happened to be sitting out in their garden. As soon as they caught sight of Shri Acharyaji, the couple said to each other: "We should take the refuge of Shri Acharyaji." So Purushottamdas jumped up and ran to Shri Acharyaji, prostrated himself and entreated him, saying: "My Lord! Have mercy upon us and take us into your refuge. Please come and grace my home."[12] In response Shri Acharyaji said: "Come to Adel and take the name of Shri

[9] Hariray's various ways of interpreting Tulsa's statement and relationship with Vitthalnath are not entirely clear. Those with whom I have read this *vārtā* in Ahmedabad have asserted that Hariray's gloss is meant to explain that Tulsa's experience of Shri Thakurji is beyond verbal expression. Because she is such a pure devotee, it would be absurd to think of her as a mere animal who eats and sleeps. She not only performs *sevā* for Thakurji and for her guru but also reads and lives by the scriptures of Vallabhacharya.

[10] *so kahāṃ tāīṃ kahiye*: "how much can be revealed," or "to what extent can it be told," is a common way in which *vārtās* are concluded in the *84VV* and *252VV*.

[11] The translated text appears in D. Parīkh, ed., *Caurāsī Vaiṣṇavan kī Vārtā*, 150–154.

[12] This is a formulaic entreaty for initiation, which appears repeatedly in the *84VV* and *252VV*.

Krishna from Shri Gusainji."[13] Purushottamdas replied: "My Lord! What's the difference between you and Shri Gusainji? You make me your *sevak*. How can I have any faith that my body will carry on? Such an opportunity to take your *darśan* may not be easy to come by later on." In this way, since he was a *daivī jīv*, Purushottamdas had become aware that Shri Acharyaji's form was divine. Then Shri Acharyaji went to Purushottamdas' home. He had Purushottamdas and Purushottamdas' wife make a dedication to Shri Krishna. Then Purushottamdas and his wife entreated Shri Acharyaji, saying: "My Lord! Now what is it that we should do?" Shri Acharyaji said: "Do the Lord's *sevā*." Then Purushottamdas said: "My Lord! Bestow Shri Thakurji upon me so that I may perform His *sevā*." But Shri Acharyaji replied: "A blemish will come upon your heads.[14] You should go to bathe in Gangaji (the revered Ganges River) and then come to Adel where I will bestow Shri Thakurji upon you. You two both have these mothers who are *āsurī jīvs* and will cause you trouble." Then Purushottamdas and his wife said: "But our mothers show a great deal of affection for us. So why would they cause any trouble?" Shri Acharyaji replied: "They have shown you affection because until now you were *not* Vaishnavas. Just see what happens when they hear that you have become Vaishnavas! I don't much like managing such troubles, so I'm taking off." Then Purushottamdas and his wife fearfully put together whatever offering they could manage and quickly presented it to Shri Acharyaji. They bade farewell to their guru who, aware of the imminent trouble, went immediately to his home in Adel. In the meantime, Purushottamdas and his wife fearfully refrained from telling their mothers that they had become Vaishnavas for three days. They sustained themselves on plain milk.[15] Then Purushottamdas' mother saw the *mālā* around his neck and said: "Son, why is there a *mālā* around your neck? Our sacred thread is paramount. Why the *mālā*?" Purushottamdas did not reply. Then the mother of Purushottamdas' wife saw her own daughter's head and neck exposed. She cried when she saw the *mālā*, thinking: "Man and wife have both become ascetics!" Then the mother of Purushottamdas' wife said to Purushottamdas' mother: "Your son and my daughter have both taken to wearing the *mālā*—they have both become ascetics. What should we do?" Then the one said to the other: "Come on, let's remove those *mālās*, otherwise both our children will surely perish!" So, both mothers came to the husband and wife and exclaimed: "Remove these *mālās* this very moment! If you don't, then you'll both destroy yourselves!" Then Purushottamdas summoned ten to twenty of his relations and addressed the mothers in front of everyone: "These *mālās* are part and parcel of who we are. We wouldn't care if our heads fall off, but we will never part with these *mālās*. What harm are the *mālās* to you? If you desire, you can continue to live with us, or, if you prefer you will be given a separate house and a man will stay there with you as your servant. Take whatever you like. If it is possible for us, then we will serve you. If you want, you can stay in this house and we will go to live in a separate home. We will do as you say, just don't cause any problems: we will absolutely not abandon our *mālās*. And we won't take food or drink touched by your hands. If you take *mālās* yourselves and become Vaishnavas

[13] Taking the *nām*, or "the name" refers to the first part of sectarian initiation when the new devotee recites a mantra stating that he or she takes refuge in Krishna. See Chapter 1 for further details about the process of initiation.

[14] The Braj Bhasha reads, "*tumhāre māthe kalaṅk āvego*"—*kalaṅk*, meaning spot or blemish.

[15] The implication of this statement is that because Purushottamdas and his wife had become Vaishnavas, they had therefore committed to only eating certain kinds of foods prepared in certain kinds of ways. Because of this, they could not accept the food their uninitiated mothers would have presumably prepared for the household.

then water from your hands will be acceptable to us." Hearing this, both mothers became angry: "You both have become ascetics and are now making us into ascetics too? We nurtured you and in your view we are nothing but lowly leather workers and sweepers, thinking: 'We won't even take their water!' We'll both die on account of you two." In this way, for five days nobody took water. All their relatives and even the leader of the village came to resolve the issue, but the two mothers would not listen. That night, while Purushottamdas and his wife were sleeping, the two mothers went to the household well, jumped into it and died. In the morning Purushottamdas performed their last rites. Then everyone in the community began to say: "Since you, man and wife, have led to your mothers' untimely end, go bathe in Gangaji. Only then may you return to our community." Man and wife thought to themselves: "We must go to Shri Acharyaji and have him establish the Lord's *sevā* for us. Let's go." Then they both left from their hometown and came to Prayag. After bathing, they came to Adel, prostrated themselves to Shri Acharyaji and Shri Gusainji, and told them everything: "My Lord! Everything happened just as you said it would. Both our mothers died and all of our afflictions have been extinguished. Now bestow upon us the Lord's *sevā*. Then Shri Acharyaji said: "Those two were *āsurī jīv*s, but now that you have become Vaishnavas they too will be sheltered by the Lord. If one person becomes a Vaishnava, then their entire family becomes spiritually accomplished. Now go do the Lord's *sevā*. In Adel there lived an old Brahmin who followed the path of *pūjā* (ritual) and who had a small Krishna *svarūp*.[16] Speaking to the Brahmin, Shri Acharyaji said: "If you can no longer perform *pūjā* for Shri Thakurji then give Him to me." In reply, the Brahmin said: "I was just thinking about who I could give Him to now that I can no longer perform *pūjā*." Then Shri Acharyaji bathed Shri Thakurji in the five holy substances and bestowed Him upon Purushottamdas. Purushottamdas stayed in Adel for a few days and after learning all the ways in which to perform *sevā*, returned to Agra. All members of the community prepared meals for Brahmins in their kitchens in order to dispel all worldly disputes and Purushottamdas and his wife began to perform the Lord's *sevā*.

Episode 1: One day Shri Gusainji came to Agra. When he came to Purushottamdas' home, Purushottamdas' wife was sequestered. Shri Gusainji asked Purushottamdas, "Where is your wife?" Purushottamdas said, "My Lord! The *janeu* (sacred thread) must have broken." Then Shri Gusainji realized that she was sitting separately. Because of this, Shri Gusainji bathed and himself prepared everything for Thakurji's meal: lentils, rice, five or six vegetables, and sweet rice pudding. When it was time to roll the bread, Purushottamdas' wife, who had just bathed, came to sit down. Then Shri Gusainji asked, "Where were you until now?" Then she said, "My Lord! I had some work to do."

> ***Bhāvprakāś***: At this time Purushottamdas' wife's fifth day of confinement due to menstruation had passed. She had remained hidden thinking: "I should not show my face to Shri Gusainji until I have bathed."[17]

[16] The comparison between *pūjā* and *sevā* is intended to further distinguish those who follow the Pushtimargi from those who do not.

[17] This is in reference to the "traditional" observances surrounding menstruation when women do not perform ritual duties, etc. Contemporary Pushtimargi women continue to observe such measures. Many of the women I am in communication with tell me that they return to performing *sevā* on the fourth day of their monthly cycles.

Then she finished rolling the bread. Shri Gusainji had also completed all the other food preparations and thus set out Shri Thakurji's meal. When Thakurji had completed the meal, Shri Gusainji prepared Shri Thakurji for *anosar* (rest). Then the couple said to Shri Gusainji, "My Lord! Take your meal on this very plate that Shri Thakurji has eaten from." Then Shri Gusainji said: "How can one take a meal on the plate of Shri Thakurji? I'll take my own meal on a leaf plate." Then Purushottamdas said, "My Lord! It's not as if our wealth has decreased or that all the coppersmiths have died. New utensils will come our way!" Reasoning in this way, Purushottamdas served the meal to Shri Gusainji on Shri Thakurji's plate.

> ***Bhāvprakāś***: From this it is known that they had devotional sentiments for Shri Gusainji. Furthermore, in *līlā* Shri Chandravaliji takes her own meal with Shri Thakurji from the very same plate. The divine form of Purushottamdas was the *sakhī* of Shri Chandravaliji, who is the divine form of Shri Gusainji. All of the refulgence of *līlā* is *sphūrti* (shines through).[18] Therefore, Purushottamdas served Shri Gusainji his meal on Shri Thakurji's plate. The man and wife had great affection for Shri Gusainji, which is why they thought, "If we bring the dish over again on a different plate, then the food will lose its taste and get cold. The delay in preparing the food is also not good." Thus, with great affection they served Gusainji the meal on the same plate that Shri Thakurji had eaten from.

Then Shri Gusainji ate his meal and sat down. Then Purushottamdas' wife came to sit down nearby and said, "My Lord! Eat this food." Then Shri Gusainji said, "I'll eat as much as I like." Then Purushottamdas' wife said: "My Lord! Would that you eat in all Vaishnavas' homes just as you eat in the home of Nandaji (Lord Krishna's adopted father as told in the *Bhāgavatapurāṇa*)."[19]

> ***Bhāvprakāś***: From this it is understood that: "in Nandaji's house you eat in accordance with the desires of the devotees." To this Gusainji said: "I'll take as much as I desire. Will this do?"

In this way, Purushottamdas and his wife spoke affectionately with Shri Gusainji. They served him further helpings of the food and Shri Gusainji was pleased. Then the couple had Shri Gusainji sleep on Shri Thakurji's bed—right there on His holy bedding and pillow—and began to worship Shri Gusainji's feet. Then Shri Gusainji said, "Now get up, you two, and go take *mahāprasād* for yourselves. Then the couple said, "My Lord! We will always take *mahāprasād*." In this way, for five to seven days they had Shri Gusainji stay with them—constantly serving him fresh things with love and firm resolve. Always new leaf plates, bed, clothing, etc., were presented. Such a husband and wife are blessed devotees.

[18] The "shining through" refers to the luminescence of *līlā* suddenly becoming apparent in the worldly context. That is, the parallel reality of the divine world is causally linked to and ever present in the *laukik* context.

[19] The point being made here is that Purushottamdas and his wife, as hosts, wish for Krishna to eat fulsomely—just as he would in Nanda's home (that is, in his own father's home) in Braj. In this context, as throughout the *vārtās*, the guru (here Gusainji) is being compared to Krishna himself.

***Bhāvprakāś*:** In this *vārtā* the following principle was established: they have more love for the guru than there is even for Shri Thakurji. If Vaishnavas act in such a way then they will reap the fruits of their deeds.

Example C: The Vārtā *of Raskhan (from the* 252VV*)*

Now is told the *bhāv* of the *vārtā* of Raskhan, a Sayed Pathan, Shri Gusainji's *sevak*.[20]

Episode 1: Raskhan lived in Delhi. He was quite attached to the boy of a certain merchant.[21] He loved the boy so much that he'd gaze upon him night and day. He even consumed the leftover food and water of anything the boy left behind. Those in Raskhan's *jātī* (community) used to spite him, saying, "Why do you eat the leftovers of a Hindu? Now you've become a *kāphar* (infidel)."[22] Replying, Raskhan would say, "I am what I am, and if you speak badly of me, I'll hit you." This is how Raskhan's love for the boy influenced him, and everyone in the community was afraid of him. Many days passed like this.

Episode 2: One day, while visiting Delhi, two Vaishnavas observed Raskhan's behavior toward the merchant's son. One Vaishnava said to the other, "Look, brother. This Raskhan models attachment. He follows that Hindu boy everywhere. He cannot live without the boy and is totally unashamed of what people say about him with respect to caste or the rest. Is this not the type of attachment one should have for the Lord?" Meanwhile, the love-struck Raskhan was standing nearby and saw how one of the Vaishnavas clapped his hand to his forehead and stuck his nose up into the air. "Was it about me that you just did that? Tell me or I'll knock you out cold!" Raskhan drew his sword and the Vaishnava cautiously explained, "If you loved the Lord as you do that boy, you'd find fulfillment." Raskhan asked, "Whom do you call "Lord"? I don't know anything about this." The Vaishnavas responded: "The Lord is the one from whom the world's magnificence emerges." Raskhan asked, "How do I come to recognize the Lord?" One of the Vaishnavas took out of his turban a painting of Krishna in the form of Shrinathji. Immediately upon viewing the painting, Raskhan's eyes welled with tears and his mind spun. His love for the boy then came to an end.

***Bhāvprakāś*:** Here it is shown that attachment, even if worldly, is divine and therefore, if sincere, can be transformed, taking a being towards God. Raskhan's attachment to that boy was sincere and real, and so he was therefore able to take that affection and become attached to Shrinathji.

Raskhan then inquired, "Where does this *mahbūb* (beloved one) stay?" One of the Vaishnavas replied, "The Beloved lives in Braj." Raskhan demanded, "Give me that painting." The Vaishnava, recognizing Raskhan to be a *daivī jīv*, gave the painting to him, and Raskhan departed for Braj. He went to many temples on his way, but nowhere did

[20] The translated text appears in D. Parīkh, ed., *Do Sau Bāvan Vaiṣṇavan kī Vārtā*, 341–347.
[21] The Braj Bhasha word used in the *vārtā* to describe Raskhan's love/attachment for the boy, and subsequently for Krishna, is *āsakta* (attachment).
[22] The Braj Bhasha word comes from the Arabic *kāfir* (infidel).

he find a deity with Shrinathji's form. At last his travels took him to Mount Govardhan, but when he tried to go into the temple there, the temple guard threw him out rudely. Raskhan went to Govind Pond nearby, thinking to himself, "I have never been thrown from a Hindu temple. This place, with such strict measures of security, must therefore be where my Beloved resides." So Raskhan sat there staring at Shrinathji's temple, saying again and again, "My Beloved resides in that temple," and swearing to not leave without having *darśan* there. Three days passed and Shrinathji thought to Himself, "Raskhan will soon die from hunger." Feeling compassion, Shrinathji appeared, along with His retinue of cows and cowherds, playing His flute at the top of Mount Govardhan. He looked exactly as He did in the painting, and so Raskhan recognized Shrinathji as his Beloved and ran to grab Him. But Shrinathji disappeared and went to the town of Shri Gokul where He awakened the sleeping Gusainji by gently stroking the hair on his head. "Praise the one who removes his devotees' suffering,"[23] Gusainji said. Shrinathji then said, "There is this *daivī jīv* who has been born into the *baṛī jātī* [lit. "senior community"; Muslim community]. I gave him *darśan* but then he ran to grab me. You initiate him, and then I shall give him refuge." Gusainji asked, "Why have You come in such a rush?" Shrinathji replied, saying, "Because he tried to touch me and it's my vow to only speak to, accept food-offerings from, and touch those you have first initiated. Without your initiation these three things will be granted to no one." Pleased, Gusainji got up, went to the banks of the Yamuna, and crossed the river in a boat. Reaching the other side, he mounted a horse and went toward Mount Govardhan where he then proceeded directly to Govind Pond where Raskhan was seated. Upon seeing Gusainji, Raskhan thought, "This man who just got down from his horse appears to be a close *mitra* (friend) of my Beloved who lives atop Mount Govardhan." He approached Gusainji and said, "My Beloved lives in that house on the hill. I am very attached to Him. I also know that you are His close associate. If you would let me meet Him, that would be truly wonderful." Gusainji was pleased with Raskhan's words and asked him, "How do you know that He's my friend?" Raskhan replied, "As you were approaching I saw that your gaze was fixed on His temple." Gusainji replied, telling him, "Now bathe in the Govind Pond's cleansing waters." After returning from his bath, Gusainji initiated Raskhan through his grace. Gusainji then had a servant take Raskhan up to Mount Govardhan, and he himself climbed to the temple and sounded the conch to wake up Shrinathji. When the temple opened, Gusainji prepared some fruits for Shrinathji's early afternoon food offering. A bit later, Raskhan entered Shrinathji's temple and was thrilled again to have *darśan*. As Raskhan was departing from the temple, Shrinathji emerged from His shrine and grabbed hold of Raskhan's arm, saying, "Hey you bastard,[24] where are you going?!" And from this day on whenever Shrinathji left to graze the cattle He would take Raskhan along. The *līlā* that Raskhan saw there he would then illustrate through his verses. It was in this manner that he acquired the *bhāv* of *gopī*. Raskhan was Shri Gusainji's blessed follower; to what extent can his story be praised?

[23] The Braj Bhasha here reads, "*bhaktāpanivārakāya namaḥ*."

[24] As noted in Chapter 1, the Braj Bhasha term used here is *sāre*—a vocative of Modern Standard Hindi's *sālā* (wife's brother or brother-in-law), and a harsh, though sometimes playful, term of abuse (the implication being that the person hurling the insult is sleeping with the other person's sister).

Glossary

Select Dramatis Personae

Acharyaji Lit. "great teacher"; an epithet for Vallabhacharya.

Dwarkadas Parikh (Dvārkādās Parīkh) 20th-century editor and commentator on *vārtā* texts whose versions of the *84VV* and *252VV* are widely read by modern Pushtimargis. Parikh's commentaries are primarily discussed in Chapter 1.

Gokulnath (1551–1640) Vaishnava theologian and Vitthalnath's fourth son. The *84VV* and *252VV* are attributed to Gokulnath (Hariray is credited as the texts' editor and commentator).

Goswami Indirabetiji (d. 2016) A Pushtimargi hereditary leader and author who lived in Baroda; an interlocutor whose experiences, *pravacan*s, and publications are discussed primarily in Chapter 5.

Gusainji An epithet for Vitthalnath.

Hariray (1590–1715; life span according to tradition) Vaishnava theologian and Vallabhacharya's great-grandson. The *Bhāvprakāś* commentaries in the *84VV* and *252VV*, among other texts (e.g., the *Baḍe Śikṣāpatra*), are attributed to Hariray.

Krishna A popular Hindu deity known for his sweetness and playful characteristics, and who is revered widely throughout Hindu traditions; the deity whose worship is primary to Pushtimargi Hinduism.

Mahaprabhuji Lit. "great lord"; an epithet for Vallabhacharya.

Megha Choksi A Pushtimargi devotee from Ahmedabad and interlocutor whose experiences are discussed primarily in Chapter 1.

Mona Desai A Pushtimargi devotee from Ahmedabad and interlocutor whose experiences are discussed primarily in Chapter 5.

Natvarlalji One of two Krishna *svarūp*s residing at the Goswami Haveli in the Kalupur neighborhood of Ahmedabad.

Rajabetiji A Pushtimargi hereditary leader from Ahmedabad and interlocutor whose experiences are discussed primarily in Chapter 4.

Shalini Goswami The wife of a Pushtimargi hereditary leader from Ahmedabad and interlocutor whose experiences are discussed primarily in Chapter 1.

Shrinathji The foremost Pushtimargi Krishna *svarūp*. A shortened title of Govardhannathji—the Lord of Mount Govardhan in Braj. The *svarūp* today resides in a *havelī* in Nathdwara, Rajasthan.

Shyam Manohar Goswami (Śyām Manohar Gosvāmī) A Pushtimargi hereditary leader and author from Mumbai; an interlocutor whose experiences, *pravacan*s, and publications are discussed primarily in Chapter 3.

Sonali Dogra A Pushtimargi devotee from Ahmedabad and interlocutor whose experiences are discussed primarily in Chapter 5.

Thakurji A proper name for the deity Krishna, often in his form as a *svarūp*. The title comes from the word *ṭhākur* (lord; chief; master).

Tilak Goswami (Madhusudanlal Goswami) A Pushtimargi hereditary leader from Ahmedabad and interlocutor whose experiences are discussed primarily in Chapter 4.

Vallabhacharya (1479–1531) The Vaishnava theologian understood to be the first preceptor of Pushtimargi Hinduism.

Vitthalnath (1515–1585) A Vaishnava theologian understood to have inherited authority from his father Vallabhacharya to lead the Pushtimarg. Vitthalnath had seven sons through whom he continued to pass on religious authority.

Yojana Mahajan, Dr. A Pushtimargi devotee from Ahmedabad and interlocutor whose experiences are discussed primarily in Chapters 4 and 5.

Significant Texts

84VV Abbreviation for *Caurāsī Vaiṣṇavan kī Vārtā*.

252VV Abbreviation for *Do Sau Bāvan Vaiṣṇavan kī Vārtā*.

Baḍe Śikṣāpatra "The Great Teaching Letters." This composite text, written partly in Braj Bhasha and partly in Sanskrit, takes the form of forty-one letters sent from *vārtā* commentator Hariray to his brother Gopeshvar on the event of the death of Gopeshvar's wife. Gopeshvar's commentaries on the letters are also included in the text, which addresses various matters but focuses on devotional living, emotional well-being, and *sevā*.

Bhāgavatapurāṇa A Sanskrit poetic work redacted in southern India during the 10th century CE. The *Bhāgavatapurāṇa*'s tenth canto famously describes the *līlā* of Krishna as a playful child and amorous youth in the celestial land of Braj.

Bhāvprakāś "An Illumination of the Text's Inner Meaning." This commentary, attributed to Hariray, circulates with one recession of the *84VV* and one recession of the *252VV* in their manuscript forms, and in most contemporary printed versions of these texts.

Caurāsī Baiṭhak Caritra "An Account of Eighty-Four Seats." A Braj Bhasha text that describes eighty-four of the primary sites where Vallabhacharya sat to recite and provide oral exegesis on the *Bhāgavatapurāṇa*.

***Caurāsī Vaiṣṇavan kī Vārtā* (abbreviated as *84VV*)** "Chronicles of Eighty-Four Vaishnavas." The earliest (17th century) and most popular *vārtā* text, which provides prose hagiographies for Vallabhacharya's beloved disciples.

Dharmaśāstra "Dharma Manuals." A genre of Sanskrit theological texts on Hindu *dharma*.

***Do Sau Bāvan Vaiṣṇavan kī Vārtā* (abbreviated as *252VV*)** "Chronicles of Two Hundred and Fifty-Two Vaishnavas." A *vārtā* text that provides prose hagiographies for Vitthalnath's beloved disciples.

Prākaṭya Vārtā See *Śrīnāthjī kī Prākaṭya Vārtā*.

Ṣoḍaśagrantha "Sixteen Treatises." This is a collection of short Sanskrit treatises attributed to Vallabhacharya. Many of these treatises are referred to and commented on in *Vārtā Sāhitya* and during readers' exegesis of the hagiographies.

***Śrīnāthjī kī Prākaṭya Vārtā* (abbreviated as *Prākaṭya Vārtā*)** "The Emergence Chronicle of Shrinathji." A text that narrates the 15th-century emergence of the Pushtimarg's primary *svarūp*, Shrinathji, and the deity's eventual movement from his emergence place at Mount Govardhan in the region of Braj to Nathdwara, Rajasthan, in the 17th century.

Subodhinī "That Which Is Greatly Enlightening." A commentarial text on the *Bhāgavatapurāṇa* attributed to Vallabhacharya.

Select Indic Terms

alaukik Otherworldly.

aparas A ritually pure state.

aṣṭachāp Lit. "eight seals"; a group of eight early modern poets whose life stories are told in the *84VV* and *252VV* and whose poem-songs are sung in the form *kīrtan* as part of Pushtimargi liturgy.

aṣṭayām sevā Eight traditionally appointed times for Pushtimargi *sevā*.

bahūjī Respected daughter-in-law; a title appointed to the wives of Pushtimargi hereditary leaders.

baniyā Merchant; often used to refer to communities who hail from traditionally merchant caste backgrounds.

bava (bāvā/bābā) In the Pushtimargi context this is a term of respect and endearment reserved for male hereditary leaders—generally those who are not the eldest direct descendants of their particular lineage (who would be referred to as Maharaj).

***ben* (*bahen*)** Sister; a suffix indicating respect and affixed to the end of women's names in Gujarati-speaking communities.

beṭījī Respected daughter; the title appointed to female descendants of Vallabhacharya.

bhakta Devotee.

bhakti Devotion; devotional.

bhāv(a) Devotional sentiments; inner meaning; affective peity.

bhog Special food items offered to Krishna as part of Pushtimargi *sevā* rituals.

brahmasambandha The second of two initiation mantras used in the Pushtimarg. The mantra is meant to bind (*sambandha*) devotees to Brahman, the Supreme Being, who is one and the same as Krishna.

Braj A region in northwest India demarcated through Krishna-centered pilgrimage routes and sacred sites, such as temples and shrines. The physical region falls partly within the contemporary state of Uttar Pradesh's Mathura District. Braj is also understood to be a celestial place and home to Krishna's otherworldly eternal *līlā*.

Braj Bhasha (Braj Bhāṣā) A regional form of Hindi. Braj Bhasha was the dominant vehicle for vernacular literature produced in many parts of northern India from the 15th to 19th centuries. It is the language Pushtimargi authors used to compose *Vārtā Sāhitya* and other early modern devotional texts.

daivī jīv Godly being. This term is used in the *84VV* and *252VV* and by contemporary Pushtimargis to refer to those figures from the *vārtā*s who are predestined to enter the fold through initiation by Vallabhacharya or Vitthalnath. Their opposites are *āsurī jīv*s (wicked beings).

darśan Auspicious sight; seeing and being seen by a deity, revered person, or sacred site.

dharma Duty; righteousness. The term has various connotations in different contexts but refers broadly to socio-religious norms.

dhoḷ Gujarati-style devotional song.

dhotī A single, long piece of cloth tied as pants. *Dhotī*s are often considered "traditional" attire for Indian men.

gopā Male cowherd; the divine counterparts of Krishna in the celestial land of Braj.

gopī Female cowherd; the divine counterparts of Krishna in the celestial land of Braj.

gosvāmī Lit. "lord of cows"; an honorary title affixed to the names of religious leaders in the Pushtimarg and also in other Hindu communities.

Govardhan A sacred site in the region of Braj specific to Krishna devotional traditions. According to classical and vernacular texts and traditions, Krishna lifted Mount Govardhan to protect his cowherd counterparts in a battle with the Vedic deity Indra. Krishna also revealed himself as manifest in the stones of Govardhan. Today Govardhan—really a hill, not a mountain as such—is an important place of pilgrimage and site of devotion for Pushtimargis and others.

granth Text; religious text.

havelī Palatial home; Pushtimargi temple.

havelī saṅgīt Music of the *havelī*; "temple" music. A particular genre of semiclassical devotional singing and musical accompaniment specific to the Pushtimarg.

jāher Public (as in, not private).

jāī Hail (as in *Jāī Shri Krishna*, "Hail to Lord Krishna").

ji (*jī*) An honorific suffix, e.g., Shrinathji.

kaliyug The degenerate age.

kathā Story, tale; storytelling, exegesis; recitations and exegesis of religious texts such as the *vārtā*s or the *Bhāgavatapurāṇa*.

kathākār Exegete.

kīrtan Devotional songs.

laukik Worldly.

līlā Divine pastimes; Krishna's playful dalliances (especially in the celestial land of Braj).

mahāprasād Consecrated food offering (also rendered *prasād*).

***maharaj* (*mahārāj*)** Lit. "great king," though "my Lord" is a more accurate translation. The oldest presiding male hereditary leader in any given Vallabha Kul family is commonly referred to as Maharaj.

mālā Garland; religious necklace signifying affiliation to a particular community.

mandir Temple; some Pushtimargis prefer to use the term *havelī* (lit. "palatial home") to distinguish their temples from temples of other communities.

nitya Eternal.

prākaṭya Emergence; divine emergence of a deity or person.

prasād Consecrated food offering (also rendered *mahāprasād*).

prasaṅg Episode or section from Pushtimargi *vārtā* texts.

pravacan Religious lecture.

pravacankār Exegete; one who delivers a *pravacan*.

Pushtimarg (*Puṣṭimārg*) The Path of Nourishment; the Krishna devotional tradition that grew around the teachings of Vallabhacharya.

Pushtimargi (*Puṣṭimārgī* or *Puṣṭimārgīy*) An adjectival term meaning "belonging" or "pertaining" to the Pushtimarg.

puṣṭi Nourishment; grace.

rāg A musical mode; refers generally to devotional singing and music and to one of three "essentials" to Pushtimargi *sevā* rituals (*rāg*, *bhog*, and *śṛṅgār*).

rasa Sap; essence. A theory of theatrical and literary aesthetics adopted by medieval and early modern theologians.

rāsa-līlā Amorous divine play of Krishna with the *gopī*s in Braj.

sabhā Assembly.

sakhā Male friend; a term used alternatively for *gopā*.

sakhī Female friend; a term used alternatively for *gopī*.

satī Lit. "virtuous" or "chaste"; refers to a so-called faithful wife who burns herself (or is made to burn herself) with her husband's corpse on his funeral pyre. It can also be an epithet of the goddess Parvati.

satsaṅg Gathering of the faithful; often used to refer to gatherings where devotees sing and read and discuss devotional literature.

sevā Loving service; Pushtimarg-specific ritual practices of caring for Krishna *svarūp*s in *havelī*s and domestic spaces through ritualized singing, dressing, bathing, and feeding.

sevak Loving servant; practitioner of *sevā*.

Shri (*Śrī*) An honorific prefix, e.g., Shri Krishna.

Shuddhādvaita Pure non-dualism; the philosophical system developed by Vallabhacharya.

śṛṅgār(a) Refers to dressing and adorning Krishna *svarūp*s and to the devotional sentiment of sweetness with reference to erotic intimacy.

svarūp Icon of a living deity; the deity's *sva* (own) *rūp* (form).

ṭīkā Commentary; commentarial writing.

vacanāmṛt Nectarous speech; direct speech or dialogue attributed to revered individuals, including Krishna, Vallabhacharya, and Vitthalnath, in the Pushtimargi *vārtā*s.

Vallabha Kul Vallabha dynasty; the family, past and present, of Vallabhacharya.

Vallabha Sampraday The following or sect of Vallabha.

varṇāśramadharma The Brahminical system by which people are ranked and expected to act in certain ways according to birth community, life stage, and gender.

Vārtā Sāhitya "Chronicle Literature." A collection of Braj Bhasha prose hagiographies, committed to writing starting in the 17th century, which recount the lives of Vallabhacharya, Vitthalnath, and their disciples.

vātsalya The devotional sentiment of parental affection.

viraha Pangs of separation, specifically from one's object(s) of devotion, namely, Krishna in the Pushtimargi context.

Bibliography

Manuscripts

Hariräy (scribe: "Sanāḍhya Brahmin from Gokul"). "*Caurāsī Vaiṣṇavan kī Vārtā*," 1697 VS (1640 CE). 68/2. Vidya Vibhāg Pustakālay, Kankroli Rajasthan.

Harirāy. "*Govardhannāthjī kī Prākaṭya Vārtā*," 1882 VS (1825 CE). Vrindavan Research Institute, Vrindavan. Harirāy (scribe: Pārekh Māyācand Kuśaldās on the behalf of Ācārya Abhirām Mahāśankar). "*Śrīnāthjī kī Prākaṭya Vārtā*," 1912 VS (1855 CE). Private Collection, Ahmedabad, Gujarat, India.

Harirāy. "*Govardhannāthjī ke Prāgaṭya kī Prakār*," 20th century CE. 423/175/. Shri Sanjay Sharma Research Institute, Jaipur.

Harirāy. "*Govardhannāthjī ke Prāgaṭya kī Prakār*," n.d. 16497 (3). Rajasthani Shodh Sansthan, Chopasani, Jodhpur.

Harirāy (scribe: V. Purohit). "*Govardhannāthjī ke Prākaṭya kī Vārtā*," n.d. 25457. Rajasthan Oriental Research Institute, Jodhpur.

Harirāy. "*Govardhannāth kī Nij Vārtā*," n.d. 12705/2. Rajasthan Oriental Research Institute, Jaipur (Rāmcandra jī kā mandir).

Harirāy. "*Govardhan Prākaṭyam*," n.d. 18019. Rajasthan Oriental Research Institute, Jodhpur (P.W.D. Road).

Harirāy. "*Śrīnāthjī kī Prākaṭya Vārtā*," n.d. Private Collection, Ahmedabad, India.

Harirāy. "*Śrīnāthjī kī Prākaṭya Vārtā*," n.d. Private Collection, Ahmedabad, India (originally from a temple collection in Bhadrapur (Bhavnagar District, Gujarat).

Books and Articles

Allocco, Amy L. "Vernacular Practice, Gendered Tensions, and Interpretive Ambivalence in Hindu Death, Deification, and Domestication Narratives." *The Journal of Hindu Studies* 13, no. 2 (2020): 144–171.

Allocco, Amy L., and Brian Pennington, eds. *Ritual Innovation: Strategic Interventions in South Asian Religion*. Albany: State University of New York Press, 2018.

Ambalal, Amit. *Krishna as Shrinathji: Rajasthani Paintings from Nathdvara*. Ahmedabad, India: Mapin Publishing, 1987.

Arney, Paul. "The *Bade Shikshapatra*: A Vallabhite Guide to the Worship of Krishna's Divine Images." In *Krishna: A Sourcebook*, edited by Edwin F. Bryant, 505–536. Oxford: Oxford University Press, 2007.

Bachrach, Emilia. "Is Guruji Online?: Internet Advice Forums and Transnational Encounters in a Vaishnav Sampraday." In *Indian Transnationalism Online: New Perspectives on Diaspora*, edited by Ajaya K. Sahoo and Johannes G. de Kruijf, 163–176. London: Ashgate, 2014.

Bachrach, Emilia. "Religious Reading and Everyday Lives." In *Text and Tradition in Early Modern India*, edited by Tyler A. Williams, Anshu Malhotra, and John Stratton Hawley, 413–433. New Delhi: Oxford University Press, 2018.

Bachrach, Emilia. *In the Service of Krishna: Illustrating the Lives of Eighty-Four Vaishnavas from a 1702 Manuscript in the Amit Ambalal Collection*. Ahmedabad, India: Mapin, 2019.

Bachrach, Emilia. "Saints and Hagiography in Hinduism." In *Oxford Bibliographies in Hinduism*, edited by Tracy Coleman. New York: Oxford University Press, 2019.

Bachrach, Emilia. "The Uncertain Self in Ethnographic Research and Writing." *Fieldwork in Religion*, 15.1–2 (2020): 113–125.

Bahūjī, Gosvāmī Rukmiṇī. "Śubhāśīrvād." In *Do Sau Bāvan Vaiṣṇavan kī Vārtā (Tīn Janma kī Līlā Bhāvnā Vālī): Dvitīya Bhāg*, edited by Dvārkādās Parīkh, 3. Indore, India: Vaiṣṇav Mitra Maṇḍal, 2009.

Bailey, Greg M., and Ian Kesarcadi-Watson, eds. *Bhakti Studies*. New Delhi: Sterling, 1992.

Bakhtin, Mikhail. *Problems of Dostoevsky's Poetics* (1929). Edited and translated by Caryl Emerson. Minneapolis: University of Minnesota Press, 1984.

Bangha, Imre, ed. *Bhakti Beyond the Forest: Current Research of Early Modern Literatures in North India, 2003–2009*. New Delhi: Manohar, 2012.

Bar, Doron, and Kobi Cohen-Hattab. "A New Kind of Pilgrimage: The Modern Tourist Pilgrim of Nineteenth-Century and Early Twentieth-Century Palestine." *Middle Eastern Studies* 39, no. 2 (2003): 131–148.

Barz, Richard K. *The Bhakti Sect of Vallabhācārya*. New Delhi: Munshiram Manoharlal, 1992.

Barz, Richard K. "Kṛṣṇadās Adhikārī: An Irascible Devotee's Approach to the Divine." In *Bhakti Studies*, edited by Greg M. Bailey and Ian Kesarcadi-Watson, 236–262. New Delhi: Sterling, 1992.

Barz, Richard K. "The *Caurāsī Vaiṣṇavan kī Vārtā* and the Hagiography of the Puṣṭimārg." In *According to Tradition: Hagiographical Writing in India*, edited by Rupert Snell and Winand M. Callwaert, 44–64. Wiesbaden: Harrassowitz, 1994.

Barz, Richard K. "Kumbhandas: The Devotee as Salt of the Earth." In *Krishna: A Sourcebook*, edited by Edwin F. Bryant, 477–504. Oxford: Oxford University Press, 2007.

Bauman, Richard, and Charles L. Briggs. *Voices of Modernity: Language Ideologies and the Politics of Inequality*. Cambridge: Cambridge University Press, 2003.

Beck, Guy L. "Haveli Sangit: Music in the Vallabha Tradition." *Journal of Vaishnava Studies* 1, no. 4 (1993): 77–86.

Beck, Guy L. "Vaishnava Music and the Braj Region of Northern India." *Journal of Vaishnava Studies* 4, no. 2 (1996): 115–148.

Bell, Claudia, and J. Lyall. *The Accelerated Sublime—Landscape Tourism and Identity*. London: Praeger, 2001.

Ben-Herut, Gil. *Śiva's Saints: The Origins of Devotion in Kannada According to Harihara's Ragaḷegaḷu*. New Delhi: Oxford University Press, 2018.

Bennett, Peter. "In Nanda Baba's House: The Devotional Experience in Pushti Marg Temples." In *Divine Passions: The Social Construction of Emotion in India*, edited by Owen M. Lynch, 182–211. Berkeley: University of California Press, 1990.

Bennett, Peter. "Krishna's Own Form: Image Worship and the Pushti Marga." *Journal of Vaishnava Studies* 1, no. 4 (1993): 109–134.

Bennett, Peter. *The Path of Grace: Social Organisation and Temple Worship in a Vaishnava Sect*. Delhi: Hindustan Publishing Corporation, 1993.

Bhalla, Tamara. *Reading Together, Reading Apart: Identity, Belonging, and South Asian American Community*. Champaign: University of Illinois Press, 2016.

Bhalodia, Aarti. "Princes, Diwans and Merchants: Education and Reform in Colonial India." PhD diss., University of Texas at Austin, 2012.

Bhāṭiyā, Bhūpendra. *Ṣoḍaśagranthāgat Upadeś ane tem-nī 28 Vārtāo (Bhāg 2)*. Rajkot, India: Purvī Press, 2008.

Bielo, James. *The Social Life of Scriptures: Cross-cultural Perspectives on Biblicism*. New Brunswick, NJ: Rutgers University Press, 2009.

Black, Brian, and Laurie Patton, eds. *Dialogue in Early South Asian Religions: Hindu, Buddhist, and Jain Traditions*. New York, Routledge, 2016.

Blackburn, Anne. "Looking for the Vinaya: Monastic Discipline in the Practical Canons of the Theravada." *Journal of the International Association of Buddhist Studies* 22, no. 2 (1999): 281–309.

Boyarin, Jonathan, ed. *The Ethnography of Reading*. Berkeley: University of California Press, 1993.

Briggs, Charles. "Literacy, Reading, and Writing in the Medieval West." *Journal of Medieval History* 26, no. 4 (2000): 397–420.

Bryant, Edwin F., trans. *Krishna: The Beautiful Legend of God (Śrīmad Bhāgavata Purāṇa Book X)*. London: Penguin, 2003.

Bryant, Edwin F., ed. *Krishna: A Sourcebook*. Oxford: Oxford University Press, 2007.

Bucar, Elizabeth M. *Creative Conformity: The Feminist Politics of U.S. Catholic and Iranian Shi'i Women*. Washington, DC: Georgetown University Press, 2011.

Busch, Allison. *Poetry of Kings: The Classical Hindi Literature of Mughal India*. New York: Oxford University Press, 2011.

Bynum, Caroline Walker. *Holy Feast and Holy Fast: The Religious Significance of Food to Medieval Women*. Berkeley: University of California Press, 1988.

Caturdevī, Viṣṇu. *Gosvāmī Harirāy aur unkā Braj Bhāṣā Sāhitya*. Mathura, India: Javāhar Pustakālya, 1976.

Certeau, Michel de. *The Practice of Everyday Life*, translated by Steven Rendall. Berkeley: University of California Press, 1984.

Clémentin-Ojha, Catherine. "A Mid-nineteenth-century Controversy over Religious Authority." In *Charisma and Canon*, edited by Vasudha Dalmia, Angelika Malinar, and Martin Christof, 183–204. Oxford: Oxford University Press, 2001.

Corbellini, Sabrina, et al., eds. *Discovering the Riches of the Word: Religious Reading in Late Medieval and Early Modern Europe*. Leiden: Brill, 2015.

Cort, John E. "The Jain Knowledge Warehouses: Traditional Libraries in India." *Journal of the American Oriental Society* 115, no. 1 (1995): 77–87.

Cort, John E. "Bhakti in the Early Jain Tradition: Understanding Devotional Religion in South Asia." *History of Religions* 42, no. 1 (2002): 59–86.

Dalmia, Vasudha. "The Establishment of the Sixth *Gaddī* of the Vallabha Sampradāy: Narrative Structure and the Use of Authority in a *Vārtā* of the Nineteenth Century." In *Studies in South Asian Devotional Literature*, edited by Alan W. Entwistle and Françoise Mallison, 94–117. New Delhi: Manohar, 1994.

Dalmia, Vasudha. "'The Only Real Religion of the Hindus': Vaiṣṇava Self-representation in the Late Nineteenth Century." In *Representing Hinduism: The Construction of Religious Traditions and National Identity*, edited by Vasudha Dalmia and Heinrich von Stietencron, 176–210. New Delhi: Sage Publications, 1995.

Dalmia, Vasudha. *The Nationalization of Hindu Traditions: Bhāratendu Hariśchandra and Nineteenth-century Banaras*. Delhi: Oxford University Press, 1997.

Dalmia, Vasudha. "Women, Duty and Sanctified Space in a Vaiṣṇava Hagiography of the Seventeenth Century." In *Constructions Hagiographiques dans le Monde Indien: Entre Myth et Histoire*, edited by Françoise Mallison, 205–219. Paris: Champion, 2001.

Dalmia, Vasudha. *Hindu Pasts: Women, Religion, History*. Albany: State University of New York Press, 2017.

Dalmia, Vasudha, Angelika Malinar, and Martin Christof, eds. *Charisma and Canon*. Oxford: Oxford University Press, 2001.

DeNapoli, Antoinette E. *Real Sadhus Sing to God: Gender, Asceticism, and Vernacular Religion in Rajasthan*. New York: Oxford University Press, 2014.

Derné, Steven. *Globalization on the Ground: New Media and the Transformation of Culture, Class, and Gender in India*. New Delhi: Sage Publications, 2008.

Desāī, Lallubhāī Chaganlāl. *Śrī Ācāryajī Mahāprabhu (Śrī Vallabhācāryajī) nā 84 Vaiṣṇav nī Vārtā*. Ahmedabad, India: Śrī Lakṣmī Pustak Bhandar, 1917.

Desāī, Lallubhāī Chaganlāl. *84 Vaiṣṇavnī Vāto*. Ahmedabad, India: Koṭhārī Prakāśan Ghar, 1970.

Desāī, Lallubhāī Chaganlāl. *252 Vaiṣṇavnī Vāto*. Ahmedabad, India: Śrī Lakṣmī Pustak Bhandar, 1976.

Deśpāṇḍe, P.G. *Gujarātī-Angrejī Koś*. Ahmedabad, India: University Granth-nirmāṇ Board, 2002.

Dharwadker, Vinay, ed. *The Collected Essays of A.K. Ramanujan*. Oxford: Oxford University Press, 1999.

Diyorā, Gosvāmī Karamśībhāī Vastabhāī. *Śrī Jamuneś Mahāprabhujīnā Jīvan Carītāmṛt*. Surat, India: Gosvāmī Vastabhāī Naraśībhāī Diyorā, 2002.

Dobbin, Christine E. *Urban Leadership in Western India: Politics and Communities in Bombay City, 1840–1885*. London: Oxford University Press, 1972.

Dobe, Timothy S. "Dayānanda Sarasvatī as Irascible *Ṛṣi*: The Person and Performed Authority of a Text." *The Journal of Hindu Studies* 4 (2011): 79–100.

Dwyer, Rachel. *The Poetics of Devotion: The Gujarati Lyrics of Dayaram*. Richmond, UK: Curzon Press, 2001.

Entwistle, Alan W. *Braj: Centre of Krishna Pilgrimage*. Groningen, Netherlands: Egbert Forsten, 1987.

Entwistle, Alan W., and Françoise Mallison, eds. *Studies in South Asian Devotional Literature*. New Delhi: Manohar, 1994.

Entwistle, Alan W., and Carol Salomon, with Heidi Pauwels and Michael C. Shapiro, eds. *Studies in Early Modern Indo-Aryan Languages, Literature and Culture*. New Delhi: Manohar, 1999.

Erzen, Tanya. *Fanpire: The Twilight Saga and the Women Who Love It*. Boston: Beacon Press, 2012.

Fish, Stanley E. *Self-Consuming Artifacts: The Experience of Seventeenth-Century Literature*. Berkeley: University of California Press, 1972.

Fish, Stanley E. "Interpreting the *Variorum*." In *Reader-Response Criticism: From Formalism to Post-Structuralism*, edited by Jane P. Tompkins, 164–184. Baltimore: Johns Hopkins University Press, 1980.

Fisher, Elaine. "Public Space, Public Canon: Situating Religion at the Dawn of Modernity in South India." *Modern Asian Studies* 42, no. 5 (2018): 1486–1541.

Flueckiger, Joyce B. *Gender and Genre in the Folklore of Middle India*. Ithaca, NY: Cornell University Press, 1996.

Flueckiger, Joyce B. "Wandering from 'Hills to Valleys' with the Goddess: Protection and Freedom in the Matamma Tradition of Andhra." In *Women's Lives, Women's Rituals in the Hindu Tradition*, edited by Tracy Pitchman, 35–54. New York: Oxford University Press, 2007.
Flueckiger, Joyce B. *When the World Becomes Female: Guises of a South Indian Goddess*. Bloomington: Indiana University Press, 2013.
Flueckiger, Joyce B. *Everyday Hinduism*. West Sussex, UK: Wiley-Blackwell, 2015.
Foley, John M. *How to Read an Oral Poem*. Urbana: University of Illinois Press, 2002.
Gade, Anna M. "Taste, Talent, and the Problem of Internalization: A Qur'ānic Study in Religious Musicality from Southeast Asia." *History of Religions* 41, no. 4 (2002): 328–368.
Gade, Anna M. *Perfection Makes Practice: Learning, Emotion, and the Recited Qur'ān in Indonesia*. Honolulu: University of Hawaii Press, 2004.
Gāndhi, Kānti R. *Bhaktiras Calke, Jīvan Madhurū Malke: Param Viḍuṣī Pūjya Gosvāmī Indirābeṭījī*. Mumbai: Paramount Printing Press, 2000.
Garlington, W. "Candrāvalī and the *Caurāsī Vaiṣṇavan kī Vārtā*." In *Bhakti Studies*, edited by Greg M. Bailey and Ian Kesarcodi-Watson, 251–262. New Delhi: Sterling, 1992.
Gaston, Anne-Marie. "Continuity of Tradition in the Music of Nathdvara: A Participant Observer's View." In *The Idea of Rajasthan: Explorations in Regional Identity*, Vol. I, edited by Karine Schomer, Joan L. Erdman, Deryck O. Lodrick, and Lloyd I. Rudolph, 238–277. New Delhi: Manohar, 1994.
Gaston, Anne-Marie. *Krishna's Musicians: Musicians and Music Making in the Temples of Nathdvara, Rajasthan*. New Delhi: Manohar, 1997.
Geertz, Clifford. "Art as a Cultural System." In *Local Knowledge: Further Essays in Interpretive Anthropology*, 94–120. New York: Basic Books, 1983.
Geertz, Clifford. "Deep Hanging Out." *The New York Review of Books* 45, no. 16 (1998): 69–72.
Genette, Gérard. *Paratexts: Thresholds of Interpretation*, translated by Jane E. Lewin. Cambridge: Cambridge University Press, 1997.
Gold, Ann Grodzins, and Gloria Goodwin Raheja. *Listen to the Heron's Words: Reimagining Gender and Kinship in North India*. Berkeley: University of California Press, 1994.
Gosh, Anindita. "An Uncertain 'Coming of the Book:' Early Print Cultures in Colonial India." *Book History* 6 (2003): 23–55.
Gosh, Anindita. *Power in Print: Popular Publishing and the Politics of Language and Culture in a Colonial Society, 1778–1905*. New York: Oxford University Press, 2006.
Gosvāmī, Śyām Manohar, ed. *Ṣoḍaśagranthāḥ*. Bombay: Sṭuḍio Bahār, 1980.
Gosvāmī, Śyām Manohar. *Puṣṭividhānam: Pāṭhāvalī*. Mumbai: Sahayog Prakāśan, 2002.
Gosvāmī, Śyām Manohar. *Ādhunak Nyāyapraṇālī no Āpasī Ṭakarāv*. Kacch, India: Śrī Vallabhācārya Ṭrasṭ, 2006.
Gosvāmī, Śyām Manohar. *Vārtāṅkī Saiddhāntik Saṅgati*. Mumbai: Ramā Arts, 2011.
Gosvāmī, Śyām Manohar. *Sevā: R̥tu, Utsav, Manorath*. Mandvi-Kacch, India: Śrī Vallabhācārya Ṭrasṭ, n.d.
Gosvāmī, Śyām Manohar, and Gosvāmī Viṭṭhalnāthjī. *Puṣṭi Siddhānt Carcā Sabhā: Saṅkṣip Vivaraṇ*. Mumbai: Narotam Bhāṭīyā, 1992.
Gosvāmī, Yogeśkumār, ed. *Puṣṭi Siddhānt Carcā Sabhā: Vistr̥t Vivaraṇ*. Mumbai: Saṃvād Sthāpak Maṇḍal, 1992.
Graham, William A. *Beyond the Written Word: Oral Aspects of Scripture in the History of Religion*. New York: Cambridge University Press, 1993.

Grierson, Sir George Abraham. *The Modern Vernacular History of Hindustan*. Calcutta: The Asiatic Society, 1889.
Griffiths, Paul J. *Religious Reading: The Place of Reading in the Practice of Religion*. New York: Oxford University Press, 1999.
Gupta, Ravi, and Kenneth Valpey, eds. *The Bhāgavata Purāṇa: Sacred Text and Living Tradition*. New York: Cambridge University Press, 2013.
Haberman, David L. "On Trial: The Love of Sixteen Thousand Gopees." *History of Religions* 33, no. 1 (1993): 44–70.
Haberman, David L. *Journey Through the Twelve Forests: An Encounter with Krishna*. New York: Oxford University Press, 1994.
Haberman, David L. *Acting as a Way of Salvation: A Study of Rāgānugā Bhakti Sādhana*. Delhi: Motilal Banarsidass, 1998.
Haberman, David L. "A Theology of Place: Pilgrimage in the *Caurāsī Baiṭhak Caritra*." In *Studies in Early Modern Indo-Aryan Languages, Literature and Culture*, edited by Alan. W. Entwistle and Carol Solomon, with Heidi Pauwels and Michael C. Shapiro, 155–166. New Delhi: Manohar, 1999.
Haberman, David L. *Loving Stones: Making the Impossible Possible in the Worship of Mount Govardhan*. New York: Oxford University Press, 2020.
Hancock, Mary E. "The Dilemmas of Domesticity: Possession and Devotional Experience Among Urban Smārta Women." In *From the Margins of Hindu Marriage: Essays on Gender, Religion, and Culture*, edited by Lindsey Harlan and Paul B. Courtright, 60–91. New York: Oxford University Press, 1995.
Hare, James P. "Garland of Devotees: Nābhādās' *Bhaktamāl* and Modern Hinduism." PhD diss., Columbia University, 2011.
Harirāy and Gopeśvar. *Śrīharirāy kṛt Baḍe Śikṣāpatra: Śrī Gopeśvar kṛt Vrajbhāṣāṭikāsahit*, edited by Śrī Subodhinī Sabha. Lucknow, India: Janakprasād Agravāl, 1972.
Harlan, Lindsey, and Paul B. Courtright, eds. *From the Margins of Hindu Marriage: Essays on Gender, Religion, and Culture*. New York: Oxford University Press, 1995.
Hatcher, Brian. Hinduism Before Reform. Cambridge, MA: Harvard University Press, 2020.
Hawley, John Stratton. "Modern India and the Question of Middle-Class Religion." *International Journal of Hindu Studies* 5, no. 3 (2001): 217–225.
Hawley, John Stratton. *The Memory of Love: Surdas Sings to Krishna*. New York: Oxford University Press, 2009.
Hawley, John Stratton. "The Four *Sampradāys*: Ordering the Religious Past in Mughal North India." *South Asian History and Culture* 2, no. 2 (2011): 160–183.
Hawley, John Stratton. "How Vallabhācārya Met Kṛṣṇadevarāya." Paper presented in Mumbai, K. R. Cama Oriental Institute, January 7, 2012.
Hawley, John Stratton. *A Storm of Songs: India and the Idea of the Bhakti Movement*. Cambridge, MA: Harvard University Press, 2015.
Hawley, John Stratton. *Krishna's Playground: Vrindavan in the 21st Century*. New York: Oxford University Press, 2020.
Hess, Linda. "Lovers' Doubts: Questioning the Tulsi *Rāmāyaṇ*." In *Questioning Ramayanas: A South Asian Tradition*, edited by Paula Richman, 25–48. Berkeley: University of California Press, 2001.
Hess, Linda. *Bodies of Song: Kabir Oral Traditions and Performative Worlds in North India*. New York: Oxford University Press, 2015.
Ho, Meilu. "The Liturgical Music of the Puṣṭi Mārg of India: An Embryonic Form of the Classical Tradition." PhD diss., University of California, Los Angeles, 2006.

Horstmann, Monika, and Anand Mishra. "Vaishnava Sampradāyas on the Importance of Ritual: A Comparison of the Two Contemporaneous Approaches by Viṭṭhalnātha and Jīva Gosvāmī." In *Bhakti Beyond the Forest: Current Research of Early Modern Literatures in North India, 2003–2009*, edited by Imre Bangha, 155–176. New Delhi: Manohar, 2012.

Hutchings, Tim. "Design and the Digital Bible: Persuasive Technology and Religious Reading." *Journal of Contemporary Religion* 32, no. 2, 2017: 205–219.

Hyder, Syed Akbar. *Reliving Karbala: Martyrdom in South Asian Memory*. New York: Oxford University Press, 2008.

Isaka, Riho. *Language, Identity, and Power in Modern India: Gujarat, c. 1850–1960*. London: Routledge, 2022.

Iser, Wolfgang. *The Act of Reading: A Theory of Aesthetic Response*. Baltimore: Johns Hopkins University Press, 1978.

Jacobs, Alan. *A Theology of Reading: The Hermeneutics of Love*. New York: Routledge, 2001.

Jacobsen, Knut A., ed. *Brill Encyclopedia of Hinduism*. Leiden: Brill, 2014.

Jassal, Smita. *Unearthing Gender: Folksongs of North India*. Durham, NC: Duke University Press, 2012.

Johnson, Helen M. "Conversion of Vikrama Saṃvat Dates." *Journal of the American Oriental Society* 58, no. 4 (1938): 668–669.

Kelley, Mary. "'A More Glorious Revolution': Women's Antebellum Reading Circles and the Pursuit of Public Influence." *The New England Quarterly* 76, no. 2 (2003): 163–196.

Kelting, M. Whitney. *Singing to the Jinas: Jain Laywomen, Mandal Singing, and the Negotiations of Jain Devotion*. New York: Oxford University Press, 2001.

Kelting, M. Whitney. *Heroic Wives: Rituals, Stories and the Virtues of Jain Wifehood*. New York, Oxford University Press: 2009.

Khandelwal, Meena. *Women in Ochre Robes: Gendering Hindu Renunciation*. Albany: State University of New York Press, 2004.

Khare, R.S., ed. *The Eternal Food: Gastronomic Ideas and Experiences of Hindus and Buddhists*. Albany: State University of New York Press, 1992.

Khare, R.S., and M.S.A. Rao, eds. *Food, Society, and Culture: Aspects in South Asian Food Systems*. Durham, NC: Carolina Academic, 1986.

Kim, Hanna. "Public Engagement and Personal Desires: BAPS Swaminarayan Temples and Their Contribution to the Discourses on Religion." *International Journal of Hindu Studies* 13 (2010): 357–390.

Kim, Hanna. "A Fine Balance: Adaptation and Accommodation in the Swaminarayan Sanstha." In *Gujarati Communities Across the Globe: Memory, Identity and Continuity*, edited by S. Mawani and A. Mukadam, 141–156. London: Trentham Books, 2012.

Klemm, David E. "Ricoeur, Theology, and the Rhetoric of Overturning." *Literature and Theology* 3, no. 3 (1989): 267–284.

Knight, Lisa. *Contradictory Lives: Baul Women in India and Bangladesh*. New York: Oxford University Press, 2011.

Kort, Wesley A. "*Take, Read*": *Scripture, Textuality, and Cultural Practice*. University Park: Pennsylvania State University Press, 1996.

Kothari, Priya. "The Aṣṭākṣara Mantra: Spiritual Growth from 'Śrī' to 'Ma' in Puṣṭimārga." *Journal of Vaishnava Studies* 24, no. 2 (2016): 197–212.

Lachaier, Pierre, and Catherine Clémentin-Ojha, eds. *Divines Richesses: Religion et Économie en Monde Marchand Indien*. Paris: École Française d'Extême-Orient, 2008.

Laramee Kidd, Susannah. "Genres of Reading/Genres of Agency: An Ethnography of Protestant Women's Reading Groups." PhD diss., Emory University, 2013.

Long, Elizabeth. *Book Clubs: Women and the Uses of Reading in Everyday Life*. Chicago: University of Chicago Press, 2003.

Love, Velma E. *Divining the Self: A Study in Yoruba Myth and Human Consciousness*. University Park: Pennsylvania State University Press, 2012.

Luhrmann, Tanya M. *When God Talks Back: Understanding the American Evangelical Relationship with God*. New York: Vintage, 2012.

Lutgendorf, Philip. *The Life of a Text: Performing the Rāmcaritmānas of Tulsidas*. Berkeley: University of California Press, 1992.

Lynch, Owen M., ed. *Divine Passions: The Social Construction of Emotion in India*. Berkeley: University of California Press, 1990.

Lyons, Tryna. *The Artists of Nathadwara: The Practice of Painting in Rajasthan*. Bloomington: Indiana University Press, 2004.

Mahmood, Saba. *Politics of Piety: The Islamic Revival and the Feminist Subject*. Princeton, NJ: Princeton University Press, 2005.

Mahodayśrī, Vāgīśkumārjī, ed. *Śrī Girdharlāljī Mahārājśrī nā 120 Vacanāmṛt*. Vadodara, India: Vākpati Foundation, 2012.

Mallison, Françoise, ed. *Constructions Hagiographiques dans le Monde Indien: Entre Myth et Histoire*. Paris: Champion, 2001.

Mamtora, Bhakti. "Smartphone Applications and Religious Reading Among Swaminarayan Hindus." *Postscripts* 12, no. 1 (2021): 21–44.

Mawani, S., and A. Mukadam, eds. *Gujarati Communities Across the Globe: Memory, Identity and Continuity*. London: Trentham Books, 2012.

McGregor, R.S., *A History of Indian Literature: Hindi Literature from Its Beginnings to the Nineteenth Century*. Wiesbaden: Harrassowitz, 1984.

McGregor, R.S., ed. *Devotional Literature in South Asia*. Cambridge: University of Cambridge Press, 1992.

McGregor, R.S. *The Oxford Hindi-English Dictionary*. Oxford: Oxford University Press, 1993.

Mehta, Makrand J., "Maharaj Libel Case: A Study in Social Change in Western India in the 19th Century." *Indo-Asian Culture* 19, no. 1 (1970): 26–39.

Miller, Daniel. *Tales From Facebook*. London: Polity, 2011.

Molekamp, Femke. *Women and the Bible in Early Modern England: Religious Reading and Writing*. New York: Oxford University Press, 2013.

Monius, Anne E. *Imagining a Place for Buddhism: Literary Culture and Religious Community in Tamil-Speaking South India*. New York: Oxford University Press, 2001.

Moodie, Deonnie. *The Making of a Modern Temple and a Hindu City: Kalighat and Kolkata*. New York: Oxford University Press, 2018.

Motiwala, B.N. *Karsondas Mulji: A Biographical Study*. Bombay: Karsondas Mulji Centenary Celebration Committee, 1935.

Mulji, Karsondas. *History of the Sect of Maharajas, or Vallabhacharyas in Western India*. London: Trübner & Co., 1865.

Narayan, Kirin. *Storytelling, Saints, and Scoundrels: Folk Narrative in Hindu Religious Teaching*. Philadelphia: University of Pennsylvania Press, 1989.

Narayanan, Vasudha. *The Vernacular Veda: Revelation, Recitation, and Ritual*. Columbia: University of South Carolina Press, 1994.

Neal, Lynn S. *Romancing God: Evangelical Women and Inspirational Fiction*. Chapel Hill: University of North Carolina Press, 2006.

Novetzke, Christian Lee. "The Theographic and the Historiographic in an Indian Sacred Life Story." *Sikh Formations* 3, no. 2 (2007): 169–184.

Olivelle, Patrick. *Renunciation in Hinduism: A Medieval Debate*. Vienna: Institut fur Indologie der Universität Wien, 1986.

Orsi, Robert A. *Between Heaven and Earth: The Religious Worlds People Make and the Scholars Who Study Them*. Princeton, NJ: Princeton University Press, 2005.

Paṇḍyā, Viṣṇulāl, ed. *Śrī Govardhannāthjī ke Prākaṭya kī Vārtā*. Bombay: Śrī Veṅkaṭeśvar, 1905.

Parīkh, Dvārkādās Puruṣottamdās. *Prācīn Vārtā Rahasya (bhāg 1–3)*. Kankroli, India: Śrī Vidyāvibhāg, 1939.

Parīkh, Dvārkādās Puruṣottamdās. *Vārtā Sāhitya-Mīmāṃsā*. N.p.: Sandeś Prakāśan, 1949.

Parīkh, Dvārkādās Puruṣottamdās, ed. *Caurāsī Vaiṣṇavan kī Vārtā (Tīn Janma kī Līlā Bhāvnā Vālī)*. Mathura, India: Śrī Govarddhan Granthmālā, 1971.

Parīkh, Dvārkādās Puruṣottamdās, ed. *Do Sau Bāvan Vaiṣṇavan kī Vārtā (Tīn Janma kī Līlā Bhāvnā Vālī): Dvitīya Bhāg*. Indore, India: Vaiṣṇav Mitra Maṇḍal, 2009.

Parīkh, Dvārkādās Puruṣottamdās, ed. *Mahāprabhujī kī Nijvārtā, Gharuvārtā, Baiṭhak Caritra ityādī*. Indore, India: Vaiṣṇav Mitra Maṇḍal, 2010.

Parīkh, Dvārkādās Puruṣottamdās, ed. *Caurāsī Vaiṣṇavan kī Vārtā (Tīn Janma kī līlā Bhāvnā Vālī)*. Indore, India: Vaiṣṇav Mitra Maṇḍal, 2011.

Parīkh, Dvārkādās Puruṣottamdās. "Granth meṁ Prāpt Puṣṭi ke Anukāraṇīy aur Mānanīy Thatyoṁ kā Saṃkalan." In *Caurāsī Vaiṣṇavan kī Vārtā (Tīn Janma kī līlā Bhāvnā Vālī)*, edited by Dvārkādās Parīkh, 33–40. Indore, India: Vaiṣṇav Mitra Maṇḍal, 2011.

Parīkh, Dvārkādās Puruṣottamdās, ed. *Śrī Harirāyjī Mahāprabhupraṇīt 41 Baḍe Śikṣāpatra*. Ahmedabad, India: Pūjā Prakāśan, 2011.

Parīkh, Rameśbhāī V., trans. "Coryāsī Vaiṣṇavo nī Vārtāo: Tūm Bīn Tattva kachu nahī Jagmeṃ (84 Bhagavadīya tatva Vicār)." In *Puṣṭimārgīy Patrācār: Śuddhādvait Sevābhūṣaṇ*, edited by Rameśbhāī V. Parīkh, 291–448. Vadodara, India: Śrī Vākpati Foundation, 2002.

Parīkh, Rameśbhāī V., ed. *Puṣṭimārgīy Patrācār: Śuddhādvait Sevābhūṣaṇ*. Vadodara, India: Śrī Vākpati Foundation, 2002.

Patel, Deven. *Text to Tradition: The Naiṣadhīyacarita and Literary Community in South Asia*. New York: Columbia University Press, 2014.

Patel, Shruti. "Beyond the Lens of Reform: Religious Culture in Modern Gujarat." *The Journal of Hindu Studies* 10, no. 1 (2017): 47–85.

Pauwels, Heidi, and Emilia Bachrach. "Aurangzeb as Iconoclast? Vaishnava Accounts of the Krishna Images' Exodus from Braj." *Journal of the Royal Asiatic Society* 28, no. 3 (2018): 485–508.

Peabody, Norbert. *Hindu Kingship and Polity in Precolonial India*. Cambridge: Cambridge University Press, 2003.

Pechilis, Karen. *Interpreting Devotion: The Poetry and Legacy of a Female Bhakti Saint of India*. New York: Routledge, 2016.

Pennington, Brian K. *Was Hinduism Invented?: Britons, Indians, and the Colonial Construction of Religion*. Oxford: Oxford University Press, 2005.

Pinch, William R. *Peasants and Monks in British India*. Berkeley: University of California Press, 1996.

Pinkney, Andrea Marion. "Prasāda." In Brill *Encyclopedia of Hinduism*, edited by Knut A. Jacobsen, 103–111. Leiden: Brill, 2014.

Pintchman, Tracy. *Guests at God's Wedding: Celebrating Kartik Among the Women of Benares*. Albany: State University of New York Press, 2005.

Pintchman, Tracy, ed. *Women's Lives, Women's Rituals in the Hindu Tradition*. Edited by Tracy Pintchman. New York: Oxford University Press, 2007.

Pramod, Amin, ed. *Vraj Venu* 1, no. 4 (Sept.-Dec, 2016): 1–36.

Prasad, Leela. *Poetics of Conduct: Oral Narrative and Moral Being in a South Indian Town*. New York: Columbia University Press, 2006.

Prasad, Leela. *Ethics in Everyday Hindu Life*. Ranikhet, India: Permanent Black, 2007.

Pocock, David F. *Mind, Body, and Wealth: A Study of Belief and Practice in an Indian Village*. Oxford: Basil Blackwell, 1973.

Purohit, Teena. *The Aga Khan Case: Religion and Identity in Colonial India*. Cambridge: Harvard University Press, 2013.

Radway, Janice A. *Reading the Romance: Women, Patriarchy, and Popular Literature*. Chapel Hill: University of North Carolina Press, 1984.

Radway, Janice A. *A Feeling for Books: The Book-of-the-Month Club, Literary Taste, and Middle-class Desire*. Chapel Hill: University of North Carolina Press, 1997.

Raj, Selva J., and Corinne G. Dempsey, eds. *Ritual Levity and Humor in South Asian Religions*. Albany: State University of New York Press, 2010.

Ramanujan, A.K. "Talking to God in the Mother Tongue." *Manushi* 50–52 (1989): 9–14.

Ramanujan, A.K. "Three Hundred *Rāmāyaṇas*: Five Examples and Three Thoughts on Translation." In *Many Ramayanas: The Diversity of a Narrative Tradition in South Asia*, edited by Paula Richman, 22–49. Berkeley: University of California Press, 1991.

Ramanujan, A.K. "On Translating a Tamil Poem." In *The Collected Essays of A.K. Ramanujan*, edited by Vinay Dharwadker, 219–231. Oxford: Oxford University Press, 1999.

Ramanujan, A.K. "On Women Saints." In *The Collected Essays of A.K. Ramanujan*, edited by Vinay Dharwadker, 270–278. Oxford: Oxford University Press, 1999.

Rangacharya, Adya, ed. and trans. *The Nāṭyaśāstra: English Translation with Critical Notes*. New Delhi: Munshiram Manoharlal, 1996.

Redington, James D. "The Last Days of Vallabhacarya." *Journal of Vaishnava Studies* 1, no. 4 (1983): 109–134.

Redington, James D. *Śrīsubodhinī: Vallabhācārya on the Love Games of Kṛṣṇa*. Delhi: Motilal Banarsidass, 1983.

Redington, James D. "Elements of a Vallabhite Bhakti-Synthesis." *Journal of the American Oriental Society* 112, no. 2 (April, 1992): 287–294.

Redington, James D. *The Grace of Lord Krishna: The Sixteen Verse-Treatises (Ṣoḍaśagranthāḥ) of Vallabhacharya*. Delhi: Sri Satguru Publications, 2000.

Report of the Maharaj Libel Case and Bhattia Conspiracy Case, Connected with It. Bombay: Bombay Gazette Press, 1862.

Richardson, E. Allen. *Seeing Krishna in America: The Hindu Bhakti Tradition of Vallabhacharya in India and Its Movement to the West*. Jefferson, NC: McFarland, 2014.

Richman, Paula. *Many Ramayanas: The Diversity of a Narrative Tradition in South Asia*. Berkeley: University of California Press, 1991.

Richman, Paula, ed. *Questioning Ramayanas: A South Asian Tradition*. Berkeley: University of California Press, 2001.

Richman, Paula, ed. *Ramayana Stories in Modern South India: An Anthology*. Bloomington: Indiana University Press, 2008.

Richman, Paula. *A Narrative and a Region: Rama and Sita in Tamil Country and Beyond*. New Delhi: Permanent Black, forthcoming.

Richman, Paula, and Rustom Bharucha, eds. *Performing the Ramayana Tradition: Enactments, Interpretations, and Arguments*. New York: Oxford University Press, 2021.

Ricoeur, Paul. *From Text to Action: Essays in Hermeneutics II*. Translated by Kathleen Blamey and John B. Thompson. Evanston, IL: Northwestern University Press, 1986.

Rinehart, Robin. *One Lifetime, Many Lives: The Experience of Modern Hindu Hagiography*. Atlanta: Scholars Press, 1999.

Rinehart, Robin. *Debating the Dasam Granth*. New York: Oxford University Press, 2011.

Ronald, Emily K. "'More than Alone with the Bible': Reconceptualizing Religious Reading." *Sociology of Religion* 73, no. 3 (2012): 323–344.

Rosen, Matthew. "Ethnographies of Reading: Beyond Literacy and Books." *Anthropological Quarterly* 88, no. 4 (2016): 1059–1083.

Rousseva-Sokolova, Galina. "Sainthood Revisited: Two Printed Versions of the *Lives of the Eighty-Four Vaishnavas* by Gokulnāth." In *Bhakti Beyond the Forest: Current Research of Early Modern Literatures in North India, 2003–2009*, edited by Imre Bangha, 91–104. New Delhi: Manohar, 2012.

Rousseva-Sokolova, Galina. "Voices from the Past. Rearranging Values in Times of Crisis: The Example of North Indian Vaishnava Hagiographies." *Journal of Human Values* 26, 1 (2020): 64–74.

Ruffle, Karen G. *Gender, Sainthood, and Everyday Practice in South Asian Shi'ism*. Chapel Hill: University of North Carolina Press, 2011.

Saha, Shandip. "Creating a Community of Grace: A History of the Puṣṭi Mārga in Northern and Western India: 1493–1905." PhD diss., University of Ottawa, 2004.

Saha, Shandip. "A Community of Grace: The Social and Theological World of the Puṣṭi Mārga Vārtā Literature." *Bulletin of SOAS* 69, no. 2 (2006): 225–242.

Saha, Shandip. "The Darbār, the British, and the Runaway Mahārāja: The Transformation of the Nathdvara-Mewar Relationship." *South Asia Research* 27, no. 3 (2007): 271–291.

Saha, Shandip. "The Movement of *Bhakti* Along a North-West Axis: Tracing the History of the Puṣṭimārg Between the Sixteenth and Nineteenth Centuries." *International Journal of Hindu Studies* 11, no. 3 (2008): 299–318.

Saha, Shandip. "From Vaiṣṇavas to Hindus: The Redefinition of the Vallabha Sampradaya in the Late Nineteenth and Early Twentieth Centuries." Paper presented at the International Conference for Early Modern Literature in North India, Shimla, India, August 3–5, 2012.

Sahoo, Ajaya K., and Johannes G. de Kruijf, eds. *Indian Transnationalism Online: New Perspectives on Diaspora*. London: Ashgate, 2014.

Said, Edward W. "The Text, the World, the Critic." *The Bulletin of the Midwest Modern Language Association* 8, no. 2, 1975: 1–23.

Said, Edward W. *The World, the Text, and the Critic*. Cambridge, MA: Harvard University Press, 1983.

Śarmā, Purṇacandra, ed. *Corāśī Vaiṣṇavnī Vārttā*. Ahmedabad, India: Hargovinddās Harjīvandās Pustakvāḷā; Rājnagar Ṭāip Fāūṇḍrī Prinṭiṅg Press, 1899.

Śarmā, Sumit Madhukarjī. *Śrī Vallabhīy Puṣṭi Sevā*. Ahmedabad, India: Puṣṭimārgīy Vaiṣṇav Pariṣad, 2010.

Saunders, Jennifer. *Imagining Religious Communities: Transnational Hindus and Their Narrative Performances*. New York: Oxford University Press, 2019.

Sawin, Patricia. *Listening for a Life: A Dialogic Ethnography of Bessie Eldreth Through Her Songs and Stories*. Logan: Utah State University Press, 2004.

Schechner, Richard. *Performance Studies: An Introduction*. New York: Routledge, 2013.
Scott, J. Barton. "Luther in the Tropics: Karsandas Mulji and the Colonial 'Reformation' of Hinduism." *Journal of the American Academy of Religion*, 83 no. 1 (2014): 181–209.
Scott, J. Barton. "How to Defame a God: Public Selfhood in the Maharaj Libel Case." *The Journal of South Asian Studies* 38, no. 3 (2015): 387–402.
Scott, J. Barton. *Spiritual Despots: Modern Hinduism and the Genealogies of Self-Rule*. Chicago: University of Chicago Press, 2016.
Sebastian, V. "Gandhi and the Standardisation of Gujarati." *Economic and Political Weekly* 44, no. 31 (2009): 94–101.
Shackle, Christopher, ed. *Urdu and Muslim South Asia: Studies in Honour of Ralph Russell*. London: SOAS, 1989.
Sharafi, Mitra. *Law and Identity in Colonial South Asia: Parsi Legal Culture, 1772–1947*. Cambridge: Cambridge University Press, 2014.
Sharma, Shital. "Negotiating Modernity." Paper presented at the 42nd Annual Conference on South Asia, Madison, Wisconsin, October 17–20, 2013.
Sharma, Shital. "A Prestigious Path to Grace: Class, Modernity, and Female Religiosity in Pustimarg Vaisnavism." PhD diss., McGill University, 2014.
Sharma, Shital. "Middle-class Modernities and the Reproduction of Sectarian Identity Among Puṣṭimārg Vaiṣṇavas in the Bombay Presidency. *The Journal of Hindu Studies* 10, no. 1 (2017): 86–111.
Sharma, Shital. "Consuming Krishna: Women, Class, and Ritual Economies in Pushtimarg Vaishnavism." In *Ritual Innovation: Strategic Interventions in South Asian Religion*, edited by Brian Pennington and Amy L. Allocco, 149–167. Albany: State University of New York Press, 2018.
Sharma, Shital, and Emilia Bachrach. "Beyond Initiation: The Social Lives of Mantra in the Puṣṭimārg." *Journal of Vaishnava Studies* 24, no. 2 (2016): 177–196.
Shodhan, Amrita. "Legal Representations of Khojas and Pushtimārga Vaishnava Polities as Communities: The Aga Khan Case and the Maharaj Libel Case in Mid-Nineteenth Century Bombay." PhD diss., University of Chicago, 1995.
Shodhan, Amrita. "Women in the Maharaj Libel Case: A Re-examination." *Indian Journal of Gender Studies* 4, no. 2 (1997): 123–239.
Shyamdas, trans. *Eighty-four Vaishnavas*. Baroda, India: Shri Vallabha Publications, 1985.
Simpson, Edward. "Why Bhatiyas Are Not "Banias" and Why This Matters: Economic Success and Religious Worldview Among a Mercantile Community of Western India." In *Divines Richesses: Religion et Économie en Monde Marchand Indien*, edited by Pierre Lachaier and Catherine Clémentin-Ojha, 91–111. Paris: École Française d'Extême-Orient, 2008.
Simpson, Edward, and Aparna Kapadia, eds. *The Idea of Gujarat: History, Ethnography and Text*. New Delhi: Orient Blackswan, 2010.
Singh, Shalini. "Secular Pilgrimages and Sacred Tourism in the Indian Himalayas." *GeoJournal* 64, no. 3 (2005): 205–223.
Smith, Frederick M. "The *Saṃnyāsanirṇayaḥ*: A Śuddhādvaita Text on Renunciation Vallabhācārya." *Journal of Vaishnava Studies* 1, no. 4 (1993): 135–156.
Smith, Frederick M. "*Nirodha* and the *Nirodhalakṣāṇa* of Vallabhācārya." *Journal of Indian Philosophy* 26, no. 6 (1998): 589–651.
Smith, Frederick M. "The Hierarchy of Philosophical Systems According to Vallabhācārya." *Journal of Indian Philosophy* 33, no. 4 (2005): 421–453.
Smith, Frederick M. "Vedic and Devotional Waters: The *Jalabheda* of Vallabhācārya." *International Journal of Hindu Studies* 10, no. 1 (2005): 107–136.

Smith, Frederick M. "Dark Matter in Vārtāland: On the Enterprise of History in Early Puṣṭimārga Discourse." *The Journal of Hindu Studies* 2, no. 1 (2009): 27–47.

Smith, Frederick M. "Predestination and Hierarchy: Vallabhācārya's Discourse on the Distinctions Between Blessed, Rule-Bound, Worldly, and Wayward Souls (the *Puṣṭipravāhamaryādābheda*)." *Journal of Indian Philosophy* 39 (2011): 173–227.

Smith, Frederick M. "Pilgrimage and Haveli Seva." Paper presented at the International Conference for Early Modern Literature in North India, Shimla, India, August 3–5.

Smith, W.L. *Patterns in North Indian Hagiography*. Stockholm: Department of Indology, University of Stockholm, 2000.

Snell, Rupert. "Raskhan the Neophyte: Hindu Perspectives on a Muslim Vaishnava." In *Urdu and Muslim South Asia: Studies in Honour of Ralph Russell*, edited by Christopher Shackle, 29–37. London: SOAS, 1989.

Snell, Rupert. *The Hindi Classical Tradition: A Braj Bhāṣā Reader*. London: School of Oriental and African Studies, 1991.

Snell, Rupert, and Winand M. Callwaert, eds. *According to Tradition: Hagiographical Writing in India*. Wiesbaden: Harrassowitz, 1994.

Sontheimer, Günther-Dietz, and Hermann Kulke, eds. *Hinduism Reconsidered*. New Delhi: Manohar, 1997.

Śrāvaṇī. *Gāvalḍī Māre Banvuṃ Che*. Baroda, India: Vraj Dham Adhyatmik Kendra, 2003.

Stark, Ulrike. *An Empire of Books: The Naval Kishore Press and the Diffusion of the Printed Word in Colonial India*. Ranikhet, India: Permanent Black, 2007.

Stewart, Tony K. *The Final Word: The* Caitanya Caritāmṛta *and the Grammar of Religious Tradition*. Oxford: Oxford University Press, 2010.

Śuklā, Rāmcandra. *Hindī Sāhitya kā Itihās*. Varanasi, India: Nāgari Pracāriṇī Sabha, 1957.

Supreme Court, Plea Side. *Maharaja Libel Case Including Bhattia Conspiracy Case, No. 12047 of 1861, Supreme Court Plea Side: Jadunathjee Bizrattanjee Maharaj Vs. Karsondass Mooljee and Nandabhai Rustamji*. Bombay: D. Lukhmidass, 1911.

Talbot, Cynthia. "Contesting Knowledges in Colonial India: The Question of Prithviraj Raso's Historicity." In *Knowing India: Colonial and Modern Constructions of the Past: Essays in Honor of Thomas R. Trautmann*, edited by Cynthia Talbot, 171–212. New Delhi: Yoda Press, 2011.

Talbot, Cynthia, ed. *Knowing India: Colonial and Modern Constructions of the Past: Essays in Honor of Thomas R. Trautmann*. New Delhi: Yoda Press, 2011.

Ṭaṇḍan, Hariharnāth. *Vārtā Sāhitya: Ek Vṛhat Adhyayan*. Aligarh, India: Bharat Prakāśan Mandir, 1960.

Ṭaṇḍan, Harimohandās. *Vraj ke Vaiṣṇav Sampradāy aur Hindī Sāhitya*. Allahabad, India: Sāhitya Bhavan, 1997.

Ṭaṇḍan, Premnārāyaṇ. *Sūrdās kī Vārtā*. Lucknow, India: Nandan Prakāśan, 1968.

Taylor, Woodman Lyon. "Picture Practice: Painting Programs, Manuscript Production, and Liturgical Performances at the Kotah Royal Palace." In *Gods, Kings, and Tigers: The Art of Kotah*, edited by Stuart Cary Welch, 61–72. Munich: Prestel Verlag, 1997.

Taylor, Woodman Lyon. "Visual Culture in Performative Practice: The Aesthetics, Politics and Poetics of Visuality in Liturgical Practices of the Vallabha Sampradaya Hindu Community at Kota." PhD diss., University of Chicago, 1997.

Toomey, Paul M. "Food from the Mouth of Krishna: Socio-Religious Aspects of Sacred Food in Two Krishnaite Sects." In *Food, Society, and Culture: Aspects in South Asian Food Systems*, edited by R.S. Khare and M.S.A. Rao, 55–83. Durham, NC: Carolina Academic, 1986.

Toomey, Paul M. "Krishna's Consuming Passions: Food as Metaphor and Metonym for Emotion at Mount Govardhan." In *Divine Passions: The Social Construction of Emotion in India*, edited by Owen M. Lynch, 157–181. Berkeley: University of California Press, 1990.

Toomey, Paul M. "Mountain of Food, Mountain of Love: Ritual Inversion in the Annakuta Feast at Mount Govardhan." In *The Eternal Food: Gastronomic Ideas and Experiences of Hindus and Buddhists*, edited by R.S. Khare, 117–146. Albany: State University of New York Press, 1992.

van Doorn-Harder, Pieternella. *Women Shaping Islam: Reading the Qur'an in Indonesia.* Bloomington: University of Indiana Press, 2006.

Varma, Dhirendra. *La Langue Braj*. Paris: Adrien-Maisonneuve, 1935.

Vaudeville, Charlotte. *Myths, Saints and Legends in Medieval India*. Delhi: Oxford University Press, 1996.

Vaudeville, Charlotte. "Multiple Approaches to a Living Hindu Myth: The Lord of the Govardhan Hill." In *Hinduism Reconsidered*, edited by Günther-Dietz Sontheimer and Hermann Kulke, 105–124. New Delhi: Manohar, 1997.

Waghorne, Joanne Punzo. "The Gentrification of the Goddess." *International Journal of Hindu Studies* 5, no. 3 (2001): 227–267.

Waghorne, Joanne Punzo. *Diaspora of the Gods: Modern Hindu Temples in an Urban Middle-Class World*. Oxford: Oxford University Press, 2004.

Waldrop, Anne. "Kitty-parties and Middle-class Femininity in New Delhi." In *Being Middle-Class in India: A Way of Life*, edited by Henrike Donner, 162–183. New York: Routledge, 2011.

Watts. James W. "The Three Dimensions of Scriptures." *Postscripts: The Journal of Sacred Texts and Contemporary Worlds* 2 (2006): 135–159.

Williams, Raymond B. *An Introduction to Swaminarayan Hinduism*. Cambridge: Cambridge University Press, 2001.

Williams, Tyler A., Anshu Malhotra, and John Stratton Hawley, eds. In *Text and Tradition in Early Modern India*. New Delhi: Oxford University Press.

Wimbush, Vincent, ed. *Theorizing Scriptures: New Critical Orientations to a Cultural Phenomenon*. New Brunswick, NJ: Rutgers University Press, 2008.

Wimbush, Vincent, ed. *African Americans and the Bible: Sacred Texts and Social Textures*. Eugene, OR: Wipf and Stock Publishers, 2021.

Yadav, K.C., ed. *The Autobiography of Dayanand Saraswati*. New Delhi: Manohar, 1987.

Yeolekar, Mugdha. "Gurucaritra Pārāyaṇ: Social Praxis of Religious Reading." PhD diss., Arizona State University, 2014.

Ziegler, Norman P. "The Seventeenth Century Chronicles of Mārvāṛa: A Study in the Evolution and Use of Oral Traditions in Western India." *History in Africa* 3(1976): 127–153.

Websites and Podcasts

Abha Shahra Shyama. "Happenings Around the Mandir." Accessed November 30, 2013, http://www.shreenathjibhakti.org/shreenathjimandir.htm.

Abha Shahra Shyama. "Live Vaartas." Accessed September 14, 2021. https://www.shreenathjibhakti.org/post/shreenathji-live-vartaas.

Britannica Academic, s.v. "Veda." Accessed January 8, 2021. https://academic-eb-com.ezproxy.oberlin.edu/levels/collegiate/article/Veda/74939.

Goodwin, Megan, and Ilyse Morgenstein Fuerst. "Episode 102: Who gets left out of "religion"?." Accessed January 29, 2020, in *Keeping 101: A Killjoy's Introduction to Religion*, podcast, audio, 01:16, https://keepingit101.com/e102.

Goswami Anandbava. "The Ego in Pushtimarg: The slip between the Cup and the Lip." Accessed August 13, 2012. http://pushtimarg.com/anandbava/2011/the-ego-in-pushtimarg-the-slip-between-the-cup-and-the-lip/.

"Indira betiji pravachan 84 vaisnav varta- 1 of 71." Accessed January 10, 2018. https://www.youtube.com/watch?v=okx9DILLBgI.

Mazzarella, William. "Middle Class." Accessed October 3, 2020. https://www.soas.ac.uk/south-asia-institute/keywords/file24808.pdf.

Nathdwara Temple Management. "Member Board Info." Accessed October 21, 2013. http://www.nathdwaratemple.org/Management/BoardMemberInfo.aspx.

Mathur, N. "Dhirendra Manharbhai (Shri) And . . . vs. State Anr. On 6 May, 2005." Accessed October 13, 2013. http://indiankanoon.org/doc/977892/?type=print.

"Our Pushti Siddhant says." Accessed August 29, 2020. https://www.instagram.com/p/CEbZOlaBu9l/.

Pushtimarg. "Pilgrimage" and "Seva." Accessed January 3, 2014; March 1, 2014. http://www.pushtimarg.net/pushti/history/pilgrimage/; http://www.pushtimarg.net/pushti/sahitya/seva/.

"Pushti Sahitya Seva." Accessed August 29, 2020. https://pushtimarg.net/seva/.

"Pushti Satsang." Accessed August 8, 2020. https://www.facebook.com/427657920746929/posts/goswami-108-shri-indira-betijimahodayashreeit-is-15-days-since-aapshris-nitya-l/630939863752066/.

"Pushtiswadhyay." Accessed December 22, 2020. https://www.youtube.com/watch?v=xKbyzEf5v60&t=2241s&ab_channel=Pushtiswadhyay-GoswamyShriShyammanoharji.

Rajasthan Government. "The Nathdwara Temple Act, 1959." Accessed October 30, 2013. https://devasthan.rajasthan.gov.in/Files/Nathdwara_Temple_Act%201959_Eng.pdf.

Rajasthan Government. "The Nathdwara Temple Act, 1973." Accessed October 30, 2013. https://devasthan.rajasthan.gov.in/Files/Upload/6262007105849AM%20NathdwaraTempleRules1973.pdf.

Shreenathji v/s Rajasthan Congress Government on Facebook. "Shreenathji v/s Rajasthan Congress Government." Accessed October 16, 2013; March 1, 2014. https://www.facebook.com/pages/Shreenathji-vs-Rajasthan-Congress- Government/522192447862408.

"Shree Vallabh Vidyapeeth (Pushtimargiya Open University)." Accessed August 16, 2018. http://www.vallabhkankroli.org/activities_shree%20vallabh%20vidhyapith.htm.

"Shrimad Bhagavat katha Part 1 By PPG 108 Shri Indirabetiji (jiji)." Accessed December 20, 2020. https://www.youtube.com/watch?v=4Y6MFSgImew.

Shrinathji Temple on Facebook. "Shrinathji Temple." Accessed December 25, 2013. https://www.facebook.com/shrinathjitemple/posts/379186805517553.

Shyam Manohar Goswami. "Upkaram 1." Accessed March 1, 2013. http://72.167.35.235/ongoing/fal_seminar_2013/01_upkaram/.

Shyam Manohar Goswami. "Shri Vallabh vachanamrut Rana vyas Ki varta." Accessed August 29, 2019. http://pushtimarg.net/video-pravachana/?post_id=4739.

"Temple Extension Plan." Accessed October 21, 2013. http://www.nathdwaratemple.org/Development/TempleExtensionPhaseI.aspx.

"Things to Do In Nathdwara." Accessed April 9, 2022. https://www.tripadvisor.com/Attractions-g1162444-Activities-Nathdwara_Rajsamand_District_Rajasthan.html.

"Travel Systems." Accessed September 27, 2020. https://hindureligiousitems.com/products/wooden-jhapiji-travel-system.

Vallabhacharya Vidyapeeth. "Activities at the Vidyapeeth." Accessed February 2, 2014. http://vallabhacharyavidyapeeth.org/activities-at-the-vidyapeeth/.

"Vallabh Youth Organization." Accessed January 12, 2020. https://vyoworld.org.

"Varta Sahitya Pravachan." Accessed December 1, 2020. https://www.youtube.com/watch?app=desktop&v=O6jQ7KIBsVs&ab_channel=BhaktiSagarPravachan.

Index

For the benefit of digital users, indexed terms that span two pages (e.g., 52–53) may, on occasion, appear on only one of those pages.

Figures are indicated by *f* following the page number. Footnotes are indicated by n. or nn. followed by the note number.

Abha Shahra Shyama, 107–9, 107n.20, 125–26
Abhinavagupta, 56n.63
Acharyaji, 38, 102, 180–81, 183–84, 205. *See also* Vallabhacharya
  vārtā of Amma, 175
  vārtā of Krishnadas, 62
  vārtā of Purushottamdas, 143–44, 145, 198–200
  vārtā of Rana Vyas, 165–66
  vārtā of Tulsa, 195, 197–98
Ādhunik Puṣṭimārgīy Bhāṣā Sāhityanī Śoc Stithi, 91–92, 91n.76
affective and embodied practice, 25, 158–60, 173, 176, 187
Akbarnāmā, 91
alaukik
  Bhāvprakāś commentary, 58–61
  biographical details of protagonists, 58–61
  defined, 207
  Desai's commentary, 87–88, 88n.68
  handling doubts about dubious actions of protagonists, 63
  Nathdwara *havelī* complex, 102
  public reading, 100–1
  Śrīnāthjī kī Prākaṭya Vārtā, 86–87
  worldly vs. otherworldly, 24–25, 43–44, 46–48, 187
Allocco, Amy, 167n.15
Ambalal, Amit, 106n.19
Amma, 174–75
Anand (Ani) (Mona's grandchild), 174, 175–76
Anandavardhana, 56n.63
Anandbava, Goswami, 112n.30
ansakhaṛī, 196–97, 196n.5
Anstey (lawyer), 73, 74
anyāśray, 149–50, 149n.47
aparas, 30–31, 207
āratī, 183, 183n.39, 195, 196–97
arcana, 133–34
Arnould, Joseph, 73, 74n.23
Arya Samaj, 75n.25
aṣṭachāp poets, 54, 54n.55, 60n.70, 61n.75, 109–10, 207
aṣṭākṣara. *See Shri Krishna śaranaṃ mama* mantra
aṣṭayām sevā, 106n.18, 117n.43, 207
ātmanivedan. *See brahmasambandha* mantra
ātma-nivedana, 133–34
Aurangzeb, 102, 113–14

bābā (*bava*; *bāvā*), 135–36, 135n.18, 207
Baḍe Śikṣāpatra (Hariray), 34–35n.9, 117n.41, 118n.44, 149n.47, 158–60, 171–72, 206
bahen (*ben*), 136n.19, 207
Bahuji, Brajlata, 184n.42
bahūjīs, 134, 178, 183–84, 207
baniyā, 9, 160, 207
BAPS (Bochasanwasi Shri Akshar Purushottam Swaminarayan Sanstha), 123–24, 123n.61
baṛī jātī, 42–43, 46–48, 47n.36, 202–3
Barz, Richard, 60–61
Bauman, Richard, 67n.1
bava (*bāvā*; *bābā*), 135–36, 135n.18, 207
Bayley (lawyer), 73
be bol, 82
ben (*bahen*), 136n.19, 207
Bengali language, 40n.24

beṭījīs, 134, 163–64, 177–78, 207
Bhāgavata kathās, 48–49n.41
Bhāgavatapurāṇa, 55–56, 197
defined, 206
devotional sentiments adopted by *bhakti* traditions, 57n.64
nine modes of *bhakti*, 133–34
nitya līlā, 117n.43
performative reading and storytelling (*kathā*), 20–21n.48, 33–34, 109n.25, 147n.41, 179–80
relationship between *vārtās* and, 37–38
religious schools, 75–76
Subodhinī commentary, 20, 37–38, 55–58
tenth canto (*Rāsapañcādhyāyī*), 20, 56n.60
vacanāmṛt, 48–49n.41
Vallabhacharya's passion for, 20n.47, 55–56
women's reading, 173, 179–80
Bhaktamāl (Nabhadas), 76–77, 91
bhaktas, defined, 207
bhakti theologies
bhāv, 132n.6
defined, 207
devotional sentiments in *Bhāgavatapurāṇa* and adopted by, 57n.64
emergence of print and vernacular book culture, 76–78
gendering of, 25–26, 26–27n.51, 52–54, 138–39
Hindu attitudes towards Muslim community, 45–46
Maharaja Libel Case, 72
nine modes of, 133–34
rasa theory, 57n.65
Bhaktivardhinī, 115–16, 132–33, 147
Bhalla, Tamara, 13–16, 159n.2
Bhargava, Kanhaiyalal, 78n.37
Bhatt, Kalyan, 19, 37
Bhatt, Krishna, 90
Bhatt-Rawat, Kashika, 93–94, 161–62
bhāv(a)
in *Bhāgavatapurāṇa* and adopted by later *bhakti* traditions, 57n.64
definitions of, 131–32, 132n.6, 195n.1, 208
Bhavika (devotee), 164–65, 166–69
Bhāvprakāś commentary (Hariray), 58–64, 68–69, 195
alignment of *vārtās* with Vallabhacharya's writings, 96–97, 117
authorship of, 36–37, 84, 90
on Chandravali, 76–77
community readings, 132–33, 149–50, 151, 155
defined, 206
Desai's commentary vs., 87–88
dialogical (conversational) quality of *vārtās*, 33–34
divine counterparts of protagonists, 46–47
modern commentaries and, 82
as natural stopping point for discussion, 43–44
Parikh's version of *84VV* and *252VV*, 34n.8
printing practices, 59n.69
Puṣṭimārgīy Patrācār course, 96
on seemingly dubious actions of protagonists, 56–58, 61–63, 73–74, 91–92
"three lives" narrative, 59–60, 88
vārtā of Krishnadas, 73–74, 91–92
vārtā of Raskhan, 41–42, 43–44
vārtā of Tulsa, 195, 196, 197–98, 198n.9
vārtās as inherently authoritative and imbued with divinity, 37–38
worldly vs. otherworldly, 58–61
Bhāvsindhu, 34–35
bhog, 56–58, 117–18, 117n.43, 146, 146n.38, 170–71, 208
Black, Brian, 44–46, 49, 64–65
Blackburn, Anne, 38
Bochasanwasi Shri Akshar Purushottam Swaminarayan Sanstha (BAPS), 123–24, 123n.61
Bodies of Song (Hess), 7n.10, 65–66
Bombay Intelligentsia, 71
Bombay Presidency, 71
Bourdieu, Pierre, 156n.63
Brahman, 30, 50n.44, 72–73. *See also* Krishna
brahmasambandha (*ātmanivedan*) mantra, 30, 30n.1, 31–32, 35–36, 50, 50n.44, 50n.46, 59n.68, 93–94, 115–16, 208

Brahmins, 9, 13–16, 50–51, 52–54, 80–81, 85n.55, 120n.55, 121, 183–84, 196n.4, 196n.6, 198–200
Braj Bhasha (Braj Bhāṣā)
aṣṭachāp poets, 54
Baḍe Śikṣāpatra, 34–35n.9
Caurāsī Baiṭhak Caritra, 55–56
defined, 4n.4, 208
dialogical prose, 44–45, 45n.29
early printed editions of *vārtās*, 79
everyday speech of *vārtās* in, 35n.11
kīrtan, 128–29
Maharaja Libel Case, 74n.22
multiple styles of, 91
Parikh's *84VV* and *252VV*, 89
performative styles of narration, 43–44
Puṣṭimārgīy Patrācār course, 95–96
"*Shri Thakurji sānubhāvatā janānā*," 39–40
Shyam Manohar Goswami, 109–10, 111
Śrīnāthjī kī Prākaṭya Vārtā, 83–84
translations from, 81–82, 82n.49
Vārtā Sāhitya, 4
women's reading, 19–20
Braj region, 20n.46, 208
Brajvilās Sārāvalī (Dhusar), 78n.37
Briggs, Charles, 10n.16, 67n.1
Buddhism and Buddhists, 45–46, 60n.72
Bynum, Caroline Walker, 147–48

Caitanyacaritāmṛta (Krishnadas Kaviraj), 40n.24
Candrāvalī (Harishchandra), 76–77
Caurāsī Baiṭhak Caritra, 34–35, 55–56, 206
Caurāsī Bārttā, 78n.37
Caurāsī Ḍhol (Dayaram), 95–96, 142–43
Caurāsī Vaiṣṇavan kī Vārtā. *See 84VV*
Certeau, Michel de, 17–18, 17n.39
Chaitanya, 40n.24, 45–46, 56–58
Champaklata, 195, 196
Chandragopalji Goswami, 184n.42
Chandravali, 59–60, 76–77, 198–200, 201. *See also* Vitthalnath
Choksi, Megha, 2–3, 30–32, 35–36, 37–38, 39–40, 44, 65–66, 79–81, 93–94, 205
Christianity and Christians, 40n.21, 147–48
Citra Gangayayani, 44–45, 49
commentarial reading, 22–23, 67–98, 188–89. *See also names of specific commentaries*
defined, 8
emergence of print and vernacular book culture, 67–68, 75–83
imagined audience including "historians and archeologists," 84–86
Maharaja Libel Case, 70–75
reauthorization of *Vārtā Sāhitya* through written commentary, 67–68, 83–97
community reading, 24–25, 128–56. *See also satsaṅgs*
at Goswami Haveli, 128–29
negotiating family dynamics, 142–51
questioning the *vārtās*, 152–56
as *satsaṅg*, 132–42
Corāśī Vaiṣṇavnī Vārttā, 81–82
Cort, John, 26–27n.51
Coryāsī Vaiṣṇavo nī Vārtāo, 142–43, 145
COVID-19 pandemic, 28n.53, 104–5, 187, 191–92

daivī jīvs, 42–43, 44, 50–51, 52–54, 87–88, 198–200, 202–3, 208
Dalmia, Vasudha, 37–38, 87n.64, 166n.13
Damodar (Yojana's husband), 171–73
Damodardas Sambhalvale, 103, 149–50
darśan, 105–6, 126–27
BAPS, 123–24
defined, 23–24, 208
Goswami Haveli, 128–29, 157
temple spaces, 23–24, 122–24, 139–40
vārtā of Raskhan, 42–43
dāsya, 57n.64, 133–34
Dayaram, 95–96, 142–43
debates, 11–13, 23–24, 76, 97, 188–91
havelī sevā and renovation debates, 1–2, 100–1, 119–23, 126–27, 189–90
healthy *puṣṭi* debate, 148–50, 154–55
over food offerings, 2–4
over sartorial propriety during *sevā*, 153–54
Puṣṭi Siddhānt Carcā Sabhā, 119–20
social media, 100n.4
DeNapoli, Antoinette E., 161–63
Desai, Lallubhai Chaganlal, 87–89, 88n.68, 93–94

Desai, Mona, 28–29, 95, 157–61, 163, 174–78, 184–85, 192–93, 205
Devakinandacharya, 75–76
devotional songs, 8, 110–11, 117–18, 169–70, 172–73
  āratī, 183n.39
  aṣṭachāp poets, 34–35n.9
  dhoḷ, 95–96, 142–43, 157–58, 208
  kīrtan, 1–2, 54–55n.56, 84n.53, 109–10, 128–29, 133–34, 134n.15, 157–58, 209
dharma
  defined, 16n.34, 208
  remaining a householder and following one's own dharma, 115–16, 147
  sanātana-dharma, 75–77
  women, 52–54, 162–63, 162–63n.9
Dharma Sabha, 76–77
Dharmaśāstras, 13–16, 207
dhoḷ, 95–96, 142–43, 157–58, 208
dhotīs, 116n.39, 152n.53, 208
Dhusar, Govardhandas, 78n.37
dialogical reading, 30–66, 187
  analysis involving living readers, 65–66
  dialogical quality of *vārtās*, 5, 6–7, 21, 22–23, 24–25
  dialogue across religious traditions, 40n.21, 44–46
  emphasis on reader rather than on text, 64–66
  grammar of devotion and tradition, 32–33, 39–40, 48
  Hariray's *Bhāvprakāś* commentary, 33–34, 58–64
  intertextual elements of *vārtās*, 33–34, 38, 49–58, 64, 66
  introduction to *84VV* and *252VV*, 34–38
  modeling devotional behavior through dialogue, 48
  performative styles of narration, 43–44
  real-life speech acts, 40
  "thinking out loud" speech, 41–43
  vacanāmṛt, 32–33, 39–48
  Vārtā Sāhitya as intertextual hagiography, 49–58
Dialogue in Early South Asian Religions (Black and Patton), 44–45
Dinesh (Bhavika's husband), 167
Dipa (devotee), 43–44, 142–43, 144, 146, 150–51
Diwali, 157–58
Dobbin, Christine E., 71
Dogra, Sonali, 157–61, 163–70, 176, 177–78, 181, 184–85, 206
Dohāvalī (Dhusar), 78n.37
Do Sau Bāvan Vaiṣṇavan kī Vārtā. *See 252VV*
Dwarkadhishji, 105
Dwarkanathji, 102–3, 183

84VV (*Caurāsī Vaiṣṇavan kī Vārtā*), 30–32, 171–72
  authorship of, 36–37, 36n.13
  Bhāvprakāś commentary, 58, 58n.66, 59n.69
  caste and gender, 52–54
  contents of, 32–33, 35–36
  defined, 206
  Desai's versions, 87–89
  dhoḷ by Dayaram, 142–43
  dialogical (conversational) quality of, 21, 22–23
  diversity of human emotions and behaviors, 50–52
  diversity of protagonists, 50–51
  emergence of print and vernacular book culture, 76–78, 78n.37, 81–82
  emotional support and mental health, 158–60, 174–75
  encounters and communication with Krishna, 40
  gift vs. giver, 65n.81
  handling doubts about dubious actions of protagonists, 61, 63–64
  as inherently authoritative and imbued with divinity, 37–38
  initiation through Vallabhacharya, 35–36
  intertextuality, 33–34, 49–52
  intimately experiencing, and knowing needs of Krishna, 39–40
  Maharaja Libel Case, 72–73
  Naval Kishore Press, 67–68
  number of hagiographies in, 35n.11
  paratextual elements, 79–80, 88–89, 93–94
  Parikh's version, 34n.8, 89–91, 195

as practical canon, 38
provenance of, 36–37, 36n.12
Puṣṭimārgīy Patrācār course, 95–96
reference to poetic works, 54–55
satsaṅgs, 132–33
Shalini Goswami's reading and exegesis, 19–20
Shyam Manohar Goswami, 113
specific dates, 86–87
temple controversies and reconstructions, 102–3
vacanāmṛt, 39–48
vārtā of Amma, 174–75
vārtā of Damodardas, 103, 149–50
vārtā of Krishnadas, 72–74, 91–92
vārtā of Purushottamdas, 142–45, 146, 147, 150, 198–202
vārtā of Rana Vyas, 111–13, 148, 164–67
vārtā of Raskhan, 40–44, 40n.23, 50–51, 56–58, 59–60, 202–3
vārtā of Tulsa, 195–98
vārtā of Vasudevdas Chakda, 120
vārtā of Virbai, 61, 152–55
worldly vs. otherworldly details of protagonists, 46–47, 59–61
Empire of Books, An (Stark), 77–78

Facebook, 99–105, 100n.4, 125–26, 182
"factual footnote" commentary (Desai), 87–89
female impersonation, 139n.27
Fish, Stanley, 65–66
Fuerst, Ilyse Morgenstein, 189–90

Gandhi, Mohandas K., 82n.49
Gattu Lalji (Govardhanlalji), 84–85, 85n.59
Gattulalji, Pandit, 75–76
Geertz, Clifford, 130–31
Genette, Gérard, 79n.41
Ghanshyam Bhatt, 85n.59
Gharu Vārtā, 34–35
*ginān*s, 69n.6
Gita (devotee), 93–94, 135–36, 136n.19
Gokulnath (Gokulnathji), 19, 36–38, 36n.13, 55–56, 58, 90, 91, 132–33, 205
Goodwin, Megan, 189–90
gopās (*sakhās*), 60–61, 60n.70, 208, 209
Gopeshvar, 34–35n.9, 120n.55
Gopinath (Gopinathji), 102–3, 117n.41
gopīs (*sakhīs*)
Chandravali, 76–77
defined, 25–26, 208, 209
rāsa-līlā, 55–58
role models, 169–70, 184n.41
vārtā of Purushottamdas, 198–200, 201
vārtā of Raskhan, 42–43, 46–47
vārtā of Tulsa, 195, 196, 196n.6, 197
women's devotional sentiments, 138–39, 160–61
worldly vs. otherworldly, 59–61, 60n.70, 62–63
Gosh, Anindita, 80n.43
gosvāmī, defined, 40n.22, 208
Goswami Haveli, 122, 128–30, 137, 152, 157
Govardhandas, 90
Govardhanlal Maharaj, 75–76
Govardhannathji. *See* Shrinathji
Govindlal Maharaj, 84–85
Govindray, 36n.13
grammar of devotion and tradition, 7, 32–33, 39–40, 48, 93–94, 167–69
*granth*s, defined, 208
Griffiths, Paul J., 13n.20, 15n.29, 37n.15, 68–69, 155, 155n.58
Gujarati
Caurāsī Ḍhol, 95–96
code-switching, 143n.34
commentaries, 82
Coryāsī Vaiṣṇavo nī Vārtāo, 142–43
Dayaram, 142–43
Desai's commentary, 87–89
devotional songs, 142–43, 157–58
early printed editions of *vārtā*s, 81–82
Indirabetiji, 179–80
Parikh's *Vārtā Sāhitya Mīmāṃsā*, 89–90
performative styles of narration, 43–44
Puṣṭimārgīy Patrācār course, 94, 95–96
Puṣṭi Siddhānt Carcā Sabhā, 119n.49
Satya Prakāś, 68n.4
Shalini Goswami, 31–32
standardization of, 82n.49
Vārtā Sāhitya, 4, 22–23
women's reading, 1–2, 31–32, 142–43, 157–58, 162–63, 179–80
*guṇ*s, 60n.72, 195n.2

Gusain (Gusainji), 180–81, 205. *See also* Vitthalnath
vārtā of Amma, 175
vārtā of Purushottamdas, 198–201
vārtā of Raskhan, 40, 40n.22, 42–43, 202–3
vārtā of Tulsa, 197–98

hagiographies. *See vārtās*
hakikat fūṭnot, 88–89
Hanumān Cālīsā, 144, 144n.36
Hariray (Harirayji), 58–64, 205. *See also* *Bhāvprakāś* commentary
Baḍe Śikṣāpatra, 34–35n.9
editing and compilation of *84VV* and *252VV*, 36–37, 36n.13
handling doubts about dubious actions of protagonists, 61–63
"*Shri Thakurji sānubhāvatā janānā*," 39–40
Śrīnāthjī kī Prākaṭya Vārtā, 84
worldly vs. otherworldly details of protagonists, 58–61
Hariray Goswami, 119–21, 120n.56
Hariścandra Candrikā, 76–77
Harishchandra, Bharatendu, 76–78, 78n.36
Harsani, Damodardas, 35–36, 49–51, 65n.81, 88, 90, 96, 105
Hastings, Warren, 70–71
havelīs. *See* temples
havelī saṅgīt, 54, 208
Hawley, John S., 40n.24, 52n.50, 54n.55, 86n.61
Heroic Wives (Kelting), 162–63
Hess, Linda, 65–66, 155
Hindi, 5, 10–11, 32–33, 79n.40, 82n.49, 102, 107–8, 107n.20. *See also* Braj Bhasha
code-switching, 143n.34
commentaries, 82
Harishchandra, 76–78
kīrtan, 1–2
Puṣṭi Siddhānt Carcā Sabhā, 119n.49
Shyam Manohar Goswami, 111
Tulsidas, 13–16
Vārtā Sāhitya, 80–81
Hindi Classical Tradition, The (Snell), 5

householder lifestyle, 52, 52n.50, 115–16, 147, 161–63, 183–84
humor, 2–3, 32–33, 33n.7, 47–48, 74–75, 111, 153–54
Hyder, Syed Akbar, 13–16
hypophora, 33–34, 63

icchā, 39–40, 161–62
Indirabetiji, Goswami, 25, 26–27, 49–50, 109–10, 112n.30, 163–64, 176–85, 191–92, 205
background of, 178
emotional well-being and contemporary life, 180–81
influence of, 184–85, 184n.42
non-renunciation, 183–84
philanthropy, 182
pravacans and *kathās*, 179–81
as a primary guru and embodiment of divinity, 177–78
initiation, 30–32, 35–36, 46–47, 59, 59n.68
of Europeans and Americans, 10, 10n.15
through Vallabhacharya, 35–36, 40
through Vitthalnath, 40, 47–48
of Vallabhacharya, 31–32, 35–36, 49–50
Instagram, 104–5
interpretive communities, 13–16, 65–66, 188–89
intertextuality, 20, 33–34, 38, 49–58, 64, 66, 74–75, 142
Islam and Muslims
baṛī jātī, 42–43, 46–48, 47n.36, 202–3
Hindu attitudes towards, 45–48, 149n.48
Ismaili Muslim Khojas, 69n.6
vārtā of Raskhan, 41, 42–43, 47–48, 202–3
itihās lekhak, 84–85

Jadunath Brijratanji Maharaj, 70–72, 74n.22, 75–76, 75n.27
Jagannath Joshi, 165–66
Jahāṃgīrnāmā, 91
Jahangir, 103n.9
jāher, 108–9, 209
jāher mandirs, 120, 125–27
jāī, 129, 144, 157, 196–97, 209

Jainism and Jains, 45–46, 60n.72, 162–63
Jalabheda, 62–63, 62n.77
jhāpījīs, 180–81
ji (*jī*), 48n.40, 209

kāch, 152, 152n.53
kaliyug, 51–52, 55, 209
Kalyanray, 36n.13
Kamala (devotee), 135–36
Karbala, 13–16
kathākārs, 48–49n.41, 179–80, 209
kathās, 80, 109n.25, 112, 132–33n.9, 147, 147n.41, 179–81, 209. *See also* public reading
Kauṣītaki Upaniṣad, 44–45, 49, 64–65
kautumbik mūlyo, 146, 146n.39, 148–49
Kelting, M. Whitney, 162–63
Kim, Hanna, 123–24, 123n.61
kīrtan, 1–2, 54–55n.56, 84n.53, 109–10, 128–29, 133–34, 134n.15, 157–58, 209
kīrtana, 133–34
Kishori (devotee), 128–29, 138
kitty parties, 167, 167n.14
Krishna. *See also* Brahman; *līlās*; Natvarlalji; *sevā* rituals; Shrinathji; *svarūps*; Thakurji
  balancing caretaking with householder lifestyle, 11–13, 24–25, 26–27, 52
  Banarasi women's rituals during Kartik, 169–70
  becoming attuned to daily needs and desires of, 26–27
  bhakti theologies, 25–26, 26–27n.51
  books as *prasād*, 170–71
  defined, 205
  dialogical (conversational) quality of *vārtās*, 21
  encounters and communication with, 39–40, 40n.21, 41–45, 47–48, 107–8
  essential nature of as Supreme Being, 36–38, 55
  hagiographies as embodiments of, 36–37
  human body as vessel for *sevā*, 167
  improved comfort for, 105, 105n.16
  initiation, 30–32
  initiation through Vallabhacharya, 35–36
  intimately experiencing, and knowing needs of, 39–40
  Mathuranathji, 195–96, 195n.3
  Narayan, 103
  offering grace through disability, 176
  passion and attachment for, 41–44, 46–48
  protection from trap of transgressive behavior, 73–74
  rasa theory, 56–58
  satsaṅgs, 132–33
  Śrīnāthjī kī Prākaṭya Vārtā, 83–84
  temple controversies and reconstructions, 23–24
  vacanāmṛt, 32–33
  women as primary caretakers, 11–13, 160–61
Krishnadas, 72–74, 91–92
Krishnadas Adhikari, 52–54, 61–63
Krishnadas Kaviraj, 40n.24
kṛpā, 1n.1, 39–40, 154–55
Kshatriyas, 198–201
Kumud (devotee), 2–3, 138–39

Ladobetiji, 85n.59
Lakshmana, 45–46
Lakshmi, 103
Lakshmi Venkateshwar Steam Press, 84–85
Lalitaji, 63, 196
laukik
  Bhāvprakāś commentary, 58–61
  biographical details of protagonists, 58–61
  defined, 209
  Desai's commentary, 87–88, 88n.68
  handling doubts about dubious actions of protagonists, 62–63, 196n.6
  luminescence of *līlā*, 201n.18
  public reading, 100–1
  Śrīnāthjī kī Prākaṭya Vārtā, 86–87
  worldly vs. otherworldly, 24–25, 43–44, 46–48, 187
Leena (devotee), 1n.2
Life of a Text, The (Lutgendorf), 13–16
Lila (devotee), 150–51, 191–92
līlās, 56n.60, 60nn.70–71, 96–97, 106–7
  Bhāvprakāś commentary, 58–61, 62–63, 177–78

līlās (*cont.*)
defined, 209
luminescence of, 201, 201n.18
model for love for the divine, 20
nitya līlā, 56–58, 59, 87–88, 117n.43, 181
rāsa-līlā, 55–58, 209
vārtā of Purushottamdas, 198–200, 201
vārtā of Raskhan, 42–43, 202–3
vārtā of Tulsa, 195, 196, 196n.6, 197
Long, Elizabeth, 11–13
Luhrmann, Tanya M., 40n.21
Lutgendorf, Philip, 13–16

Madhavi, 198–200
mādhurya. *See śṛṅgār(a)*
Madhusudanlal Goswami. *See* Tilak Goswami
Mahābhārata, 55
Mahajan, Yojana, 158–61, 163–64, 206
gurus and their families, 163
Indirabetiji, 177–78, 184–85
pseudonym, 134n.16
Puṣṭimārgīy Patrācār course, 95
satsaṅgs, 134–35, 141, 141n.31, 142–43, 144–46, 147, 148–49, 150–51, 187
Shyam Manohar Goswami, 112
well-being and "meditative state," 170–73, 176, 190–91
Mahaprabhuji, 31–32, 33n.6, 58, 111, 174–75, 205. *See also* Vallabhacharya
mahāprasād (*prasād*), 121, 121–22n.59, 122–23, 146n.38, 165–66, 170–71, 175, 183, 195–97, 201, 209
Maharaj (*mahārāj*), 47–48, 209
Maharaja Libel Case, 22–23, 69–75, 83–84, 87, 96–98, 188–89
context of, 71
"debased" traditions, 71–72
emergence of print and vernacular book culture following, 75–76
overview of, 70–71
vārtā of Krishnadas, 72–74, 91–92
mahbūb, 42–43, 47–48, 202–3
mālās, 59n.68, 143–44, 145, 147, 198–200, 209
Malati, 198–200
mandirs, 23–24, 119, 209. *See also* temples
maṅgalācaraṇ, 109–10
Manikundala, 195, 196
Manish (devotee), 58–59
Manju (devotee), 5
Manjula (devotee), 122–23
maryādāmārg, 56–58
Mathuranathji, 195–96, 195n.3
Mathureshji Maharaj, 183n.38
McGregor, R.S., 91n.74
merchant communities, 71, 71n.13, *See also baniyā*
Miller, Daniel, 100n.4
Mirabai, 52–54
mitras, 42–43, 47–48, 202–3
mlecch, 149–50, 149n.48
modernities, 67–68, 67n.1
Mohanmālā (Dhusar), 78n.37
Molekamp, Femke, 169n.18
Mount Govardhan
defined, 42n.26, 208
Śrīnāthjī kī Prākaṭya Vārtā, 83–84
vārtā of Krishnadas, 61–62
vārtā of Raskhan, 42–43, 202–3
Mughal emperors, 91, 102, 103n.9, 113–14
Mukhavatar, 48–49n.41
Mulji, Karsandas, 70–72, 73, 74, 188–89
Mumbai ul-Ulum Press, 77–78, 78n.37
Mundaka Kanni Amman temple, 105n.16
Munjee, Runchor, 72–73, 74–75

Nabhadas, 91
Naiṣadhīya, 188–89
nām nivedan. *See Shri Krishna śaranaṃ mama* mantra
Nanda (Nandaji), 104–5, 201
Narayan, 103
Narhar Sannyasi, 51–52
Nathdwara *havelī*, 99–100, 102–9, 106n.19, 112–13, 115n.37, 121, 125–26, 167–69
Natvarlalji, 122, 128–29, 157, 205. *See also* Krishna
Nāṭyaśāstra, 56n.63
Naval Kishore Press, 67–68, 77–78, 78nn.36–37, 84–85
Navaratna, 96
Neha (devotee), 138–39, 144, 145
nibandhs, 82

nij mandir, 106n.19
Nij Vārtā, 34–35
nirguṇ, 60n.72
nitya, 209
nitya līlā, 56–58, 59, 87–88, 117n.43, 181

Orsi, Robert, 17n.36, 155–56
Ortegren (Jennifer), 163n.9

pāda-sevana, 133–34
Padmanabhadas, 118n.44, 195, 196, 197–98
pān, 122
Pandya, Mohanlal Vishnulal, 84–86, 85n.55
Parabrāhmaṇa, 55
paratextual elements, 79–80, 79n.41, 84–85, 88–89, 93–94, 98
Parekh, Lallubhai Pranvallabhdas, 76n.30
paricāy, 82
Parikh, Dwarkadas (Dvārkādās Parīkh), 34n.8, 68–69, 89–94, 195, 205
Parikh, Ramesh, 94, 95–97
Parimal (Mona's husband), 174, 175–76
Parvati, 60, 88n.68, 165n.12
Patel, Deven, 14n.26, 188–89
Pathan, 41n.25, 46–47
Patton, Laurie, 44–46, 49, 64–65
Pauwels, Heidi, 55n.59, 84, 84n.52, 85n.60
performative canon and narrative style, 6–8, 20–21n.48, 21–22, 28–29, 33–34, 43–44, 66, 109n.25, 125–27, 147n.41, 179–80, 188–89
pilgrimage, 9–10, 34–35, 42n.26, 55–56, 72–73, 99–100, 104–5, 106–7, 108–9, 108n.23, 116n.40, 179
Pinch, William, 78
Pintchman, Tracy, 169–70
Prabhuji, Gopendra, 179
prācīn padārthān ke shodhak, 84–85
Practice of Everyday Life, The (Certeau), 17–18
prākaṭya, 174–75, 209
Prākaṭya Vārtā. *See Śrīnāthjī kī Prākaṭya Vārtā*
prasād. *See mahāprasād*
prasaṅgs, 35–36, 209
prastāvnā, 82, 84–85
pravacankārs, 109–10, 209
pravacans, 8, 9–10, 49–50, 100–1, 119. *See also* public reading
  BAPS, 123–24
  defined, 8, 109n.25, 209
  Indirabetiji, 176–77, 179–81, 182–83
  nibandhs, 82
  reasons for attending, 135–36
  Shyam Manohar Goswami, 109–17, 109n.24, 125–26
  virtual, 125–26, 187
Preetha (devotee), 181
psychoanalysis, 112, 189–90
public reading, 23–24, 99–127, 189–90
  defined, 100–1
  performative canon, 125–27
  Puṣṭi Siddhānt Carcā Sabhā, 119–25
  Shyam Manohar Goswami, 109–18
  temple controversies and reconstructions, 99–100, 102–9, 106n.17
Purushottamdas, 142–45, 146, 147, 150, 198–201
"Pushti Doctrine Colloquium" (*Puṣṭi Siddhānt Carcā Sabhā*), 119–22, 124–26
Pushtimarg and Pushtimargi Hindus and Hinduism
  academic scholarship on aspects of, 6n.7
  accepted texts as inherent to *Vārtā Sāhitya*, 34–36
  authority inherited through male primogeniture, 25, 52, 177–78
  author's archival research and ethnographic fieldwork, 9–11
  centrality of reading in process of becoming Pushtimargi, 30–32
  class and caste privilege, 9, 30–32
  context sensitivity and changing with the times, 191–92
  emergence of print and vernacular book culture, 67–69
  encounters and communication with Krishna, 39–40
  everyday experiences and religious reading, 9–10
  festivals, 71–72n.16
  infinite power of possibility, 131–32

Pushtimarg and Pushtimargi Hindus and Hinduism (*cont.*)
initiation, 30–32, 35–36, 59, 59n.68
initiation of Europeans and Americans, 10, 10n.15
literacy, 10–11, 10n.16, 80–81
Maharaja Libel Case, 22–23, 69–76
meshing tradition with contemporary world through reading, 3–4
ocean-like quality of hagiographies, 5–6
personal, subjective perception, 192–93
Pushtimarg, defined, 209
Pushtimargi, defined, 3n.3, 209
reauthorization of tradition and literature, 11–13, 22–23, 67–68, 76–77, 83–97, 100–1, 188–89
translation of term, 1–2, 1n.1
vibrancy, 122–23
weekly gatherings for reading, 3–4
"what did you learn" questions, 192
Pushtimargiya Open University (Vallabha Vidyapith; Vallabha University), 94, 176
puṣṭi, 1n.1, 56–58, 120n.55, 144, 145, 148–49, 150–51, 154–55, 177–78, 209
Puṣṭimārgīy Patrācār course, 94–97, 97n.84
Puṣṭi Siddhānt Carcā Sabhā ("The Pushti Doctrine Colloquium"), 119–22, 124–26

Radha (Svamini), 59–60, 138–39. *See also* Vallabhacharya
rāg, 56–58, 117–18, 117n.43, 209
Rajabetiji (Raja), 148–50, 151, 154–55, 191–92, 205
rājasī, 60, 60n.72
Rajasthan Oriental Research Institute, 84
Rajnagar Type Foundry Printing Press, 81–82, 86n.61
Rakesh Maharaj, 103
Raksha (Yojana's daughter), 171–72, 172n.22
Rama, 13–16, 45–46, 144n.36
Ramanujan, A.K., 45–46, 53n.54
Rāmāyaṇa, 13–16, 45–46, 155
Rāmcaritmānas, 13–16
Ram Singh II, 84–85
Rana Vyas (Ranaji), 111–13, 148, 164–67
rāsa-līlā, 55–58, 209
Rāsapañcādhyāyī, 56n.60
Rasasiddha (Rasasiddhā), 46–47, 59–60
rasa theory, 56–58, 56n.61, 56n.63, 57n.65, 209
rāsa, 56n.61
Raskhan, 40–44, 40n.23, 45–48, 50–51, 56–58, 59–60, 202–3
"Raskhan the Neophyte" (Snell), 45–46
Ravana, 45–46
reauthorization of tradition and literature, 11–13, 22–23, 67–68, 76–77, 83–97, 100–1, 188–89
religious reading. *See also* commentarial reading; community reading; dialogical reading; public reading; women and women's reading
affective and embodied practice, 25, 158–60, 173, 176, 187
author's interest in, 5
celebrating and (re)articulating individual and community identity and devotional practice and tradition, 3–4, 11–13, 27–29
centrality of in process of becoming Pushtimargi, 30–32
considering through theoretical or "ideal" readers, 16–17, 16n.35
context sensitivity and changing with the times, 191–92
diversity of conversations arising from, 11
ethonographic consideration of, 11–13
existing scholarship on, 13–17
grammar of devotion and tradition, 7, 32–33, 39–40, 48, 93–94, 167–69
infinite power of possibility, 131–32
meaning of "reading," 3–4, 10
neither text nor interpretation immutable, 187
questioning process and interpretation, 155
reader-centered model of study, 11–17
readers as permanent residents in habitats built (at least in part) by texts, 17–18, 191–92
scholarship on reading vs. overreliance on textual study, 189–90

- as social practice, 16–17
- studying readers and texts as relationally performative, 7
- texts as communicative act across time and space, 17–18
- vernacular Indian vs. Sanskrit-language texts, 11

Reliving Karbala (Hyder), 13–16
Richman, Paula, 13–16
Ricoeur, Paul, 131–32, 151
Rinehart, Robin, 63–64
ṛṣi, 55, 75n.25
Ruffle, Karen, 131–32
Rukmini Bahuji, Goswami, 132
Rupa Gosvamin, 56–58

*sabhā*s
- defined, 209
- Dharma Sabha, 76–77
- *Puṣṭi Siddhānt Carcā Sabhā*, 119–22, 124–26
- *sabhā hol*s, 139–40

Sādhanadīpikā, 117n.41
sāgar, 5–6
Saha, Shandip, 91n.74
Said, Edward W., 17, 18n.41, 187
sakhaṛī, 196–97, 196n.5
*sakhā*s (*gopā*s), 60–61, 60n.70, 208, 209
*sakhī*s. *See gopī*s
sakhya, 57n.64, 133–34
Saloni (devotee), 52–54
sāmagrī, 120, 120n.56
sanātana-dharma, 75–77
Sanjay (devotee), 104–6
Sanskrit, 11, 34–35n.9, 38, 40n.24, *See also Bhāgavatapurāṇa*; *Subodhinī* commentary
- elite treatises, 13–16
- *maṅgalācaraṇ*, 109–10
- *Naiṣadhīya*, 188–89
- *Nāṭyaśāstra*, 56n.63
- *Puṣṭimārgīy Patrācār* course, 95–96
- *rasa* theory, 56–58
- *Sādhanadīpikā*, 117n.41
- "Sanskritization," 76–77
- Shastras, 73–74
- *Siddhāntarahasya*, 49–50
- *Vallabhadigvijaya*, 77n.31
- *Veda*s, 55n.57, 69–70
- *Vivekadhairyāśraya*, 145
- *Yamunāṣṭaka*, 144–45

*sansthān*s, 124, 124n.65
śānta, 57n.64
sār, 82, 87–88
Saraswati, Dayanand, 75n.25
sāre, 43n.28, 47–48, 203n.24
satī, 165–67, 165n.12, 210
*satsaṅg*s. *See also* women and women's reading
- children and youth, 137, 137n.22
- community reading, 24–25, 132–42
- defined, 8, 132–33, 210
- membership, 136–37
- men's participation in, 138n.23, 139–40
- modes of *bhakti*, 133–34
- "moistening the heart," 132–34, 136
- negotiating family dynamics, 142–51
- paratextual elements and, 79–80
- *Puṣṭimārgīy Patrācār* course, 94–96
- questioning the *vārtā*s, 152–56
- reading the *vārtā*s, 141
- reasons for attending, 135–36
- reasons for starting, 134–35
- temple vs. home-based, 134, 139–40
- travel distance and scheduling, 140–41
- virtual, 95, 187
- women, 137–39

sāttvik, 60n.72, 195, 195n.2, 197
Saurbha, 196
Sausse, Matthew, 70–71
Sawin, Patricia, 162–63
Sejal (Indirabetiji's attendant), 177–78, 182–83
self-study reading, 93–97
*sevak*s, 56–58, 104, 106–7, 112–13, 116, 121, 167–69
- defined, 30–31, 210
- *vārtā* of Purushottamdas, 198–201
- *vārtā* of Raskhan, 202
- *vārtā* of Tulsa, 195
- women, 183, 183n.40

sevā rituals
- *aṣṭayām sevā*, 106n.18, 117n.43, 207
- balancing caretaking of Krishna with householder lifestyle, 26–27, 52, 146, 162–63

sevā rituals (*cont.*)
defined, 8, 210
donated ritual materials, 120
entering "meditative state," 172–73
establishment of, 83–84
food preparation, 121–22
gendered nature of, 25–26, 138–39, 160–61
handling doubts about dubious actions of protagonists, 61–62
havelī sevā, 100–1, 106–7, 106n.19, 109, 112–18, 119–25, 126–27, 129–30, 183, 189–90
human body as vessel for, 167
intimate knowing of Krishna, 39–40
issues of "purity and pollution" during, 61, 149–50, 152–53
lunisolar calendars, 26–27
maxi garments vs. saris, 152–53
men's participation in, 139–40
"moistening the heart," 132–34
newly initiated, 30–32
observant devotees, 160n.3
pre-*sevā satsaṅg*, 171–73
rasa theory, 56–58
sacred and mundane, 13–16
sevā bhūṣaṇ, 94
śṛṅgār sevā, 196–97, 196n.7
vittajā sevā, 115–16
worldly vs. otherworldly, 60
Shah, Deepa (devotee), 105–6, 105n.16
Shalini Goswami (Goswami Shalini Bahuji), 19–20, 21–22, 30–32, 33–34, 35–36, 37–38, 48, 63–64, 65–66, 134–35, 205
Sharma, Shital, 76n.30, 158n.1, 178, 183n.40, 184n.42
Sharma, Sumit, 152n.53
Shastras, 73–75
Shi'ism, 131–32
Shobha (devotee), 150–51
Shravani, 179–80. *See also* Indirabetiji, Goswami
"Shreenathji v/s Rajasthan Congress Government" Facebook page, 99–105
Shri (*śrī*), 19n.43, 48n.40, 210
Shriji. *See* Shrinathji
Shri Krishna śaranaṃ mama (*nām nivedan*; *aṣṭākṣara*) mantra, 30, 30n.1, 59n.68, 165–66
Shrinathji (Govardhannathji; Shriji), 26*f*, 205. *See also* Krishna
community contributions to *sevā* rituals, 120–21
84VV and *252VV*, 34–36
havelī sevā and renovation debates, 100–2, 103, 106–9
Nathdwara *havelī* complex, 106–7, 106n.19
sevā after death of Vitthalnath, 113–14
Śrīnāthjī kī Prākaṭya Vārtā, 83–84, 102
tilkāyat, 103, 103n.9, 104–5
Vallabhacharya's initiation, 49–50
vārtā of Krishnadas, 61–62
vārtā of Raskhan, 41–43, 44, 47–48, 202–3
vārtā of Vasudevdas Chakda, 120
śhuddhādvaita, 20, 210
Shukla, Bhavesh, 122–24
Shvetaketu, 44–45, 49
Shyam Manohar Goswami (Śyām Manohar Gosvāmī), 50n.45, 96–97, 108–22, 148, 178, 189–90, 206
historicizing the *vārtās*, 113–14, 114n.36
homiletic style, 110–12
modern lifestyles, 115–16, 125, 125n.66
pilgrimage, 116n.40
pravacan sessions, 109–10, 125–26
public vs. private *sevā* rituals, 112–18, 119
Puṣṭi Siddhānt Carcā Sabhā, 119–22, 124–25
Vallabhacharya Vidyapith, 124n.65
siddhānt, 26–27, 90, 96–97, 117–18, 134–35, 151
Siddhāntarahasya, 49–50, 52n.50
smaraṇa, 133–34
Snell, Rupert, 5, 45–46, 47–48, 47n.36
social media, 99–105, 100n.4, 189–90
Ṣoḍaśagrantha, 50, 50n.45, 62–63, 96, 110–11, 115–16, 145, 171–72, 207
śravaṇa, 133–34
Śrī Ācāryajī Mahāprabhu (Śrī Vallabhācāryajī) nā 84 Vaiṣṇav nī Vārtā (Desai), 87–89

Śrīnāthjī kī Prākaṭya Vārtā (*Prākaṭya Vārtā*), 34–35, 83–87
  authorship of, 84, 84n.53
  contents of, 83–84
  defined, 207
  historiographic texture, 86–87
  paratextual elements, 84–85
  provenance of, 84–85, 84n.53
  Shyam Manohar Goswami, 113–14
  temple controversies and reconstructions, 102
  tilkāyat, 103n.9
Śrī Vallabhācāryajī (Śrī Ācāryajī Mahāprabhu) nā 84 Vaiṣṇav nī Vārtā (Desai), 87–89
śṛṅgār sevā, 196–97, 196n.7
śṛṅgār(a) (*mādhurya*), 56–58, 56–57nn.63–64, 117–18, 117n.43, 210
Stark, Ulrike, 77–78, 78nn.35–36, 80–81
Stewart, Tony K., 28–29, 32n.4
sthāyībhāvas, 56–58, 56nn.62–63
storytelling, 8, 13–16, 22–23, 24–25, 33–34, 161–62, 169–70, 173. *See also kathās*
strī dharma, 162–63, 162–63n.9
Subodhinī (*Subodhinījī*) commentary, 19, 20, 37–38, 55–58, 68–69, 132–33, 207
Sucharita, 60
Suraj (Yojana's son), 171–72
Surdas, 109–10, 197–98
Surekha (devotee), 150–51
Svamini (Radha), 59–60, 138–39. *See also* Vallabhacharya
svarūps, 28*f*, *See also names of specific* svarūps; *sevā* rituals
  bridge between two worlds, 60–61
  care for when traveling, 150–51, 180–81, 191–92
  defined, 8, 30n.2, 210
  "emergence" *vārtās*, 34–35
  food preparation, 121–22
  initiation, 59n.68
  issues of "purity and pollution" during *sevā*, 61
  temple spaces, 105n.16, 106n.19, 113–16, 119
  vārtā of Amma, 175
  vārtā of Purushottamdas, 198–200
  vārtā of Tulsa, 195, 195n.3
  vārtā of Vasudevdas Chakda, 120
  vārtā of widowed woman and her Thakurji, 21
  women as primary caretakers, 25–26
Swaminarayan temples, 122–24
Swapna (devotee), 144, 170
Śyām Manohar Gosvāmī. *See* Shyam Manohar Goswami

Tadiya Samaj, 76–77
tāmasī, 60n.72
teliyo rājā, 149n.46
temples (*havelīs*)
  BAPS, 122–24
  darśan, 23–24, 122–24, 139–40
  defending the benefits of collective, temple *sevā*, 119–25
  defined, 208
  Mundaka Kanni Amman temple, 105n.16
  Nathdwara board and renovations, 99–100, 102–9, 112–13, 115n.37, 121, 125–26, 167–69
  newer temples, 106n.19, 123–24
  satsaṅgs in temple spaces, 139–40
  Shyam Manohar Goswami on *havelī sevā*, 112–18
  Swaminarayan temples, 122–24
  Vallabh Sadan temple, 134, 142
  Vraj Dham Haveli, 182–83
textual autonomy, 36–37, 37n.15
Thakurji, 1n.2, 206. *See also* Krishna
  balancing caretaking with householder lifestyle, 146
  becoming attuned to daily needs and desires of, 39–40
  bhog, 118nn.44–45
  books as *prasād*, 170–71
  care for *svarūp* when traveling, 150–51, 180–81, 191–92
  discussion over whether to serve pizza to, 1–4, 11–13, 153–54, 191–92
  image of, 2*f*, 22*f*
  issues of "purity and pollution" during *sevā*, 152–53
  language, 44
  member of family, 131–32, 138–39, 167–69

Thakurji (*cont.*)
pre-*sevā satsaṅg*, 171–73
vārtā of Amma, 175
vārtā of Purushottamdas, 198–202
vārtā of Tulsa, 196–98
vārtā of widowed woman and her Thakurji, 1–2, 21–22, 22*f*
women as primary caretakers, 160–61
ṭīkā, 82, 82n.51, 210
Tilak Goswami (Madhusudanlal Goswami; Tilak Bava), 128–29, 128n.1, 134, 138n.23, 148–49, 152–53, 154–55, 206
tilkāyat, 103–5, 103n.9, 108
Tīn Janma kī Bhāvnā, 59, 59n.67, *See also* *Bhāvprakāś* commentary
Tulsa, 195–98
Tulsidas, 13–16
252VV (*Do Sau Bāvan Vaiṣṇavan kī Vārtā*)
authorship of, 36–37, 36n.13
Bhāvprakāś commentary, 58, 58n.66, 59n.69
caste and gender, 52–54
contents of, 32–33, 35–36
defined, 206, 207
Desai's versions, 87–89
diversity of human emotions and behaviors, 50–51
diversity of protagonists, 50–51
emergence of print and vernacular book culture, 81–82
encounters and communication with Krishna, 40
handling doubts about dubious actions of protagonists, 61, 63–64
intertextuality, 33–34, 49–52
intimately experiencing, and knowing needs of Krishna, 39–40
Maharaja Libel Case, 72–73
number of hagiographies in, 35n.11
paratextual elements, 79, 88–89
Parikh's version, 34n.8, 89–91, 195
provenance of, 36–37, 36n.12
reference to poetic works, 54–55
specific dates, 86–87
vacanāmṛt, 39–48
worldly vs. otherworldly details of protagonists, 46–47, 59–60

Uddalaka Aruni, 44–45, 49
University of Texas at Austin, 5
Upanishads (*upaniṣads*), 44–45, 45n.32, 49, 64–65
Urdu, 77–78
Uttarārdha Bhaktamāl (Harishchandra), 76–77

vacanāmṛt, 21–22, 32–33, 125–26
in analysis of the *purāṇa*, 48–49n.41
defined, 210
in *84VV*, 39–40, 43–44, 45–47
hereditary leaders' exegesis, 135–36
Shyam Manohar Goswami, 110–11, 112
in *252VV*, 39–44, 45–48
undoubted veracity of, 90–91
Vacanāmṛtsaṃkalan (Shyam Manohar Goswami), 110–11
Vaishnavas, defined, 19n.42, *See also* *84VV*; *252VV*
Vakpati Foundation, 94–95, 176
Vallabhācārya Mat Khaṇḍan, 75n.25
Vallabhacharya, 206. *See also 84VV*; Mahaprabhuji
accepted texts as inherent to *Vārtā Sāhitya*, 34–36
authority inherited through descendance from, 25, 31–32, 177–78
Bhāgavatapurāṇa, 20, 20n.47, 55–56, 179–80
Bhaktivardhinī, 147
danger of prostitutes and other "debased" individuals, 62–63
dialogical (conversational) quality of *vārtās*, 21
divine counterpart Svamini (Radha), 59–60, 138–39
hagiographies, 4
honorifics, 47–48
householder lifestyle, 52, 52n.50, 115–16
initiation of, 31–32, 35–36, 49–50
initiation through, 35–36, 40
intertextual elements of *vārtās*, 33–34, 49–58
Maharaja Libel Case, 70–71, 75–76
making sense of teachings that don't align with *vārtās*, 61
Mukhavatar, 48–49n.41

non-renunciation, 183–84
positions on caste and gender, 52–54
proselytizing pilgrimages, 55–56
providing narrative contexts for works attributed to, 49–50
renunciation, 51–52, 52n.49
Saṃnyāsanirṇaya treatise, 51–52
Sanskrit commentaries and treatises attributed to, 38
satsaṅgs, 132–33
Shyam Manohar Goswami's positions on teachings of, 110–11, 112, 113–16, 117–18
Śrīnāthjī kī Prākaṭya Vārtā, 83–84
story of widowed disciple, 1–2
Subodhinī commentary, 20, 20n.47, 37–38, 55–58
tilkāyat, 103n.9
vacanāmṛt, 21, 32–33, 39–40, 90–91, 110–11, 112, 125–26
Vallabhadigvijaya, 77n.31
vārtā of Damodardas, 103, 149–50
Veda, 55
Vivekadhairyāśraya, 145
worldly vs. otherworldly details of protagonists, 59
Yamunāṣṭaka, 144–45
Vallabhacharya Vidyapith, 124n.65
Vallabhadigvijaya, 77n.31
Vallabha Kul, 31–32, 31n.3, 52, 75–76, 84–85, 88, 94, 103n.9, 110–11, 112, 113–14, 114n.36, 116, 117n.43, 120–21, 135–36, 135n.18, 148–49, 163–64, 178–79, 178n.25, 183–84, 210
Vallabha Vidyapith (Vallabha University; Pushtimargiya Open University), 94, 176
Vallabh Sadan temple, 134, 142
vandana, 133–34
Varma, Dhirendra, 91, 91nn.73–74
Varma, Thakur Giriprasad, 78
varṇāśramadharma, 52–54, 210
Vārtānkī Saiddhāntik Saṅgati (Shyam Manohar Goswami), 33n.6, 117
vārtās. *See also 84VV*; *252VV*; *Vārtā Sāhitya*; *and names of other specific* vārtās
accepted texts as inherent to *Vārtā Sāhitya*, 34–36
affordable published editions, 22–23
author's research into recorded reception history, 10
authorship of, 20, 20–21n.48
bridging between Krishna's *līlā* and devotees' everyday lives, 187–89
canonical status, 32–33
caste and gender, 52–54
"closed" canon, 6
collections of, 4
community reading and questioning of, 152–56
defined, 4
depiction of marital tensions, 167n.15
dialogical (conversational) quality of, 5, 6–7, 21, 24–25
differences in textual authority, 11
divine vs. pedestrian, 46–48, 48n.40
as embodiments of Krishna, 36–37
emergence of print and vernacular book culture, 68–69, 75–83
encounters and communication with Krishna, 39–40
"factual" nature of, 87–89
grammar of devotion and tradition, 32–33, 39–40, 48, 93–94, 167–69
handling doubts about dubious actions of protagonists, 61–63
historicizing, 83–91, 113–14, 114n.36
as inherently authoritative and imbued with divinity, 37–38
initiation, 46–47
insiders vs. outsiders (belonging vs. "Otherness"), 45–46, 48
intertextuality, 20, 33–34, 38, 49–58, 64, 66, 74–75, 142
Maharaja Libel Case, 69–70, 72–76
meshing tradition with contemporary world, 24–25
modeling devotional behavior through dialogue, 48
ocean-like quality of, 5–6
"Otherness", 45–46, 47–48
paratextual elements, 79–80, 79n.41, 84–85, 88–89, 93–94, 98
performative canon and narrative style, 6–7, 8, 21–22, 33–34, 43–44
as primary religious texts, 11

vārtās (*cont.*)
providing narrative contexts for works attributed to Vallabhacharya, 49–50
providing *siddhānt* and *dṛṣṭānt*, 26–27
real-life speech acts, 40
reauthorization of, 22–23, 67–68, 83–97, 188–89
relationship between *Bhāgavatapurāṇa* and, 37–38
satsaṅgs, 141
solo study guides, 28–29
specific dates, 86–87
storytelling mode, 8, 24–25, 33–34
"thinking out loud" speech, 41–43
vacanāmṛt, 21–22, 32–33
vārtā of Amma, 174–75
vārtā of Damodardas, 103, 149–50
vārtā of Krishnadas, 72–74, 91–92
vārtā of Purushottamdas, 142–45, 146, 147, 150, 198–202
vārtā of Rana Vyas, 111–13, 148, 164–67
vārtā of Raskhan, 40–44, 40n.23, 50–51, 56–58, 59–60, 202–3
vārtā of Tulsa, 195–98
vārtā of Vasudevdas Chakda, 120
vārtā of Virbai, 61, 152–55
women's discussion over whether to serve pizza to Thakurji, 1–3, 153–54
worldly vs. otherworldly, 24–25, 43–44, 46–48, 58–61
written commentaries, 22–23, 82
Vārtā Sāhitya
accepted texts as inherent to, 34–36
author's research into recorded reception history, 10
becoming attuned to Krishna's daily needs and desires, 26–27
"closed" canon, 6, 34–35
community reading, 129, 131–32
defined, 210
Desai's "factual footnote" commentary, 87–89
dialogical (conversational) quality of, 5
emergence of print and vernacular book culture, 80–81
foremost text in genre, 30–31
gender and *sevā* rituals, 25–26
grammar of devotion and tradition, 7
importance of, 4
intertextuality, 49–58
Maharaja Libel Case, 22–23, 69–75
Parikh's *Vārtā Sāhitya Mīmāṃsā*, 89–92
as performative canon, 6–7, 28–29, 33–34
as primary religious texts, 11
public readings and exegesis for income, 179–80
Puṣṭimārgīy Patrācār and self-study reading, 93–97
reauthorization of through written commentary, 76–77, 83–97
Shalini Goswami's reading and exegesis, 19–20
Shyam Manohar Goswami, 109–10, 115–16
Śrīnāthjī kī Prākaṭya Vārtā, 83–87
translation into modern Gujarati, 22–23
using stories about early disciples to relate Vallabhacharya's teachings, 19, 20
vacanāmṛt, 21–22
Vallabhacharya's initiation, 31–32
Vārtā Sāhitya Mīmāṃsā, 89–92
vernacular synthesis, 38
Vārtā Sāhitya Mīmāṃsā (Parikh), 89–92
Vasudevdas Chakda, 120
vātsalya, 57n.64, 210
Vedas, 45n.32, 55, 55n.57, 69–70
Vicārdhārā (Varma), 91, 91n.73
Vikram Samvat calendar, 34n.8
viraha, 28–29, 76–77, 152, 171–72, 210
Virbai, 61, 152–55
Vishal Goswami, 104–5, 105n.16
Vishnu, 19n.42, 103
Vitthalnath, 32–33, 206. *See also 252VV*
accepted texts as inherent to *Vārtā Sāhitya*, 34–36
divine counterpart Chandravali, 59–60, 76–77
gift vs. giver, 65n.81
honorifics, 47–48
initiation through, 40, 47–48
intertextual elements of *vārtās*, 33–34
proselytizing pilgrimages, 55–56
Sanskrit commentaries and treatises attributed to, 38

Shrinathji's *sevā* after death of, 113–14
tilkāyat, 103n.9
vacanāmṛt, 90–91
worldly vs. otherworldly details of protagonists, 59
Vitthalray, 103n.9
Vivekadhairyāśraya, 145
Vrajbhamini Goswami, 153
Vraj Dham Haveli, 182–83
Vrajeshkumar Maharaj, 36n.12
Vrajraman Goswami, 120–21
Vrindavan Research Institute, 84
Vyaghrapad Press, 78, 84–85
Vyasa, 55

Waghorne, Joanne, 105n.16
Watts, James W., 101n.6
WhatsApp, 9–10, 158–60, 187
Wimbush, Vincent L., 13–16
women and women's reading, 25–27, 157–86
absence of women's interpretations, 7
affective and embodied practice, 158–60, 173, 176
author's early experience with group, 5–6
balancing caretaking of Krishna with householder lifestyle, 24–25, 26–27, 160–61, 160n.4, 162–63, 190–91
Banarasi women's rituals during Kartik, 169–70
becoming attuned to Krishna's daily needs and desires, 26–27
conversations about family dynamics, 157–58
"creative conformity," 162–63
demographics, 160
devotional sentiments, 138–39, 160–61
discussion over whether to serve pizza to Thakurji, 1–4, 153–54, 191–92
entering "meditative state," 170–73, 190–91
forming and fostering relationships, 169–70
gendered nature of *sevā*, 25–26, 138–39
gopīs, 25–26
Indirabetiji, 177–85
informal, gender-segregated meetings, 138n.23
issues of "purity and pollution" during, 61, 149–50, 152–53, 200n.17
meshing tradition with contemporary world, 3–4, 11–13
promoting welfare of faraway kin, 174
reading through "joys and sorrows," 174–77
satsaṅgs, 137–39
satsaṅgs and negotiation of family dynamics, 142–48, 158, 167–69, 171–73
satsaṅgs and women's "mental health," 164–70
sevaks, 183, 183n.40
Shalini Goswami's reading and exegesis, 19–20
strī dharma, 162–63, 162–63n.9
varṇāśramadharma, 52–54
well-being, 158–60, 163, 190–91
women as primary caretakers, 11–13, 160–61
women's "inherent qualities," 25–26
Women's College of Baroda, 178

Yamunabetiji (Yamunesh Prabhuji), 179
Yamuna Devi, 144–45, 177–78
Yamunāṣṭaka, 144–45, 172n.22
Yashoda, 25–26, 138–39
YouTube, 104–5, 109n.24, 176–77